Lecture Notes in Artificial Intelligence 8801

Subseries of Lecture Notes in Computer Science

Maosong Sun Yang Liu Jun Zhao (Eds.)

Chinese Computational Linguistics and Natural Language Processing Based on Naturally Annotated Big Data

13th China National Conference, CCL 2014 and
Second International Symposium, NLP-NABD 2014
Wuhan, China, October 18-19, 2014
Proceedings

Volume Editors

Maosong Sun
Yang Liu
Tsinghua University
Department of Computer Science and Technology
Haidian District, Beijing 100084, China
E-mail: {sms, liuyang2011}@tsinghua.edu.cn

Jun Zhao
Chinese Academy of Sciences
Institute of Automation
Beijing 100190, China
E-mail: jzhao@nlpr.ia.ac.cn

ISSN 0302-9743 e-ISSN 1611-3349
ISBN 978-3-319-12276-2 e-ISBN 978-3-319-12277-9
DOI 10.1007/978-3-319-12277-9
Springer Cham Heidelberg New York Dordrecht London

Library of Congress Control Number: 2014950449

LNCS Sublibrary: SL 7 – Artificial Intelligence

Typesetting: Camera-ready by author, data conversion by Scientific Publishing Services, Chennai, India

Printed on acid-free paper

Springer is part of Springer Science+Business Media (www.springer.com)

Preface

Welcome to the proceedings of the 13th China National Conference on Computational Linguistics (13th CCL) and the Second International Symposium on Natural Language Processing Based on Naturally Annotated Big Data (2nd NLP-NABD). The conference was hosted by Central China Normal University.

CCL is an annual conference (bi-annual before 2013) that started in 1991. It is the flagship conference of the Chinese Information Processing Society (CIPS), which is the largest NLP scholar and expert community in China. CCL is a premier nation-wide forum for disseminating new scholarly and technological work in computational linguistics, with a major emphasis on computer processing of the languages in China such as Mandarin, Tibetan, Mongolian, and Uyghur.

Affiliated with the 13th CCL, the Second International Symposium on Natural Language Processing Based on Naturally Annotated Big Data (NLP-NABD) covered all the NLP topics, with a particular focus on methodologies and techniques relating to naturally annotated big data. In contrast to manually annotated data such as treebanks that are constructed for specific NLP tasks, naturally annotated data come into existence through users' normal activities, such as writing, conversation, and interactions on the Web. Although the original purposes of these data typically were unrelated to NLP, they can nonetheless be purposefully exploited by computational linguists to acquire linguistic knowledge. For example, punctuation marks in Chinese text can help word boundaries identification, social tags in social media can provide signals for keyword extraction, and categories listed in Wikipedia can benefit text classification. The natural annotation can be explicit, as in the above examples, or implicit, as in Hearst patterns (e.g., "Beijing and other cities" implies "Beijing is a city"). This symposium focuses on numerous research challenges ranging from very large scale unsupervised/semi-supervised machine leaning (deep learning, for instance) of naturally annotated big data to integration of the learned resources and models with existing handcrafted "core" resources and "core" language computing models. NLP-NABD 2014 is supported by the National Key Basic Research Program of China (i.e., "973" Program) "Theory and Methods for Cyber-Physical-Human Space Oriented Web Chinese Information Processing" under grant no. 2014CB340500.

The Program Committee selected 113 papers (86 Chinese papers and 27 English papers) out of 233 submissions from China, Hong Kong (region), and Macau (region) for publication. The 27 English papers cover the following topics:

- Word segmentation (1)

- Syntactic analysis and parsing the Web (1)
- Lexical semantics and ontologies (2)
- Semantics (2)
- Discourse, coreference and pragmatics (1)
- Textual entailment (1)
- Language resources and annotation (2)
- Sentiment analysis, opinion mining and text classification (2)
- Large-scale knowledge acquisition and reasoning (1)
- Text mining, open-domain information extraction and machine reading of the Web (2)
- Machine translation (4)
- Multilinguality in NLP (3)
- Underresourced languages processing (2)
- NLP applications (3)

The final program for the 13th CCL and the Second NLP-NABD was the result of a great deal of work by many dedicated colleagues. We want to thank, first of all, the authors who submitted their papers, and thus contributed to the creation of the high-quality program that allowed us to look forward to an exciting joint conference. We are deeply indebted to all the Program Committee members for providing high-quality and insightful reviews under a tight schedule. We are extremely grateful to the sponsors of the conference. Finally, we extend a special word of thanks to all the colleagues of the Organizing Committee and Secretariat for their hard work in organizing the conference, and to Springer for their assistance in publishing the proceedings in due time.

On behalf of the Program and Organizing Committees, we hope the conference was interesting for all the participants and that their visit to Wuhan, a famous and beautiful historical and cultural city in China, was a really valuable experience.

August 2014

Maosong Sun
Jun Zhao
Guodong Zhou
Xuanjing Huang
Dekang Lin
Ting Liu

Organization

General Chairs

Wushour Silamu	Xinjiang University, China
Yuming Li	Beijing Language and Culture University, China

Program Committee

13th CCL Program Chair

Maosong Sun	Tsinghua University, China

13thCCL Program Co-chairs

Jun Zhao	Institute of Automation, Chinese Academy of Sciences
Guodong Zhou	Soochow University, China
Xuanjing Huang	Fudan University, China

13th CCL Area Co-chairs

Linguistics and Cognitive Science

Yulin Yuan	Peking University, China
Weiguang Qu	Nanjing Normal University, China

Theory and Methods for Computational Linguistics

Houfeng Wang	Peking University, China
Donghong Ji	Wuhan University, China

Information Retrieval, Information Extraction, Question Answering, Text Classification, and Summarization

Bing Qin	Harbin Institute of Technology, China
Bin Wang	Institute of Computing Technology, Chinese Academy of Sciences

Machine Translation and Multilingual Information Processing

Tiejun Zhao	Harbin Institute of Technology, China
Jiajun Chen	Nanjing University, China

Language Resource and Evaluation

Erhong Yang	Beijing Language and Culture University, China
Ru Li	Shanxi University, China

Social Computing and Sentiment Analysis

Ting Liu	Harbin Institute of Technology, China
Hongfei Lin	Dalian University of Technology, China

NLP Applications

Xiaojie Wang	Beijing University of Posts and Telecommunications, China
Hongying Zan	Zhengzhou University, China

13th CCL Technical Committee

Rangjia Cai	Qinghai Normal University, China
Dongfeng Cai	Shenyang Aerospace University, China
Baobao Chang	Peking University, China
Qunxiu Chen	Tsinghua University, China
Xiaohe Chen	Nanjing Normal University, China
Xueqi Cheng	Institute of Computing Technology, Chinese Academy of Sciences
Key-Sun Choi	KAIST, Korea
Li Deng	Microsoft Research, USA
Alexander Gelbukh	National Polytechnic Institute, Mexico
Josef van Genabith	Dublin City University, Ireland
Randy Goebel	University of Alberta, Canada
Tingting He	Central China Normal University, China
Isahara Hitoshi	Toyohashi University of Technology, Japan
Heyan Huang	Beijing Polytechnic University, China
Xuanjing Huang	Fudan University, China
Donghong Ji	Wuhan University, China
Turgen Ibrahim	Xinjiang University, China
Shiyong Kang	Ludong University, China
Sadao Kurohashi	Kyoto University, Japan
Kiong Lee	ISO TC37, Korea
Hang Li	Huawei, Hong Kong, SAR China
Ru Li	Shanxi University, China
Dekang Lin	Google, USA
Qun Liu	Institute of Computing Technology, Chinese Academy of Sciences
Shaoming Liu	Fuji Xerox, Japan

Qin Lu	Polytechnic University of Hong Kong, SAR China
Wolfgang Menzel	University of Hamburg, Germany
Jian-Yun Nie	University of Montreal, Canada
Yanqiu Shao	Beijing Language and Culture University, China
Xiaodong Shi	Xiamen University, China
Rou Song	Beijing Language and Culture University, China
Jian Su	Institute for Infocomm Research, Singapore
Benjamin Ka Yin Tsou	The Hong Kong Institute of Education, SAR China
Haifeng Wang	Baidu, China
Fei Xia	University of Washington, USA
Feiyu Xu	DFKI, Germany
Nianwen Xue	Brandeis University, USA
Erhong Yang	Beijing Language and Culture University, China
Tianfang Yao	Shanghai Jiaotong University, China
Shiwen Yu	Peking University, China
Quan Zhang	Institute of Acoustics, Chinese Academy of Sciences
Jun Zhao	Institute of Automation, Chinese Academy of Sciences
Guodong Zhou	Soochow University, China
Ming Zhou	Microsoft Research Asia, China
Jingbo Zhu	Northeastern University, China
Ping Xue	Research & Technology, The Boeing Company, USA

2nd NLP-NABD Program Chairs

Maosong Sun	Tsinghua University, China
Dekang Lin	Google, USA
Ting Liu	Harbin Institute of Technology, China

2nd NLP-NABD Technical Committee

Key-Sun Choi	KAIST, Korea
Li Deng	Microsoft Research, USA
Alexander Gelbukh	National Polytechnic Institute, Mexico
Josef van Genabith	Dublin City University, Ireland
Randy Goebel	University of Alberta, Canada
Isahara Hitoshi	Toyohashi University of Technology, Japan
Xuanjing Huang	Fudan University, China
Donghong Ji	Wuhan University, China
Sadao Kurohashi	Kyoto University, Japan
Kiong Lee	ISO TC37, Korea

Hang Li	Huawei Hong Kong, SAR China
Hongfei Lin	Dalian Polytechnic University, China
Qun Liu	Institute of Computing Technology, Chinese Academy of Sciences
Shaoming Liu	Fuji Xerox, Japan
Ting Liu	Harbin Institute of Technology, China
Yang Liu	Tsinghua University, China
Qin Lu	Polytechnic University of Hong Kong, SAR China
Wolfgang Menzel	University of Hamburg, Germany
Hwee Tou Ng	National University of Singapore, Singapore
Jian-Yun Nie	University of Montreal, Canada
Jian Su	Institute for Infocomm Research, Singapore
Zhifang Sui	Peking University, China
Le Sun	Institute of Software, Chinese Academy of Sciences
Benjamin Ka Yin Tsou	The Hong Kong Institute of Education, SAR China
Fei Xia	University of Washington, USA
Feiyu Xu	DFKI, Germany
Nianwen Xue	Brandeis University, USA
Jun Zhao	Institute of Automation, Chinese Academy of Sciences
Guodong Zhou	Soochow University, China
Ming Zhou	Microsoft Research Asia, China
Ping Xue	Research & Technology, The Boeing Company, USA

13th CCL and 2nd NLP-NABD Local Arrangements Chair

Tingting He	Central China Normal University, China

13th CCL and 2nd NLP-NABD Local Arrangements Co-chair

Maoyuan Zhang	Central China Normal University, China

13th CCL and 2nd NLP-NABD System Demonstration Chair

Jingbo Zhu	Northeastern University, China

13th CCL and 2nd NLP-NABD Publications Co-chairs

Yang Liu	Tsinghua University, China
Zhiyuan Liu	Tsinghua University, China

Table of Contents

Word Segmentation

Syntactic Analysis and Parsing the Web

Lexical Semantics and Ontologies

Semantics

Discourse, Coreference and Pragmatics

Textual Entailment

Language Resources and Annotation

Sentiment Analysis, Opinion Mining and Text Classification

Large-Scale Knowledge Acquisition and Reasoning

Text Mining, Open IE and Machine Reading of the Web

Machine Translation

Multilinguality in NLP

Underresourced Languages Processing

NLP Applications

Unsupervised Joint Monolingual Character Alignment and Word Segmentation

Zhiyang Teng[1,2], Hao Xiong[2,3], and Qun Liu[2,4]

[1] University of Chinese Academy of Sciences
[2] Institute of Computing Technology, Chinese Academy of Sciences
[3] Torangetek Information Technology (Beijing) Ltd.
[4] Centre for Next Generation Localisation
Faculty of Engineering and Computing, Dublin City University
{tengzhiyang,xionghao,liuqun}@ict.ac.cn

Abstract. We propose a novel Bayesian model for fully unsupervised word segmentation based on monolingual character alignment. Adapted bilingual word alignment models and a Bayesian language model are combined through product of experts to estimate the joint posterior distribution of a monolingual character alignment and the corresponding segmentation. Our approach enhances the performance of conventional hierarchical Pitman-Yor language models with richer character-level features. In the conducted experiments, our model achieves an 88.6% word token f-score on the standard Brent version of the Bernstein-Ratner corpora. Moreover, on standard Chinese segmentation datasets, our method outperforms a baseline model by 1.9-2.9 f-score points.

Keywords: unsupervised word segmentation, word alignment, Gibbs sampling; Pitman-Yor process.

1 Introduction

Many advanced natural language processing applications, such as dependency parsing and machine translation, use words as basic units. Unlike English, there are no white spaces between words in many Asian languages. Therefore, identifying word boundaries is a fundamental task of processing these languages.

There are two major categories of machine learning approaches: supervised methods and unsupervised methods. Supervised methods rely heavily on labeled data of a given language, thus they require much manual work. On the other hand, unsupervised methods have become increasingly important in research due to their independence of human efforts, as well as adaptability to any domains. In addition, the unsupervised learning process shows insights on how human beings acquire lexical knowledge.

In general, many previous unsupervised methods can be classified into two categories. The first category focuses on making use of heuristic rules based on local statistics such as the cohesion and the separating degree of resulting units [1] [2]. The second category evaluates probability of a segmentation of a given string based on explicit probabilistic models via nonparametric Bayesian inference [3–5]. Bayesian methods become popular because of its simplicity, interpretability and high accuracy. While a challenge

M. Sun et al. (Eds.): CCL and NLP-NABD 2014, LNAI 8801, pp. 1–12, 2014.

for Bayesian unsupervised word segmentation is how to model contextual dependencies. Contextual information plays a significant role in evaluating segmentation scores. Contextual dependencies include word-level dependencies and character-level dependencies. Several hierarchical Bayesian models are capable to capture continuous word-level dependencies [3–5]. Besides, [4] considered continuous character dependencies and [5] characterized a wider range of inter-word dependencies by adaptor grammars which is the state-of-the-art model. But adaptor grammars for segmentation is dependent on language. Different grammars need to be carefully designed for different languages. It is still expensive to apply adaptor grammar on natural text corpora due to high computational cost.

In addition to normal word-level dependencies, our approach utilizes character-level dependencies from three perspectives. Firstly, we try to explore not only continuous character groups but also gappy character patterns among different words. For example, we intend to learn the extremely meaningful gappy pattern "h...t" among words such as "**h**a**t**", "**h**i**t**","**h**o**t**" and "**h**ur**t**". Similar patterns also can be easily found in Chinese. Pattern "计...器" appears in words such as "计算器 (calculator)", "计时器 (timer)", "计分器 (scoring indicator)" and "计程器 (taximeter)". When we come to a plausible word of this pattern, it might be reasonable to assign this word high probability. Secondly, We pay direct attention to the location of a character. The location of a character in a string have great impacts on whether the character should be merged into left, right or as a separate word. For example, given an English string "**a**sm**a**rtboy", the first letter "a" tends to be a separate word, but the fourth letter "a" tends to be combined with other characters. Thirdly, we show emphasis on the fertility of a character. Fertility means that how many characters a character usually related to. It has an implicit influence on word length which is believed to be an important factor for unsupervised word segmentation.

Word alignment models for SMT are very good at inducing lexical association, locality and fertility parameters. [6] exploited monolingual word alignments to extract collocations. [7] demonstrated that these factors were surprisingly effective for the unsupervised dependency parsing under a monolingual alignment model. We are inspired to treat the word segmentation as a problem of monolingual character alignment. By taking the source side and the target side as the same sequence of monolingual characters, we can produce an alignment inside a string. When we produce a character alignment, we simultaneously obtain a segmentation that each word is consistent with the character alignment by a mapping algorithm. A Gibbs sampler samples every candidate alignment position for each character. The posterior distribution is product of experts of IBM Models 1-3 [8], hidden markov alignment model [9], as well as a hierarchical Pitman-Yor language model [10]. After several iterations, most frequent samples are selected to be final segmentation results.

Our model achieves an 88.6% word token F-score on English phonetic transcripts corpora [11], which outperforms the best model in [4] by more than 16.5% in F-score and approaches the state-of-art model [5]. On standard Chinese text datasets, we also improve the segmentation accuracy by 1.9 to 2.9 F-score points compared to [1].

The rest of the paper is organized as follows. After introducing background and related works, we describe the joint model. Then we explain the Gibbs sampling algorithm. In the last two sections, we show the experimental results and draw conclusions.

2 Background and Related Work

2.1 Word Alignment

Given a foreign sentence $\mathbf{f} = (f_1, ..., f_J)$ and an English sentence $\mathbf{e} = (e_1, ..., e_I)$, to model the translation probability from $\mathbf{e}$ to $\mathbf{f}$, a hidden alignment variable a is introduced, $Pr(\mathbf{f}|\mathbf{e}) = \sum_a Pr(\mathbf{f}, a|\mathbf{e})$, where $a = (a_1, ..., a_J)$ and $a_j \in \{0, ..., I\}$. IBM model 1 only considers lexical translation probability $t(f_j|e_{a_j})$. Model 2 adds an explicit alignment model $a(a_j|j, I, J)$, which considers the impact of location. Model 3 adds a fertility model $n(\phi_i|e_i)$ to indicate how many words e usually translates to. In Hidden Markov alignment model, an alignment is dependent of the previous one.

The word alignment problem was joint inference with segmentation learning in [12], [13] and [14]. But all these works rely on bilingual information.

2.2 Introduction to Pitman-Yor Process

A Pitman-Yor Process (PYP) [15] is a stochastic process that generates power-law distributions. It is governed by a discount parameter $0 \leq d < 1$, a strength parameter $a > -d$ and a base distribution G_0. The generated distribution G is marked as $G \sim PYP(a, d, G_0)$. The discount parameter d is responsible for probability smoothing while the strength parameter a controls the similarity between G_0 and G.

The generative procedure of PYP can be represented by a variant of the Chinese Restaurant Process (CRP). CRP can be described using the analogy of a restaurant has an infinite number of tables, each of which has an infinite capacity for customers. Customers enter the restaurant one by one and each chooses to sit at a table. The first customer always sits at the first table. Suppose after a time, a restaurant already has n customers and m occupied tables. The next customer either selects an occupied table $(1 \leq k \leq m)$ or an empty table $(k = m+1)$ to seat. Let z_i be the table index of the i-th customer. Then the table choosing probability

$$p(z_{n+1} = k|z_1, ..., z_n) = \begin{cases} \dfrac{c_{t_k} - d}{n+a} & 1 \leq k \leq m \\ \dfrac{d * m + a}{n+a} & k = m+1 \end{cases} \tag{1}$$

where c_{t_k} is the number of customers seated at table k in $z_1, ..., z_n$.

For the labeled PYP, we can regard "label" as a dish served to customers. When a customer seat an occupied table, he can share the dish labeling that table with others. Otherwise, the table he takes will be labeled by a dish h with probability $G_0(h)$. Let l_i denote the label of table i. Given previous label and table assignments, we can sum over all the tables labeled with h,

$$p(l_{n+1} = h|z_1, ..., z_n, l_1, ..., l_n) = \frac{c_h - d * m_h + (d * m + a) * G_0(h)}{n+a} \tag{2}$$

where m_h is the number of tables served with the dish h and c_h is the number of customers who are served with the dish h in the previous table assignments.

Labeled PYP is used by many bayesian unsupervised word segmentation models. The hierarchical Pitman-Yor language model describes the n-gram language model in a way that the $(n-1)-$gram probability distribution is used as the base distribution to generate n-gram probability distribution. The unigram model $G_1 = \{P_1(\cdot)\}$ is generated as $G_1 \propto PYP(a_1, d_1, G_0)$, the bigram model $G_2 = \{P_2(\cdot|w)\}$ is generated as $G_2 \propto PYP(a_2, d_2, G_1)$ and so on. G_0 is a probability distribution of words in the corpus vocabulary. [4] employs a nested hierarchical Pitman-Yor language model. The base distribution $G_0 = \{P_0(\cdot)\}$ is also generated as $G_0 \propto PYP(a_0, d_0, G_c)$, where G_c is a character-level n-gram language model and G_c is generated in the same way of word-level distributions. Dirichlet Process and Hierarchical Dirichlet Process are also used for segmentation in [3][16]. Dirichlet Process is a special case of PYP with discount parameter equals to zero. Adaptor grammars also uses PYP to describe the probability distribution of a parsing rule [5].

3 Joint Model of Character Alignment and Word Segmentation

3.1 Monolingual Character Alignment (MCA)

Given a string $\mathbf{s} = c_1...c_n$, the character alignment $a^* = \{(j, a_j)|j \in [1...n], a_j \in [0...n]\}$ is computed by equation (4).

$$a^* = \arg\max_a P(a|\mathbf{s}) \tag{3}$$

$a_j = i$ means character c_j aligns to character c_i. $a_j = 0$ means character c_j aligns to "NULL". Monolingual character alignment (MCA) prevents each character is aligned to itself at the same position. Without this constraint, each character will tend to align to itself. That kind of alignments make no sense for segmentation. Figure 1 shows two MCA examples of string "asmartboy".

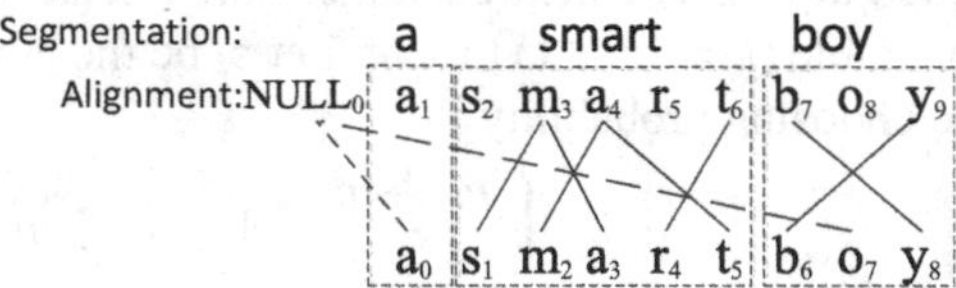

(a) A correct segmentation example

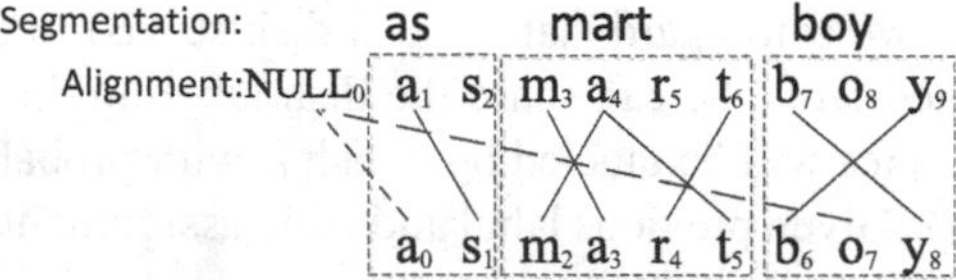

(b) A wrong segmentation example

Fig. 1. Two alignment examples of string "asmartboy". The subscript number stands for the corresponding position in a string. (a) has a good derivation for correct segmentation , "a smart boy". (b) leads to a bad result,"as mart boy".

3.2 Generative Story

Given a string s, our model maximizes the probability of a character alignment a and a word segmentation w by equation (5).

$$(a^*, w^*) = \underset{a,w}{\arg\max}\, p(a, w|\mathbf{s}, \Theta) \tag{4}$$

Θ is hyperparameter. We apply generative models to decompose $p(a, w|\mathbf{s}, \Theta)$.

Two-Stage Model: The simplest way is to employ a two-stage model. Firstly, we generate a character alignment inside the given string. Then, we deduce a word segmentation result from the character alignment. The decomposing procedure is shown in equation (6).

$$p(a, w|\mathbf{s}, \Theta) = p(a|\mathbf{s}, \Theta) * p(w|a, \mathbf{s}, \Theta) \tag{5}$$

$p(a|\mathbf{s}, \Theta)$ is the alignment model and $p(w|a, \mathbf{s}, \Theta)$ is the segmentation model. But the two-stage model has two disadvantages. First, the alignment a is very sparse. The segmentation model has little effect on the alignment model. The purpose of MCA is to infer a good segmentation, rather than to capture translation clues. We suppose character alignment and word segmentation benefit from each other. A good character alignment could lead to a good word segmentation and vice versa. Second, the computational cost of $p(w|a, \mathbf{s}, \Theta)$ is relatively expensive since every alignment has the probability to be mapped to several segmentations according to different heuristic rules. The segmentation selection procedure is relatively slow.

One-Step Model: In order to overcome defects of the two-stage model, the one-step model produce word segmentation and character alignment simultaneously. The generating procedure is shown in equation (7).

$$p(a, w|\mathbf{s}, \Theta) = p(a|\mathbf{s}, \Theta) * p(w_a|\mathbf{s}, \Theta) \tag{6}$$

w_a denotes the corresponding segmentation according to character alignment a. This model generates a character alignment a first. At the same time, it converts a to a unique segmentation w_a. The segmentation result is the side product of character alignment. One advantage of this model is that it makes a tighter connection between character alignment and word segmentation. When generating a character alignment, the probability of the corresponding segmentation must be considered. For example, if we want to compare the two alignments in Figure 1, we need to consider the plausibility of related segmentations, "a smart boy" and "as mart boy". Another advantage is that it is efficient because it performs a unique mapping from character alignment to segmentation and only requires a single step computing.

3.3 Mapping Alignment to Segmentation

We design a mapping algorithm for extracting segmentation $\mathbf{w} = w_1 ... w_2$ from character alignment $\mathbf{a}$ according to **alignment consistency**. Statistical machine translation models often make use of alignment consistency to extract bilingual phrase pairs. A span $c_i ... c_j$ is consistent with character alignment if their alignments satisfy two conditions. (1) $\forall k$, if $i \leq k \leq j$, then $a_k \in 0 \cup [i, j]$; (2) $\forall k$, if $k < i$ or $k > j$, then $a_k \notin [i, j]$; We assume if a span consistent with character alignment then this span is a high plausible word. Considering length factors, we choose **smallest non-crossed span** as a word. In figure 1(a), span "asmart" is a valid span of alignment consistency, but it is too long. Instead, we regard two smaller spanes "a" and "smart" as words. In monolingual character alignment, a span consistent with alignment may cover another one. In figure 1(a), "o" is a span consistent with alignment, but links "b-y" and "y-b" cross this span, therefore we choose the longer span "boy" as a word. The smallest non-crossed strategy try to control the length of a word as well as to bond connected characters as many as possible into a word. The mapping algorithm is shown in Algorithm 1.

In Algorithm 1, we do a greedy search to find smallest non-crossed span set w. Line 1-3 is initiation. f stands for the start point of the next smallest non-crossed span. P stands for the alignment boundary of the previous character. C stands for the alignment boundary of the current character. The alignment boundary of a character means the minimum value and maximum value of the set of its position, the position it aligned to and all positions aligned to it. For example, in figure 1(a), the alignment boundary of m_3 is $< 2, 4 >$. Line 4-14 traverse remained characters one by one. According to the relationship of P and C, word boundaries are determined. Line 6-10 means if P and C are not intersected, then we find a target span $[f, i-1]$ and update the value of P and f. Line 11-14 means if P and C are intersected, then we merge P and C. $P \oplus C = [\min(P.l, C.l), \max(P.r, C.r)]$. At last, we add the tail span to w at line 15. According to Algorithm 1, two character alignments and their corresponding segmentations are shown in Figure 1.

3.4 Product of Experts

We decompose $p(\mathbf{a}|\mathbf{s}, \Theta)$ in equation (7) into four sub-models according to IBM Models and Hidden Markov alignment model. Those models are used to exploit literal, position and fertility factors for segmentation. Considering character alignment and word segmentation could have effect on each other in the one-step model, we use a product of experts (PoE) to combine them. PoE multiplies several probability distribution together and has bias toward samples which have high probability in all sub-models. Let random variable aw be the pair of a and w. The probability distribution $P(aw|\mathbf{s}, \Theta)$ under PoE is shown in Equation (8).

$$P(aw|s) = \frac{\prod_i P_i(aw|s)}{\sum_{aw'} \prod_i P_i(aw'|s)}, \quad i \in \{m_1, m_2, m_3, m_h, m_s\} \tag{7}$$

m_1, m_2, m_3 and m_h are adapted from alignment models IBM Model 1-3 and HMM model respectively. m_s is a model for segmentation. Distributions over these five sub-models and their Pitman-Yor priors are shown in Table 1.

Character Association Model: Characters with high co-occurrence will tend to be bound together. IBM Model 1 is changed to model the character association probability in MCA.

$$P_{m_1}(aw|s) = P_{m_1}(a|s) = \prod_{i=1}^{l} P_{m_1}(c_i|c_{a_i}) \tag{8}$$

l is the length of s. $P_{m_1}(c_j|c_i)$ describes the probability c_j is connected to c_i. In Table 1, $|V|$ is the number of character types in the corpus.

Table 1. Distributions over five sub-models and their Pitman-Yor priors.

model	distribution
m_1	$c_j\|c_i; G_1^{m_1}(c_i) \sim PYP(a^{m_1}, d^{m_1}, G_0^{m_1}),\ G_0^{m_1} \sim U(\frac{1}{\|V\|})$
m_2	$m_i\|n_i; G_1^{m_2}(n_i) \sim PYP(a^{m_2}, d^{m_2}, G_0^{m_2}),\ G_0^{m_2} \sim U(\frac{1}{D})$
m_3	$\phi_i\|c_i, G_1^{m_3}(c_i) \sim PYP(a^{m_3}, d^{m_3}, G_0^{m_3}),\ G_0^{m_3} \sim U(\frac{1}{F})$
m_h	$hd_i\|hc_i, G_1^{m_h}(hc_i) \sim PYP(a^{m_h}, d^{m_h}, G_0^{m_h}),\ G_0^{m_h} \sim U(\frac{1}{T})$
m_s	$w_i\|w_{i-1}; G_2^{m_s} \sim PYP(a_2^{m_s}, d_2^{m_s}, G_1^{m_s})$ $w_i; G_1^{m_s} \sim PYP(a_1^{m_s}, d_1^{m_s}, G_0^{m_s})$

Location Model: We use a same alternate distance model described in [7].

$$P_{m_2}(aw|s) = P_{m_2}(a|s) = \prod_{i=1}^{l} P_{m_2}(a_i - i|c_i, l) \tag{9}$$

In Table 1, $m_i = a_i - i$ and $n_i = (c_i, l)$, $P_{m_2}(m_i|n_i)$ describes the probability of the alignment offset of n_i is m_i. D is the types of possible values of m_i. We use $D = 10$ in this paper. The valid value of m_i is restricted to $[-5, 5]$. We prevent too long alignments because it will cause the under-segmentation problem. When $a_i = 0$, we use a similar method used in [17] by viewing every character is preceded by a NULL token. It means that if $a_i = 0$ then $a_i - i$ is set to be 1. Location model tries to make the same character behave differently in different positions.

Fertility Model: IBM Model 3 introduces two kinds of probability, NULL insertion probability and fertility probability. NULL insertion can not be applied to MCA. Because source side and target side are the same in MCA, so we do not need to insert NULL tokens in target side. Also in MCA all characters are allowed to be aligned to NULL, Thus $l - \phi_0$ might be zero. ϕ_0 denotes the number of characters aligned to NULL. Instead, we directly handle the alignment probability from NULL by

$$P_{m_3}(aw|s) = P_{m_3}(a|s) = \binom{l}{\phi_0} p_1^{\phi_0} p_0^{l-\phi_0} \prod_{i=1}^{l} \phi_i! n(\phi_i|c_i) \tag{10}$$

$n(\phi_i|c_i)$ indicates the probability of ϕ_i characters are aligned to c_i. In Table 1, F is types of character fertilities. We use $F = 5$ in this paper. p_1 is the probability of a character linked to NULL, $p_0 = 1 - p_1$. A character which prefers to distribution over greater value of ϕ has a tendency of forming multi-character words with neighboring aligned characters. We use $p_1 = 0.2$ in this paper.

Transition Model: [9] proposed a HMM-based alignment model. Similar to the Location Model, we reformulate the transition probability as:

$$P_{m_h}(aw|s) = P_{m_h}(a|s) = \prod_{i=1}^{l} P_{m_h}(a_i - a_{i-1}|c_{a_{i-1}}, l) \tag{11}$$

In Table 1, $hd_i = a_i - a_{i-1}$ and $hc_i = (c_i, l)$. T is the number of distance types. We make $T = 5$ in this paper. This model depicts the first order dependence of jump over characters. Jump distance is usually small inside a word but large between word boundaries. When $a_i = 0$, the same method mentioned in Location Model is used to calculate the distance.

Segmentation Model: A bigram Pitman-Yor language model is adopted as:

$$P_{m_s}(aw|s) = P_{m_s}(w_a|s) = \prod_{i=1}^{l+1} P_{m_s}(w_i|w_{i-1}) \tag{12}$$

A special marker \$ is added to both the start and the end of the word sequence. In Table 1, the spelling model $G_0^{m_s}(w)$ is the same as [12]:

$$G_0^{m_s}(w) = \frac{e^{-\lambda_0}{\lambda_0}^k}{k!}\frac{1}{|V|^k} \tag{13}$$

where k is the length of w. Different from [12], we use a method proposed in [4] to estimate λ_0 by a Gamma Prior during each iteration instead of leaving it as a constant.

Algorithm 1: Converting Alignment to Segmentation

```
Input: string s, alignment boundary b
Output: word spanes w
w ← φ
f ← 1
P ←< b[1].l, b[1].r >
for i ← 2...|s| do
    C ←< b[1].l, b[1].r >
    if !P ∩ C then
        w ← w ∪ [f, i − 1]
        f ← i
        P ← C
    end
    else
        P ← P ⊕ C
    end
end
w ← w ∪ [f, |s|]
```

Algorithm 2: Gibbs sampler of MCA

```
Input: S, B
Output: Θ
Initialize segmentations w and alignments A;
for m = 1 to B do
    for a in A do
        Remove customers of w_a from Θ;
        for i = 1 to |a| do
            Remove (i, a_i) from Θ;
            Draw a_i according to equation (14);
            Add (i, a_i) to Θ;
        end
        Add customers of w_a to Θ
    end
    Sample Hyperparameters of Θ;
end
```

4 Gibbs Sampling

It is hard to do exact inference due to the exponential alignments in equation (8). Therefore, we use Gibbs sampling to simulate the procedure of character alignment. Gibbs sampling is a special case of Monte Carlo Markov Chain method, and it is guaranteed to converge to the true posterior distribution. The denominator in equation (8) is expensive to track, therefore we ignore the denominator. Assume before a sampling iteration the segmentation of a string $\mathbf{s}$ is w. The distribution of candidate alignments of a position i conditioned on other values is:

$$P(a_i = j|\mathbf{A}_{-i}, \mathbf{S}; \mathbf{\Theta}) \propto P_{m_s}(w'_{a_i=j}|\mathbf{W}(\mathbf{A})_{-w_a}; \mathbf{\Theta}) \times \prod_k P_k(a_i = j|\mathbf{A}_{-i}, \mathbf{S}; \mathbf{\Theta}) \tag{14}$$

where $k \in \{m_1, m_2, m_3, m_h\}$, the subscript $-i$ denotes the exclusion of current position, $-w_a$ denotes the exclusion of current segmentation. $w'_{a_i=j}$ means the new segmentation after setting $a_i = j$.

The sampling algorithm is described in Algorithm 2. S is the monolingual corpus, B is the number of burn-in iterations. The Gibbs sampler first randomly initializes word boundaries of a string and then randomly assigns an alignment connected to characters in the same word for each character. After initialization, the Gibbs sampler repeatedly samples a reasonable alignment for each character conditioned on all other alignments and segmentations. A blocked computing is performed by moving an alignment from one position to another since each movement might result in different segmentations. An example of counts change during one movement is shown in Table 3. After B burn-in iterations, we collect K segmentation samples for each string s. The most frequent sample will be the final result. As for the hyper-parameter sampling, we use a slice sampler [5] by putting a flat beta prior $Beta(1, 1)$ on the discount parameter d and a vague prior $Gamma(10, 0.1)$ on the strength parameter a.

5 Experiments

To evaluate the efficiency of our model, we conducted experiments on two kinds of corpus. One of them is the public SIGHAN Bakeoff 2005 dataset [18]. This dataset contains four kinds of data, i.e. CITYU, MSR, PKU and AS. CITYU and AS are traditional Chinese text. MSR and PKU are simplified Chinese text. We only use the test set data for alignment. The other corpus consists of English phonetic scripts made by Brent of the Bernstein-Ratner corpus [11] in the CHILDES database [19]. A line of this corpus is "yuwanttusiD6bUk" and the corresponding English text is "you want to see the book". We need to segment the phonetic script into "yu want tu si D6 bUk". Details of all corpora are shown in Table 2.

For Chinese, punctuation and consecutive non-Chinese characters are recognized as a single character,such as English letters and Arabic numerals. We make use of them to segment a long string into several shorter strings. This preprocessing is beneficial for string alignment to overcome a part of sparsity of sentence length. We compare our result with models that also encode the information of punctuation or word types.

For each corpus, we simultaneously ran 4 chains. Each chain employs a Gibbs sampler for 501 iterations, including 250 burn-in iterations. In order to speed up convergence, we use a simulated annealing procedure, which cools down the Gibbs sampler from a high temperature $T_0 = 10$ to a final temperature $T_f = 1$ with geometric decline $(\frac{T_f}{T_0})^{\frac{1}{n}}$. n is the number of burn-in iterations. After each 10 iteration, we sample hyperparameters for 20 iterations.

Generally, We use word token precision(P), recall(R), F1-measure(F) to evaluate the performance. For phonetic scripts, we also calculate the same metrics(LP, LR, LF) over induced lexicons.

5.1 English phonetic transcripts

On English phonetic transcripts, we compared our model with Hierarchical Dirichlet Process based model (HDP), Nested Hierarchical Pitman-Yor Langauge model (NPY)

Table 2. Statistics of five corpora. W: words. C: characters. AC: the average count of a word. Word tokens divided by word types equals AC. Seg_sents: the number of sentences after preprocessing.

Corpus	W			C		Sents	Seg_sents
	AC	Types	Tokens	Types	Tokens		
CITYU	4.5	9001	40937	2953	66346	1492	11584
AS	6.5	18811	122613	3884	196299	14432	36392
PKU	7.9	13149	104373	3433	168975	1946	31128
MSR	8.3	12923	106873	3341	180987	3985	33189
Brent	25.3	1321	33399	50	95809	9791	9791

and Adaptor Grammar based model (AG). Table 4 shows the accuracy of segmentation results. Word token accuracy of our model has surpassed both HDP and NPY. It is surprised that the result of MCA is so close to AG, even MCA has a weaker ability to identify word-level collocations compared to a three layers of collocation-syllable structure in AG. One significant difference between AG and MCA is that AG models the relationship between characters in terms of a hierarchical syllable structure while MCA applies an alignment structure.

5.2 Model Comparison

We design experiments to show the effectiveness of five sub-models. Results of multiple combinations are shown in Table 5. m_1 and m_s are essential for basic segmentation. We include them in all combinations. By comparison setting (1) to (2), (3) to (4) and (4) to (6), we can find F value increase by 25.2, 16.9 and 18.6 points respectively. It approves our hypothesis that location factor m_2 plays a crucial role in improving segmentation result. Another interesting phenomenon we observed is that model m_3 always helps improve the recall value. With analysis of setting (2) and (3) together with setting (5) and (6), we can infer that the precision value does not change too much, but the recall value both increase by 5.7 points. This result can explain our fertility factor m_3 is capable of overcoming the under-segment problem to some extent. Although m_h also is a location factor, it is less powerful than m_2. But combining these two overlapped factors still achieve a valuable improvement.

5.3 Chinese Word Segmentation

For each Chinese corpus, we only use the test set data. As far as we known, ESA [1] has reported results under the same experimental conditions. NPY model used additional training data. So we use ESA as our baseline model. Results are shown in Table 6.

Our model gains an accuracy improvement from 1.9 points to 2.9 points. Even when compared to NPY model, we outperform them on MSR data set with 1.7 points improvement. However, MCA loses to NPY on CITYU corpus. We can infer from Table 2 that CITYU is a smaller corpus compared to another three Chinese corpora, and the AC value is the smallest. It tends to have a positive correlation between AC and the accuracy improvements. The greater AC value is, the more times a word appears from a corpora. Characters inside general words will have stronger relationships. NPY has good performance on smaller corpus while MCA might show its potential on larger corpus. Some examples of segmentation of MSR corpus are" 但 做 一些 **力所能及** 的 小事 的 机会 却 很多 。 有些 大 学生 **眼高手低** ， 不 屑于 做 小 事情". From these results, we can see that our method can recognize some words with complex character structures, such as "力所能及" and "眼高手低". Some words are over-segmented. "大 学生" should be merged as a whole word. "大" can be regarded as affix characters, it often appears in the boundary of a word. Therefore, they are more probable to align to NULL. This phenomenon can lead to some fine-grained segmentation results. But fine-grained segmentation results might be more suitable for SMT, we will evaluate them in future.

Table 3. Counts change when the alignment of s_1 moves from m_3 to a_1, as shown from Figure 1(a) to Figure1(b)

model	decrement	increment
m_1	$(s\|m)$	$(s\|a)$
m_2	$(2\|s,9)$	$(0\|s,9)$
m_3	$(1\|m),(0\|a)$	$(1\|a),(0\|m)$
m_h	$(2\|s,9),(1\|m,9)$	$(0\|s,9),(3\|m,9)$
m_s	\$ a smart boy \$	\$ as mart boy \$

Table 4. Segmentation accuracies on Brent Corpus. NPY(n) denotes n-gram NPY language model. HDP refers to the result reported in [16].

Model	P	R	F	LP	LR	LF
HDP	75.2	69.6	72.3	**63.5**	55.2	**59.1**
NPY(2)	74.8	76.7	75.7	57.3	56.6	57.0
NPY(3)	74.8	75.2	75.0	47.8	**59.7**	53.1
AG	-	-	**89**	-	-	-
MCA	**87.0**	**90.4**	88.6	63.2	52.9	57.6

Table 5. F-measure comparsion using various model combinations on English phonetic transcripts

Model	P	R	F
$(1)m_1 + m_s$	65.7	53.5	**59.0**
$(2)m_1 + m_2 + m_s$	85.7	**82.7**	**84.2**
$(3)m_1 + m_2 + m_3 + m_s$	85.4	**88.4**	**86.9**
$(4)m_1 + m_h + m_3 + m_s$	72.7	62.0	**70.0**
$(5)m_1 + m_2 + m_h + m_s$	86.2	**84.7**	85.4
(6)All	87.0	**90.4**	**88.6**

Table 6. Segmentation accuracy on Chinese corpora. ESA_{best} denotes setting 4 in [1]. Marker '+' shows the increment from ESA_{best} to MCA.

Model	CITYU	PKU	MSR	AS
ESA_{best}	76.0	77.8	80.1	78.5
NPY(2)	**82.4**	-	80.2	-
NPY(3)	81.7	-	80.7	-
MCA	77.9 (+1.9)	**80.7** (+2.9)	**82.4** (+2.3)	**80.6** (+2.1)

6 Conclusion and Future Work

We present that it is beneficial to incorporate global character features into hierarchical bayesian models for unsupervised word segmentation. We adopt a joint model to produce monolingual character alignment and word segmentation at the same time. Through experiments, we show that this model plays a significant role in improving word segmentation accuracy on both phonetic scripts and Chinese natural text corpus. In the future, we will work out character to block alignment models instead of transforming character to character alignment models at hand.

Acknowledgements. Work supported by National Natural Science Foundation of China (Contract 61202216) and CAS Action Plan for the Development of Western China (No. KGZD- EW-501).

References

1. Wang, H., Zhu, J., Tang, S., Fan, X.: A new unsupervised approach to word segmentation. CL 37, 421–454 (2011)
2. Sun, M., Shen, D., Tsou, B.K.: Chinese word segmentation without using lexicon and hand-crafted training data. In: Proceedings of the Joint Conference of ACL and COLING, Montreal, Quebec, Canada, pp. 1265–1271. ACL (1998)
3. Goldwater, S., Griffiths, T.L., Johnson, M.: Contextual dependencies in unsupervised word segmentation. In: Proceedings of the Joint Conference of ACL and COLING, ACL-44, Stroudsburg, PA, USA, pp. 673–680 (2006)
4. Mochihashi, D., Yamada, T., Ueda, N.: Bayesian unsupervised word segmentation with nested pitman-yor language modeling. In: Proceedings of the Joint Conference of ACL and IJCNLP, ACL 2009, Stroudsburg, PA, USA, pp. 100–108 (2009)
5. Johnson, M., Goldwater, S.: Improving nonparameteric bayesian inference: experiments on unsupervised word segmentation with adaptor grammars. In: Proceedings of Human Language Technologies: The 2009 NAACL, NAACL 2009, Stroudsburg, PA, USA, pp. 317–325 (2009)
6. Liu, Z., Wang, H., Wu, H., Li, S.: Collocation extraction using monolingual word alignment method. In: Proceedings of EMNLP, Singapore, pp. 487–495 (2009)
7. Brody, S.: It depends on the translation: unsupervised dependency parsing via word alignment. In: Proceedings of EMNLP, EMNLP 2010, Stroudsburg, PA, USA, pp. 1214–1222 (2010)
8. Brown, P.F., Pietra, V.J.D., Pietra, S.A.D., Mercer, R.L.: The mathematics of statistical machine translation: Parameter estimation. Comput. Linguist. 19, 263–311 (1993)
9. Vogel, S., Ney, H., Tillmann, C.: Hmm-based word alignment in statistical translation. In: Proceedings of COLING, COLING 1996, Stroudsburg, PA, USA, pp. 836–841 (1996)
10. Teh, Y.W.: A hierarchical bayesian language model based on pitman-yor processes. In: Proceedings of the Joint Conference of ACL and COLING, ACL-44, Stroudsburg, PA, USA, pp. 985–992 (2006)
11. Bernstein-Ratner, N.: The phonology of parent-child speech. In: Nelson, K., van Kleeck, A. (eds.), vol. 6. Erlbaum, Hillsdale (1987)
12. Xu, J., Gao, J., Toutanova, K., Ney, H.: Bayesian semi-supervised Chinese word segmentation for statistical machine translation. In: Proceedings of COLING, COLING 2008, Stroudsburg, PA, USA, pp. 1017–1024 (2008)
13. Nguyen, T., Vogel, S., Smith, N.A.: Nonparametric word segmentation for machine translation. In: Proceedings of COLING, COLING 2010, Stroudsburg, PA, USA, pp. 815–823 (2010)
14. Chung, T., Gildea, D.: Unsupervised tokenization for machine translation. In: Proceedings of EMNLP, EMNLP 2009, Stroudsburg, PA, USA, pp. 718–726 (2009)
15. Pitman, J., Yor, M.: The two-parameter Poisson-Dirichlet distribution derived from a stable subordinator (1995)
16. Goldwater, S., Griffiths, T.L., Johnson, M.: A bayesian framework for word segmentation: Exploring the effects of Context. Cognition 112, 21–54 (2009)
17. Och, F.J., Ney, H., Josef, F., Ney, O.H.: A systematic comparison of various statistical alignment models. Computational Linguistics 29 (2003)
18. Tom, E.: Second international Chinese word segmentation bakeoff (2005)
19. MacWhinney, B., Snow, C., et al.: The child language data exchange system. Journal of Child Language 12, 271–296 (1985)

Improving Multi-pass Transition-Based Dependency Parsing Using Enhanced Shift Actions

Chenxi Zhu, Xipeng Qiu, and Xuanjing Huang

[1] Shanghai Key Laboratory of Intelligent Information Processing
[2] School of Computer Science, Fudan University, Shanghai, China
{13210240078,xpqiu,xjhuang}@fudan.edu.cn

Abstract. In multi-pass transition-based dependency parsing algorithm, the *shift* actions are usually inconsistent for the same node pair in different passes. Some node pairs have a indeed dependency relation, but the modifier node has not been a complete subtree yet. The bottom-up parsing strategy requires to perform *shift* action for these node pairs. In this paper, we propose a method to improve performance of parsing by using enhanced *shift* actions. These actions can be further used as features for the next parsing decision. Experimental results show that our method is effective to improve the performance of parsing.

1 Introduction

In recent years, data-driven deterministic dependency parsing has received an increasing amount of interests. Dependency parsing uses dependency representation of syntactic structure, which directly reflects relationships among the words in a sentence. Dependency parsing is usually more efficient and accurate than constituency parsing, since dependency trees are inherently lexicalized and do not need full structure grammar and extra non-terminal nodes. Therefore, dependency parsing is widely used in a variety of practical tasks, especially for web-scale data.

Currently, there are two main kinds of approaches for data-driven dependency parsing: graph-based [10] and transition-based methods [18, 12].

The graph-based methods generate dependency trees by considering all possible spanning trees [10]. Graph-based methods usually consist of two stages. In the scoring stage, a classifier is used to score all possible edges (or other small substructures), in the decoding stage, the highest scoring parse tree is found from all possible outputs by combinatorial optimization algorithm. When the dependency tree is projective, the time complexity is $O(n^2)$ for first-order models using a minimum directed spanning tree algorithm [4, 8].

The transition-based methods use a classifier to make greedy decisions of parsing actions locally [18, 12]. Transition-based parsing gives complexities as low as $O(n)$ or $O(n^2)$ for parsing.

Although the transition-based methods usually run fast and performs accurately, they suffer the problems of error propagation. Therefore, their performances are slightly below the graph-based methods[2, 11]. However, recent researches on transition-based dependency parsing have therefore explored different ways of improving their accuracy

M. Sun et al. (Eds.): CCL and NLP-NABD 2014, LNAI 8801, pp. 13–22, 2014.

[19, 1, 17]. With these methods, transition-based parsers have reached state-of-the-art accuracy for a number of languages.

The state-of-the-art transition-based parsers use only one shift action, which obviously loses some information which will be helpful for the dependency parsing. Especially in multi-pass transition-based dependency parsing algorithm, the *shift* actions are usually inconsistent for the same node pair in different passes. Some node pairs have a indeed dependency relation, but the modifier node has not been a complete subtree yet. The bottom-up parsing strategy requires to perform *shift* action for these node pairs.

In this paper, we explore a new approach to improve the accuracy of transition-based parsers by using the enhanced shift actions, which combine the actions and the relations between the target nodes. Our method can give a link between actions and the real relations between the target nodes. While all previous transition systems ignore shift information, our new system distinguishes the shift action by the relation between the two target nodes. With the more detailed actions, the parser can predict more accurately when it has to decide whether the action should be left or right after several *shift* actions between the target nodes. Besides, the previous actions can be helpful for next decision by using these actions as features.

The experiments show that our method leads to significant improvements in parsing accuracy, compared to a baseline parser. Our parser also performs better than Maltparser [12], which is one of the most widely used state-of-the-art transition-based systems.

The rest of the paper is organized as follows: We first describe the multi-pass transition-based parsing in section 2 and give a discussion for the shift action used in current state-of-the-art algorithm in section 3. Then we propose our method on section 4. The experimental results are given in section 5. Finally, we introduce the related work in section 6 and conclude our work in section 7.

2 Multi-pass Transition-Based Dependency Parsing

Our work is based on the Yamada's algorithm [18], which performs multi-pass scans of a partially built dependency structure.

In a transition-based system, an input sentence is usually processed from left to right. Yamada's algorithm uses a deterministic analyzing model based on shift-reduce algorithm. It performs multi-pass scans of a partially built dependency structure. At each point, it focuses on a pair of adjacent nodes in the partial dependency structure and uses a support vector machine to decide whether to create a dependency link between them or to shift the focus to the next pair of heads.

There are three following deterministic actions:

shift No construction of dependencies between these target nodes, and the position of focus simply moves to the right.

left A dependency relation is constructed between two neighboring nodes where the right node of target nodes becomes a child of the left one.

right A dependency relation is constructed between two neighboring nodes where the left node of target nodes becomes a child of the right one.

Yamada' parsing algorithm consists of three steps: (i) Estimate the appropriate parsing actions using contextual information surrounding the target nodes, (ii) constructs a dependency tree by executing the estimated actions, (iii) if there is no construction in one pass, get the left or right action which has the max probability in the dependency tree to construct.

The pseudo-code of our parsing algorithm is shown in Algorithm 1.

We use T to represent the sequence of nodes consisting of m elements $t_m (m \leq n)$, each element of which represents the root node of a sub-tree constructed in the parsing process (initially all t_i is a word w_i).

During the execution, the parsing action $y_i \in \{Right; Left; Shift\}$ is estimated for the focus nodes pair $< t_i, t_{i+1} >$. Meanwhile, we use y_i' to record the substitute action if $y_i = shift$. y_i' is the action with second largest score s_i' given by a classifier.

If every action $y_i = shift$ for $i = 1, \cdots, T - 1$ in one pass, no construction is executed and the variable $no\_construction = true$. We select the action y_j' and make the construction. $j = \arg\max_i s_i'$.

The contextual features x are extracted from the context surrounding $< t_i, t_{i+1} >$. Then an appropriate parsing action $y \in \{Right; Left; Shift\}$ is estimated by one or more classifiers.

```
input  : Input Sentence: (w1, w2 ··· wn)
output: dependency tree T and |T| = 1
Initialize:
  i = 1 ;
  T = w1, w2 ··· wn ;
  no_construction = true ;
  while |T| ≥ 1 do
    if i == |T| then
      if no_construction == true then
        find the substitute action y'j with largest score j = arg max_i s'i
        construct(T, j, y'j);
        no_construction = false ;
        i = j ;
      end
    end
    get the contextual features x;
    estimate the substitute action y;
    construction(T, i, y) ;
    if y == left or right then
      no_construction = false ;
    else
      estimate the substitute action y'i and its score s'i ;
    end
  end
  return T ;
```

Algorithm 1. Parsing Algorithm

The complexity of the algorithm is $O(n^2)$ in worst case because it takes up to $n1$ passes to construct a complete dependency tree. However, it runs in linear time in practice.

3 Discussion of Shift Action in Multi-pass Transition-Based Parsing

Due to the bottom-up regulation, a dependency relation $h \leftarrow d$ can be constructed only after all modifiers of the d have been constructed. Therefore, there are two cases for *shift* action in Yamada's algorithm: (a) there is no dependencies relation between the node pair, (b) there is dependency relation between the node pair, but the modifier node has not been a complete subtree yet. These two cases are shown in Figure 1. ABC is a word sequence.

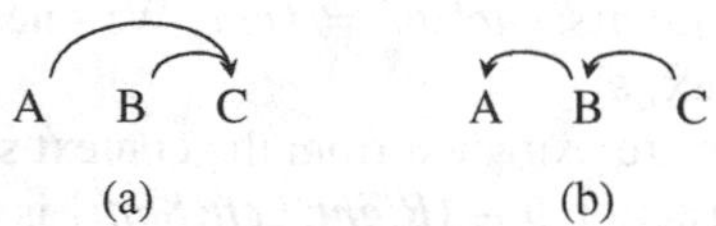

Fig. 1. Two Cases of Shift Action (The arc is from the modifier to its governor.)

Shift action is executed for pair of (A, B) for both cases at the first pass. However, for case (b), it need predict to take left action at node pair (A, B) at the second pass. The difference between two predictions is whether C has been attached as a dependent of node B. This might cause a degradation of performance since that the prediction is often made with linear classifier. The features extracted from this two situations have a lot of overlap. So the prediction of (A, B) is very difficult and may cause error propagation. If it predicts *left* action on (A, B) at the first pass, the predict head of C will be never right due to the bottom-up regulation.

The main reason of the problem is that the parser ignores the potential relation between the target node pair when it predicts a *shift* action. In order to cope with this problem, Yamada and Matsumoto [18] suggested to divide the action *shift* into two kinds of actions, *shift'* and *wait* for two cases respectively. These new actions are the same behavior in parsing process. However, they do not report any experimental result for their suggestion.

4 Dependency Parsing Using Enhanced Shift Actions

In this paper, we deal with this problem with two improvements. First, we modify the actions of the transition system. Second, we extend the feature set for parsing based on our improved actions.

4.1 Enhanced Shift Actions

We expand the parsing action by adding two actions: *shift-left* and *shift-right*.

left let the right node become a child of the left one.
right let the left node become a child of the right one.

shift let the point of focus moves to the right. And there is no relation between target nodes.

shift-right let the point of focus moves to the right. And there is a right relation between target nodes but we can just shift because dependent child still have further dependent children in the sentence.

shift-left let the point of focus moves to the right. And there is a left relation between target nodes.

Compared to set of actions of Yamada's algorithm, we split the original *shift* action into *shift*, *shift-left* and *shift-right*, which is used to distinguish the relation between the target node pair. The *shift-left* and *shift-right* actions can be also called *pseudo shift* actions.

We count these three *shift* actions in parsing process on Chinese dataset of the CoNLL 2009 shared task[9]. The *pseudo shift* actions are more than 20%. The detailed information is shown in Table 1.

Table 1. Statistics of Three Shift-related Actions

(a) Training Dataset

	Number	Percent
Shift	694460	77.68%
Shift-Left	156644	17.52%
Shift-Right	42886	4.80%
Total	893990	

(b) Test Dataset

	Number	Percent
Shift	83455	77.77%
Shift-Left	20104	18.50%
Shift-Right	5139	4.73%
Total	108698	

Figure 2 gives real examples *shift-left* and *shift-right* actions.

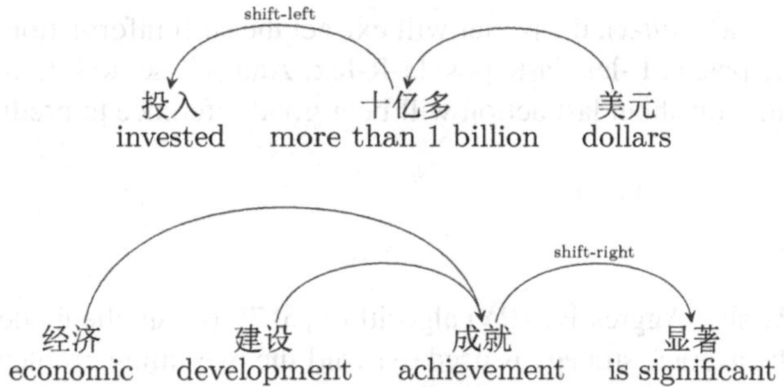

Fig. 2. Examples of *shift-left* and *shift-right* Actions(The arc is from the modifier to its governor.)

4.2 Feature Extraction

Let i and $i+1$ be the indexes of the left and right of target nodes in T. The left context is defined as the nodes on the left side of the target nodes: $t_l(l < i)$, and the right context is defined as those on the right: $t_r(i+1 < r)$. Context lengths (l, r) represents the numbers of nodes within the left and right contexts. We choose the context lengths (2, 2).

A feature can be represented as triplet (p, k, v), in which p is the position from the target nodes, k denotes the feature type, and v is the value of the feature. If $p < 0$, it represents the node in the left context, $p = 0-; 0+$ denotes the left or right node of target nodes. $p > 0$ denotes those in the right context. The feature type k and its value v are summarized in the Table 2.

Table 2. Summary of the features

	Type	Value
Traditional Features	pos	POS tag string
	lex	word string
	ch-L-pos	POS tag string of the child node modifying to the parent node from left side
	ch-L-lex	word string of the child node node modifying to the parent node from left side
	ch-R-pos	POS tag string of the child node modifying to the parent node from right side
	ch-R-lex	word string of the child node modifying to the parent node from right side
Action-based Features	**la**	last action if it is *shift-x*
	la-L-pos	POS tag string of the left target node in the last action
	la-L-lex	word string of the left target node in the last action
	la-R-pos	POS tag string of the right target node in the last action
	la-R-lex	word string of the right target node in the last action

Besides the traditional features, we also extract the features based on previous action. These features are shown in bold in Table 2. If the last action is *shift*, *shift-left* or *shift-right*(referred as *shift-x*), the parser will extract the shift information of last action including la, la-L-pos, la-L-lex, la-R-pos, la-R-lex. And p is set to 0 to make a formal unity. The information about last action will be a good reference to predict the current action.

4.3 Training

We use online Passive-Aggressive (PA) algorithm [6, 7] to train the model parameters. Following [5], the average strategy is used to avoid the overfitting problem.

First, we need to build instance list of training data sets $(\mathbf{x}, \mathbf{y})$. The algorithm of building instance list is just like the parsing algorithm. Here, x is the contextual features and y is the parsing action. We can get all the instances from training corpus.

Given an example $(\mathbf{x}, \mathbf{y})$, $\hat{\mathbf{y}}$ are denoted as the labels with the highest score

$$\hat{\mathbf{y}} = \arg\max_{\mathbf{z}} \mathbf{w}^T \Phi(\mathbf{x}, \mathbf{z}). \quad (1)$$

where $\mathbf{w}$ is the parameter of score function, and $\Phi(\mathbf{x}, \mathbf{y})$ is the feature vector consisting of lots of overlapping features, which is the chief benefit of discriminative model.

For the training data sets, given an example $(\mathbf{x}_i, \mathbf{y}_i)$, we compare the $\mathbf{y}_i$ and $\hat{\mathbf{y}}_i$ as the hinge-loss function. If $\hat{\mathbf{y}}_i = \mathbf{y}_i$, the resulting algorithm is passive, that is, $\mathbf{w}_{k+1} = \mathbf{w}_k$ as we expected. In contrast, when $\hat{\mathbf{y}}_i \neq \mathbf{y}_i$, the algorithm aggressively forces $\mathbf{w}_{k+1}$ to satisfy the constraints. We define the following constrained optimization problem to update the new weight vector $\mathbf{w}_{k+1}$ based on weight vector $\mathbf{w}_k$. The **margin** $\gamma(\mathbf{w}; (\mathbf{x}, \mathbf{y}))$ is defined as

$$\gamma(\mathbf{w}; (\mathbf{x}, \mathbf{y})) = \mathbf{w}^T \Phi(\mathbf{x}, \mathbf{y}) - \mathbf{w}^T \Phi(\mathbf{x}, \hat{\mathbf{y}}). \tag{2}$$

Thus, we calculate the **hinge loss** $\ell(\mathbf{w}; (\mathbf{x}, \mathbf{y}))$, (abbreviated as ℓ_w) by

$$\ell_w = \begin{cases} 0, & \gamma(\mathbf{w}; (\mathbf{x}, \mathbf{y})) > 1 \\ 1 - \gamma(\mathbf{w}; (\mathbf{x}, \mathbf{y})), & \text{otherwise} \end{cases} \tag{3}$$

In round k, the new weight vector $\mathbf{w}_{k+1}$ is calculated by

$$\mathbf{w}_{k+1} = \arg\min_{\mathbf{w}} \frac{1}{2} ||\mathbf{w} - \mathbf{w}_k||^2 + \mathcal{C} \cdot \xi,$$

$$\textbf{s.t. } \ell(\mathbf{w}; (\mathbf{x}_k, \mathbf{y}_k)) \leq \xi \textbf{ and } \xi \geq 0 \tag{4}$$

where ξ is a non-negative slack variable, and $\mathcal{C}$ is a positive parameter which controls the influence of the slack term on the objective function.

Following the derivation in PA [7], we can get the update rule,

$$\mathbf{w}_{k+1} = \mathbf{w}_k + \tau_k (\Phi(\mathbf{x}_k, \mathbf{y}_k) - \Phi(\mathbf{x}_k, \hat{\mathbf{y}_k})), \tag{5}$$

where

$$\tau_k = \min(\mathcal{C}, \frac{\ell_{w_k}}{||\Phi(\mathbf{x}_k, \mathbf{y}_k) - \Phi(\mathbf{x}_k, \hat{\mathbf{y}_k})||^2}) \tag{6}$$

5 Experiments

Our experiments were conducted on Chinese dataset of the CoNLL 2009 shared task[9]. The detailed information is shown in Table 3. FORM/LEMMA OOV (out-of-vocabulary) is the percentage of FORM/LEMMA tokens not found in the respective vocabularies derived solely from the training data.

Table 3. Data Statistics for the Chinese Dataset of CoNLL-2009 Shared Task

Training data size (sentences)	22,277
Training data size (tokens)	609,060
Avg. sentence length (tokens)	27.3
Evaluation data size (sentences)	2,556
Evaluation data size (tokens)	73,153
Evaluation FORM OOV	3.92%
Evaluation LEMMA OOV	3.92%

We compare the accuracy of our model against Maltparser [14] and Yamada's algorithm. The MaltParser is an efficient deterministic dependency parser that is gaining popularity. Similar to Yamada's algorithm, the MaltParser relies on a discriminative classifier to choose its actions. However, by employing the arc-eager algorithm presented in [12], the parser can build the complete parse tree in a single pass and therefore it guarantees $O(n)$ complexity in the worst case.

We trained all parsers up to 50 iterations.

The following measures were used to evaluate parsing performance.

$$UAS = \frac{\langle \sharp \text{ of tokens with correct heads} \rangle}{\langle \sharp \text{ of tokens} \rangle}$$

$$LAS = \frac{\langle \sharp \text{ of tokens with correct heads and labels} \rangle}{\langle \sharp \text{ of tokens} \rangle}$$

$$CM = \frac{\langle \sharp \text{ of correctly parsed sentences} \rangle}{\langle \sharp \text{ of sentences} \rangle}$$

The test results are shown in Table 4.

Considering UAS, our method provides an improvement of 1.66 over the baseline and 0.72 over the maltparser. Considering LAS, we achieve improvements of 1.71 and 0.86, respectively.

The improvement of our method can be ascribed to two contributions.

The first contribution is the enhanced actions, which is introduced in section 4.1. These enhanced actions avoid the inconsistent actions for the same nodes pair in different passes. Furthermore, they also improve the accuracy of classifier.

The second contribution is the new features based on the additional actions by recording last shift action, which introduced in section 4.2. When the previous action is *shift-left*, we can derive that the current action may not be *right*. Otherwise, there would be two heads for one node.

Table 4. Accuracy on test set, excluding punctuation, for unlabeled attachment score (UAS), labeled attachment score (LAS) and Complete Match (CM)

	UAS	LAS	CM
Maltparser	82.31	80.64	28.17
Top CoNLL 2009[15] (Transition-based)	81.22	79.19	-
Che et al. [3] (Graph-based)	-	75.49	-
Baseline(Yamada's algorithm)	81.37	79.79	26.41
Baseline + enhanced actions	82.59	81.07	27.66
Baseline + enhanced actions + action-based features	**83.03**	**81.50**	**29.11**

6 Related Works

Yamada and Matsumoto [18] is in the light of the target nodes, and determines what kind of action to do. This can be treated as a multi-class classification problem. It also uses the the left and right context information of the target nodes and their children's information to exclude ambiguity. However, this method suffers from the inconsistent action problem. It is caused by the strict bottom-up strategy, which requires each node to have found all its dependents before it is combined with its head.

Nivre [13] handles the inconsistent action problem by modifying the parsing strategy. It combines the bottom-up and top-down processing. It has four actions: Left-arc, Right-arc, Reduce and Shift. And it to some extent eases the contradiction between restrict parsing framework and the structure of the dependency tree.

Rush and Petrov [16] propose a multi-pass coarse-to-fine architecture for dependency parsing using linear-time vine pruning and structured prediction cascades. Their first-, second-, and third-order models achieve accuracies comparable to those of their unpruned counterparts, while exploring only a fraction of the search space.

Sartorio et al. [17] present a transition-based, greedy dependency parser which implements a flexible mix of bottom-up and top-down strategies. The new strategy allows the parser to postpone difficult decisions until the relevant information becomes available.

7 Conclusion

In this paper, we investigate to use the enhanced shift actions to improve the transition-based parsing. Our method is based on the multi-pass parsing algorithm. The experiments show the effectiveness of our parser over the baseline and Maltparser.

Our future work is to explore more in the shift information to improve the accuracy of the transition-based dependency parser. We also wish to apply our strategy in the one-pass transition-based parsing algorithm.

Acknowledgments. We would like to thank the anonymous reviewers for their valuable comments. This work was funded by NSFC (No.61003091) and Science and Technology Commission of Shanghai Municipality (14ZR1403200).

References

[1] Bohnet, B.: Very high accuracy and fast dependency parsing is not a contradiction. In: Proceedings of the 23rd International Conference on Computational Linguistics, pp. 89–97. Association for Computational Linguistics (2010)

[2] Buchholz, S., Marsi, E.: Conll-x shared task on multilingual dependency parsing. In: Proceedings of the Tenth Conference on Computational Natural Language Learning, pp. 149–164. Association for Computational Linguistics (2006)

[3] Che, W., Li, Z., Li, Y., Guo, Y., Qin, B., Liu, T.: Multilingual dependency-based syntactic and semantic parsing. In: Proceedings of the Thirteenth Conference on Computational Natural Language Learning: Shared Task, pp. 49–54. Association for Computational Linguistics (2009)

[4] Chu, Y.J., Liu, T.H.: On shortest arborescence of a directed graph. Scientia Sinica 14(10), 1396 (1965)

[5] Collins, M.: Discriminative training methods for hidden markov models: Theory and experiments with perceptron algorithms. In: Proceedings of the 2002 Conference on Empirical Methods in Natural Language Processing (2002)
[6] Crammer, K., Singer, Y.: Ultraconservative online algorithms for multiclass problems. Journal of Machine Learning Research 3, 951–991 (2003)
[7] Crammer, K., Dekel, O., Keshet, J., Shalev-Shwartz, S., Singer, Y.: Online passive-aggressive algorithms. Journal of Machine Learning Research 7, 551–585 (2006)
[8] Edmonds, J.: Optimum branchings. Journal of Research of the National Bureau of Standards B 71(233-240), 160 (1967)
[9] Hajič, J., Ciaramita, M., Johansson, R., Kawahara, D., Martí, M., Màrquez, L., Meyers, A., Nivre, J., Padó, S., Štěpánek, J., et al.: The CoNLL-2009 shared task: Syntactic and semantic dependencies in multiple languages. In: Proceedings of the Thirteenth Conference on Computational Natural Language Learning: Shared Task, pp. 1–18. Association for Computational Linguistics (2009)
[10] McDonald, R., Crammer, K., Pereira, F.: Online large-margin training of dependency parsers. In: Proceedings of the 43rd Annual Meeting on Association for Computational Linguistics, pp. 91–98 (2005)
[11] Nilsson, J., Riedel, S., Yuret, D.: The conll 2007 shared task on dependency parsing. In: Proceedings of the CoNLL Shared Task Session of EMNLP-CoNLL, pp. 915–932. sn (2007)
[12] Nivre, J.: An efficient algorithm for projective dependency parsing. In: Proceedings of the 8th International Workshop on Parsing Technologies (IWPT). Citeseer (2003)
[13] Nivre, J.: Incrementality in deterministic dependency parsing. In: Proceedings of the Workshop on Incremental Parsing: Bringing Engineering and Cognition Together, pp. 50–57. Association for Computational Linguistics (2004)
[14] Nivre, J., Hall, J., Nilsson, J., Chanev, A., Eryigit, G., Kübler, S., Marinov, S., Marsi, E.: Maltparser: A language-independent system for data-driven dependency parsing. Natural Language Engineering 13(2), 95–135 (2007)
[15] Ren, H., Ji, D., Wan, J., Zhang, M.: Parsing syntactic and semantic dependencies for multiple languages with a pipeline approach. In: Proceedings of the Thirteenth Conference on Computational Natural Language Learning: Shared Task, pp. 97–102. Association for Computational Linguistics (2009)
[16] Rush, A.M., Petrov, S.: Vine pruning for efficient multi-pass dependency parsing. In: Proceedings of the 2012 Conference of the North American Chapter of the Association for Computational Linguistics: Human Language Technologies, pp. 498–507. Association for Computational Linguistics (2012)
[17] Sartorio, F., Satta, G., Nivre, J.: A transition-based dependency parser using a dynamic parsing strategy. In: Proceeding of the 51st Annual Meeting of the Association for Computational Linguistics (2013)
[18] Yamada, H., Matsumoto, Y.: Statistical dependency analysis with support vector machines. In: Proceedings of the International Workshop on Parsing Technologies (IWPT), vol. 3 (2003)
[19] Zhang, Y., Clark, S.: A tale of two parsers: Investigating and combining graph-based and transition-based dependency parsing using beam-search. In: Proceedings of the Conference on Empirical Methods in Natural Language Processing, pp. 562–571. Association for Computational Linguistics (2008)

Diachronic Deviation Features in Continuous Space Word Representations

Ni Sun[1,2], Tongfei Chen[1], Liumingjing Xiao[1], and Junfeng Hu[1,2,*]

[1] School of Electronics Engineering & Computer Science, Peking University, Beijing, P.R. China
[2] Key Laboratory of Computational Linguistics (Ministry of Education)
{sn96,ctf,hujf}@pku.edu.cn,
xlmj531@163.com

Abstract. In distributed word representation, each word is represented as a unique point in the vector space. This paper extends this to a diachronic setting, where multiple word embeddings are generated with corpora in different time periods. These multiple embeddings can be mapped to a single target space via a linear transformation. In this target space each word is thus represented as a distribution. The deviation features of this distribution can reflect the semantic variation of words through different time periods. Experiments show that word groups with similar deviation features can indicate the hot topics in different ages. And the frequency change of these word groups can be used to detect the age of peak celebrity of the topics in the history.

Keywords: Lexical semantics, diachronic corpora, semantic distribution, hot topics.

1 Introduction

Representation of words as dense, real-valued vectors can be trained via a neural network language model[1,7]. It has been shown that these distributed representations of words can be used to improve the performance of many NLP systems[3].

However, despite such models' successful application, most of these models do not consider the concept of diachronicity, i.e. the change of the semantics of the words through different time periods is not taken into account. In this paper, we devised a feature vector that represents the semantic variation of a word in a diachronic corpus.

Mikolov et al. [8] demonstrated that it is possible to produce a linear projection between vector spaces of words that represent different languages. We adopt the idea to vector spaces of words that represents texts of different time periods. Word embeddings learned from different time periods are projected to the same vector space (target space).

* Corresponding author.

M. Sun et al. (Eds.): CCL and NLP-NABD 2014, LNAI 8801, pp. 23–33, 2014.

For a specific word, a multinomial Gaussian distribution is defined to fit all the projections in the target space. The deviation feature vector drawn from this distribution reflects the stability of the semantic of this word in a diachronic corpus. Experiments showed that these deviation features can be used in mining hot topics in different ages.

The rest of this paper is organized as follows. Section 2 elaborates the details of the mapping of different vector spaces. Section 3 illustrates our diachronic deviation feature vector, and its use in topic clustering. In Section 4, evaluations are presented to illustrate the effectiveness of the diachronic deviation feature, and the application of the topic cluster is also presented. The final section concludes this paper and discusses possible future work.

2 Linear Projection between Spaces

Given a diachronic corpus, we seek to split it into diachronic sections, under the assumption that each section is synchronic. For each section a distributed representation of words is trained via the method proposed by Mikolov et al. [7]. Then, by analogy of the method proposed by Mikolov et al. [8], a linear projection is built to transform all these vector spaces into a target space. It serves as a transformation that transforms all spaces to a uniform one. The symbols used in this section are described below:

Table 1. Symbols

Symbol	Definition
$\mathbf{x}(w, s)$	Vector representation of word w in slice s
$\mathbf{T}_{st}$	Transformation matrix from slice s to t

2.1 Splitting the Diachronic Corpus

A sliding-window based scheme is used to split the diachronic corpus. The splitting is dependent on two variables: window size and window increment. For example, in Figure 1, the window size is 5 years and the window increment is 1 year.

Using this method a diachronic corpus (year 1947 to 1996 in Figure 1) can be split into multiple (46 here) segments, in which each segment contains a time-consecutive portion of the original corpus, while large enough to train a reliable distributed representation of words. Additionally, overlapping of the slices, instead of using disjoint slices, produces more samples.

2.2 Training the Linear Projection

In order to observe the representation of words over different time periods, a liner transformation is used here to project all the different vector spaces into a target space.

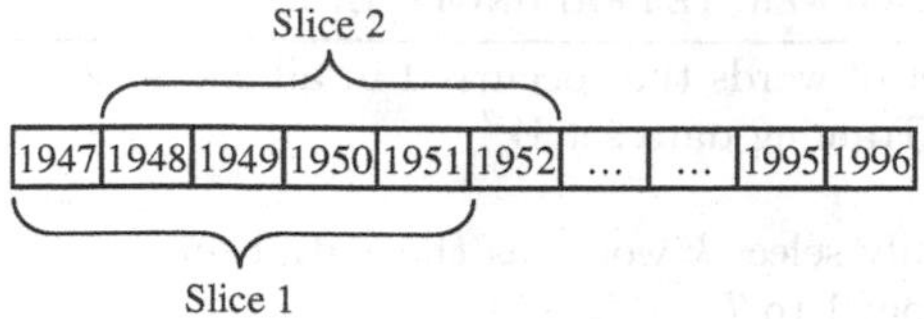

Fig. 1. Sliding window scheme

In our experiments, the *target space* is generated by training the entire diachronic corpus using the neural network model. We seek to transform each vector space of a time period (*source space*) to the target space. This problem is formulated below:

Problem Description: Given a set of words and their associated vector representations in two time periods

$$(\mathbf{x}(w,s), \mathbf{x}(w,t))_{i=1}^{n} , \tag{1}$$

find a transformation matrix $\mathbf{T}_{st}$ such that $\mathbf{T}_{st}\mathbf{x}(w,s)$ approximates $\mathbf{x}(w,t)$.

In practice, $\mathbf{T}_{st}$ can be learned by the following optimization problem:

$$\min_{\mathbf{T}_{st}} \sum_{i=1}^{n} \|\mathbf{T}_{st}\mathbf{x}(w_i,s) - \mathbf{x}(w_i,t)\|^2 . \tag{2}$$

This is solved using batch gradient descent.

After the transformation matrix $\mathbf{T}_{st}$ is trained, we can transform every vector in the source space to the target space by computing

$$\hat{\mathbf{x}}(w,t) = \mathbf{T}_{st}\mathbf{x}(w,s) . \tag{3}$$

Despite its simplicity, this linear transformation worked well between different languages Mikolov et al. [8], and it performed effectively in our experiments as well.

2.3 Generating the Training Data Set

One of the key problems that influence the result of the transformation matrix is the proper choice of the training set. In this section we focus on how to build an appropriate training set for the optimization problem stated above, i.e. a set of words with their associated vector representations in two spaces.

In this task, a set of words whose semantics are stable over time periods is desired. To avoid overfitting, the size of this set should be relatively small. In our experiments 100 words are selected for both Chinese and English corpus. First, we build this training set beginning from a randomly selected set. Initial transformation matrices are trained from this initial training set with the target

Algorithm 1. GenerateTrainingDataSet

Input: Set of words that occurred in all slices W
Output: Training data set W'

```
begin
    Randomly select k words as the initial set
    for i from 1 to T
        Train the transformation matrix T_{i0} for slice i
    end
    for w ∈ W
        for i from 1 to T
            d(w,i) = ||x(w,0) − T_{i0} x(w,i)||
        end
        v(w) = var(w,·)
    end
    Return the top n words with the smallest v(w)
end
```

space. Then word whose variances of the error between the actual representation and the predicted representation are lowest is selected. In Algorithm 1, the target space is numbered 0.

Table 2 presents the generated training set of words (top 25 shown here) on two diachronic corpora: one in Chinese (*People's Daily*) and one in English (*New York Times*).

Table 2. Generated training data set for building the linear transformation matrix. (top 24 shown here).

Chinese (*People's Daily*)		English (*New York Times*)	
不仅(not only)	而且(and)	while	usually
例如(such as)	但是(but)	and	which
当时(at that time)	以前(previously)	now	place
还要(still)	地方(place)	although	industry
就是(exactly)	因为(because)	called	but
因此(hence)	这个(this)	similarly	still
这些(these)	等等(and so on)	also	presumably
同时(meanwhile)	原来(it turns out)	quietly	whereas
所以(therefore)	至于(as for)	mostly	suddenly
并且(as well as)	经过(after)	supposedly	apparently
除了(except)	虽然(although)	continually	with
只是(just)	当然(of course)	fully	however

From the generated words we could see that the training set generated mostly contains conjunctions and adverbs or some common concepts in both Chinese and English. The semantics of these words are mostly stable in diachronic corpora, thus serving as a good training set for the training of the linear transformation model over time periods.

3 Diachronic Deviation Feature

From the linear transformation procedure described above, for each word w, we have a set of vector representations drawn from different time periods all projected to the same space, namely

$$S(w) = \{\mathbf{T}_{s0}\mathbf{x}(w, s)\}_{s=1,\cdots,T}. \tag{4}$$

This set of vectors $S(w)$ is fit to a multidimensional Gaussian distribution, namely the *diachronic representation distribution* $N(\boldsymbol{\mu}_w, \boldsymbol{\Sigma}_w)$.

From the word representation model it can be assumed that the dimensions of the representation space are mutually independent. Thus, the covariance matrix $\boldsymbol{\Sigma}_w$ is reduced to a diagonal matrix. We define the deviation features as the variance of each dimension:

$$\varphi_w = (\Sigma_{ii})_{i=1,\cdots,D} \ , \tag{5}$$

where D is the dimensionality of the vector space. A min-max scaling is performed on these features:

$$\tilde{\varphi}_w^{(i)} = \frac{\varphi_w^{(i)} - \min \varphi_{(\cdot)}^{(i)}}{\max \varphi_{(\cdot)}^{(i)} - \min \varphi_{(\cdot)}^{(i)}} \ . \tag{6}$$

Here $\varphi^{(i)}$ denotes the ith dimension of vector $\boldsymbol{\varphi}$. The scaled vector $\tilde{\boldsymbol{\varphi}}$ is our diachronic deviation feature vector.

4 Evaluation

In this section, we demonstrate that clustering result of words using the diachronic deviation feature vectors is correlated with time-specific topics.

4.1 Corpus and Experiment Settings

Experiments are conducted on one Chinese real-word corpora: *People's Daily* of 50 years (from 1947 to 1996). ICTCLAS[9] is applied to segment the raw text. Window size is 5 years and window increment is set to be 1 year. Each text slice contains approximately 30 million words.

For each text slice, the vector representation is learned using the method by Mikolov et al. [7]. The dimension of the vectors is set to be 50. The target vector space is trained by the entire corpus. The words used for clustering are words that are prevalent in every time slice; i.e. the number of occurrence of a specific word in any time slice is greater than a minimum threshold. The actual number of words for clustering is approximately 10000.

4.2 Clustering

A diachronic deviation feature vector is generated for each word using the method described in Section 3. We use the cosine similarity measure as the similarity measure between the feature vectors. And we used the hierarchical word clustering scheme described by He et al. [4]. It uses the hyper-link induced topic search algorithm [5] to produce clusters of words. The number of clusters is determined after the completion of the algorithm, thus it is not necessary for the users to specify the number of clusters. The algorithm is shown below.

Algorithm 2. HierarchicalClustering

Input: Level-1 concept set C, level n, Similarity matrix of words M_0
Output: Hierarchical clustering tree H
begin
  for l from 2 to n
    $M_l \leftarrow$ Similarity matrix in level-$(l-1)$ concepts
    Perform initial clustering according to M_l
    while maximum iteration count not reached
      Run HITS on each concept to get authority score a
      Adjust the clustering result according to a
    end
    Write the clustering result of level-l to H
  end
end

We present several clusters produced by our method in Table 3. It can be seen that the produced clusters are largely correlated with topics instead of synonyms. Namely, The words in the same cluster have a tendency to occur in a specific time period, and they are correlated with a same hot topic in that period.

4.3 Case Study on *People's Daily*

In this section we present the experimental results on the Chinese corpus People's Daily (from 1947 to 1996). Table 4 is a cluster generated using the method described in Section 4.2.

It can be seen that the words in the cluster are closely related to topics concerning with exploiting class and revolution. The normalized frequency of these terms in the entire diachronic corpus is illustrated in Figure 2, where the frequency is divided by the total frequency of all the terms of each year. An abrupt change of frequency can be noticed around 1967.

Frequency of these terms is not uniformly distributed with respect to time; the terms have a tendency to occur in a specific time period. Then we choose the year(1967) with the highest frequency of these terms, and run a latent Dirichlet allocation (LDA) [2] on it to observe the topic distribution of these terms.

Table 3. Examples of clusters produced by the similarity of deviation features

Higher education	师范大学(normal university), 清华大学(Tsinghua University), 北京大学(Peking University), 学院(College), 工学院(College of Engineering), 医学院(College of Medicine), 师范学院(Normal College), 研究室(Laboratory), 院校(Institute)
Cities	西安市(Xi'an), 杭州市(Hangzhou), 沈阳市(Shenyang), 广州市(Guangzhou), 武汉市(Wuhan), 长春市(Changchun), 南京市(Nanjing), 天津市(Tianjin), 上海市(Shanghai), 长沙市(Changsha), 包头(Baotou), 北京市(Beijing), 重庆市(Chongqing)
Meteorological phenomena	洪水(flood), 山洪(mountain torrents), 雨(rain), 风沙(sandwind), 霜(frost), 雹(hail), 猛涨(surge), 风暴(storm)
Kinships	哥哥(elder brother), 姐姐(elder sister), 女儿(daughter), 妻子(wife), 父亲(father), 弟弟(younger brother), 母亲(mother), 丈夫(husband), 家里(at home), 儿子(son), 爱人(lover), 老乡(folks), 生病(sick), 妹妹(younger sister), 照料(taking care of), 孩子(child), 叔叔(uncle), 娃娃(kid), 孙子(grandchild), 邻居(neighbor)

Table 4. A cluster of words generated from *People's Daily*

统治(rule), 统治者(ruler), 封建(feudal), 官僚(bureaucrat), 专制(despotism), 势力(force), 统治阶级(ruling class), 剥削阶级(exploiting class), 推翻(overturn), 剥削(exploit), 封建主义(feudalism), 资产阶级(bourgeoisie), 右派(the Right), 国民党(Kuomingtang), 资本家(capitalist), 残余(remnant), 左派(the Left), 农奴(serf), 执政(be in power), 地主(landlord), 压迫(oppress), 腐败(corrupt), 改组(reorganize), 殖民(colonization), 派别(faction), 反动(reaction), 垄断(monopoly), 瓦解(disintegration)

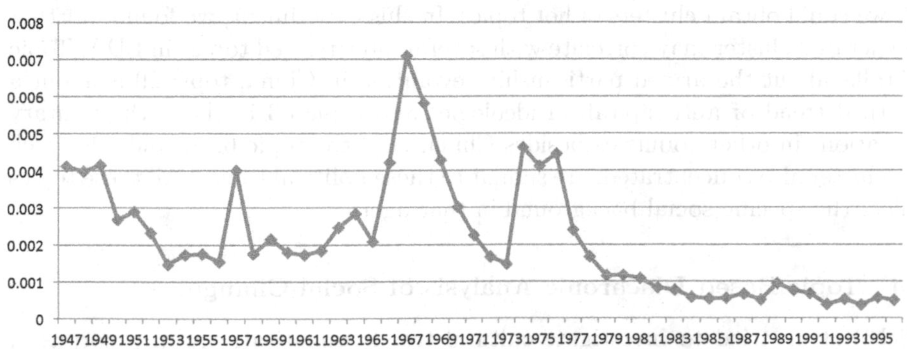

Fig. 2. The normalized frequency of words in the cluster of exploiting class and revolution in the diachronic corpus

For each word in the produced cluster in Table 4, we observe its top 5 topics in LDA with the highest probability. We count the word number for each topic, and the relation between the frequencies of words with respect to the topics generated by LDA is shown in Figure 3. The terms in this cluster concentrates heavily on topic 17, 29, and 83. The words in those corresponding topics are shown in Table 5.

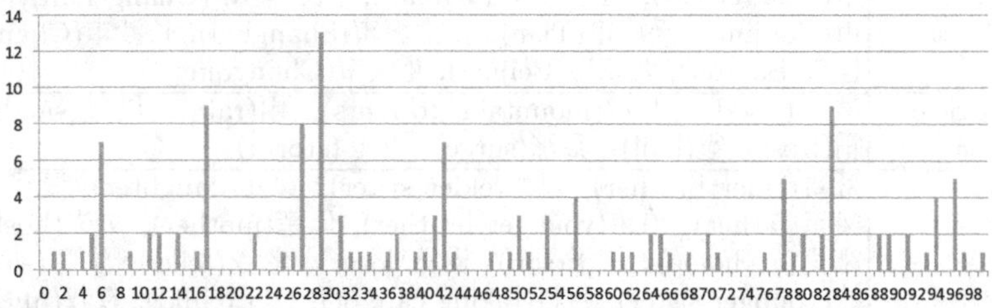

Fig. 3. Topic distribution of words in the cluster of exploiting class and revolution. y-axis indicates the frequency of words in a specific topic.

Table 5. Words in related LDA topics from *People's Daily*

Topic #17	党(Party) , 领导(lead) , 武装(armed) , 斗争(struggle) , 共产党(Communist party), 革命(revolution), 建立(establish) , 中国(China) , 政权(regime)
Topic #29	文化(culture) , 社会(society), 阶级(class), 思想(thoughts), 资产阶级(bourgeoisie), 生活(life), 制度(institution), 剥削阶级(exploiting class), 统治(rule)
Topic #83	印度(India) , 政府(government) , 武装(armed) , 地区(region), 反动(reactionary) , 农民(peasants), 军事(military), 挑衅(provoke), 巴基斯坦(Pakistan)

According to the deviation features and a hierarchical word clustering scheme [4], we could obtain clusters of hot topics. In this experiment, we found out that a generated cluster may correlate with several inter-related topics in LDA. Topic 17 talks about the armed partisanship revolution in China, topic 29 is about a political trend of anti-capitalism ideologies and topic 83 is about the military operations in other countries besides China. And the topic 6, 27 and 42, which the cluster also concentrated, are similar to these political topics. All these topics reflect the specific social background in that age.

4.4 Topic Based Diachronic Analysis of Social Change

Michel et al. tried to investigate cultural trends quantitatively in a corpus of digitized texts containing about 4% of all books ever printed[6]. By tracking the usage frequency of words picked carefully in different years, they highlight that the cultural change guides the concepts we discuss (hot topics). An example is shown in Figure 4, in which they plotted the median frequency in German over

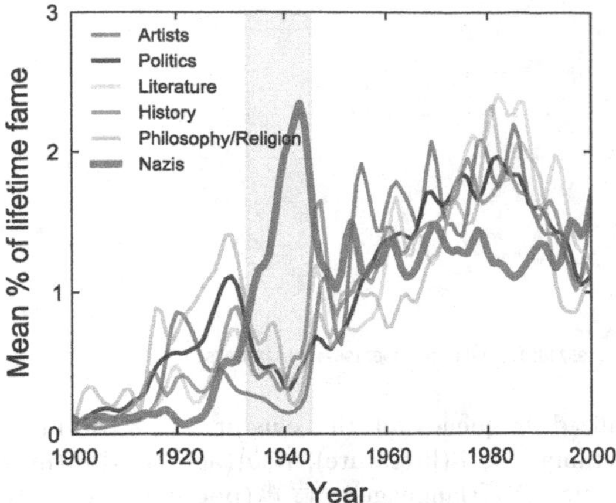

Fig. 4. Artists and writers in various disciplines were suppressed by the Nazi regime (red highlight). In contrast, the Nazis themselves (thick red line) exhibited a strong fame peak during the war years.[6].

time for five lists of names and a collection of Nazi party members(547 names) to probe the impact of censorship on a person's cultural influence in Nazi Germany.

Therefore, tracking the frequency of some certain words could detect the age of peak celebrity of some topics and study the human culture. While these special words were chose manually in Michel's work[6], by our deviation features and clustering method, the clusters with words belong to a same topic were generated automatically. With this method, the topic based diachronic analysis of social and culture change is more effective then.

We have shown an example above in Figure 2 (also the red line in Figure 5). As this cluster of exploiting class and revolution was active before the founding of the People's Republic, it had relatively high frequency. And the frequency of it peaked in 1967, which is the beginning of the Cultural Revolution. Since the Cultural Revolution eulogized revolutionary violence, and some claustrophobic restrictions was proposed, the political-related topic developed. After this period, with the reform and open policy carrying on, the revolution and military operations stepped down from the stage of history so that the frequency declined gradually.

Another example is shown in Figure 5, which is a cluster about literature and art. Its frequency was low during the war years but soared since the founding of PRC (1949), and retained high for nearly 20 years, but then underwent a rapid decay in 1967 reversely, dropping the bottom over 10 years. And returned to the average level before 1967. This is because the artistic creation was significantly influenced by ideological factors in the Cultural Revolution (1967-1977) but reached its peak accompanying economic development.

This analysis illustrates that the frequency change of topics can reflect the culture change.

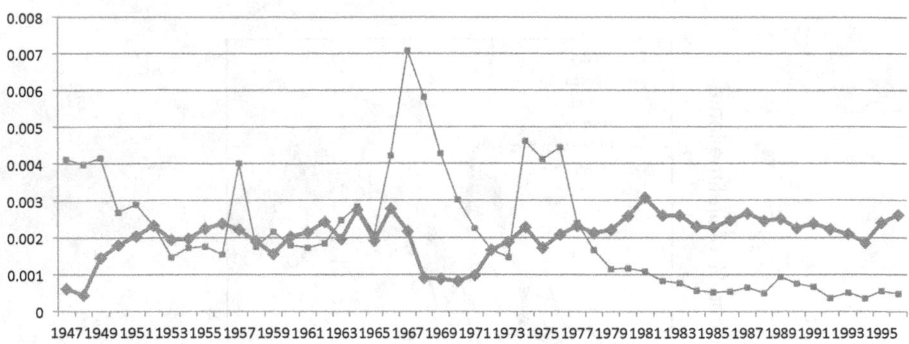

Fig. 5. The normalized frequency of the cluster "话剧(drama), 作品(words), 创作(creation), 戏剧(drama), 文学(literature), 演员(actor), 音乐(music), 连环画(comic strip), 绘画(drawing), 语言(language), 诗歌(poetry), 故事(story), 诗人(poet), 杂技(acrobatics), 现实主义(realism), 文艺(literature and art), 作家(writer), 电影(movie), 油画(painting), 歌剧(opera), 影片(film), 民歌(folk song), 小说(novel), 纪录片(documentary), 美术(art), 编排(arrange), 艺术(art), 鲁迅(Xun Lu)" (blue line) compare with the frequency of the cluster of exploiting class and revolution (red line).

5 Conclusion and Future Work

This paper proposed deviation features of the diachronic word semantic distribution, which represents the stability of the word-meaning over time periods. The word semantic distribution can be learned via linear transformations of the word embedding results generated from the different time periods of text in the diachronic corpora. We demonstrated that the clustering result of words using these deviation vectors is correlated with time-specific topics. The frequency changes of these word clusters can indicate the social and culture changes in history.

Our future work includes exploiting this feature to other NLP tasks including diachronic topic mining or semantic change mining, and it can be also applied to the social linguistics and historical linguistics.

Acknowledgments. This work is supported by the NNSF of China (grant No. M1321005).

References

1. Bengio, Y., Ducharme, R., Vincent, P., Jauvin, C.: A neural probabilistic language model. JMLR 3, 1137–1155 (2003)
2. Blei, D.M., Ng, A.Y., Jordan, M.I.: Latent dirichlet allocation. JMLR 3, 993–1022 (2003)
3. Collobert, R., Weston, J., Bottou, L., Karlen, M., Kavukcuoglu, K., Kuksa, P.: Natural language processing (almost) from scratch. JMLR 12, 2493–2537 (2011)

4. He, S., Zou, X., Xiao, L., Hu, J.: Construction of diachronic ontologies from people's daily of fifty years. In: LREC (2014)
5. Kleinberg, J.M.: Hubs, authorities, and communities. ACM Computing Surveys 31(4es), 5 (1999)
6. Michel, J.B., Shen, Y.K., Aiden, A.P., Veres, A., Gray, M.K., Pickett, J.P., Hoiberg, D., Clancy, D., Norvig, P., Orwant, J., et al.: Quantitative analysis of culture using millions of digitized books. Science 331(6014), 176–182 (2011)
7. Mikolov, T., Chen, K., Corrado, G., Dean, J.: Efficient estimation of word representations in vector space. arXiv preprint arXiv:1301.3781 (2013)
8. Mikolov, T., Le, Q.V., Sutskever, I.: Exploiting similarities among languages for machine translation. arXiv preprint arXiv:1309.4168 (2013)
9. Zhang, H.P., Yu, H.K., Xiong, D.Y., Liu, Q.: Hhmm-based chinese lexical analyzer ictclas. In: SIGHAN, pp. 184–187 (2003)

Ontology Matching with Word Embeddings

Yuanzhe Zhang[1], Xuepeng Wang[1], Siwei Lai[1], Shizhu He[1], Kang Liu[1], Jun Zhao[1], and Xueqiang Lv[2]

[1] National Laboratory of Pattern Recognition
Institute of Automation, Chinese Academy of Sciences
{yzzhang,xpwang,swlai,shizhu.he,kliu,jzhao}@nlpr.ia.ac.cn
[2] Beijing Key Laboratory of Internet Culture and Digital Dissemination Research
Beijing Information Science & Technology University
lxq@bistu.edu.cn

Abstract. Ontology matching is one of the most important work to achieve the goal of the semantic web. To fulfill this task, element-level matching is an indispensable step to obtain the fundamental alignment. In element-level matching process, previous work generally utilizes WordNet to compute the semantic similarities among elements, but WordNet is limited by its coverage. In this paper, we introduce word embeddings to the field of ontology matching. We testified the superiority of word embeddings and presented a hybrid method to incorporate word embeddings into the computation of the semantic similarities among elements. We performed the experiments on the OAEI benchmark, conference track and real-world ontologies. The experimental results show that in element-level matching, word embeddings could achieve better performance than previous methods.

Keywords: Ontology Matching, Element-level Matching, WordNet Similarity, Latent Semantic Analysis, Word Embeddings.

1 Introduction

The semantic web is receiving increasing attentions because of its bright future. In the semantic web, ontologies are essential components which are explicit specifications of conceptualization [10]. Thus, a large number of ontologies have been created in the last decade. Although many of them describe the same domain, they cannot share information with each other since they are designed by different conventions. Hence, ontology matching is required due to the heterogeneous and distributed nature of ontologies [4].

Many ontology matching systems have been designed in recent years. Element-level techniques [7] are widely utilized. They take advantage of lexical information as essential elements. However, merely employing the string surface similarity is impracticable. For example, "journal" and "periodical" cannot be matched, while "journal" and "journey" actually might be aligned. To settle this problem, WordNet similarity [22] was employed to obtain the semantic similarities among elements. But the weakness is that the words in WordNet are insufficient. Many elements in ontologies cannot find their correspondences in WordNet. As a result, it is impossible to compute the semantic similarities between these elements with others.

M. Sun et al. (Eds.): CCL and NLP-NABD 2014, LNAI 8801, pp. 34–45, 2014.

We aim to acquire the semantic similarity without the scale constraint of WordNet. So we introduce word embeddings to this task. Word embeddings are able to represent a majority of words as vectors in a semantic space. The words' similarities then can be worked out by using simple strategies, such as the cosine similarity, Euclidean distance, etc. Word embeddings have been proved to be effective in several NLP tasks, such as named entity recognition, part-of-speech tagging and semantic role labeling [5]. However, there is no straightforward evidence that word embeddings are effective for ontology matching. Thus, in this paper, we learn word embeddings using Wikipedia as training data, and testify the capacity of them.

Compared with edit distance, word embeddings can deeply capture the real meaning behind the words. Compared with WordNet, word embeddings already contain more words. Moreover, we proposed a hybrid method to combine word embeddings and edit distance together. To the best of our knowledge, this is the first usage of word embeddings in ontology matching field.

We conducted several experiments on several open datasets, such as Ontology Alignment Evaluation Initiative (OAEI) 2013[1] benchmark and conference track, real-world ontologies (Freebase [2], YAGO2 [11] and DBpedia [1]). Concretely, we compared the performance of edit distance, WordNet, Latent Semantic Analysis (LSA), word embeddings and a hybrid method using both edit distance and word embeddings. The results demonstrate that the performance of the hybrid method outperforms the others.

The rest of this paper is organized as follows. Section 2 reviews related work. In Section 3, we describe the setup of the paper. Section 4 presents our matching algorithm in detail. Section 5 shows the experiments and the analysis. We conclude this paper in the final section.

2 Related Work

Ontology matching, a solution to the semantic heterogeneity problem [23], is a crucial part to achieve the goal of the semantic web. So far, dozens of ontology matching systems have been created. Lexical information, including names and labels describing entities are valuable to matching systems. Essential correspondences between two ontologies are found by element-level matchers. A simple and efficient method is to calculate the surface similarity between the strings. Most of the string-based metrics have been evaluated [25,3]. Edit distance was widely adopted by many matching systems, such as RiMOM [14], ASMOV [12] and AgreementMaker [6], to measure the similarity between two words.

It is evident that string surface similarity fails to capture the semantics behind the strings, like "journal" and "periodical". To deal with this problem, WordNet [20] was employed for ontology matching. Most of the state of the art matching systems took advantage of WordNet [17]. There are three principal ways to obtain WordNet similarity [17], namely edge-based method, information based method and hybrid method. WordNet definitely discovers the meaning of a word and resolves part of the synonym problem. The biggest shortcoming of WordNet is its low coverage. If either of the two words is out of range, the WordNet similarity between them cannot be figured out.

[1] http://oaei.ontologymatching.org/2013/

Distributed word representations are called word embeddings which are trained through deep neural networks. Each dimension of the embeddings represents a latent feature of the word, hopefully capturing useful syntactic and semantic properties [26].

Word embeddings have been used in many NLP tasks and have received a number of positive results. These tasks include parsing [24], language modeling [19] and sentiment classification [9], etc. Collobert et al. [5] proposed a unified neural network architecture and learning algorithm, which improved the performance of named entity recognition, part-of-speech tagging and chunking. However, to the best of our knowledge, there is little work which employed word embedding in the task of ontology matching.

3 Setup

3.1 Problem Statement

We define an ontology O by a simplified 3-tuple (C, P, I). C stands for the *classes*, denoting the concepts. P represents the *properties*, indicating the relations within the ontology. I means the *individuals*, which are the instances of classes. Classes, properties and individuals are collectively referred to as e, *entities*. Entities have several lexical descriptions, i.e., *names,labels* and *comments*. For instance, an entity's name is "Journal";its label is "Journal or magazine" and its comment is "A periodical publication collecting works from different authors".

The task of ontology matching is to find the alignment between entities in a source ontology O_1 and a target ontology O_2. We define an alignment as a set, $\{(e_1, e_2, con)|e_1 \in O_1, e_2 \in O_2\}$. Every element in the set is called a correspondence. e_1 is an entity in O_1, and e_2 is an entity in O_2. con is the confidence of the correspondence.

Our algorithm offers an implement of an element-level matcher. We declare two preconditions in advance. First, the hierarchy structure is not taken into account. It is because the structure-level matchers are error-prone and strongly depend on the results of element-level matchers [21]. Only contrasting the performance of the element-level matchers makes it easier to discover the capability of the newly added word embeddings method. Second, following the convention of OAEI 2013 benchmark and conference track, the correspondences only have equivalence ($\equiv$) relations.

3.2 WordNet Similarity

There are many proposed ways to use WordNet to acquire word similarity. In this paper, we employ three representative methods.

Edge-based method. Wu and Palmer [27] define the similarity between two concepts taking advantage of common super-concept and paths.

$$Sim(C_1, C_2) = \frac{2 \times N_3}{N_1 + N_2 + 2 \times N_3} \tag{1}$$

Where C_3 is the least common superconcept of C_1 and C_2. N_1 is the number of nodes on the path from C_1 to C_3. N_2 is the number of nodes on the path from C_2 to C_3. N_3 is the number of nodes on the path from C_3 to root.

Information-based method. Lin [16] presents an information-based similarity computational method. It bases on the idea that the similarity between A and B is measured by the ratio between the amount of information needed to state the commonality of A and B and the information needed to fully describe what A and B are. The final formula is as follows.

$$Sim(x_1, x_2) = \frac{2 \times \log P(C_0)}{\log P(C_1) + \log P(C_2)} \quad (2)$$

Where $x_1 \in C_1$ and $x_2 \in C_2$. C_0 is the most specific class that subsumes both C_1 and C_2.

Hybrid method. Jiang and Conrath [13] propose a combined model, adding information content to edge-based method to measure the semantic similarity between words.

$$Dist(w_1, w_2) = IC(c_1) + IC(c_2) - 2 \times IC(LSuper(c_1, c_2)) \quad (3)$$

where $c_1 = sen(w_1)$ and $c_2 = sen(w_2)$. $sen(w)$ denotes the set of possible senses for word w. $IC(c_1)$ and $IC(c_2)$ are the information content of c_1 and c_2 respectively. $LSuper(c_1, c_2)$ denotes the lowest super-ordinate of c_1 and c_2.

3.3 Latent Semantic Analysis

LSA assumes that there are some underlying structures in the pattern of words. Given training data, LSA first generates a matrix of co-occurrences of each word in each document, and the sequential order of the words is not concerned. Then singular-value decomposition (SVD) is applied. Instead of representing documents and terms directly as vectors of independent words, LSA represents them as continuous values on each of the k orthogonal indexing dimensions derived from the SVD analysis [8]. Thus we harvest a word represented by a vector in a latent semantic space. It is expected that synonyms will be mapped to the same direction in the latent semantic space.

In our experiment, we train LSA in Wikipedia to get semantic vectors. An open source software named S-Space[2] is available to train LSA models. We finally generate words represented by 50-dimensional vectors for experiments.

3.4 Word Embeddings

Deep learning approaches gain focus owing to the great success of their applications in fields like computer visions. Tremendous researches have investigated the effectiveness of deep learning methods on NLP tasks. Word embeddings are trained by deep neural networks, and manage to demonstrate their powers in many traditional NLP tasks. In the field of ontology matching, however, they have never been utilized. Inspired by the potential of word embeddings, they are given great expectations to leverage the semantics of words. We are not intended to describe the training detail because it is complicated and not closely related to ontology matching task itself. But it is necessary to explain the word embeddings we use.

[2] https://github.com/fozziethebeat/S-Space

We train our own word embeddings on Wikipedia (version 20130805). *Word2Vec* is an efficient implementation of the continuous bag-of-words and skip-gram architectures for computing vector representations of words. The theory is detailed in [18]. In practice, we discard less frequent words that occur less than five times in the whole corpus. We generate unified 50-dimensional word embeddings.

4 Our Matching Algorithm

4.1 Element-level Matching Algorithm

The input of the matching system is two ontologies, i.e., O_1 and O_2. The input ontologies are first parsed by JENA API[3]. Then the entities in both ontologies are preprocessed. We mainly extract the lexical information, e.g., names, labels and comments of an entity, in this step. Then element-level matching is implemented. Finally the evaluation module provides the matching results.

Algorithm 1. Element-level matching algorithm

```
alignment, Entity1, Entity2 = φ
Entity1 = C1 ∪ P1 ∪ I1
Entity2 = C2 ∪ P2 ∪ I2
for each e1 ∈ Entity1 do
  maxSim = 0
  candidate = null
  for each e2 ∈ Entity2 do
    sim = max{Sim(name1, name2),
        Sim(label1, label2),
        Sim(comment1, comment2)}
    if sim > maxSim then
      maxSim = sim
      candidate = e2
    end if
  end for
  alignment ← alignment + (e1, candidate, maxSim)
end for
return alignment;
```

Our strategy is maximum matching. For every entity e_1 in the source ontology $O_1 = \{C_1, P_1, I_1\}$, find the most similar entity e_2 in the target ontology $O_2 = \{C_2, P_2, I_2\}$. The correspondence (e_1, e_2, con) is then added to the alignment, the confidence *con* is the similarity between $e1$ and $e2$. The full algorithm is described in Algorithm 1. Notice that in the hybrid method, $Sim(name_1, name_2)$, $Sim(label_1, label_2)$ and $Sim(comment_1, comment_2)$ are the maximal value of edit distance similarity and word embeddings similarity.

[3] `http://jena.apache.org/`

The reason of using maximum matching is that in the element-level matching phase, the main concern is to guarantee recall. The results of the element-level matcher is usually filtered by some constraint and further used by the structure-level matchers. Promoting the recall of element-level matcher is of great importance.

4.2 Sentence Similarity Algorithm

In most scenarios, an entity in ontology is described by sentences consisting of more than one word. Sometimes entities have multi-word names, not to mention their labels and comments. How to get the similarity between these sentences becomes an obstacle for element-level ontology matching. To cope with this problem, we propose a heuristic method to compute sentence similarities. The basic idea of this method is that if more words in one sentence having similar words in the other, the two sentences are more similar. This method is similar to the way of getting the semantic similarity between sentences [15].

Algorithm 2. Sentence Similarity between S_1 and S_2

```
sum = 0
for each w1 ∈ S1 do
    maxSim = 0
    for each w2 ∈ S2 do
        sim = Sim(w1, w2)
        if sim > maxSim then
            maxSim = sim
        end if
    end for
    sum ← sum + maxSim
end for
sum ← sum/N;
return sum;
```

Assume sentence S_1 has N words; sentence S_2 has M words, and $N > M$. The similarity between S_1 and S_2 can be acquired by Algorithm 2. Where $Sim(w_1, w_2)$ is the similarity between word w_1 and word w_2. If w_1 and w_2 are represented by vectors, we use their dot product as similarity. In practice, we found that most words in a sentence have corresponding vectors. If a sentence contains many words that cannot be represented by vectors, it is probably that the sentence cannot be aligned by other sentences. So the proposed algorithm is rational.

In WordNet method, if either w_1 or w_2 is not in WordNet, $Sim(w_1, w_2)$ will be zero. This is common because of the low coverage of WordNet. Likewise, in word embeddings method, if either w_1 or w_2 is not in the training data, $Sim(w_1, w_2)$ will be zero.

5 Experiment

Data Sets: The data sets we use contain two parts:

1) OAEI 2013 benchmark and conference track. The benchmark test suits are systemically generated from a seed bibliographic reference. This seed ontology is modified to generate new ontologies, and the task is matching the new ones to the original ontology. The goal of the conference track is to find alignments within a collection of seven ontologies describing the domain of organizing conferences. The ontologies are from different origins to make sure the heterogeneity.

2) Real-world ontologies, i.e., Freebase, YAGO2 and DBpedia. Freebase has more than 7000 properties, and we chose the most frequent 88 properties. YAGO2 has 125 properties, and we extract 1370 properties from DBpedia.

Evaluation: OAEI 2013 benchmark and conference track both have gold standards respectively, hence the performance could be measured by precision, recall and F-measure. There are dozens of test cases in each track, so the final results are given by the harmonic means according to [21].

$$\begin{cases} H(p) = \frac{\sum_{i=1}^{n}|C_i|}{\sum_{i=1}^{n}|A_i|} \\ H(r) = \frac{\sum_{i=1}^{n}|C_i|}{\sum_{i=1}^{n}|R_i|} \\ H(f) = \frac{2\times H(p)\times H(r)}{H(p)+H(r)} \end{cases} \quad (4)$$

Where $|A_i|$ denotes the correspondences found by matching system in each alignment, $|C_i|$ refers to correct correspondences and $|R_i|$ is the reference answers.

Real-world ontologies do not have gold standards, so we ask two persons to check the output alignments independently. Only the correspondences accepted by both the checkers are labeled as correct.

Table 1. Results of benchmark

Methods	Precision	Recall	F-measure
Edit Distance	**0.993**	0.622	**0.765**
WordNet (Wup)	0.862	0.510	0.641
WordNet (Lin)	0.990	0.557	0.713
WordNet (Jcn)	0.949	0.535	0.684
LSA	0.993	0.615	0.760
Word Embeddings	0.990	0.616	0.760
Hybrid	0.990	**0.623**	**0.765**

For comparisons we select several methods as follows:

1) Edit distance. Using edit distance to measure the similarities between elements.

2) WordNet. There are three principal ways to compute WordNet similarity. We employ Wu and Palmer [27]'s method to obtain edge-based similarity; employ Lin

[16]'s method to obtain information-based similarity; employ Jiang and Conrath [13]'s method to obtain hybrid WordNet similarity. We use *WordNet (Wup)*, *WordNet (Lin)* and *WordNet (Jcn)* to represent them in the results.

3) LSA. Words are represented by vectors in a latent semantic space after using LSA on training data, thus the similarities can be calculated as cosine similarities. We train LSA on Wikipedia (version 20130805) to acquire semantic vectors.

5.1 Benchmark and Conference

The benchmark results are given in Table 1. Particularly, we conducted experiments on benchmark test case 205, which replaces some names of entities with their synonyms. It is because we believe that word embeddings are adept in dealing with synonyms. The results of test case 205 can be seen in Table 2. The results of conference track are given by Table 3.

Table 2. Results of benchmark test case 205

Methods	Precision	Recall	F-measure
Edit Distance	0.351	0.351	0.351
WordNet (Wup)	0.287	0.258	0.272
WordNet (Lin)	0.386	0.330	0.356
WordNet (Jcn)	0.373	0.320	0.344
LSA	0.358	0.351	0.354
Word Embeddings	0.421	0.412	0.417
Hybrid	**0.433**	**0.433**	**0.433**

Table 3. Results of conference

Methods	Precision	Recall	F-measure
Edit Distance	0.860	0.482	0.618
WordNet (Wup)	0.786	0.469	0.587
WordNet (Lin)	**0.877**	0.466	0.608
WordNet (Jcn)	0.770	0.462	0.578
LSA	0.876	0.462	0.605
Word Embeddings	0.872	0.469	0.610
Hybrid	0.875	**0.482**	**0.622**

In the results, we obtained the following observation:

1) Word embeddings method always achieves higher F-measure than WordNet methods do.

2) Word embeddings mehtod is good at dealing with synonyms.

3) The hybrid method achieves the best performance (in terms of F-measure) in both benchmark and conference track.

5.2 Real-World Ontologies

The matching tasks between these ontologies will yield three alignments. Our algorithm only generates the alignments of properties, because the alignments of classes and individuals are too large to evaluate. The final results are shown in Table 4.

In the results, we obtained the following observation:

Table 4. Results of matching real-world ontologies

Methods	Freebase-DBpedia	Freebase-YAGO2	YAGO2-DBpedia
Edit Distance	30	7	11
WordNet (Wup)	28	3	11
WordNet (Lin)	29	7	12
WordNet (Jcn)	23	6	11
LSA	**33**	7	14
Word Embeddings	**33**	**8**	**15**
Hybrid	**33**	**8**	**15**

1) The found correspondences are relatively scarce, because not all properties have appropriate matching.

2) Word embeddings method finds more correct correspondences than WordNet methods in all the three tasks.

3) The hybrid method does not find more correct correspondences than word embeddings method. It is because edit distance does not contribute to the hybrid method in these three tasks.

5.3 Comparisons among Word Embeddings

In order to discover the influence of using different word embeddings, we utilized two other word embeddings to fulfil the ontology matching tasks. These two word embeddings are *C&W by Turian* [26] and *SENNA* [5]. The comparisons are given by Figure 1 and Figure 2.

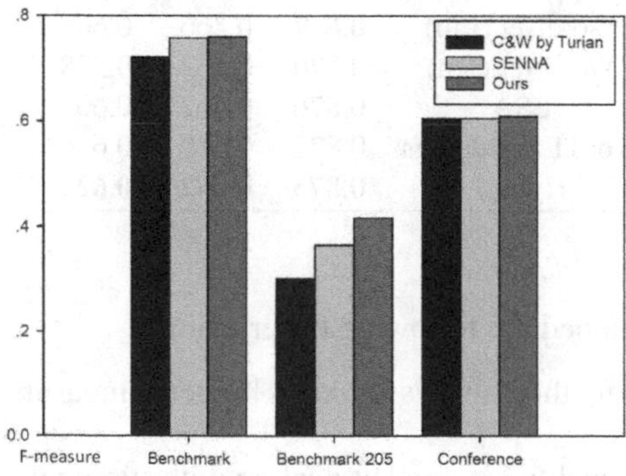

Fig. 1. Comparisons of different word embeddings on OAEI tracks

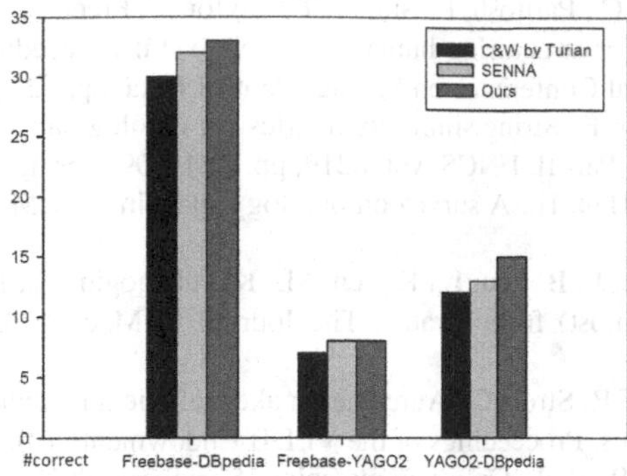

Fig. 2. Comparisons of different word embeddings on real-world ontologies

From the figures we can see that the matching performance is influenced by different word embeddings, and our word embeddings achieve better results than the other two. The reason is that these word embeddings are trained by different data. *C&W by Turian* uses Reuters RCV1 as training data; *SENNA* uses partial Wikipedia and Reuters RCV1 as training data; our training data is the whole Wikipedia. This result indicates that the performance is influenced by the training data.

6 Conclusion

In this paper, we have introduced word embeddings to ontology matching. The experiments show that using word embeddings as a supplement is preferable in ontology matching. The hybrid method combining edit distance and word embeddings achieves the best results.

There are several directions of promotions in the future. The most promising one is training word embeddings specifically. For example, when dealing with biomedical ontologies, we can use relative training data instead of Wikipedia. This amounts to using external resources. It is hopeful since training corpus affect the performance dramatically as our experiments demonstrated. Another possible improvement could be generated by a proper matching strategy. Assigning different weights to semantic similarity and traditions ones appropriately will boost the performance.

Acknowledgement. This work was supported by the National Natural Science Foundation of China (No.61202329, 61272332, 61333018), CCF-Tencent Open Research Fund and the Opening Project of Beijing Key Laboratory of Internet Culture and Digital Dissemination Research(ICDD201301).

References

1. Auer, S., Bizer, C., Kobilarov, G., Lehmann, J., Cyganiak, R., Ives, Z.G.: Dbpedia: A nucleus for a web of open data. In: Aberer, K., et al. (eds.) ISWC/ASWC 2007. LNCS, vol. 4825, pp. 722–735. Springer, Heidelberg (2007)

2. Bollacker, K., Evans, C., Paritosh, P., Sturge, T., Taylor, J.: Freebase: A collaboratively created graph database for structuring human knowledge. In: Proceedings of the 2008 ACM SIGMOD International Conference on Management of Data, pp. 1247–1250. ACM (2008)
3. Cheatham, M., Hitzler, P.: String similarity metrics for ontology alignment. In: Alani, H., et al. (eds.) ISWC 2013, Part II. LNCS, vol. 8219, pp. 294–309. Springer, Heidelberg (2013)
4. Choi, N., Song, I.Y., Han, H.: A survey on ontology mapping. ACM Sigmod Record 35(3), 34–41 (2006)
5. Collobert, R., Weston, J., Bottou, L., Karlen, M., Kavukcuoglu, K., Kuksa, P.: Natural language processing (almost) from scratch. The Journal of Machine Learning Research 12, 2493–2537 (2011)
6. Cruz, I.F., Antonelli, F.P., Stroe, C.: Agreementmaker: efficient matching for large real-world schemas and ontologies. Proceedings of the VLDB Endowment 2(2), 1586–1589 (2009)
7. Euzenat, J., Shvaiko, P., et al.: Ontology matching. Springer (2007)
8. Foltz, P.W.: Latent semantic analysis for text-based research. Behavior Research Methods, Instruments, & Computers 28(2), 197–202 (1996)
9. Glorot, X., Bordes, A., Bengio, Y.: Domain adaptation for large-scale sentiment classification: A deep learning approach. In: Proceedings of the 28th International Conference on Machine Learning (ICML 2011), pp. 513–520 (2011)
10. Gruber, T.R., et al.: A translation approach to portable ontology specifications. Knowledge Acquisition 5(2), 199–220 (1993)
11. Hoffart, J., Suchanek, F.M., Berberich, K., Weikum, G.: Yago2: a spatially and temporally enhanced knowledge base from wikipedia. Artificial Intelligence 194, 28–61 (2013)
12. Jean-Mary, Y.R., Shironoshita, E.P., Kabuka, M.R.: Ontology matching with semantic verification. Web Semantics: Science, Services and Agents on the World Wide Web 7(3), 235–251 (2009)
13. Jiang, J.J., Conrath, D.W.: Semantic similarity based on corpus statistics and lexical taxonomy. arXiv preprint cmp-lg/9709008 (1997)
14. Li, J., Tang, J., Li, Y., Luo, Q.: Rimom: A dynamic multistrategy ontology alignment framework. IEEE Transactions on Knowledge and Data Engineering 21(8), 1218–1232 (2009)
15. Li, Y., McLean, D., Bandar, Z.A., O'shea, J.D., Crockett, K.: Sentence similarity based on semantic nets and corpus statistics. IEEE Transactions on Knowledge and Data Engineering 18(8), 1138–1150 (2006)
16. Lin, D.: An information-theoretic definition of similarity. In: Proc. 15th International Conf. on Machine Learning, vol. 98, pp. 296–304 (1998)
17. Lin, F., Sandkuhl, K.: A survey of exploiting wordnet in ontology matching. In: Bramer, M. (ed.) Artificial Intelligence in Theory and Practice II. IFIP, vol. 276, pp. 341–350. Springer, Heidelberg (2008)
18. Mikolov, T., Sutskever, I., Chen, K., Corrado, G., Dean, J.: Distributed representations of words and phrases and their compositionality. In: Proceedings of NIPS (2013)
19. Mikolov, T., Zweig, G.: Context dependent recurrent neural network language model. In: SLT, pp. 234–239 (2012)
20. Miller, G.A.: Wordnet: a lexical database for English. Communications of the ACM 38(11), 39–41 (1995)
21. Ngo, D., Bellahsene, Z., Todorov, K.: Opening the black box of ontology matching. In: Cimiano, P., Corcho, O., Presutti, V., Hollink, L., Rudolph, S. (eds.) ESWC 2013. LNCS, vol. 7882, pp. 16–30. Springer, Heidelberg (2013)
22. Pedersen, T., Patwardhan, S., Michelizzi, J.: Wordnet:: Similarity: Measuring the relatedness of concepts. Demonstration Papers at HLT-NAACL 2004, pp. 38–41. Association for Computational Linguistics (2004)
23. Shvaiko, P., Euzenat, J.: Ontology matching: State of the art and future challenges. IEEE Transactions on Knowledge and Data Engineering, 158–176 (2013)

24. Socher, R., Lin, C.C., Manning, C., Ng, A.Y.: Parsing natural scenes and natural language with recursive neural networks. In: Proceedings of the 28th International Conference on Machine Learning (ICML 2011), pp. 129–136 (2011)
25. Stoilos, G., Stamou, G., Kollias, S.D.: A string metric for ontology alignment. In: Gil, Y., Motta, E., Benjamins, V.R., Musen, M.A. (eds.) ISWC 2005. LNCS, vol. 3729, pp. 624–637. Springer, Heidelberg (2005)
26. Turian, J., Ratinov, L., Bengio, Y.: Word representations: a simple and general method for semi-supervised learning. In: Proceedings of the 48th Annual Meeting of the Association for Computational Linguistics, pp. 384–394. Association for Computational Linguistics (2010)
27. Wu, Z., Palmer, M.: Verbs semantics and lexical selection. In: Proceedings of the 32nd Annual Meeting on Association for Computational Linguistics, pp. 133–138. Association for Computational Linguistics (1994)

Exploiting Multiple Resources for Word-Phrase Semantic Similarity Evaluation

Xiaoqiang Jin, Chengjie Sun, Lei Lin, and Xiaolong Wang

School of Computer Science and Technology
Harbin Institute of Technology, China
{xqjin,chjsun,linl,wangxl}@insun.hit.edu.cn

Abstract. Previous researches on semantic similarity calculating have been mainly focused on documents, sentences or concepts. In this paper, we study the semantic similarity of words and compositional phrases. The task is to judge the semantic similarity of a word and a short sequence of words. Based on structured resource (WordNet), semi-structured resource (Wikipedia) and unstructured resource (Web), this paper extracts rich effective features to represent the word-phrase pair. The task can be treated as a binary classification problem and we employ Support Vector Machine to estimate whether the word and phrase is similar given a word-phrase pair. Experiments are conducted on SemEval 2013 Task5a. Our method achieves 82.9% in accuracy, and outperforms the best system (80.3%) that participates in the task. Experimental results demonstrate the effectiveness of our proposed approach.

Keywords: word-phrase Semantic Similarity, Support Vector Machine.

1 Introduction

Semantic similarity calculation plays an important role in natural language processing, such as information retrieve, automatic question answering, word sense disambiguation and machine translation. Most previous studies about semantic similarity calculation mainly focus on documents, sentences or concepts, while ignore the fine-grained word-phrase semantic similarity which has been a research hot topic. In this paper, we study the semantic similarity of words and compositional phrases.

The word-phrase semantic similarity evaluation task is to judge the semantic similarity of a word and a short sequence of words. In each word-phrase pair, the word is a noun and the phrase is made up of an adjective and a noun pair. The task can be treated as a binary classification which judge the word-phrase pair is similar or not in semantic space. As the word-phrase pair lack of context, in this paper, we propose to extract rich features from multiple resources to represent word-phrase pair, including structured resource (WordNet), semi-structured resource (Wikipedia) and unstructured resource (Web). Totally, 27 features are obtained. Through feature selection, we finally get the best feature subset. Then we use a supervised learning algorithm—Support Vector Machine

M. Sun et al. (Eds.): CCL and NLP-NABD 2014, LNAI 8801, pp. 46–57, 2014.

(SVM) to judge whether the word-phrase pair is similar or not in semantic space. We conduct experiments on SemEval 2013 Task5a. Our method achieves 82.9% in accuract beyond the best system (80.3%) that participates in the task. Experimental results demonstrate the effectiveness of our approach.

2 Related Work

According to the technology used, semantic similarity mainly could be divided into three categories: purely statistical techniques , knowledge-based techniques and hybrid techniques[10]. The researching objects have been mainly focused on article, sentence and concept.

Vector Space Model (VSM) is a purely statistical technique, which use the distributional hypothesis [2,3,4,5] that words that occur in similar contexts tend to have similar meanings. The distributional hypothesis could be explained as that statistical pattern of human word usage can be used to figure out what people mean. When calculate word-word semantic similarity, VSM represents the word as a point of the high dimension of the text by counting the frequency of the word. Then the semantic similarity could be calculated by comparing the distance of the point. VSM has been widely used in the information retrieval area. VSM has been modified to calculate the semantic similarity between words,documents and patterns[1]. Many methods have improved VSM , Deerwester et al. (1990)[6] used truncated Singular Value Decomposition (SVD) on the term-document matrix to improve similarity measurements. Landauer and Dumais (1997)[7] applied truncated SVD to word semantic similarity, achieving human-level scores on multiple-choice synonym questions from the Test of English as a Foreign Language (TOEFL). Truncated SVD applied to document semantic similarity is called Latent Semantic Indexing (LSI), but it is called Latent Semantic Analysis (LSA) when applied to word semantic similarity.

Web-based methods also use purely statistical techniques. It bases on the huge Web corpus and usually uses search engine to get the statistical information. Based on the AltaVista search engine, Turney P (2001) [21] used pointwise mutual information(PMI) to recognize synonyms. Hsin-Hsi et al(2006) [22] proposed a web search with double checking model to explore the web as a live corpus. GANG LU et al(2010) [23] proposed a semantic similarity measurement method using the information page count and snippets. Danushka Bollegala et al(2008) [24] proposed an approach to compute semantic similarity using automatically extracted lexical-syntactic patterns from text snippets.

WordNet based methods are based on the knowledge. It encodes the important relations between the words such as synonymy, hypernymy and meronymy. In WordNet text semantic similarity is mapped to word sense traced as the concept. Methods [13,14,15,16,17,18] based on WordNet employ the structure of the WordNet, sometimes combing the information content.

Wiki-based methods are based on knowledge-Wikipedia. Like WordNet based methods, Wiki-based methods [9,10,11,12] either use the content in the page or the structure between the page. Explicit semantic analysis [9,10] (ESA) treats each article in Wikipedia as a concept and map any text into the high dimension of concept, besides, ESA has also measured the link between the pages. Hybrid methods have used both the statistical techniques and knowledge-based techniques. Mihalcea et al (2006) [25] and Bar et al (2012) [26] used hybrid method to measure text semantic similarity.

Despite many methods have been used to calculate the semantic similarity, different methods focus on different lengths of texts and the effect of each semantic similarity is mainly dependent on the resource. There are three main resources frequently used: structured resource, semi structured resource and unstructured resource. VSM and ESA perform better in long text while WordNet and Web-based methods in word. Structured resource(e.g. WordNet) could provide more information about semantic similarity but a lower coverage, Besides it is difficult to update. Unstructured resource(e.g. Web) have a higher coverage but provide less information. Semi structured resource(e.g. Wikipedia) combine the advantages of structured resource and unstructured resource. But at the same time, it gets the drawbacks of them. Though the length of phrase is shorter than long text, we can still treat a phrase as a long text. Besides the semantic similarity of phrase can be calculated by word-word semantic similarity. To obtain the advantage of multiple resources and methods, we use multiple semantic similarities as the features of word-phrase pair and employ a supervised learning algorithm to calculate the semantic similarity of word-phrase.

3 Method

The word-phrase semantic similarity evaluation task is to judge whether the word and phrase in a given pair is similar in semantic space or not. We treat the task as a binary classification problem and employ SVM to solve it. The representation of word-phrase pair has a significant influence on the final performance. Therefore we focus on the feature crafting. In consideration of the lack of sufficient context information, we propose to exploit three kinds of resources, i.e. structured resource (Wordnet), semi-structured resource (Wikipedia) and unstructured resource (Web), to extract rich features for word-phrase pair representation. To combine the features from different resources, we employ a feature selection algorithm to select effective features. In the following, we first introduce three kind of features, and then give the details of the feature selection algorithm.

3.1 WordNet Based features

Adjective in English mostly act as a modifier, that is to say we can neglect the adjective in phrase without losing much information. Besides WordNet organizes same part of speech in a tree, it performs worse when used to measure the semantic similarity of words which have different part of speeches. Here to simplify the method to get the features, we use word-word semantic similarity as the feature instead of word-phrase semantic similarity. Many methods have been proposed to calculate word-word semantic similarity using WordNet. These methods are mainly based on structure in the WordNet or information content. Since a word in WordNet is represented by its synsets[1], we cannot calculate the word-word semantic similarity directly. Usually, we can use the following formula to get the word-word semantic similarity, by selecting for any given pair of words those two meanings that lead to the highest concept-concept semantic similarity.

$$Sim(w_1, w_2) = max_{c_1 \in SC_1 c_2 \in SC_2} Sim(c_1, c_2) \quad (1)$$

where w_1 and w_2 are the words which need to calculate the semantic similarity and w_1 and w_2 have the same part of speech, SC_1 and SC_2 are the synsets of w_1 and w_2 in the WordNet.

Here we give a short description of methods that are frequently used. Path semantic similarity method proposed by S&P[13] is defined as:

$$Sim_{S\&P}(c_1, c_2) = 2 * depthMax - len(c_1, c_2) \quad (2)$$

Where the $depthMax$ is the maximum depth of the taxonomy, $len(c_1, c_2)$ is the length of the shortest path between the concepts c_1 and c_2 using node counting.

Wup (Wu & Palmer 1994)[14] semantic similarity metric use the length of two given concepts in the WordNet taxonomy and the depth of the least common subsume(LCS).

$$Sim_{W\&P} = \frac{2 * depth(msc(c_1, c_2))}{len(c_1, c_2) + 2 * depth(msc(c_1, c_2))} \quad (3)$$

Lch(Leacock& Chodorow)[15] semantic similarity method is described as:

$$Sim_{L\&C} = -log(\frac{len(c_1, c_2)}{2 * depthMax}) \quad (4)$$

Res semantic similarity method introduced by Resnik (Resnik 1995)[16] use the information content(IC) of the LCS of the two concepts.

$$Sim_{res}(c_1, c_2) = IC(msc(c_1, c_2)) \quad (5)$$

Lin semantic similarity method[17], building on the Resnik's method ,adds a normalization factor consisting of the information content of the two input concepts:

$$Sim_{Lin}(c_1, C_2) = \frac{2 * IC(msc(c_1, c_2))}{IC(c_1) + IC(c_2)} \quad (6)$$

Jcn semantic similarity[18] is described as the following:

$$Sim_{jcn} = \frac{1}{IC(c_1) + IC(c_2) - 2 * IC(msc(c_1, c_2))} \quad (7)$$

We use six methods above to calculate the semantic similarity. The metrics can be easily achieved by using the WordNet-based implementation NLTK package[2].

[1] Sometimes synset is also called word concept.

[2] This package is implemented by Python, one can easily get the tool at the web site: http://www.nltk.org/

3.2 Wikipedia Based features

We get the Wikipedia based features mainly using the method Explicit Semantic Analysis (ESA) and Vector Space Model (VSM). ESA represents meaning of text in a high-dimensional space of concepts derived from Wikipedia, thus the meaning of any text can be represented in terms of Wikipedia-based concepts. The semantic similarity of the text can be valued by comparing the Wikipedia-based concepts vectors. Since ESA can process the text of arbitrary length, we can easily get the word-phrase semantic similarity. VSM builds a matrix of Term Frequency-Inverse Document Frequency (TF-IDF), in which rows correspond to terms and columns correspond to documents in the Wikipedia. Each word can be represented by a vector in the matrix of TF-IDF. We can get the word-word semantic similarity by comparing the vector in terms of the word. In order to get word-phrase semantic similarity, we use two methods. The first one is the same as the WordNet feature extraction, we use noun word-noun word semantic similarity to represent the word-phrase semantic similarity. The second one counts each word's weight contributing to the text semantic similarity, it use word-word semantic similarity to represent word-phrase semantic similarity. The following is the formula[25] that we use to get the semantic similarity:

$$\begin{aligned} Sim(T_1, T_2) = \frac{1}{2} * (&\frac{\sum_{w \in \{T_1\}} maxsim(w, T_2) * idf(w)}{\sum_{w \in \{T_1\}} idf(w)} \\ &+ \frac{\sum_{w \in \{T_2\}} maxsim(w, T_1) * idf(w)}{\sum_{w \in \{T_2\}} idf(w)}) \end{aligned} \quad (8)$$

Where $maxsim(w, T)$ is the highest semantic similarity between word w and w' which is a word in text T. The Formula (8) builds a bridge from word-word semantic similarity to text-text semantic similarity when calculating the semantic similarity. In this paper, we use the Wikipedia snapshot as November 1, 2012 to implement our ESA and VSM model. Following procedures have been used to process the Wikipedia XML dump:

1. Turn the Wikipedia dump format from XML to text using the tool Wikipedia_Extractor[3];
2. Stem the word[4] and change the capital case to lower case;
3. Filter out the concept[5] which has fewer than 200 words;
4. Filter out non-English characters and numbers;
5. Filter out the stop words;

[3] This is a tool to parse Wikipedia backup XML to separate text files, it could be downloaded at the website: `http://medialab.di.unipi.it/wiki/Wikipedia_Extractor`

[4] This paper uses porter2 algorithm implemented by the stemming tool: `https://pypi.python.org/pypi/stemming/1.0`

[5] In Wikipedia an concept is same as a article.

After parsing the Wikipedia XML dump, we got 9.4 Gb of text in 1,542,428 articles and 3,323,004 distinct terms, which served for representing Wikipedia concepts as attribute vectors.

To compare the vector's similarity, we use four metrics: cosine, euclidean ,manhattan and jaccard. Giving two vector:

$$w = (w_1, w_2, ..., w_N)$$

$$v = (v_1, v_2, ..., v_N)$$

We can get the metrics using the following formula:

$$cos < w, v >= \frac{\sum_{i=1}^{N} w_i * v_i}{\sqrt{\sum_{i=1}^{N} w_i^2} * \sqrt{\sum_{i=1}^{N} v_i^2}} \tag{9}$$

$$eul < w, v >= \sqrt{\sum_{i=1}^{N} (w_i - v_i)^2} \tag{10}$$

$$man < w, v >= \sum_{i=1}^{N} |w_i - v_i| \tag{11}$$

$$jac < w, v >= \frac{\sum_{i=1}^{N} w_i * v_i}{\sum_{i=1}^{N} w_i^2 + \sum_{i=1}^{N} v_i^2 - \sum_{i=1}^{N} w_i * v_i} \tag{12}$$

There are three kinds of methods to get the semantic similarity vector. And we use four metrics to evaluate the distance between vectors. Totally, 12 features are obtained based on Wikipedia.

3.3 Web Based Features

Web Based features use the word co-occurrence[19]. The core idea is that "a word is characterized by the company it keeps" [20]. Since the Web page is too huge to get the date local for us, we mostly use the search engine to get the statistical information about the term in the Web. So many metrics could be used to measure the degree of the word co-occurrence. In this paper, we get the word statistical information through AltaVista and use Pointwise Mutual Information (PMI), Jaccard coefficient and Dice coefficient to measure the word co-occurrence. If we define the $p(query)$ as the following[21]:

$$p(query) \approx \frac{hits(query)}{N} \tag{13}$$

Giving two query q_1, q_2 , the definitions of the metrics could be represented as follow formula:

$$WebDice(q_1, q_2) = log_2(\frac{2 * hits(q_1 \wedge q_2)}{hits(q_1) + hits(q_2)}) \tag{14}$$

$$WebPMI(q_1, q_2) = log_2(\frac{hits(q_1 \wedge q_2)/N}{(hits(q_1)/N) * (hits(q_2)/N)} \tag{15}$$

$$WebJaccard(q_1, q_2) = log_2(\frac{2 * hits(q_1 \wedge q_2)}{hits(q_1) * hits(q_2) - hits(q_1 \wedge q_2)}) \tag{16}$$

Where hits(q) is the number of the web page returning by the search engine containing the query q; N is the number of the total web pages, usually $N = 10^{13}$[21].

From the four different types of queries suggested by Turney (2001)[21], we are using the NEAR query (co-occurrence within a ten-word window), which is a balance between accuracy (results obtained on synonymy tests) and efficiency (number of queries to be run against a search engine)[25]. Specifically, the co-occurrence query could be defined as the follow to collect counts from the AltaVista search engine.

$$hits(q_1 \wedge q_2) = hits(q_1 NEAR\ q_2) \tag{17}$$

This paper use three ways to get the web based features:

1. Use noun word-noun word semantic similarity to represent word-phrase semantic similarity.
2. Use word-word semantic similarity to get the semantic similarity of word-phrase, which can be achieved by formula(8).
3. Treat the phrase as 'word', use the Web-based method to get the semantic similarity directly.

Here three metrics are used to evaluate the word co-occurrence, finally we achieve 9 features based on Web.

3.4 Feature Combination

Based on three resources: Wikipedia, WordNet and Web corpus, We total get 27 features. According to the method used to get the semantic similarity of word-phrase, we classify the features into three categories. To make the feature notations more readable, we use a capital letter as a prefix before method to represent the category and the letters after '-' to denote the metric we use.

1. Use word-to-word semantic similarity to represent word-to-phrase semantic similarity, here we use the prefix—'W' before methods to represent this category:

   (a) WVSM-COS,WVSM-EUL,WVSM-JAC,WVSM-MAN[6]
   (b) WIR-JAC,WIR-DICE,WIR-PMI
2. Use noun word-to noun word semantic similarity to represent word-to-phrase semantic similarity,here we use the prefix—'N' before methods to represent this category:
   (a) NLIN,NWUP,NRES,NPATH,NLCH,NJCN
   (b) NESA-COS,NESA-EUL,NESA-JAC,NESA-MAN[7]
   (c) NIR-JAC,NIR-DICE,NIR-PMI
3. Directly calculate word-phrase semantic similarity, here we use prefix—'D' before methods to represent this category:
   (a) DESA-COS,DESA-EUL,EDSA-JAC,DESA-MAN
   (b) DIR-JAC,DIR-DICE,DIR-PMI

Here we treat each semantic similarity as feature of word-phrase pair, thus each instance can be represented as a vector of 27 features.

We use two ways to combine feature. One way is to combine all the features to calculate the semantic similarity and the other is through feature selection. We use the symbols FAll and FSubset to represent the ways of feature combination separately.

Here, we use a heuristic search procedure—forward search [27] to find a good feature subset. We employ SVM[8] as the evaluation function of feature selection. The forward search can be represented as follow:

1. Initialize $\mathcal{F} = \emptyset$.
2. Repeat
   (a) For $i = 1, 2, ..., n$ if $i \notin \mathcal{F}$,let $\mathcal{F}_i = \mathcal{F} \cup \{i\}$, and use 5-flod cross validation to evaluate features $\mathcal{F}_i$.(Train the learning algorithm(SVM) using only the features in $\mathcal{F}_i$,and estimate its accuracy.)
   (b) Set $\mathcal{F}$ to be the best features subset found on step (a)
3. Select and output the best feature subset that was evaluated during the entire search procedure.

The outer loop of the algorithm can be terminated either when $\mathcal{F} = \{1, ...n\}$ is the set of all features, or when $|\mathcal{F}|$ exceeds some pre-set threshold(corresponding to the maximum number of features that you want the algorithm using).

Through feature selection, we get the best feature subset. The best feature subset—FSubset is as follow:

FSubset = {NESA-JAC,WVSM-EUC,WVSM-MAN,DESA-EUC,DESA-JAC, NIR-PMI,DIR-DICE, WIR-JAC,WIR-PMI,NLCH,NRES }

---

[6] When use word-to-word semantic similarity to calculate word-phrase semantic similarity, ESA and VSM are the same.

[7] When use noun word-to-noun word semantic similarity to calculate word-phrase semantic similarity, ESA and VSM are the same.

[8] This paper use the open source tool libsvm: `http://www.csie.ntu.edu.tw/~cjlin/libsvm/`

4 Experiments

4.1 Data Set

The data we use are from SemEval2013-Task5a[9]. The train data set consists of 5861 negative instances and 5861 positive instances. In the test set, 3906 instances are provided. The format of instance (e.g. time particular vs moment) in train and test data are the same. The first part of the instance is a noun and the second is a phrase which consists of an adjective and a noun.

4.2 Results and Discussion

To see the performance of each previous semantic similarity on word-phrase, we use each semantic similarity of word-phrase as the feature vector of word-phrase. Then we use the SVM to get the final results. This paper use three main metrics in SemEval2013-Task5a to evaluate results. According to the resources, we organize the results into three tables 1,2,3.

Table 1. The results of Wikipedia-based methods

Feature Symbol	Accuracy	Precision	Recall
NESA-COS	0.636	0.803	0.361
NESA-EUC	0.514	0.593	0.090
NESA-MAN	0.500	1.000	0.001
NESA-JAC	0.556	0.853	0.136
WVSM-COS	0.661	0.826	0.407
WVSM-EUC	0.518	0.573	0.141
WVSM-MAN	0.507	0.935	0.015
WVSM-JAC	0.582	0.868	0.195
DESA-COS	0.663	0.813	0.424
DESA-EUC	0.522	0.574	0.172
DESA-MAN	0.500	1.000	0.001
DESA-JAC	0.586	0.849	0.209

The table 1 shows the results of Wikipedia-based methods, as we can see, DESA* methods perform better than others. It can be explained as that ESA treats the phrase as a whole while others whether measure the partial information or measure the semantic similarity indirectly. Among all the metrics used to compare vector's similarity, cosine and jaccard have a better result in all the methods.

The table 2 reports the results of Web-based method. Based on the results, We find that most WIR* methods perform better than NIR* methods, We explain this as that though adjacent pay less contributions to semantic similarity than noun,it still has some contributions. DIR* methods preform worse than WIR*

Table 2. The results of Web-based methods

Feature Symbol	Accuracy	Precision	Recall
DIR-JAC	0.644	0.915	0.318
DIR-DICE	0.645	0.915	0.320
DIR-PMI	0.641	0.913	0.312
WIR-JAC	0.754	0.779	0.709
WIR-DICE	0.754	0.778	0.712
WIR-PMI	0.676	0.704	0.607
NIR-JAC	0.735	0.725	0.758
NIR-DICE	0.735	0.727	0.754
NIR-PMI	0.731	0.725	0.746

Table 3. The results of WordNet-based methods

Feature Symbol	Accuracy	Precision	Recall
NWUP	0.730	0.868	0.544
NJCN	0.646	0.922	0.320
NLCH	0.738	0.785	0.655
NLIN	0.673	0.841	0.428
NPATH	0.718	0.938	0.467
NRES	0.719	0.824	0.557

methods and NIR* methods, we conjecture that there is a main reason for the phenomena : this is due to the rare occurrence of phrase in the Web.

When we compare the data between table1, table2 and table3, we note WordNet-based methods perform better than other resources. It is because WordNet has much more information about semantic similarity than others.

Table 4. The result of top three in the SemEval 2013 task5a & feature combinations

Feature Symbol	Accuracy	Precision	Recall
	Top three in the SemEval2013-task5a		
1st	0.803	0.837	0.752
2nd	0.794	0.867	0.685
3rd	0.794	0.856	0.707
	Feature Combination		
FAll	0.814	0.851	0.760
FSubset	0.829	0.872	0.771

Table 4 shows the results of feature combination, besides the results of top three in SemEval 2013 task5a are also given. It is obvious that previous semantic similarity method is effective when we employ them to calculate the semantic similarity of word-phrase. We find that the result of FAll is significantly improved

[9] `http://www.cs.york.ac.uk/semeval-2013/task5/index.php?id=full`

and FSubset preforms even better. Different features of semantic similarity based on different resources may figure out the different aspects of semantic similarity of word-phrase. That is key point to explain why FAll obtains a better result. Because of the information redundancy between features, that is why FSubset perform better than FAll. We also find that both the FAll and FSubset perform better than the top one in the Evaluating Phrasal Semantics task in three main metrics. That demonstrates the effectiveness of our approach.

5 Conclusion

In this paper we focus on the task to judge whether the word-phrase is similar or not in semantic space. Based on multiple resources, this paper extracts rich effective features to represent the word-phrase pair. After a feature combination, we employ SVM to estimate whether the word and phrase is similar or not in semantic space. Experimental results conducted on SemEval2013-Task5a's data set demonstrate the effectiveness of our approach.

Although the approach performs better than the best result in the Evaluating Phrasal Semantics task at SemEval-2013 in three main metrics, there is still room for improvement. There may be more effective features to calculate the semantic similarity. And other classifier excluding SVM, may have a better performance.

Acknowledgment. This work is supported by the Key Basic Research Foundation of Shenzhen (JC201005260118A) and National Natural Science Foundation of China (61100094 & 61300114).The authors are grateful to the anonymous re-viewers for their constructive comments. Special thanks to Yaming Sun for insightful suggestions.

References

1. Turney, P.D., Pantel, P.: From frequency to meaning: Vector space models of semantics. Journal of Artificial Intelligence Research 37(1), 141–188 (2010)
2. Wittgenstein, L.: Philosophical Investigations. Blackwell. Translated by Anscombe, G.E.M. (1953)
3. Harris, Z.: Distributional structure. Word 10(23), 146–162 (1954)
4. Weaver, W.: Translation. In: Locke, W., Booth, D. (eds.) Machine Translation of Languages: Fourteen Essays. MIT Press, Cambridge (1955)
5. Firth, J.R.: A synopsis of linguistic theory 1930-1955. In: Studies in Linguistic Analysis, pp. 1–32. Blackwell, Oxford (1957)
6. Deerwester, S.C., Dumais, S.T., Landauer, T.K., Furnas, G.W., Harshman, R.A.: Indexing by latent semantic analysis. Journal of the American Society for Information Science (JASIS) 41(6), 391–407 (1990)
7. Landauer, T.K., Dumais, S.T.: A solution to Plato's problem: The latent semantic analysis theory of the acquisition, induction, and representation of knowledge. Psychological Review 104(2), 211–240 (1997)
8. Han, E.-H(S.), Karypis, G.: Centroid-based document classification: Analysis and experimental results. In: Zighed, D.A., Komorowski, J., Żytkow, J.M. (eds.) PKDD 2000. LNCC (LNAI), vol. 1910, pp. 424–431. Springer, Heidelberg (2000)

9. Gabrilovich, E., Markovitch, S.: Computing Semantic Relatedness Using Wikipedia-based Explicit Semantic Analysis. In: IJCAI, vol. 7, pp. 1606–1611 (2007)
10. Gabrilovich, E., Markovitch, S.: Wikipedia-based semantic interpretation for natural language processing. Journal of Artificial Intelligence Research 34(2), 443 (2009)
11. Strube, M., Ponzetto, S.P.: WikiRelate! Computing semantic relatedness using Wikipedia. In: AAAI, vol. 6, pp. 1419–1424 (2006)
12. Witten, I., Milne, D.: An effective, low-cost measure of semantic relatedness obtained from Wikipedia links. In: Proceeding of AAAI Workshop on Wikipedia and Artificial Intelligence: An Evolving Synergy, pp. 25–30. AAAI Press, Chicago (2008)
13. Resnik, P.: Semantic similarity in a taxonomy: An information-based measure and its application to problems of ambiguity in natural language. arXiv preprint arXiv:1105.5444 (2011)
14. Wu, Z., Palmer, M.: Verbs semantics and lexical selection. In: Proceedings of the 32nd Annual Meeting on Association for Computational Linguistics, pp. 133–138. Association for Computational Linguistics (1994)
15. Leacock, C., Chodorow, M.: Combining local context and WordNet similarity for word sense identification. WordNet: An Electronic Lexical Database 49(2), 265–283 (1998)
16. Resnik, P.: Using information content to evaluate semantic similarity in a taxonomy. arXiv preprint cmp-lg/9511007 (1995)
17. Lin, D.: An information-theoretic definition of similarity. In: ICML, vol. 98, pp. 296–304 (1998)
18. Jiang, J.J., Conrath, D.W.: Semantic similarity based on corpus statistics and lexical taxonomy. arXiv preprint cmp-lg/9709008 (1997)
19. Manning, C.D., Schütze, H.: Foundations of Statistical Natural Language Processing. MIT Press, Cambridge (1999)
20. Firth, J.R.: A Synopsis of Linguistic Theory 1930-1955. In: Studies in Linguistic Analysis, pp. 1–32. Philological Society, Oxford (1957), Reprinted in Palmer, F.R. (ed.): Selected Papers of J.R. Firth 1952-1959. Longman, London (1968)
21. Turney, P.: Mining the Web for Synonyms: PMI-IR versus LSA on TOEFL (2001)
22. Chen, H.H., Lin, M.S., Wei, Y.C.: Novel association measures using web search with double checking. In: Proceedings of the 21st International Conference on Computational Linguistics and the 44th Annual Meeting of the Association for Computational Linguistics, pp. 1009–1016. Association for Computational Linguistics (2006)
23. Lu, G., Huang, P., He, L., et al.: A new semantic similarity measuring method based on web search engines. WSEAS Transactions on Computers 9(1), 1–10 (2010)
24. Bollegala, D., Matsuo, Y., Ishizuka, M.: Measuring semantic similarity between words using web search engines. In: WWW, vol. 7, pp. 757–766 (2007)
25. Mihalcea, R., Corley, C., Strapparava, C.: Corpus-based and knowledge-based measures of text semantic similarity. In: AAAI, vol. 6, pp. 775–780 (2006)
26. Bar, D., Biemann, C., Gurevych, I., Zesch, T.: Ukp: Computing semantic textual similarity by combining multiple content similarity measures. In: Proceedings of the First Joint Conference on Lexical and Computational Semantics-vol. 1: Proceedings of the Main Conference and the Shared Task, and vol. 2: Proceedings of the Sixth International Workshop on Semantic Evaluation, pp. 435–440. Association for Computational Linguistics (2012)
27. Ng, A.: Regularization and model selection, CS 229 Machine Learning Course Materials, pp. 4–5

Dependency Graph Based Chinese Semantic Parsing

Yu Ding[1], Yanqiu Shao[2], Wanxiang Che[1], and Ting Liu[1]

[1] Harbin Institute of Technology, Harbin, China
{dingyu008,wanxiang}@gmail.com, tliu72@vip.126.com
[2] Beijing Language & Culture University, Beijing, China
yqshao163@163.com

Abstract. Semantic Dependency Parsing (SDP) is a deep semantic analysis task. A well-formed dependency scheme is the foundation of SDP. In this paper, we refine the HIT dependency scheme using stronger linguistic theories, yielding a dependency scheme with more clear hierarchy. To cover Chinese semantics more comprehensively, we make a break away from the constraints of dependency trees, and extend to graphs. Moreover, we utilize SVM to parse semantic dependency graphs on the basis of parsing of dependency trees.

Keywords: semantic analysis, semantic dependency graph, auto parsing of dependency graph.

1 Introduction

Semantic analysis is the ultimate goal of natural language processing on sentence level. For sentences as "张三(Tom)吃(eat)了(already)苹果(apple)" and "苹果(apple) 被(been) 张三(Tom) 吃(eat) 了(already)," both of which are semantically identical though with different forms of expression, Their semantic form is "吃(eat)(张三(Tom)，苹果(apple))" .This semantic information is helpful to word-sense disambiguation, information retrieval, machine translation and so on.

SDP integrates dependency structure and semantic information in the sentence, based on dependency grammar [1], which is a deep semantic analysis task. SDP consists of two steps, the first is to construct a dependency structure according to dependency grammar, i.e. to find out all pairs of words with direct semantic relations in a sentence, and then assign semantic labels between each word pairs.

The corpora with semantic-oriented dependencies already exist. [2,3] have annotated a corpus in the scale of one million words manually. They adjusted the semantic relations defined by HowNet, combining similar labels, eliminating those rarely used and revising those with semantic blurs and differences.

HIT semantic dependency is established by Research Center for Social Computing and Information Retrieval in Harbin Institute of Technology in 2011. It is also based on the semantic framework of HowNet, with the combination of LuChuan and Yuan Yulin semantic representation systems. [4] annotated 10 thousand of sentences in Penn

M. Sun et al. (Eds.): CCL and NLP-NABD 2014, LNAI 8801, pp. 58–69, 2014.

Chinese Treebank. [5] organized the international public assessment in SemEval-2012 using this corpus. Many research institutions in China participated in this share task. However, flaws of HIT semantic dependency exist 1) there are too many fine-grained labels, many of which are rarely mentioned or used; 2) HIT corpus is annotated on news corpus, Whether it is able to cover complex linguistic phenomena is in question; and 3) there are much overlapping between labels. Thus it needs further improvement.

SDP is studied based on dependency trees. But semantic structure in Chinese often cannot be completely expressed by trees. For instance, "我们(we) 选(select) 他(he) 当(as) 班长(monitor)." The head of "他（he）" is "选(select)" referring to a patient relation, but there is also a relation between "当(as)" and "他(he)." Another example is "我(I)头(head)痛(ache)的(de)厉害(serious)，还(still)流(flow)鼻涕(snot)" According to the tree, the head of "我(I)" is "头(head)", referring to a possessive relation; yet there is also a semantic relation between "流(flow)鼻涕(snot)" and "我(I)." Thus limitation of dependency trees is obvious.

Due to the mentioned flaws, in this paper we introduce a semantic dependency scheme with stronger theory foundations on the basis of HIT's. To cover Chinese semantics in a more all-round way, we propose semantic dependency graphs on the extension of the dependency tree structure. This paper parses dependency graphs on the basis of a parser for dependency trees and a SVM classifier.

2 The Dependency Graph Scheme

2.1 Structure of Semantic Dependency Graphs

According to real corpus on large scale and considering that Chinese is a kind of parataxis language with little syntactic restrictions, we extend the traditional structure of dependency trees to dependency graphs.

Definition: Semantic Dependency Graphs are directed acyclic graphs. Nodes refer to words and sides refer to semantic relations between words with one semantic label. There is one and only one node without any head as the center of whole graph.

The graphs overcome the limitation of dependency trees, allowing the existence of more than one head on certain nodes, as well as crossing of arcs. As in Figure 1 and Table 1, node "她(she)" has semantic relations with both "脸色(face)" and "病(disease)," which means that there are two heads for "她(she)"(notice that semantic parsing here is different from topics in pragmatics)，meanwhile arcs (病(disease), 她(she)) and (难看(terrible-looking), 现在(now)) cross.

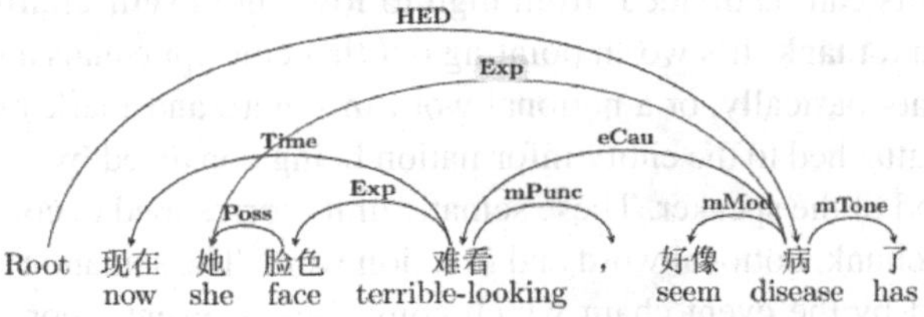

Fig. 1. An example of dependency graph

Table 1. Table form of dependency graph

Word Index	Word	Head Index	Head Word	Semantic	Descriptions
1	现在	4	难看	Time	Time
2	她	3	脸色	Poss	Possessor
2	她	7	病	Exp	Experiencer
3	脸色	4	难看	Exp	Experiencer
4	难看	7	病	eCau	Event Cause
5	，	4	难看	mPunc	Punctuation
6	好像	7	病	mMod	Modal Mark
7	病	0	HED	HED	--
8	了	7	病	mTone	Tone Mark

There are basically four rules in the theory of traditional dependency grammar (DG)[1]. Dependency graphs break the rules of traditional DG on “No element depends directly on more than one others” and “no crossings of arcs are allowed”. But its core idea still inherits from DG, for example the relations are transitive, irreflexive, and anti-symmetric. Therefore dependency graph is an extension of the DG.

2.2 Semantic Relation Scheme on the Basis of Chinese Parataxis Network

There are several problems in HIT semantic dependency scheme. There are too many semantic labels, and some of which only appear a few times. Much overlapping also appeared. HIT corpus is annotated on news corpus, but news sentences cover only limited means of Chinese expression. Thus it needs further improvement.

On the basis of Chinese parataxis network of semantic relations defined by Lu Chuan[6], this paper borrows relation labels, the classification of semantic units and the idea of semantic combination, and also integrates the characteristics of DG, to construct a semantic relation scheme of more clarity.

2.2.1 Semantic Units and Semantic Combination

The semantic units can be divided, from high to low, into **event chain**, **event**, **argument**, **concept** and **mark**. It’s worth pointing out that concept equals a simple concept in human thoughts basically, or a notional word in syntax and mark means the information which is attached to the entity information being conveyed by speakers, such as the tone and mood of the speaker. These sematic units correspond to complex sentence, minor sentence, chunk, notional word and function word. The semantic of one sentence can be expressed by the event chain which comprises of events represented by each minor sentence. The semantic of minor sentences can be expressed by the central and side arguments, while the semantic of central argument is expressed by predication concept and side argument by other referential or defining concepts. Concepts are related by marks.

The semantics of sentences comprises of semantic units, and combination ways between these units including semantic relations and semantic attachments. The semantic attachment refers to the marks of semantic units. Semantic relation includes symmetric and asymmetric relation. Symmetric relation includes coordination, selection and equivalence relations. Meanwhile, asymmetric relation includes:

Cooperative relation happens between the central concept and side concept. For example, in "工人(worker)修理(repair)管道(pipeline)", "管道(pipeline)"is the patient of "修理(repair)" and they form cooperative relation. Semantic roles usually refer to cooperative relations, and this paper defines 31 semantic roles, see appendix. **Additional relation** refers to the modification between additional concept and the central concept within the side argument, includes all kinds of roles, e.g. "地下(underground)的(de)管道(pipeline)" (管道(pipeline), 地下(underground): Loc). **Connectional relation** means the bridging relation between two events that are of neither symmetric nor nested relation. For example, "如果(If) 天气(weather)好(good), 我(I) 会(will) 去(go) 颐和园(the Summer Palace)." the former event is the hypothesis of the latter event. There are 15 relations with respect to event in the new semantic scheme.

This paper is an improvement of the existing HIT semantic dependency scheme. It provides re-organization of HIT semantic dependency system on above theoretical basis. All semantic relations are shown in appendix.

2.2.2 Important Rules

Firstly, if two words are semantic associated in a sentence, then the dependency structure must reflect this association, either through direct or transitive arc. But for the sake of simplification, if two associated words have already got indirect dependency arcs and the relation can be inferred, then there's no need for direct arc. Secondly, Chinese will not generate modifying circles, so does semantic dependency graphs.

2.2.3 Special Situations

(1) Reverse relations

When the modifier in a phrase is a predication concept, it is marked as reverse relation. For example, in phrase "出现(emerge)的(de)彗星(comet)" the head of 出现(emerge) is 彗星(comet), and "彗星(comet)的(de) 出现(emerge)." the head of 彗星(comet) is 出现(emerge). Though they are different in syntactic structure and syntactic hierarchy, semantic relations on both arcs are the same, apart from the opposite direction of arcs. To distinguish them, "r" is added to sematic roles. This is consistent with HIT semantic dependency scheme.

(2) Nested events

If two events have a nested relation, namely that one event is degraded as a constituent of another and then they are "nested". For example, in the sentence "爷爷(grandpa)看见(see)他(he)的(de)小(little)孙女(granddaughter)在(is)玩(play)计算机(computer).", the underlined part is degraded as a content of the action “看见(see)”. The nested relation is labeled as “d-role”.

3 Semantic Dependency Graph Analysis

This part will provide detailed analysis of dependency graphs.

An analysis of corpus data reveals that the occurrence of crossed arcs can be divided into following categories.1) many omissions exist in recount structures; 2) the omission of central predicates can easily lead to crossed arcs; 3) in some sentences, the important part is pre-posed and later referred to by pronouns, namely the occurrence of equivalence relation is often accompanied by crossed arcs; and 4) flexible “ba”-sentences. Following are corresponding examples.

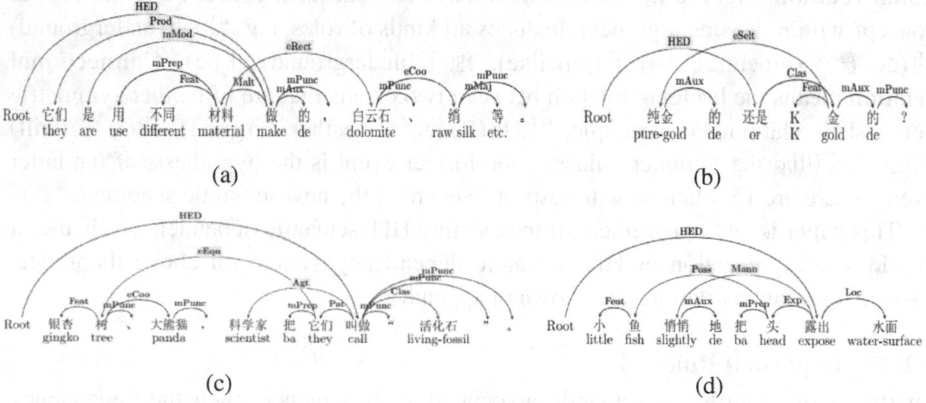

Fig. 2. Examples of crossed dependency arcs

The occurrence of nodes with multiple heads can be divided into 1) pivotal sentences caused by the causatives; 2) the reference of pronouns often cause multiple heads; 3) in a sentence comprising of several clauses, when the latter clause omits its subject and its subject is different from the former clause, there is a need for labeling the relation between predicate in the latter clause and its corresponding subject, As shown in figure 3 c), the subject of “流(flow)” is “我(I)” while the subject of “痛(pain)” is “头(head)”. It is easy to treat “头(head)” as the subject of “流(flow)” mistakenly with the induction of dependency arcs if omit the arc of “流(flow)” and “我(I)”. 4) An interlock takes place as the event degraded and the central word in the interlocking structure does not have direct semantic association with the modified part. Figure 4 gives examples under each situation.

In traditional SDP, the dependency arcs beyond the trees are omitted, such as (“采(pick)”,“自己(self)”: Agt) ，(“他(he)”,“汤姆(Tom)”: eEqu), (“流(flow)”,“我(I)”: Agt) and (“谈论(discuss)”,“话题(topic)”: rCont). Clearly, the omission of these arcs is a loss of the semantic in Chinese.

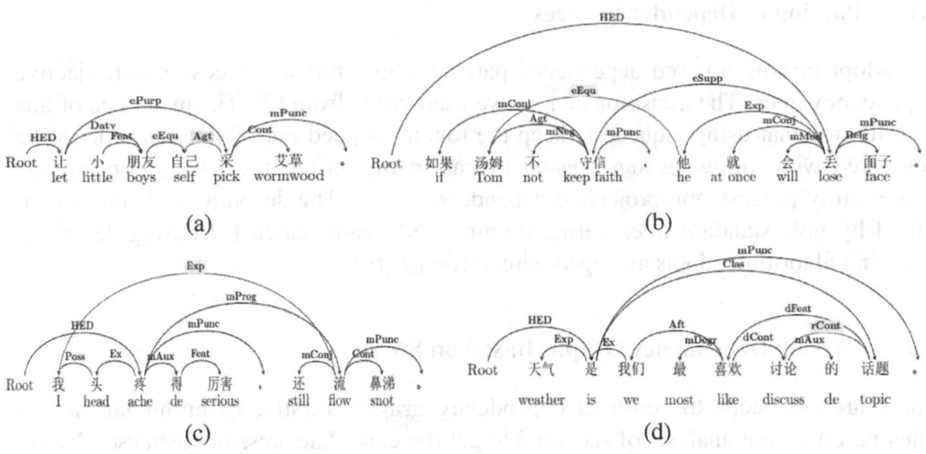

Fig. 3. Examples of nodes with multiple heads

It is known from the above analysis that, these non-projective dependency trees and dependency graphs are common language phenomena in Chinese and have a considerable quantity.

4 Automatic Parsing of Semantic Dependency Graph

Semantic dependency graph is an extension of dependency tree, which supplement relations discarded by trees. So based on the parsing of dependency trees, we use SVM to find arcs didn't appear in the trees and then assign semantic labels to each arcs.

Table 2. Statistics of all types of sentences

	Number	Sent Percentage	Arc Percentage
all sentences	10501	--	--
with crossed arcs	374	3.56%	0.33%
with multiple arcs	1025	9.77%	1.02%
with both	264	2.51%	--

We annotated 10,501 sentences, which mainly come from primary textbooks and Chinese-English bilingual corpus. The average length is 18 words. The statistics of sentences with crossed arcs and nodes with multiple heads is shown in table 2.

4.1 Parsing of Dependency Trees

We adopt transition-based dependency parsing algorithm to process non-projective dependency trees. The transition actions we used come from [7]. The main idea of this algorithm is that using a queue to keep the tokens popped out of stack in order to be compared with following unprocessed tokens in the buffer, thus this algorithm can successfully process non-projective dependency trees. The decoding decision is consulted by gold-standard trees during training and beam-search [8] during decoding. Learning algorithm adopts averaged-perceptron [9, 10].

4.2 Parsing Dependency Graphs Based on SVM

There are two steps to construct dependency graphs. Firstly, set up human-written rules based on the analysis of section 3 to get the candidate arcs, and then use SVM to select the arcs really needed to be incorporated. Finally, carry out another SVM on selected arcs and determine the semantic relations.

SVM classification relies on the design of features [11, 12]. We use some features proposed by [13] as the basis, such as the unigram bigram trigram features. Apart from those, we also add feature about the frequency of dependency arcs within the training corpus and about the two words' nearest common ancestor, including morphology, distances to ancestor and postags on the path to common ancestor respectively.

Analysis of real corpus reveals that dependency arcs existing beyond the dependency trees have numerable semantic relations. Therefore, the process of assigning semantic labels can be treated as a multi-classification problem. The features used here are the same as arcs identification used.

4.3 Results and Analysis of Dependency Tree Parsing

Table 3 shows the corpus statistics of our experimental data. The result of parsing of dependency tree is that UAS is 85.38% and LAS is 69.37%.

Table 3. Corpus statistics of our experiments

	Total	Project Trees	Graphs	Non-Project Trees
Train	8082	7206	790	86
Test	2015	1800	195	20
Dev	404	360	40	4

It is relatively low for LAS. In annotating stage, to further clarify the annotation, the hierarchy of the labels is clearly set, we can first pin down the main category of a sentence and find out the specific label later on, but all labels are equally treated by the parser. All together 98 labels are processed, thus the training is insufficient.

Table 4. Results of postags

Postag	UAS	LAS
NN	86%	58%
VV	78%	60%
VE	71%	61%
NT	84%	65%
VC	73%	66%
VA	81%	66%

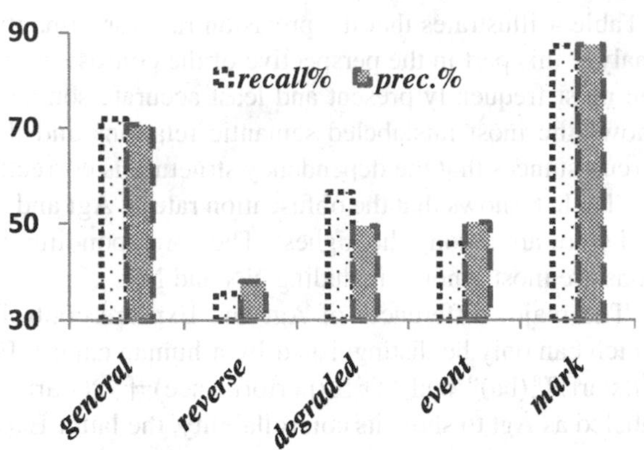

Fig. 4. Prec., Recall of semantic category

Figure 4 demonstrates reverse relations, nested relations and event relations have a relatively low rate of precision and recall. Semantic roles correspond to reverse relations and nested relations. In the training set, reverse relations and nested relations rarely exist. Thus the training on these two kinds of relations is not sufficient enough.

Semantic relations between events are similar to syntactic relations between them and no further features could help, and the arc length is longer on average. As a result, the precision of event relations is also relatively low. Whereas semantic marks is relatively higher, since more adverbs and conjunctions make up semantic marks and all the words included in each mark can be enumerated.

Table 4 shows that verbs have low rate of UAS and LAS. The following are reasons. Firstly, the existence of compressed sentences makes labeling of verbs more difficult. Two verbs form many relations, for example, eSucc, ePurp, dMann and so on. Secondly, Pivotal phrases in pivotal sentences usually express different meanings, and lead to multiple semantic relations between two actions, as eResu and eCau etc. Thirdly, relations between two clauses are represented by two kernel words of the two events. Mostly, the kernel words are verbs. However, according to our previous analysis, event relations have a relatively low rate of precision.

Table 5. Labels Prec., Recll

Label	Recall%	Prec.%
Belg	65.85	33.96
Cont	63.72	44.16
Pat	43.07	57.21
Exp	62.72	63.37
Datv	63.64	67.53
Agt	77.40	72.11
Feat	81.91	72.88

Table 6. Confusion Statistics of labels

Label	Freq	Prec.%	Confuse Label	Percent
Datv	451	64.71	Cont	7.54
Exp	1258	59.60	Agt	9.38
Cont	623	42.05	Pat	10.43
Agt	1146	66.91	Exp	10.99
Pat	534	55.97	Cont	21.16
Prod	126	49.12	Cont	26.82

Table 4 illustrates that the precision rate for semantic relations of nouns is low. We analyze this part in the perspective of the confusion of semantic relations. We statistic the most frequently present and least accurate semantic relations in Table 5. Table 6 shows the most mislabeled semantic relations and the rate of mislabeling under the circumstances that the dependency structure is correctly constructed.

Table 6 shows that the obfuscation rate of Agt and Exp, Cont and Pat, as well as Pat and Cont are among the highest. The corresponding postags of these 4 semantic relations are mostly noun, including NN and NR.

The major differences of Agt and Exp are controllability and non-controllability, which can only be distinguished by a human expert. For instance, "让(let)我们(we)开始(start)吧(ba)" and "演出(performance)开始(start)了(le)." The former sentence is labeled as Agt to show its controllability, the latter Exp to show the opposite. The main differences between Pat and Cont are "whether or not have been directly changed by subject." However, this "change" is subtle; Prod is the object been newly created or produced by subject, otherwise the object is Cont. The distinguishing of these two pairs needs human knowledge, and is difficult for machines to learn. Datv is the non-direct participant of the action, such as the receiver of things or information, the company, the excluder, the relevant party and the casualty in an event. It is normally the indirect object to the verb with a direct object. This direct object could be a Cont, e.g. 他(he)给(give)他的(his)弟弟(brother)一支(a)笔(pen), in which (给(give),弟弟(brother): Datv) and (给(give), 笔(pen): Cont). This is hard for machine to distinguish clearly.

4.4 Results and Analysis of Appending Additional Arcs

The experimental data is the test set in part 4.2. There are 195 Sentences with 210 extra arcs. Using rules to select candidate arcs, the recall is 98.86%. However, the recall in test set is only 76.42%. False arcs and labels created by auto-parsing fail the rules. To control the scale of candidate arcs, we cannot over generalize these rules. So the recall here is a compromise. The average amount of candidate arcs for each sentence is 6.8.

Table 7. The evaluation of positive instances

Feature Set	P%	R%	F%
basic	60.00	52.67	56.15
+ Word_pair_freq	62.29	51.90	56.62
+ Nearest_common_ancestor	68.57	50.00	57.83

The evaluation result in positive instances is shown in Table 7.When add two features subsequently, the result rises 1.68%. The feature of word pair frequency helps on finding heads of arcs. The common ancestor features help to distinguish whether two words are in the same semantic chunk and to find distance between two words. This is helpful to eEqu, since if two words are close to their common ancestor, even if they are distant from one another they can still express relatively close semantic information.

After analyzing the erroneous sentences, it is clearly illustrated that the majority of errors occur with eEqu mainly in the sentences with multiple nouns and pronouns, For instance, "古董商(antique dealer)告诉(tell)妈妈(mother)货箱(packing box)到(arrive)了(le),但是(but)她(she)嫌(feel)麻烦(trouble)不(not)想(like)把(ba)它(it)打开(open)." There are 5 nouns and pronouns in the sentence. However, "货箱(packing box)" and "它(it)" share a real link, while "妈妈(mother)" and "她(she)" share another link, which is not easy for machines to distinguish. The coreference resolution of pronoun is of great difficulty, But eEqus between closer nouns or pronouns are recognized better than far distance.

Errors produced by the tree parser is cascaded here, features extracted for SVM is partly wrong. This is another important reason affecting the result of classification. Both of these problems stand in the way of the construction of semantic dependency graphs.

Categorizing the previously classified dependency arcs to different semantic labels, we have a precision of 71.96%.

5 Conclusion

At the beginning, we analyzed the flaws of HIT semantic dependency scheme, to refine it, We utilized strong linguistic theories to propose a new scheme with clear semantic hierarchy and more standard labels. Moreover, it extends, on the basis of DG, the structure to dependency graphs, which are more suitable for Chinese semantics. We annotated 10 thousand sentences with our dependency scheme. In the later part, we will share the corpus with other researchers. Lastly, we introduce an auto parsing system of semantic dependency graphs. The serial process of the system led to cascading errors, causing parsing results of low accuracy. How to enhance the parsing of dependency graphs is our main work in the future.

Acknowledgement. We thank the anonymous reviewers for their constructive comments, and appreciatively acknowledge the support of the National Natural Science Foundation of China (NSFC) via Grant 61170144, 61133012 and 61370164.

References

1. Robinson, J.J.: Dependency structures and transformation rules. Language 46(2), 259–285 (1970)
2. Li, M., Li, J., Dong, Z., Wang, Z., Lu, D.: Building a large Chinese corpus annotated with semantic dependency. In: Proceedings of the Second SIGHAN Workshop on Chinese Language Processing (2003)
3. Li, M., Li, J., Wang, Z., Lu, D.: A Statistical Model for Parsing Semantic Dependency Relations in a Chinese Sentence. Chinese Journal of Computers 12(27), 1680–1687 (2004)

4. Wang, L.: Chinese Semantic Dependency Parsing. Harbin Institute of technology, Harbin (2010)
5. Che, W., Zhang, M., Shao, Y., Liu, T.: Semeval-2012 task 5: Chinese semantic dependency parsing. In: Proceedings of SemEval 2012, Montréal, Canada, June 7-8, pp. 378–384. Association for Computational Linguistics (2012)
6. Lu, C.: The Parataxis of Chinese Grammar. Commercial printing house (2001)
7. Choi, J.D., McCallum, A.: Transition-based dependency parsing with selectional branching. In: Proceedings of the 51st Annual Meeting of the Association for Computational Linguistics, Sofia, Bulgaria (2013)
8. Zhang, Y., Clark, S.: Syntactic processing using the generalized perceptron and beam search. Computational Linguistics 37(1), 105–151 (2011)
9. Collins, M.: Discriminative training methods for hidden Markov models: Theory and experiments with perceptron algorithms. In: Proceedings of the EMNLP Conference, Philadelphia, PA, pp. 1–8 (2002)
10. Collins, M., Roark, B.: Incremental parsing with the perceptron algorithm. In: Proceedings of ACL, Barcelona, Spain, pp. 111–118 (July 2004)
11. Cortes, C., Vapnik, V.: Support-vector networks. Machine Learning 20(3), 273–297 (1995)
12. Vapnik, V.N.: The Nature of Statistical Learning Theory. Springer (1995)
13. Park, K.-M., Hwang, Y.-S., Rim, H.-C.: Two-Phase Semantic Role Labeling based on Support Vector Machines. In: Proceedings of CoNLL (2004)

Appendix

Table of whole semantic dependency relations

Semantic roles	
Subject roles	Agent(Agt), Experiencer(Exp), Affection(Aft), Possessor(Poss)
Object roles	Patient(Pat),Content(Cont),Product(Prod),Origin(Orig),Dative(Datv)
Copular roles	Belongings(Belg), Classification(Clas), According(Accd)
Cause roles	Reason(Reas), Intention(Int), Consequence(Cons)
Condition roles	Manner(Mann), Tool(Tool), material(Matl)
Space-time roles	Time(Time), Location(Loc), Direction(Dir),Process(Proc), Scope(Sco)
Measurement roles	Quantity(Quan),Quantity-phrase(Qp),Frequency(Freq),Sequence(Seq)
Other roles	Feature(Feat), Host(Host), Comparison(Comp) , Name-modifier(Nmod), Time-modifier(Tmod)
Reverse relations	
r + semantic roles	
Nested relations	
d + semantic roles	
Event relations	
Symmetric relations	Coordination(eCoo), Selection(eSelt), Equivalent(eEquv)
Consecutive relations	Precedent(ePrec), Successor(eSucc), Progression(eProg), adversative(eAdvt), Cause(eCau), Result(eRes), Inference(eInf), Condition(eCond), Supposition(eSupp), Concession(eConc), Method(eMetd), Purpose(ePurp), Abandonment(eAban), Preference(ePref), Summary(eSum), Recount(eRect)
Semantic marks	
Relation marks	Conjection(mConj), Auxiliary(mAux), Preposition(mPrep)
Attachment marks	Tone(mTone), Time(mTime), Range(mRang), Degree(mDegr), Frequency(mFreq), Direction(mDir), Parenthesis(mPars), Negation(mNeg), Modal(mMod)
Other marks	Punctuation(mPunc), Majority(mMaj), Vain(mVain), Separation(mSepa)

A Joint Learning Approach to Explicit Discourse Parsing via Structured Perceptron

Sheng Li, Fang Kong*, and Guodong Zhou

School of Computer Sciences and Technology,
Soochow University, Suzhou, Jiangsu, 215006, China
qcl6355@gmail.com, {kongfang,gdzhou}@suda.edu.cn

Abstract. Discourse parsing is a challenging task and plays a critical role in discourse analysis. In this paper, we focus on building an end-to-end PDTB-style explicit discourse parser via structured perceptron by decomposing it into two components, i.e., a connective labeler, which identifies connectives from a text and determines their senses in classifying discourse relationship, and an argument labeler, which identifies corresponding arguments for a given connective. Particularly, to reduce error propagation and incorporate the interaction between the two components, a joint learning approach via structured perceptron is proposed. Evaluation on the PDTB corpus shows that our two-components explicit discourse parser can achieve comparable performance with the state-of-the-art one. It also shows that our joint learning approach can significantly outperform the pipeline ones.

1 Introduction

Discourse parsing determines the internal structure of a text, e.g., the discourse relationship between its text units. Recently it has become the research focus due to its critical importance on the downstream natural language processing (NLP) applications, such as coherence modeling [1,11], text summarization [9], statistical machine translation [14] and information extraction [16].

As the largest discourse corpus, the Penn Discourse TreeBank (PDTB) corpus [19] adds a layer of discourse annotations on the top of the Penn TreeBank (PTB) corpus [13] and has attracted increasing attention in current discourse related work [5,18,10,20,7,6,12]. However, although much research work has been carried out on certain components since the release of the PDTB corpus, there is little work on constructing an end-to-end discourse parser.

In this paper, we focus on building an end-to-end PDTB-style discourse parser for explicit connectives. Particularly, we decompose the explicit discourse parser into two component, i.e., a connective labeler, which identifies connectives from a text and determines their senses in classifying discourse relationship, and an argument labeler, which identifies corresponding arguments for a given connective. Besides, a joint learning approach via structured perceptron is introduced

* Corresponding author.

M. Sun et al. (Eds.): CCL and NLP-NABD 2014, LNAI 8801, pp. 70–82, 2014.

to reduce error propagation and incroporate the interaction between the two components. Evaluation on the PDTB corpus shows the appropriateness of our framework and the effectiveness of our joint learning approach.

The rest of this paper is organized as follows. After introducing the PDTB corpus in Section 2, we briefly review the related work on explicit discourse parser on the PDTB corpus in Section 3. Section 4 describes our end-to-end explicit discourse parser in detail. Then our joint learning approach is proposed in Section 5. After reporting the experiment results, we give a discussion in Section 6. Finally, we conclude the paper in Section 7.

2 Penn Discourse Tree Bank

The PDTB corpus follows the lexically grounded, predicate-argument approach in the D-LTAG framework [21]. It regards discourse connectives as discourse-level predicates that take exactly two text spans as their arguments. The span to which the connective is syntactically bound is labeled Arg2, while the other is labeled Arg1.

In the PDTB corpus, there are two types of discourse connectives, either explicit or implicit, among which explicit connectives occupy 53.49% (18459 tokens). Besides, each connective is assigned a sense from a three-level hierarchy, as shown in table 1 [19]. In this paper, we limit to the 16 Level-2 types.

Table 1. The hierarchy structures on discourse relationship of the PDTB corpus, Level-3 is not showed

Level-1	Temporal	Contingency	Comparison	Expansion
Level-2	Synchrony	Cause	Contrast	Conjunction
	Asynchronous	Pragmatic Cause	Pragmatic Contrast	Instantiation
		Condition	Concession	Restatement
		Pragmatic Condition	Pragmatic Concession	Alternative
				Exception
				List

Example 1 shows an explicit discourse relation from the article wsj_2337 with the connective while underlined, the Arg1 span *italicized*, and the Arg2 span **bold**. The last line of this example shows the relation sense. It will be used as a running example throughout this paper.

(1) *Total advertising linage was modestly lower as classified-ad volume increased,* while **there was softer demand for detail and national ad linage.**

(Comparison-Contrast)

3 Related Work

Since the release of the PDTB corpus, much research work has been carried out on certain components of discourse parsing, with focus on explicit connectives. For example, Pitler and Nenkova[18] proposed various kinds of syntactic features to identify explicit connectives and determine the sense of an exlicit connective on marking the discourse relationship. On gold parse trees, they achieved 94.19% in F-measure and 94.15% in accuracy for the connective identification and the Level-1 sense disambiguation, respectively. Dinesh et al.[4] introduced a tree subtraction algorithm for labeling only subordinate discourse connectives [1]. Wellner and Pustejovsky [22] proposed several machine learning approaches to identify the head words of the two arguments for an explicit connective. Following this work, Elwell and Baldridge [5] combined several general and connective specific rankers to improve the performance of labeling the head words of the two arguments. Ghosh et al.[7] viewed argument labeling as a sequence labeling problem, and used two conditional random fields (CRFs) to label Arg1 and Arg2, respectively. Besides, they exploited the sense of connective to improve the performance of argument labeling.

Compared with the research on certain components of explicit discourse parsing, there is little work on constructing a complete end-to-end explicit discourse parser. The only exceptions are Lin et al. [10,12], which designed an end-to-end explicit discourse parser into three components, i.e., a connective identifier, which identifies connectives from a text, a connective sense disambiguator, which determines the sense of a given connective, and an argument labeler, which identifies corresponding arguments for a given connective.

In this paper, we propose an end-to-end PDTB-style explicit discourse parser. Different from Lin et al. [10,12], we decompose it into two components, i.e., a connective labeler and an argument labeler, by combing the connective identifier and and the connective sense disambiguator into a single connective labeler. Particularly, a joint learning approach is proposed to reduce error propagation and capture the interaction between the two components.

4 End-to-End Explicit Discourse Parsing

In this section, we will introduce our end-to-end PDTB-style explicit discourse parser, which consists of two components, i.e. a connective labeler, which identifies connectives from a text and determines their senses in classifying discourse relationship, and an argument labeler, which identifies corresponding arguments for a given connective.

4.1 Connective Labeling

Since only true connectives can convey the sense of a discourse relationship, we view the non-discourse usage of a connective candidate as special sense "Nil".

[1] According to the PDTB, from the grammatical usage, connective can divide in three types: subordinate, coordinate and discourse-adverbial.

As this paper deals with the 16 Level-2 types in the connective sense hierachy, our connective labler becomes as a 17-category classfication task.

Table 2 lists various kinds of lexical and syntactic features employed in our connective labeler with the fourth column showing the feature instances corresponding to the gold parse tree of Example 1 as shown in Figure 1, taking [$_{IN}$ while] as the given connective candidate in question.

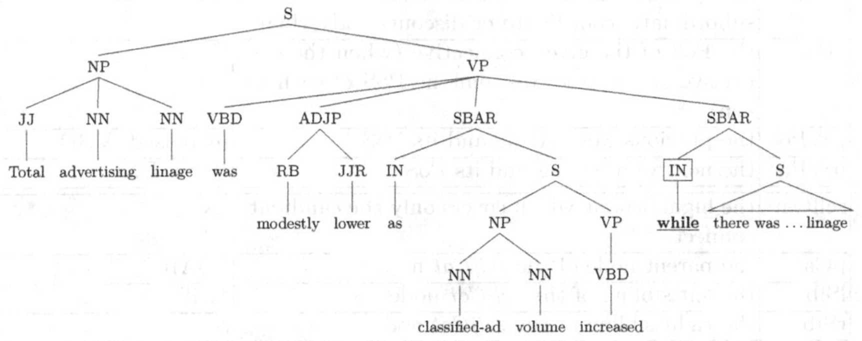

Fig. 1. Gold parse tree corresponding to Example 1

4.2 Argument Labeling

As stated above, the PDTB views a connective as the predicate of a discourse relation. Similar to semantic role labeling (SRL), we propose a constituent-based approach to do this task.

Firstly, a simple prune algorithm is employed to remove the constituents which are clearly not arguments to the connective in question, and all the remaining constituents are kept as the argument candidates of the given connective. Here, the pruning algorithm works recursively. Starting from the lowest node dominating the connective (called the connective target node), it collects all the siblings of the connective target node as argument candidates, moves on to the parent of the connective target node and collects its siblings as argument candidates. This process repeats until it reaches the root of the parse tree. Please note that, if the connective target node does not cover the connective exactly, the children of the connective target node are also collected as argument candidates. On the gold parse tree as shown in Figure 1 and given [$_{IN}$ while] as connective. We can get five argument candidates, i.e. [$_S$ there was ... linage], [$_{SBAR}$ as classified-ad volume increased], [$_{ADJP}$ modestly lower], [$_{VBD}$ was], [$_{NP}$ Total advertising linage].

Secondly, a machine learning approach is employed to determine the role of each argument candidate as whether "Arg1", "Arg2", or "Nil". Prasad et al. [19] reported that Arg1 can be located within the same sentence as the connective (SS), in some previous sentence of the connective (PS), or in some sentence following the sentence containing connective (FS). Our statistics on the PDTB corpus shows that in the PS case, the distribution of immediate previous sentence

Table 2. Features employed in our discourse relation classification

Cat.	Feature	Description	Example
Lex.	cStr	the string of the candidate connective (case-sensitive)	while
	cStrLc	the lower case string of the candidate connective	while
	cCat	the syntactic usage of the candidate connective: subordinate, coordinate or discourse adverbial	subordinate
	cPos	the PoS of the given connective (when the connective is a phrase, we combine PoS of each token)	IN
	pWPos	the previous word string and its PoS	increased, VBD
	nWPos	the next word string and its PoS	there, EX
Syn.	selfCat	the highest node which covers only the candidate connective	IN
	pCat	the parent node of the *selfCat* node	SBAR
	lSib	the left sibling of the *selfCat* node	"Nil"
	rSib	the right sibling of the *selfCat* node	S
	rVp	whether the right sibling contains a VP	yes
	pToRt	the syntactic path from *selfCat* node to the root	IN ↑ SBAR ↑ VP ↑ S
	cPToRt	the compressed syntactic path from *selfCat* node to the root	IN ↑ SBAR ↑ VP ↑ S

as Arg1 accounts 76.9% (5549 of 7215). Thus we can resolve the PS case by viewing the root of the parse tree of the immediate previous sentence as a special argument candidate. Table 3 lists various kinds of lexical and syntactic features used in our argument labeler, on reflecting the properties of the connective, the argument candidate and the relationship between them, with the fourth of column showing the feature instances corresponding to Figure 1, given$[_{IN}$ while] as the connective and $[_S$ there was ... linage] as the argument candidate in question.

Finally, we merge all the determined candidates to obtain Arg1 and Arg2 respectively.

5 Joint Learning via Structured Perceptron

With the sequential pipeline architecture as described in Section 4, our two-components explicit discourse parser ignores the interaction between the connective labeler and the argument labeler. To reduce error propagation and capture the interaction between the two components, we propose a joint learning approach via structured perceptron.

Structured perceptron is an extension to the stand linear perceptron for structured prediction, which was proposed in [2]. Given an instance $x \in X$, which in our case is a set of constituent nodes in a parse tree, the algorithm involves the

Table 3. Features used in our argument labeling

Cat.	Feature	Description	Example
Lex.	cStr	the string of the given connective (case-sensitive)	while
	connStrLc	the lowercase of the given connective	while
	cCat	the syntactic usage of the given connective: subordinate, coordinate, or discourse adverbial	subordinate
	cSen	the Level-2 relation sense conveyed by the given connective	Contrast
Syn.	nLSib	number of left siblings of the connective	0
	nRSib	number of right siblings of the connective	1
	ctOfNode	the context of the constituent node. We use PoS combination of the constituent, its parent, left sibling and right sibling to present this feature. When no parent or siblings, it is marked Nil	S-SBAR-IN-Nil
	pToConn	the syntactic path from the parent node the given connective to the constituent node	S ↑ SBAR ↓ IN
	rPOfNode	the relative position of the constituent node to the given connective: left, right or previous	right
	phToCSib	the syntactic path from the parent node of the connective to the constituent node and whether the number of the left siblings of the connective is greater than one	S ↑ SBAR ↓ IN:¡1

following decoding problem which finds the best configuration $d \in Y$ according to the current model w:

$$d = \mathop{\mathbf{arg\,max}}_{d' \in Y(x)} \quad \mathbf{w} \cdot \mathbf{f}(x, d') \tag{1}$$

where $\mathbf{f}(x, d')$ represents the feature vector of instance x under configuration d'.

5.1 Training

The perceptron learns the model w in an online fashion. Let $D = (x^i, y^i)_{i=1}^N$ be the set of training instances. In each iteration, the algorithm finds the best configuration d for instance x under current model w (Eq 1). If d is incorrect, the weights are updated as follows:

$$\mathbf{w} = \mathbf{w} + \mathbf{f}(x, y) - \mathbf{f}(x, d) \tag{2}$$

Figure 2 describes the general training framework of structured perceptron algorithm. The key step of the training and testing is the decoding procedure, which aims to find the best configuration under current model parameters. As like many NLP tasks (e.g., syntactic parsing, part-of-speech tagging) have too many states, the exact inference is often intractable. Instead, we employ beam-search to perform inexact inference. Collins and Roark [3] proposed the early-update idea for inexact inference, and later Huang et al [8] proved that structured

```
Input: Training data D = (x^i, y^i)_{i=1}^N, T iteration number, N training data
       number
Output: Model parameters w
Initialization: Set w = 0
for t ← 1 to T do
    for i ← 1 to N do
        d^i ← decode(x^i, y^i, w)
        if d^i ≠ y^i then
            w ← w + f(x^i, y^i_{[1:|d^i|]}) − f(x^i, d^i)
        end
    end
end
```

Fig. 2. General structured perceptron training framework. Here $y_{[1:i]}$ indicates previous i elements.

perceptron could converge even under exact inference, and they pointed out "violation" is just the need for the algorithm. Based on these suggestions and in order to reduce overfitting, we use a variant of stand perceptron called averaged perceptron [2] with beam-search for inexact inference to train our explicit discourse parser.

5.2 Decoding

Our decoding algorithm will joint two components. Here we use $\mathcal{R}$ to denote the discourse sense label alphabet, where $\mathcal{R}$ consists of 16 Level-2 sense types and a "Nil" sense which indicates non-discourse usage. Similarly, $\mathcal{A} = \{Arg1, Arg2, Nil\}$ denotes the argument label alphabet. We use $\mathcal{K}$ to denote the beam-size for the decoding procedure.

Let $x = (c, a_1, \ldots, a_m)$ be input of decoding algorithm, where c represents a given connective, and $a_1, \ldots, a_m$ are the pruning argument candidates. We use $y = (g(c), g(a_1), \ldots, g(a_m))$ to denote the corresponding oracle output, where function $g(\cdot)$ maps current constituent node to its output label. Consider Example 1, we have c=[$_{IN}$ while], and a_1=[$_S$ there was ... linage], ...,a_5=[$_{NP}$ Total advertising linage]. Finally, the input is $x = (c, a_1, a_2, a_3, a_4, a_5)$, and according to the annotation, the output is $y = (Contrast, Arg2, Arg1, Arg1, Arg1, Arg1)$.

Figure 3 shows the beam-search algorithm with early-update for explicit discourse parsing. For each instance, there are two sub-steps:

- **connective labeling** We enumerate all possible sense label alphabet, and select K best sense candidates for current connective.
- **argument labeling** After the relation step, we traverse all configurations in the beam. Then the procedure would select K best argument labels based on previous configuration.

```
Input: Instance x = (c, a_1, ..., a_m), and the oracle output y
K: beam size; R: relation sense label alphabet; A: argument label alphabet
Output: the best prediction d for instance x
Initialization: B ← [ε], t ← [ε]
for d' ∈ B do // search relation senses
  | t ← t ∪ {d' ⊕ r|r ∈ R}
end
B ← K-Best(t, K, c, f_c) // f_c:connective feature function
if y_[1] ∉ B then
  | return B_[0] // early-update
end
for i = 1 to m do // search argument roles
  | for d' ∈ B do
  |   | t ← t ∪ {d' ⊕ s|s ∈ A}
  | end
  | B ← K-Best(t, K, a_i, f_a) // f_a:argument feature function
  | if y_[1:i+1] ∉ B then
  |   | return B_[0] // early-update
  | end
end
return B_[0]
```

Fig. 3. Decoding algorithm for explicit discourse parsing, $d \oplus s$ means append s in d

After the second step, the rank of different sense assignments can be changed because of the argument candidates selection. Likewise, the choice of later argument candidates would be affected by previous argument assignments.

5.3 Features and Representation

In this joint framework, we use the same features as described in Table 2 and Table 3. In general, each feature f is a function $f : X \times Y \rightarrow R$, which maps x and y to a feature value. In this framework, we use indicator function to represent each feature like the following format:

$$f_1(x, i, y_i) = \begin{cases} 1 \text{ if } y_i = \text{“Contrast” and } x_i = \text{“while”} \\ 0 \text{ otherwise} \end{cases}$$

6 Experimentation

We have systematically evaluated our end-to-end explicit discourse parser on the PDTB corpus, with focus on the effectiveness of joint learning via structured perceptron.

6.1 Experimental Setting

We follow the PDTB recommendation [17] to use Section 02-21 in the PDTB for training, Section 22 for development, and Section 23 for testing. All staged classifiers are trained with the OpenNLP maximum entropy package[2] with default parameters.

We evaluate our discourse parser using gold and automatic parse trees, respectively. We use the NIST text segmenter[3] to split sentences and the Charniak parser[4] to parse sentences.

In the PDTB, some explicit relations are annotated with two senses. During training we chose the first sense as training instance. During test if the classifier assigns either of the two senses, we consider it as correct. For fair comparison with the state-of-the-art system, we report 16 types sense performance excluding "Nil" senses which indicate non-discourse connective usage. We evaluate our argument labeling using exact match metric [15] without all punctuation at the boundaries.

6.2 Parameters Selection

There are two important parameters in our joint learning framework: the maximum iteration number T and the beam size K. The harmonic mean of discourse relation classification F_1 and two arguments both right F_1 using gold parse trees is employed to measure the overall performance of our system on the development set.

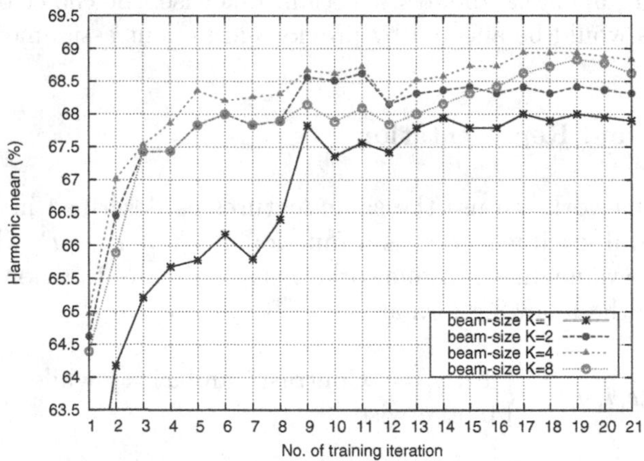

Fig. 4. Learning curves using harmonic mean on development set under different beam size settings

[2] http://maxent.sourceforge.net/

[3] http://duc.nist.gov/duc2004/software/duc2003.breakSent.tar.gz

[4] ftp://ftp.cs.brown.edu/pub/nlparser

Figure 4 shows the learning curves under four different beam size settings. As we can see that almost all curves converge around iteration 19. We also find that our system can achieve the best performance on the development set when beam-size $K = 4$. At this point, discourse relation classification achieves 83.67% in F_1, argument labeling achieves 58.61% in two arguments both right F_1, and the harmonic mean equals 68.93%. Therefore we set the maximum iteration number $T = 19$ and beam-size $K = 4$ for the remaining experiments.

6.3 Results and Analysis

Table 4. Performance on test set using gold stand parse tree and charniak auto parse tree

	Systems	Relation Classification (%)			Argument Labeling (%)		
		P	R	F_1	Arg1 F_1	Arg2 F_1	Both F_1
Gold	Lin et al.[12]	83.19	82.65	82.92	57.64	79.80	52.29
	Our pipeline system	81.93	79.09	80.49	61.08	80.93	54.13
	Our joint system	82.93	81.04	81.97	60.27	78.25	53.48
Auto	Lin et al.[12]	81.19	80.04	80.61	47.68	70.27	40.37
	Our pipeline system	81.04	77.36	79.16	49.78	75.28	43.35
	Our joint system	81.55	79.96	80.74	53.94	73.41	46.94

For comparison, We also construct an end-to-end explicit discourse parser in pipeline way (thereafter called as "our pipeline system"). Table 4 lists the results of three different systems on test set using gold and automatic parse trees, respectively. [5] From the results, we can find that:

- On the necessary of independent connective identification:

  In comparison with Lin et al. [12], using gold and automatic parse trees, the performance of discourse relation classification of our pipeline system reduces about 2.5% and 1.5% in F-measure, respectively. Just noted above, the only difference between these two systems is with or without independent connective identification component. With it, and selecting specific features for connective identification and discourse relation classification respectively, we can achieve better performance of discourse relation classification. Without it, however, we can simplify the following joint learning framework and be helpful for unified resolving of explicit and implicit discourse relations. Furthermore, joint learning approach can improve the performance of discourse relation classification without independent connective identification.
- On the impact of parse trees:

  Three systems achieve better results on both components using gold parse trees than automatic parse trees.

[5] All the improvements in this paper are significant with $p < 0.001$.

For relation classification, using automatic parse trees, the performance of Lin et al. [12] reduces about 2.3% in F-measure. Accordingly, our pipeline and joint learning systems reduce about 1.3% and 1.2% in F-measure, respectively. In comparison with Lin et al. [12], our connective labeler reduces the dependency to the parser's performance. We employ the same features (containing the features employed in connective identification and discourse relation classification) as Lin et al. [12] to classify discourse relation. The difference between our approach and Lin et al. [12] is that we cast connective identification as a part of discourse relation classification. So without independent connective identification component can reduce the dependency to the parser.

For argument labeling, all the three systems heavily depend on the parse trees. Using automatic parse trees, the performance of Lin et al. [12] and our pipeline system reduce more than 10% in both arg1 and arg2 F-measure. Accordingly, the performance of our joint learning system reduces about 6.5% in both arg1 and arg2 F-measure. So our joint learning approach can reduce argument labelings' dependency to the parser.

- On the impact of joint learning:

  In comparison with our pipeline system, using gold parse trees, our joint learning approach can improve the performance of discourse relation classification and slightly reduce the performance of argument labeling. It may be due to that our constituent-based argument labeling system can work well with gold parse trees and the additional iteration in our joint learning system will introduce some noise. When using automatic parse trees, our joint learning approach can improve the performance of both discourse relation classification and argument labeling.

  In comparison with Lin et al. [12], using gold or automatic parse trees, our joint learning approach can achieve better performance on argument labeling and comparable performance on discourse relation classification.

7 Conclusion

In this paper, we focus on building an end-to-end PDTB-style explicit discourse parser by decomposing it into two components, i.e., a connective labeler, which identifies connectives from a text and determines their senses in classifying discourse relationship, and an argument labeler, which identifies corresponding arguments for a given connective. Particularly, to reduce error propagation and incorporate the interaction between the two components, a joint learning approach via structured perceptron is proposed. Experimental results show that our end-to-end explicit discourse parser can perform well using both gold and automatic parse trees.

Acknowledgements. This work is supported by grants from National Natural Science Foundation of China (No. 61333018, No. 6127320), and National 863 program of China (No.2012AA01112).

References

1. Barzilay, R., Lapata, M.: Modeling local coherence: An entity-based approach. In: Proceedings of the 43rd Annual Meeting of the Association for Computational Linguistics (ACL 2005), pp. 141–148. Association for Computational Linguistics, Ann Arbor (2005), `http://www.aclweb.org/anthology/P05-1018`
2. Collins, M.: Discriminative training methods for hidden markov models: Theory and experiments with perceptron algorithms. In: Proceedings of the ACL 2002 Conference on Empirical Methods in Natural Language Processing, vol. 10, pp. 1–8. Association for Computational Linguistics (2002)
3. Collins, M., Roark, B.: Incremental parsing with the perceptron algorithm. In: Proceedings of the 42nd Annual Meeting on Association for Computational Linguistics, p. 111. Association for Computational Linguistics (2004)
4. Dines, N., Lee, A., Miltsakaki, E., Prasad, R., Joshi, A., Webber, B.: Attribution and the (non-)alignment of syntactic and discourse arguments of connectives. In: Proceedings of the Workshop on Frontiers in Corpus Annotations II: Pie in the Sky, CorpusAnno 2005, pp. 29–36. Association for Computational Linguistics, Stroudsburg (2005), `http://dl.acm.org/citation.cfm?id=1608829.1608834`
5. Elwell, R., Baldridge, J.: Discourse connective argument identification with connective specific rankers. In: 2008 IEEE International Conference on Semantic Computing, pp. 198–205 (2008)
6. Ghosh, S.: End-to-End Discourse Parsing with Cascaded Structured Prediction. Ph.D. thesis, University of Trento (2012)
7. Ghosh, S., Johansson, R., Riccardi, G., Tonelli, S.: Shallow discourse parsing with conditional random fields. In: Proceedings of 5th International Joint Conference on Natural Language Processing, pp. 1071–1079. Asian Federation of Natural Language Processing, Chiang Mai (2011), `http://www.aclweb.org/anthology/I11-1120`
8. Huang, L., Fayong, S., Guo, Y.: Structured perceptron with inexact search. In: Proceedings of NAACL 2012 (2012)
9. Lin, Z., Liu, C., Ng, H.T., Kan, M.Y.: Combining coherence models and machine translation evaluation metrics for summarization evaluation. In: Proceedings of the 50th Annual Meeting of the Association for Computational Linguistics (vol. 1: Long Papers), pp. 1006–1014. Association for Computational Linguistics, Jeju Island (2012), `http://www.aclweb.org/anthology/P12-1106`
10. Lin, Z., Ng, H.T., Kan, M.Y.: A pdtb-styled end-to-end discourse parser. Technical report, School of Computing. National University of Singapore (2010)
11. Lin, Z., Ng, H.T., Kan, M.Y.: Automatically evaluating text coherence using discourse relations. In: Proceedings of the 49th Annual Meeting of the Association for Computational Linguistics: Human Language Technologies, vol. 1, pp. 997–1006. Association for Computational Linguistics (2011)
12. Lin, Z., Ng, H.T., Kan, M.Y.: A pdtb-styled end-to-end discourse parser. Natural Language Engineering FirstView, 1–34 (August 2013), `http://journals.cambridge.org/article_S1351324912000307`
13. Marcus, M., Santorini, B., Marcinkiewicz, M.A.: Building a large annotated corpus of English: The penn treebank. Computational Linguistics 19(2), 313–330 (1993)
14. Meyer, T., Webber, B.: Implicitation of discourse connectives in (machine) translation. In: Proceedings of the Workshop on Discourse in Machine Translation, pp. 19–26. Association for Computational Linguistics, Sofia (2013), `http://www.aclweb.org/anthology/W13-3303`

15. Miltsakaki, E., Prasad, R., Joshi, A., Webber, B.: The penn discourse treebank, pp. 2237–2240 (2004), http://www.lrec-conf.org/proceedings/lrec2004/pdf/618
16. Ng, J.P., Kan, M.Y., Lin, Z., Feng, W., Chen, B., Su, J., Tan, C.L.: Exploiting discourse analysis for article-wide temporal classification. In: Proceedings of the 2013 Conference on Empirical Methods in Natural Language Processing, pp. 12–23. Association for Computational Linguistics, Seattle (2013), http://www.aclweb.org/anthology/D13-1002
17. The PDTB Research Group: the Penn Discourse Treebank 2.0 Annotation Manual (December 2007)
18. Pitler, E., Nenkova, A.: Using syntax to disambiguate explicit discourse connectives in text. In: Proceedings of the ACL-IJCNLP 2009 Conference Short Papers, pp. 13–16. Association for Computational Linguistics, Suntec (2009), http://www.aclweb.org/anthology/P/P09/P09-2004
19. Prasad, R., Dinesh, N., Lee, A., Miltsakaki, E., Robaldo, L., Joshi, A., Webber, B.: The penn discourse treebank 2.0, pp. 2961–2968 (2008), http://www.lrec-conf.org/proceedings/lrec2008/pdf/754
20. Prasad, R., Joshi, A., Webber, B.: Exploiting scope for shallow discourse parsing. In: Calzolari, N. (Conference Chair), Choukri, K., Maegaard, B., Mariani, J., Odijk, J., Piperidis, S., Rosner, M., Tapias, D. (eds.) Proceedings of the Seventh Conference on International Language Resources and Evaluation (LREC 2010). European Language Resources Association (ELRA), Valletta (2010)
21. Webber, B.: D-ltag: Extending lexicalized tag to discourse. Cognitive Science 28(5), 751–779 (2004)
22. Wellner, B., Pustejovsky, J.: Automatically identifying the arguments of discourse connectives. In: Proceedings of the 2007 Joint Conference on Empirical Methods in Natural Language Processing and Computational Natural Language Learning (EMNLP-CoNLL), pp. 92–101. Association for Computational Linguistics, Prague (2007), http://www.aclweb.org/anthology/D/D07/D07-1010

Chinese Textual Entailment Recognition Based on Syntactic Tree Clipping

Zhichang Zhang, Dongren Yao, Songyi Chen, and Huifang Ma

School of Computer Science and Engineering, Northwest Normal University, Lanzhou, China
{zzc,mahuifang}@nwnu.edu.cn, {wade330628704,snail200x}@163.com

Abstract. Textual entailment has been proposed as a unifying generic framework for modeling language variability and semantic inference in different Natural Language Processing (NLP) tasks. This paper presents a novel statistical method for recognizing Chinese textual entailment in which lexical, syntactic with semantic matching features are combined together. In order to solve the problems of syntactic tree matching difficulty and tree structure errors caused by Chinese word segmentation, the method firstly clips the syntactic trees into minimum information trees and then computes syntactic matching similarity on them. All features will be used in a voting style under different machine learning methods to predict whether the text sentence can entail the hypothesis sentence in a text-hypothesis pair. The experimental results show that the feature on changing structure of syntactic tree is effective and efficient in Chinese textual entailment.

Keywords: Textual Entailment, Minimum information tree, Syntactic tree clipping, Machine learning.

1 Introduction

The Recognizing Textual Entailment (RTE) challenge focuses on detecting the directional entailment relationship between pairs of text expressions, denoted by T (the entailing "Text") and H (the entailed "Hypothesis"). We say that T entails H if human reading T would typically infer that H is most likely true.

RTE is proposed as a generic task that captures the semantic inference demand with a wide range of natural language applications. For example, a question answering system needs to recognize the text whether entails a hypothesized answer, e.g., given the question "*Which team won the NBA championship in* 2012-2013?", the text "*James led Miami Heat to their second straight title on June* 20,2013" entails the hypothesized answer form "*Miami Heat win the championship in* 2012-2013".

RTE has attracted extensive attention ever since it was proposed, and researchers have developed many methods to solve this problem. These methods can be roughly classified into five categories.

1. ***Logic-based recognition Approaches*** [2, 3]. These approaches map the language expression T(Text) and H(Hypothesis) to logical meaning representations Φ_T and

M. Sun et al. (Eds.): CCL and NLP-NABD 2014, LNAI 8801, pp. 83–94, 2014.

Φ_H , then check if Φ_H can be inferred from Φ_T using many kinds of entailment rules and common sense knowledge *B* possibly by invoking theorem provers. But it is very difficult to convert the language expressions into logical forms concerning limited performance of current natural language processing tools.

2. ***Decoding based recognition approaches***[4,11]. Given many entailment rules like the following forms,

   X bought Y => X owned Y

   X loves Y => X likes Y

   X brought a lawsuit against Y => X sued Y

   These approaches are to search for a sequence of rule applications that turn *T* expression (or its syntactic or semantic representation) to *H* expression. If such a sequence is found, the two expressions constitute a positive textual entailment pair, depending on the rules used; otherwise, the pair is negative. Unfortunately, try to build these rules in a hierarchical way could not be easy no matter in theory or practice.
3. ***Transformation-based approaches***[23,24,25]. Transformation-based approaches use a set of rules to perturb the entailment pair with the goal of making the Text and Hypothesis identical. After the rule set has been exhausted (when either no more changes can be effected by apply rules, or some heuristic limited is reached), if the Text and Hypothesis match, the entailment pair is labeled as "entails", and if they don't, it is labeled as "not entailment".
4. ***Alignment and similarity measures based recognition approaches***. These approaches are to measure a kind of similarity or distance between text *T* and hypothesis *H*, and then classify the pair into positive or negative example by comparing the similarity or distance with a threshold. The similarity measure used can be computed at different levels including surface lexical string [7, 22], syntactic tree structure [9, 10], or latent semantic representations [12, 13]. And quite a few successful approaches also treat RTE as an alignment problem [8, 21]. Thesaurus like WordNet, Hownet [20] can be useful in these approaches.
5. ***Machine learning based recognition approaches***[5, 6, 14, 15]. These approaches treat the entailment judgment problem between two texts *T* and *H* as a binary classification problem, then supervised machine learning methods can be used to make the textual entailment decision. Each pair of input language expressions $<T, H>$ is represented by a feature vector $<f_1, \ldots, f_m>$ containing the scores of different similarity measures applied to the pair, and possibly other features. A supervised machine learning algorithm train a classifier on manually classified vectors corresponding to training input pairs. Once trained, the classifier can classify unseen pairs as correct or incorrect textual entailment pairs by examining their features.

This paper explores the methods for recognizing Chinese textual entailment. The difficult problems for this task include the lack of Chinese textual entailment rules, and word segmentation as well as other language processing errors, and it is also very hard to convert the language expressions T and H into logical forms to infer H from T. Therefore, we use a machine learning based Chinese textual entailment recognization method in which a new syntactic tree clipping and matching feature we presented is combined with other traditional different similarity features. With clipping and transforming the original syntactic tree structure into the "minimum information tree", the matching between T and H can be more accuracy and tolerant of word segmentation error. The experimental result shows that the clipping on syntactic tree structure is effective for Chinese textual entailment recognization.

The remainder of this paper is composed as follows. In section 2 we introduce the rules to clip a syntactic tree structure to a "minimum information tree" and the similarity measure between different "minimum information tree". In section 3 we present other features and machine learning methods used in our system. In section 4 we show the experimental results on the test data and give some analysis. Finally, we summarize our work and outline some ideas for future research.

2 Approach

Our approach also treat recognizing Chinese textual entailment as a binary classification problem. We believe that a Hypothesis *H* with "similar" content to the Text *T* is more likely to be entailed by that Text *T* than one with "less similar" content, therefore using matching similarity between *T* and *H* should be an important feature for entailment classification. In this paper we match *T* and *H* at different levels including lexical level, syntactic level, and shallow semantic level. At syntactic level, firstly we clip and transform the two original syntactic trees of *T* and *H* into "minimum syntactic trees", then search for their common structure and compute matching similarity.

2.1 Clipping Syntactic Tree

The main idea of syntactic tree clipping is to delete meaningless nodes by aggregating those nodes of syntactic tree. Based on syntactic tree, the first operation is to aggregate the common subsequence into one node. Secondly, aggregate those strings which can be treated as "common similar subtrees". Finally, we will get a tree with minimum information by saving related links of notes and deleting redundant information (nodes without any operation).

2.1.1 Common Subsequence Aggregation

In this step, we aggregate all common nodes by searching all subsequences. After this step, some entities can be extracted to reduce the Chinese word segmentation errors and the syntactic tree will be less complex. The following example (Marked as Example 1)is taken from NTCIR-10's data:

T: 张艺谋执导的新作《十面埋伏》上映4天票房已突破6300万元人民币，超过同期《英雄》的票房记录.

H: 《十面埋伏》上映4天票房突破6300万元人民币.

Two syntactic trees of *T* and *H* in the example is as following(ignore all punctuations) :

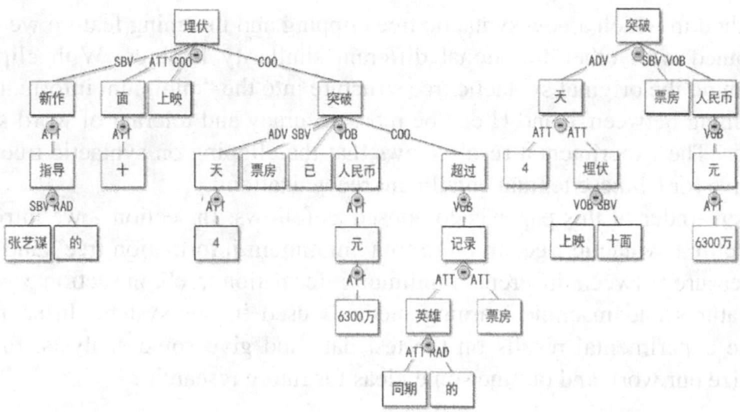

Fig. 1. Syntactic trees of T and H in Example 1

Common subsequence can fix the errors as Example 1 shows. In this example, "十面埋伏" should not be separated into three nodes, and we need to treat them as an entirety. But even two equal single nodes couldn't be treated as common subsequence. After aggregating the nodes, the "minimum information trees" would be as follows:

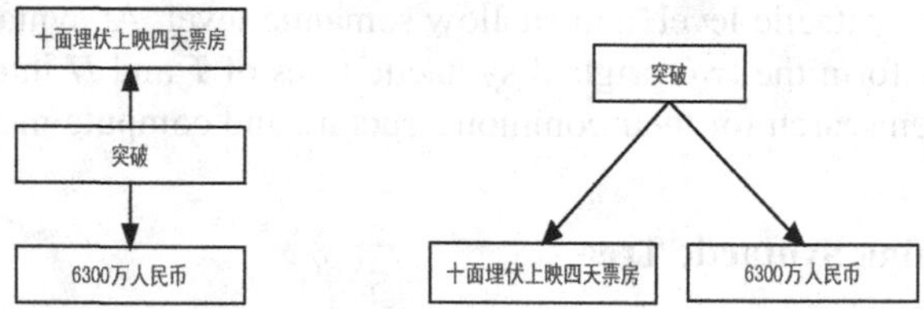

Fig. 2. "Minimum information trees" in Example

2.1.2 Common Similar Subtree Aggregation

We define the similar subtrees as such kinds of trees that have similar format and generated from syntactic analysis. Those similar subtrees will be aggregated during the step of syntactic tree clipping. Our approach judges those similar subtrees by single word's overlap. With constraint in syntactic structure and core words' similarity we can determine whether these subsequences should be aggregated or not. Another example (Marked as Example 2) selected from NTCIR-10:

T: 二次世界大战时日本广岛遭投原子弹

H: 广岛在二次世界大战时遭原子弹轰炸

Two syntactic trees of *T* and *H* in this example are as following(ignore all punctuations) :

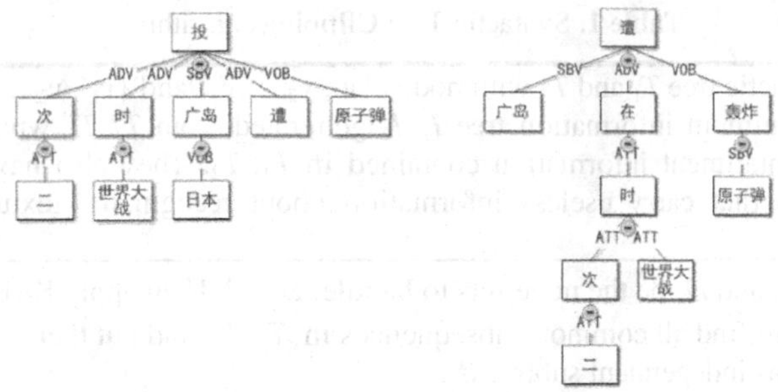

Fig. 3. Syntactic trees of T and H in Example 2

Here "二次世界大战时" is a common subsequence, "广岛" and "日本" would be name entities appearing in each text. The left one with "投" and "遭" and "原子弹" consist a subtree try to compare with the subtree which consists of "遭" and "轰炸" and "原子弹". The score of similarity greater than threshold after calculation, then aggregate those nodes into one. The final "Minimum information trees" are:

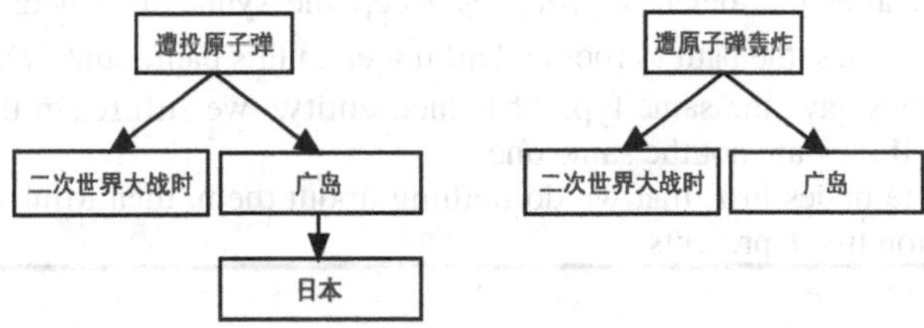

Fig. 4. "Minimum information trees" in example 1

What we had mentioned before, the equation for calculating the similarity between different subtrees is defined as:

$$Sim_{subtree} = \alpha(\text{core vocabulary similarity}) + \beta(\text{syntactic structure similarity}) \quad (1)$$

Here $0 \le \alpha, \beta \le 1$, $\alpha+\beta=1$. Via manual work, when $\alpha=0.55$ and $\beta=0.45$ this similarity work best in distinguishing the synonymy between two subtrees.

2.2 The Syntactic Tree Clipping Algorithm

The algorithm to clip the original syntactic trees of *T* and *H* into minimum information trees is as follows.

Table 1. Syntactic Tree Clipping algorithm

Input: Syntactic tree T_1 and T_2 with nodes $\{v_1, v_2,\ldots,v_n\}$ and $\{v_1', v_2',\ldots,v_n'\}$,
Output: Minimum information tree I_1, I_2 generated from T_1, T_2, which remain the entailment information contained in T_1, T_2. They also have deleted nodes that carry useless information about recognizing textual entailment.

Step1. Let D_1 and D_2 be the node sets to handle, $D_i=\emptyset$. Then apply KMP algorithm to find all common subsequences in T_1, T_2, and put them into D_i (i =1,2) as independent subtree d_{ij}.
Step2. Use the smaller one as beginning, find all common similar subtrees in T_1, T_2. The way to find all subtrees need two steps. First, use the degree of word overlap to find some pairs of subtrees, 0.76 will be the threshold to the first screen. Then those pairs through discriminant function $Sim_{subtree}$ will select the similar subtree. Let them join the set of D_i as the original way d_{ik}, until they traverse all tree. We won't deal the nodes already done in step1.
Step3. Transforming T_i, take nodes in D_i, aggregate them which in the same subtree. New nodes location depends on parent node of those aggregated node, after this delete it from D_i. Keep the syntactic structure between these nodes, the path to root and all nodes in this path, until $D_i=\emptyset$. If two subtrees have the same type of named entity, we still retain those nodes even if they are not the same one.
Step4. Delete nodes in T_i that we do nothing about them, then Minimum information tree I_i presents.

2.3 The Similarity Computing between Minimum Information Trees

Although using clipping method will decrease the number of nodes, we still can't just employ statistical features to make the entailment prediction correctly. The minimum information trees still keep semantic features. Therefore, the following Equation (2) for the similarity calculation is necessary:

$$Sim_{Tree} = \left(\frac{1}{3}\right)^{SBV} \left(\frac{1}{3}\right)^{NED} \frac{\sum Max\{Sim(Node_T, Node_H)\}}{Min(Node_T, Node_H)} \tag{2}$$

In the equation, SBV stands for the syntactic subject-predicate dependency relation while only considering those nodes around root one:

$$SBV=\begin{cases} 0\ , & \text{if the relation between nodes is different} \\ 1\ , & \text{else} \end{cases} \tag{3}$$

NED stands for the result of named entity discrimination:

$$NED=\begin{cases} 1\ , & \text{if two texts contain the identical named entity or named entity type} \\ 0\ , & \text{others} \end{cases} \tag{4}$$

3 Traditional Features

The statistical machine learning models are trained to classify whether T in a given text-hypothesis pair entail H, and some traditional features including statistical and lexical semantic features are also used in these models. The following table 2 and table 3 illustrate these features and computational equations for them.

Table 2. Statistical features

Feature Name	Comment	Formula
Word overlap	The overlap of word between two texts	$E_1=\|T \wedge H\|/\|H\|$ $E_2=\|T \wedge H\|/\|T\|$ $E=(2*E_1*E_2)/(E_1+E_2)$
Length difference	Using text length to distinguish entailment direction	$Lt(T,H) = \| Len(T) - Len(H) \|$
Cosine similarity	Representing the text pair as vectors, then calculating their cosine similarity	$Sim_{cos}(T,H) = \frac{\sum_{i=1}^{n} t_i * h_i}{\sqrt{\sum_{i=1}^{n} t_i} * \sqrt{\sum_{i=1}^{n} h_i}}$ n is vector dimensions

Table 3. Lexical semantic features

Feature Name	Comment	Formula
HowNet semantic similarity	Using HowNet to calculate the similarity between different words	See Equation 5
Tongyicilin semantic similarity [16]	Using Tongyicilin to calculate the similarity between different words	See Equation 5
The number of antonyms	Using the Web resource to count the number of antonyms	None
The number of negative words	Combining the number of antonyms to assist the decision	None
The overlap of named entity	Named entities can show the text topics in a way	$T_{NE}=\|T \wedge H\|/\|H\|$ $H_{NE}=\|T \wedge H\|/\|T\|$ $L_{NE}=(2*T_{NE}*H_{NE})/(T_{NE}+H_{NE})$

$$Sim=\frac{1}{2}\left[\frac{\sum_{i=1}^{m} max\{sim_w(w_{1i},w_{2j}) | 1 \le j \le n\}}{m} + \frac{\sum_{j=1}^{n} max\{sim_w(w_{1i},w_{2j}) | 1 \le i \le m\}}{n}\right] \quad (5)$$

What need to be illustrated is that although the equations of HowNet and Tongyicilin similarity are same, the same formula is only to sum the similarity which has already been calculated. The value of similarity in different features calculates in different ways.

4 Experimental Result and Analysis

4.1 Data and Evaluation Standards

The National Institute of Informatics (NII) of Japan organized the NTCIR [19] RITE (Recognizing Inference in TExt) competition [17] since 2011. RITE is to evaluate one system's ability about recognizing specific entailment relationship between two sentences. Therefore, we use NTCIR-10 RITE evaluation dataset as our experimental data, in which 814 text-hypothesis sentence pairs will employed as the training set, and other 781 pairs be the test set. The semantic relationship between every sentence pair has been already labeled as entailment or not entailment. We also use Precision, Recall and F-measure as system performance evaluation criterion. They are defined as follows.

$$Pre = \frac{\#\,right\ decisions}{\#\,all\ decisions} \tag{6}$$

$$Re = \frac{\#\,right\ decisions}{\#\,all\ pairs\ in\ one\ relation} \tag{7}$$

$$F\text{-}measure = \frac{2 * Pre * Re}{Pre + Re} \tag{8}$$

4.2 Experimental Result and Analysis

We implemented two systems NLPWM-01 and NLPWM-02 for experimental evaluation. NLPWM-01 uses all features mentioned in section 3, and NLPWM-02 added further the minimum information tree similarity feature of text pair. We define those *T-H* test text pairs in which the entailment relationship exists as positive instances, and others as negative instances. Being similar to confusion matrix, Table 4 presents the prediction numbers of two systems for positive and negative test instances respectively.

Table 4. Experimental result

System	#correct predication for positive pairs	#incorrect prediction for positive pairs	#correct prediction for negative pairs	#incorrect prediction for negative pairs
NLPWM-01	371	51	171	188
NLPWM-02	393	29	**202**	157

From Table 4 we can see that the precision increases after adding the minimum information tree feature, especially for negative test text pairs. The reason for performance improvement can be explained as: 1) After clipping the syntactic tree, the noise in recognizing process decreased; 2) Equation 2 solved some problems such as the only difference in subject or object, reverse of subject and object, and so on.

Figure 5 shows the achieved F-measure values by different models including Decision Tree, SVM and Naïve Bayes based on Gaussian distribution machine learning methods [18]. Different machine learning methods cause different results. SVM which is regarded as the best supervised learning method in general text classification didn't obtain the best result. Meanwhile, naïve Bayes approach gets the highest score in both prediction. And apparently, when adding the minimum information tree feature, the performance is always improved under these different prediction models.

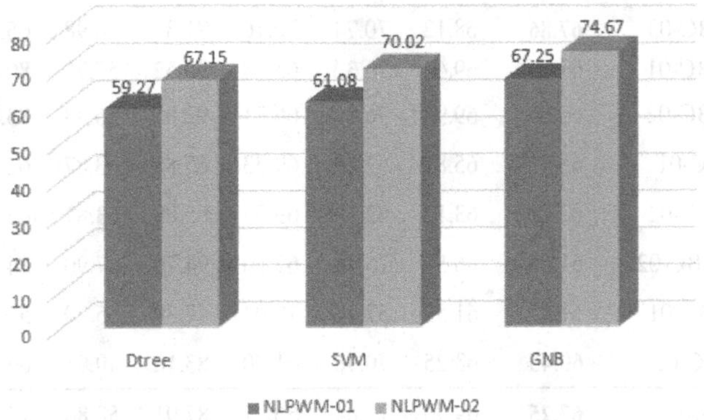

Fig. 5. Different machine learning methods achieve different F-measures

Figure 6 demonstrates the effect of different features in Naïve Bayes decision model. Features are put into vector in an order from bottom to the top. The more features join the vector, the better accuracy would be.

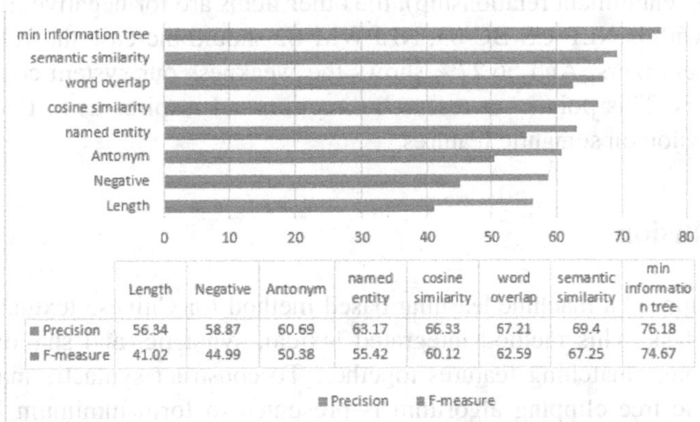

	Length	Negative	Antonym	named entity	cosine similarity	word overlap	semantic similarity	min informatio n tree
Precision	56.34	58.87	60.69	63.17	66.33	67.21	69.4	76.18
F-measure	41.02	44.99	50.38	55.42	60.12	62.59	67.25	74.67

Fig. 6. Each feature effect the Naïve Bayes decision

For all features as showed in figure 6, minimum information tree feature makes the biggest change in F-measure except the first change. These results show the minimum information tree feature is effective in textual entailment classification.

Table 5 compare the performance of our systems with those participated NTCIR-10 challenge.

Table 5. NTCIR-10 RITE Result (without percent)

System	MacroF1	Acc.	Y-F1	Y-Prec.	Y-Rec.	N-F1	N-Prec.	N-Rec
bcNLP-CS-BC-03	**73.84**	74.65	78.43	72.58	85.31	69.25	78.25	62.12
MIG-CS-BC-02	68.09	68.50	71.72	69.64	73.93	64.45	66.97	62.12
CYUT-CS-BC-03	**67.86**	68.12	70.74	70.16	71.33	64.98	65.63	64.35
bcNLP-CS-BC-01	67.04	69.65	76.32	65.98	90.52	57.75	80.20	45.13
bcNLP-CS-BC-02	66.89	69.91	76.89	65.71	92.65	56.88	83.33	43.18
MIG-CS-BC-01	65.71	65.81	67.56	69.33	65.88	63.87	62.11	65.74
CYUT-CS-BC-02	63.11	63.12	62.50	69.36	65.88	63.87	62.11	65.74
WHUTE-CS-BC-02	61.65	66.58	75.40	62.60	94.79	47.90	84.51	33.43
CYUT-CS-BC-01	61.17	61.59	57.14	71.94	47.39	65.20	55.86	78.27
IASL-CS-BC-02	60.45	63.25	70.98	61.90	83.18	49.91	66.82	39.83
NLPWM-01	**67.25**	69.40	75.64	66.37	87.91	58.86	77.03	47.63
NLPWM-02	**74.67**	**76.18**	80.86	71.45	93.13	68.48	87.45	**56.27**

The performance results of top-10 systems are listed in Table 5. In these performance criterions, MacroF1 is the average value of Y-F1 and N-F1. Items starting with "Y" show the prediction performances of different systems for positive instances (i.e., text pairs being entailment relationship), the other items are for negative instances.

Compared with bcNLP-CS-BC-03, NLPWM-02 should increase the value of recall in not entailment pairs. And 56.27% shows the weakness our system copes with not entailment pairs. This points our research direction and inspires us to find more reasonable expression on semantic features.

5 Conclusion

This paper proposed a machine learning based method for Chinese textual entailment recognization task. This method integrated lexical, syntactic, and shallow semantic levels of language matching features together. To construct syntactic matching feature, a syntactic tree clipping algorithm is presented to form minimum information trees of *T* and *H* for matching. The experimental result shows the minimum information tree feature is effective.

The approach still has two deficiencies: First, the time complexity in clipping algorithm isn't good enough; Second, the lack of resource make the system weak in dealing with not entailment pairs

Our future work is two-fold. The judgment on not entailment pairs is not successful, we therefore should find new feature or new method to express entailment relationship better. Meanwhile we also need to focus on the multi-direction in Chinese textual entailment recognizing, and this challenge requires entailment system developed in a more robust and reasonable way.

Acknowledgments. This work was sponsored by the National Natural Science Foundation of China (No. 61163039, No. 61163036, No. 61363058) and the Young Teacher Research Ability Enhancement Project of Northwest Normal University of China (NWNU-LKQN-10-2). We thank the anonymous reviewers for their insightful comments.

References

1. Dagan, I., Glickman, O.: Probabilistic textual entailment: generic applied modeling of language variability. In: PASCAL Workshop on Learning Methods for Text Understanding and Mining, Grenoble, France (2004)
2. Tatu, M., Moldovan, D.: COGEX at RTE 3. In: Proc. of the ACL-PASCAL Workshop on Textual Entailment and Paraphrasing, Prague, Czech Republic, pp. 22–27 (2007)
3. Bos, J.: Is there a place for logic in recognizing textual entailment? Linguistic Issues in Language Technology 9 (2013)
4. Harmeling, S.: Inferring textual entailment with a probabilistically sound calculus. Nat. Lang. Engineering 15(4), 459–477 (2009)
5. Quiñonero-Candela, J., Dagan, I., Magnini, B., d'Alché-Buc, F. (eds.): MLCW 2005. LNCS (LNAI), vol. 3944. Springer, Heidelberg (2006); De Raedt, L., et al. (eds.), vol. 6. Springer (2012)
6. Pham, Q.N.M., Nguyen, L.M., Shimazu, A.: A machine learning based textual entailment recognition system of jaist team for ntcir9 rite. In: Proceedings of the 9th NII Test Collection for Information Retrieval Workshop, NTCIR 2011 (2011)
7. Malakasiotis, P., Androutsopoulos, I.: Learning textual entailment using SVMs and string similarity measures. In: Proceedings of the ACL-PASCAL Workshop on Textual Entailment and Paraphrasing, pp. 42–47. Association for Computational Linguistics (2007)
8. Wang, X.-L., Zhao, H., Lu, B.-L.: BCMI - NLP Labeled - Alignment - Based Entailment System for NTCIR - 10 RITE - 2 Task. In: Proceeding of the 10th NTCIR Conference, Tokyo, Japan (2013)
9. Kouylekov, M., Magnini, B.: Recognizing textual entailment with tree edit distance algorithms. In: Proceedings of the First Challenge Workshop Recognising Textual Entailment, pp. 17–20 (2005)
10. Alabbas, M., Ramsay, A.: Natural Language Inference for Arabic Using Extended Tree Edit Distance with Subtrees. Journal of Artificial Intelligence Research 48, 1–22 (2013)
11. Bar-Haim, R., Berant, J., Dagan, I.: A compact forest for scalable inference over entailment and paraphrase rules. In: Proceedings of the 2009 Conference on Empirical Methods in Natural Language Processing, vol. 3, pp. 1056–1065. Association for Computational Linguistics (2009)
12. Wu, X., Zong, C.: An Approach to News Paraphrase Recognition Based on SRL. Journal of Chinese Information Processing 24(5), 3–9 (2010)
13. Burchardt, A.: Ph.D. Dissertation. Modeling Textual Entailment with Role-Semantic Information (2008)

14. Burrows, S., Potthast, M., Stein, B.: Paraphrase acquisition via crowdsourcing and machine learning. ACM Transactions on Intelligent Systems and Technology (TIST) 4(3), 43 (2013)
15. Galitsky, B.: Machine learning of syntactic parse trees for search and classification of text. Engineering Applications of Artificial Intelligence 26(3), 1072–1091 (2013)
16. Tian, J.-L., Zhao, W.: Words Similarity Algorithm Based on Tongyici CiLin in Semantic Web Adaptive Learning System. Journal of Jilin University 28(6), 602–608 (2010)
17. Liu, M., Li, Y., Ji, D.: Event Semantic Feature Based Chinese Textual Entailment Recognition. Journal of Chinese Information Processing 27(5), 129–136 (2013)
18. Pedregosa, et al.: Scikit-learn: Machine Learning in Python. JMLR 12, 2825–2830 (2011)
19. Watanabe, Y., Miyao, Y., Mizuno, J., et al.: Overview of the Recognizing Inference in Text (RITE-2) at NTCIR-10. In: Proceedings of the 10th NTCIR Conference (2013)
20. Dong, Z., Dong, Q.: HowNet and the Computation of Meaning. World Scientific, Singapore (2006)
21. Turchi, M., Negri, M.: ALTN: Word Alignment Features for Cross-Lingual Textual Entailment, Atlanta, Georgia, USA, p. 128 (2013)
22. Graham, Y., Salehi, B., Baldwin, T.: Umelb: Cross-lingual Textual Entailment with Word Alignment and String Similarity Features, Atlanta, Georgia, USA, p. 133 (2013)
23. Stern, A., Dagan, I.: A confidence model for syntactically-motivated entailment proofs. In: Proceedings of the International Conference on Recent Advances in Natural Language Processing, p. 96 (2011)
24. de Salvo Braz, R., Girju, R., Punyakanok, V., Roth, D., Sammons, M.: An inference model for semantic entailment in natural language. In: Proceedings of the National Conference on Artificial Intelligence (AAAI), pp. 1678–1679 (2005), doi:10.1007/11736790_15. 41, 90, 93, 162
25. Dagan, I., Roth, D., Sammons, M., Zanzotto, F.M.: Recognizing Textual Entailment: Models and Applications. Synthesis Lectures on Human Language Technologies, pp. 1–220. Morgan & Claypool Publishers (2013) ISBN 9781598298345

Automatic Collection of the Parallel Corpus with Little Prior Knowledge

Shutian Ma[1] and Chengzhi Zhang[1,2,*]

[1] Department of Information Management, Nanjing University of Science and Technology, Nanjing, China 210094

[2] Jiangsu Key Laboratory of Data Engineering and Knowledge Service (Nanjing University), Nanjing, China 210093

mashutian0608@hotmail.com, zhangcz@njust.edu.cn

Abstract. As an important resource for machine translation and cross-language information retrieval, collecting large-scale parallel corpus has been paid wide attention. With the development of the Internet, researchers begin to mine the parallel corpora from the multilingual websites. They use some prior knowledge like ad hoc heuristics or calculate the similarity of the webpages structure and content to find the bilingual webpages. This paper presents a method that uses the search engine and little prior knowledge about the URL patterns to get the bilingual websites from the Internet. The method is fast for its low time cost and there is no need for large-scale computation on URL pattern matching. We have collected 88 915 candidate parallel Chinese-English webpages, which average accuracy is around 90.8%. During the evaluation, the true bilingual websites that we found have high similar html structure and good quality translations.

Keywords: Parallel pages, Bilingual website, URL pattern, Web mining.

1 Introduction

As an important resource for many natural language processing applications, such as cross-language retrieval [1], machine translation [2], parallel corpus have been one of the key resources. Currently, various websites are bilingual or multilingual. For some international organizations or educational institutions, they will build the webpages in several languages on the site to share the information oversea. The websites in some countries where people speak two or more languages will also have bilingual or multilingual webpages. It becomes more and more common to find the parallel corpora from some known bilingual websites. For example, in Hong Kong governmental websites, there are lots of English-Chinese bilingual webpages, while in Canadian governmental websites, we can find many English-French bilingual webpages as well. Many available systems can find these bilingual websites and they detect the parallel URLs with the URL naming rules, e.g., STRAND [3,4,5], PTMiner [6], PupSniffer [7].

A typical strategy of collecting parallel corpora from bilingual websites involves four fundamental steps: (1) Locating the candidate bilingual websites; (2) Crawling

* Corresponding author.

M. Sun et al. (Eds.): CCL and NLP-NABD 2014, LNAI 8801, pp. 95–106, 2014.

for URLs of candidate parallel web pages; (3) Matching and filtering parallel web pages; (4) Extracting parallel text pairs from the obtained webpages.

Prior knowledge has been widely used when locating the candidate bilingual websites. Most of the systems use the word lists of one language or some anchor information to search on the search engine [5, 6]. Then the search engines will return the URLs of candidate bilingual websites. After crawling for the URLs of webpages, researchers need to find the true parallel webpages within candidate bilingual websites. Due to some constructing rules, when building a bilingual website, some given pairing patterns will be inserted into the parallel webpage URLs, such as the 'english' and 'chinese' in the following pair of bilingual webpages:

Webpage in English: http://www.swd.gov.hk/vs/english/police.html
Webpage in Chinese: http://www.swd.gov.hk/vs/chinese/police.html

In the third step, researchers will use some pre-defined patterns to figure out the correct pairing patterns in candidate bilingual websites. The algorithm of patterns matching results in large-scale computation. Meanwhile the URL pattern-based mining may raise concerns on high bandwidth cost and slow download speed. Some researchers try to find more bilingual webpages via link analysis and they also find out the list of bilingual URL pattern pairs with high credibility [7]. Based on this work, we utilize the search rules of search engine websites and URL patterns with high credibility to obtain bilingual websites from the Internet. The method avoids getting too much irrelevant websites from the search engine and costs less time.

The paper is structured as follows: Section 2 gives a brief review of the related work in the field. Section 3 provides the methodology of our experiment. Section 4 presents the evaluation and analysis that we obtain from the data. Section 5 draws some conclusions and we point out the shortages of our experiment and future works.

2 Related Works

For many data-driven task of NLP, how to get parallel corpora in an efficient way has been the focus in many research projects for years. There are numerous systems automatically acquiring parallel corpora from multilingual websites, for example, STRAND [3,4,5], PTMiner [6]. Many researchers are trying to improve the acquisition performance, such as PupSniffer [7], BITS [8], WPDE [9], the DOM tree alignment model [10] and Bitextor [11]. Some researchers use search engines to find parallel webpages. Microblog has also been one of the resources to get parallel corpora [12]. Among the relevant research, we can find two main types of detecting parallel webpages: the way based on the URL patterns and the way based on the HTML structure. Researchers make use of anchor texts or HTML files in order to find some apparent patterns in the websites or in the URLs which represent different languages, especially the language pattern pairs in the URLs to find more parallel websites. In this paper, we find the parallel webpages via high credible URL patterns using the search engine.

The way based on URL patterns aims at using naming rules of URLs to detect bilingual websites. In early times, researchers are using the re-defined substrings [5, 9] and then comes some automatic ways [13]. Finally, extracted URL pairs are verified based on automatic string pattern recognition instead of prior knowledge [14]. Ye,

S.et al [13] made a research of relationship between the content and structure of bilingual websites URLs. The URL patterns and HTML structure have also been combined to find parallel websites [15]. They use the HTML structure to go through the directed graph of bilingual websites simultaneously.

The way based on HTML structure advocates using the structure information of HTML. If the two webpages are parallel to each other, they may have corresponding websites links in the HTML content that connect to another pair of parallel webpages. However, in this way we may just find a little amount of parallel webpages and calculations will be much more than the way based on URL patterns. What's more, in the same bilingual website, content structure of the two languages pages may not be totally same like each other.

In our approach, we search for bilingual websites with language-specific URL substrings and replace the bilingual URL patterns to find a likely candidate pair of parallel URLs. Here we use patterns of high credibility. So what is the credibility of the patterns that we find out in the research? In the research of Kit and Ng [14], they define the linking power of pattern based on the number of URL pairs that it can match. Enhanced algorithms are proposed based on their research to match more bilingual webpages. Zhang and Yao [7] get the global credibility of pattern based on statistical analysis about the link relationship of seed websites available. They also defined the bilingual credibility of a website via link analysis. Depending on the data that we get from their research, we don't need to download all the parallel websites or do any complex pattern matching algorithm within a website.

3 Methodology

This section firstly introduces the idea of exploring parallel websites via the search engine and then it continues to show the detailed steps of the approach.

3.1 Can We Collect Bilingual Websites with Little Priori Knowledge?

There are large-scale of parallel webpages on the Internet. Some researchers explore bilingual websites based on the bilingual URL patterns and they also give the credibility of identified URL patterns [7]. We first make simple search queries with high credible URL patterns, like '*en*', '*eng*', '*english*'. The search query is made according to the search rule of '*inurl:*' in order to find URLs that contains the character, '*en*', '*eng*', '*english*' respectively. We give an example of search query: '*inurl:/en/*'. In this study, we use Google as the search engine. Table 1 shows the numbers of websites after we eliminated the duplicated ones.

Table 1. Numbers of the websites that we get from the search engine

inurl	Websites	Multilingual websites	Multilingual websites with Chinese language	Multilingual websites/All websites	Multilingual with Chinese language/All websites
en	412	323	117	78.40%	28.40%
eng	492	311	106	63.21%	21.54%
english	456	207	93	45.39%	20.39%

From the Table 1, we can see that a certain number of multilingual websites are found by limiting the URL. Multilingual websites containing the Chinese language are around 20% of all the websites from search engine. In the front part of returning results, websites are basically the English pages of those multilingual websites.

3.2 Framework and Key Technologies

Based on above observations, we can make search rules of 'inurl: source language pattern' to locate webpages in the source language of bilingual websites. Then, we use identified URL pattern pairs to find the existing URL in the target language of bilingual websites. Finally, we will get parallel webpages in a bilingual website. The whole procedure of this method can be divided into two steps:

I. Get the URLs of candidate bilingual websites in the source language;
II. Get the URLs of candidate parallel websites in the target language.

Figure 1 shows the overall framework of our approach.

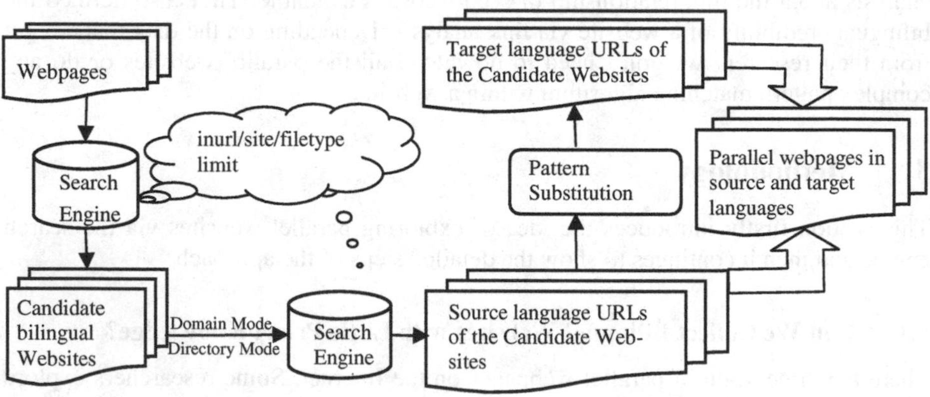

Fig. 1. Framework of our approach

Firstly, with search engine and search rules, we get some candidate bilingual websites, most of these sites are the source language pages of parallel sites.

Secondly, URLs of seed websites were processed in two modes in order to make new search terms. Under the conditions of new search rules, we use the new search terms for a second batch of search and collect the results. From our point of view, the results are actually the websites in the source language of candidate parallel websites.

Thirdly, URLs of the results will have a small substitution. We replaced the source language pattern of each URL with target language pattern to generate a new URL. These pattern pairs are given in the previous research (Zhang and Yao, 2013). If the generated URL is judged to be an existing website, we assume that the new URL and former URL is a pair of parallel websites in the candidate parallel websites. We made a final evaluation for all the URL pairs at last.

Source Language URLs of the Candidate Parallel Websites Detection
One feature of our way is we make use of search rules to find high quality parallel websites from the search engine. When we use the search rules of '*inurl:*', we can find a certain number of multilingual websites from the search engine and some of them have parallel webpages in the site. In this way, we try to add more search rules to define the URL. Then we can get source language URLs of the candidate parallel websites. The main steps of this part are as follows:

i. Search candidate bilingual websites
ii. Search webpages of candidate bilingual websites in the source language

The first step is finding candidate bilingual websites. In this study, the source language is English and target language is Chinese. We aim at the governmental (gov.hk), educational (edu.hk) and organizational (org.hk) types of websites in Hong Kong. To limit the websites types, we add the search rule of '*site:*'. In order to avoid getting too many PDF files, the search rule of '*filetype:html*' is included. Here is an example of the first search query we put in the search box of Google engine.

inurl:en site:gov.hk filetype:html

The second step of this part is finding URLs of candidate parallel websites that in English language. The first thing is reprocessing the URLs of websites that we get from the first search. Then we search again on the search engine with the reprocessed ones. The URLs from the first search are processed in two ways, we call them 'Domain Mode' and 'Directory Mode' here.

(1) Domain Mode: We eliminate the duplicated webpages of seed websites, and keep the second-level domain of each URL. For example, the original URL is'*http://www.immd.gov.hk/en/services/hk-visas/visit-transit.html*'. After processing, the domain mode URL is '*www.immd.gov.hk*'. Then we eliminate the duplicated ones again and check the second-level domain one by one to see if it is subsistent on the Internet. Because of expirations, web server changes or other reasons, some domains are invalid. So we just make use of the accessible ones and a new search query is shown here:

inurl:en site:www.immd.gov.hk filetype:html

In this mode, the file type is defined as html, htm, asp, aspx and php. If the number of the search results is below 100, we get rid of the file type definition. Here is an example of the search query.

inurl:en site:www.immd.gov.hk

(2) Directory Mode: We keep each seed websites URL of the web directory of '*/en/*', '*/eng/*' ,'*/english/*'. We will also give an example here, the original URL is '*http://www.immd.gov.hk/en/services/hk-visas/visit-transit.html*'. After processing, the directory mode URL is '*www.immd.gov.hk/en/*'. Also we eliminate the duplicated ones again and a new search query is shown here:

site: www.immd.gov.hk/en/ filetype:html

The file type is also defined as html, htm, asp, aspx and php and we collect all the search results during Directory Mode no matter if the number of URLs is below 100.

We also do the search without file type definition. You can see that we are trying to find the websites under the web directory of '*www.immd.gov.hk/en/*' as many as possible.

Finally, the search results that we get from the search engine in these two modes are seen as the URLs of candidate websites that in English language. We will use these URLs in the succeeding part.

Target Language URLs Generation

Our study is conducted on the basis of identified bilingual URL pairing patterns as described in Zhang and Yao [7]. Their research is conducted on top of the re-implementation of the intelligent web agent to automatically identify bilingual URL pairing patterns as described in Kit and Ng [13]. For some engineering purposes, the web builders will put some static pairing patterns in the pairs of parallel webpages within the same domain. So in the research, they first detected the candidate pairing patterns from candidate URL pairs. For example, the candidate pattern <en,tc> can be detected from the following URL pairs:

Webpage in English: http://www.hkgb.gov.hk/en/news/press_20120227.html
Webpage in Chinese: http://www.hkgb.gov.hk/tc/news/press_20120227.html

Then they use the detected URL patterns to match URLs in a web domain for identifying bilingual webpages [7]. The noisy patterns would be filtered out by thresholding the credibility of a pattern, which can be defined as:

$$C(p,w) = \frac{N(p,w)}{|w|} \tag{1}$$

Where *N(p,w)* is the number of webpages matched into pairs by pattern *p* within website *w*, and */w/* the size of w in number of webpages.

There are some patterns generalizing across domains. They set the *global credibility* of such a pattern p like this:

$$C(p) = \sum C(p,w)N(p,w) \tag{2}$$

We make use of the patterns with high credibility which are given in their research. The search results that we get from the previous part are the URLs including the character strings like '*en*', '*eng*', '*english*'. For each pattern '*en*', '*eng*', '*english*', we choose 5 candidate pairing patterns respectively to do the substitution according to their credibility in the research of Zhang and Yao (2013). Then we replace the character string like '*en*', '*eng*', '*english*' in the URL with corresponding character string. For instance, the chosen pairing pattern is <en,tc>, <en,b5>,<en,utf-8>...(credibility from high to low order), and we have the URL:

http://www.immd.gov.hk/en/home.html

And a new URL after replacing will be like:

http://www.immd.gov.hk/tc/home.html

Special attention should be paid here. We didn't just replace the '*en*' with '*tc*'. We replace the '*/en/*' with '*/tc/*'. If not it will appear such circumstance, the original URL is:

http://www.csb.gov.hk/mobile/english/info/2047.html

The new URL will be like:

http://www.csb.gov.hk/mobile/tcglish/info/2047.html

So the replacement doesn't make any sense.

Also, for a pairing pattern <english,chinese>, if the '*english*' character string in the URL is in the form of '*/~english/*', we will replace it with '*/~chinese/*'. There are many similar situations during the replacement.

Then new URL is checked after replacing to see whether it exists or not. If the returned http response code of the URL is 200, we assume that the original URL and generated URL is a pair of bilingual parallel websites. Otherwise we keep replacing with the lower credibility bilingual URL pairing patterns until we find an existing website. If the five generated URLs are all checked nonexistent, then we will filter this one and move to the next URL. After the replacements of all the URLs which we get from Section 3.2, we get pairs of URLs which are all existed. One is the URL of candidate websites that in English language. Another one is the URL that we generated with candidate pairing patterns. We assume that these pairs of URL are actually the pairs of parallel webpages in candidate bilingual websites.

4 Experiment and Results Evaluation

4.1 Experimental Data

In this paper, we focused on the governmental, educational and institutional types of sites in Hong Kong when obtaining parallel pages. These three types of the websites are much standard than other types of websites in the content organization and HTML structure. Table 2 shows the number of websites that we get at first.

Table 2. Numbers of the candidate bilingual websites that we get

	site:gov.hk	site:edu.hk	site:org.hk	total
inurl:en	749	1 000	1 000	2 749
inurl:eng	806	992	952	2 750
inurl:english	801	803	671	2 275
Total	2 356	2 795	2 623	7 774

We deal with this websites in two modes: 'Domain Mode' and 'Directory Mode' to get candidate bilingual websites and do the next search.

In the Domain Mode, we keep the second-level domain of each URL from seed websites and eliminate the duplicated ones. Table 3 shows the data of websites that we get after processing. The percentage of English-Chinese websites is higher than the first observation data. Then we just choose the domain that in English-Chinese language to be candidate websites.

In the Directory Mode, we keep each seed websites URL to the web directory of '*/en/*', '*/eng/*' ,'*/english/*', after eliminating the duplicated ones, we get the data in Table 4. We use all the websites in the directory mode to be candidate websites.

Table 3. Numbers of the websites in domain mode

Inurl	Total domains	Total existing domains	English-Chinese domains	English-Chinese / Total domains
en	214	203	193	90.19%
eng	277	264	211	76.17%
english	260	253	139	53.46%

Table 4. Numbers of the websites in directory mode

Web directory	Total Number
www.*./en/	274
www.*./eng/	364
www.*./english/	225

Note: '*' denotes the other strings of the web directory before the /en/,/eng/,/english/

After reprocessing the websites that we get at first, we get candidate websites. Then we make new search queries with search rules and candidate websites limit. After eliminating the duplicated ones in the search results, what we get finally is actually the websites in English language of candidate parallel websites.

The next step is pattern replacing. Table 5 shows the top 5 identified bilingual URL pairing patterns list that we get from the Pupsniffer Evaluation Website[1], a website designed by Zhang and Yao (2013). They released their research data on this website and do the evaluation.

Table 5. Identified bilingual URL pairing patterns list

	en	Credibility	eng	Credibility	english	Credibility
1	en<->tc	13 997.36	eng<->tc	12 869.56	english<->tc_chi	11 436.12
2	en<->b5	5 019.14	eng<->chi	7 824.86	english<->chinese	11 032.46
3	en<->utf-8	4 505.10	eng<->tch	5 281.43	english/<->	261.41
4	en<->ch	3 658.65	eng/<->	1 663.40	english<->traditional	227.37
5	en<->zh	3 460.32	eng<->cht	1 390.22	english<->chi	180.18

Finally we get the pairs of candidate bilingual web pages. The web pages in English language are the search results of candidate websites generated via two modes. The websites in Chinese language are the existing websites after replacing URL patterns. Table 6 shows the number of search results in two modes and the number of existing websites after we checked those replaced URLs. The duplicated ones have been eliminated here. We can see that more than half of the candidate websites have corresponding websites after URL pattern substitution.

[1] Pupsniffer Evaluation Website, `http://mega.ctl.cityu.edu.hk/~czhang22/pupsniffer-eval/`

Table 6. Numbers of the websites that we get through the two modes

	Total Websites	Existing Websites	Existing /Total
Domain mode	92 050	55 603	60.41%
Directory mode	109 462	62 034	56.67%
Total	153 683	88 915	57.86%

4.2 Results Evaluation

A web interface was implemented in the Pupsniffer Evaluation Website2 for evaluating the candidate English-Chinese webpage pairs which we finally get. The quality of bilingual webpages found by us is evaluated manually. Two people (one PhD and one master student) took part in this evaluation. Due to the large amount of retrieved pairs, we only randomly sampled and evaluated part of all pairs.

(1) Result of Bilingual Web Pages Collecting
88 915 web pages pairs[3] are found totally via two modes of searching ways. We made an evaluation of 4 460 pairs randomly and the number of the false bilingual web pages pairs is 409. Table 7 shows the precisions by different methods.

Table 7. Performance of different methods

Type of Algorithm	All Pairs	Sampling Ratio	Random Sampling		
			True Pairs	False Pairs	Precision
Kit and Ng(2007)	290 247	3.50%	9 541	603	94.06%
Zhang and Yao (2013)	348 058	4.95%	16 313	910	94.72%
Our method	88 915	5.02%	4 051	409	90.83%

The precision of our method is 90.8%4 and lower than the results of other two methods. However, there are several advantages we need to mention here. Our proposed method has lower time cost. In the other methods, they have to match a mass of the URL patterns within a website in order to find the true parallel webpages. We just make use of the few certain URL patterns pairs based on the previous works. By using the URL patterns of corresponding languages, we don't need to detect the language of websites in advance. Moreover, the method is independent of languages. There is no complex algorithm and we don't need to waste too much time on calculating. All we need is the search engine and a little prior knowledge about URL pairing patterns with high credibility. That is to say, our method is fast and easy while the precision is not low as well.

[2] The login webpage of the Pupsniffer Evaluation Website, `http://mega.ctl.cityu.edu.hk/~czhang22/pupsniffer-eval/login.html`

[3] The 88 915 web pages pairs result on the Pupsniffer Evaluation Website, `http://mega.ctl.cityu.edu.hk/~czhang22/pupsniffer-eval/Data/ccl2014_data.sql`

[4] The evaluation result on the Pupsniffer Evaluation Website, `http://mega.ctl.cityu.edu.hk/~czhang22/pupsniffer-eval/result.jsp?recordtype=6`

(2) Error Analysis

According to Table 7, there are 409 false bilingual web pages pairs. We analyze these false pairs and classify them into four categories shown in Table 8.

Table 8. Types of Errors

Type of Error	Examples
Monolingual	www.family.org.hk/lang/en-us/carnival.html www.family.org.hk/lang/tc/carnival.html
Fake Bitext	www.tytaps.edu.hk/worksheet2/3A/English/8.pdf www.tytaps.edu.hk/worksheet2/3A/chinese/8.pdf
Error of the Content	www.chamber.org.hk/en/events/doc/M130519FF.pdf www.chamber.org.hk/tc/events/doc/M130519FF.pdf
Invalid Websites	www.polyu.edu.hk/fh/en-us/useful_links www.polyu.edu.hk/fh/tc/useful_links

I: Monolingual: The pairs URLs are in the same language.

II: Fake Bitext: The pairs URLs are false bitext according to their content.

III: Error of the content: One of the pages or both of the pages have been mentioned to have moved to other pages or not to exist in the certain websites any more.

IV: Invalid Websites: After the loading of the websites, it shows '404' or other hint that the web page is invalid.

Table 9 shows the distribution of false pairs. Nearly half of the incorrect pairs are due to the monolingual reason and another problem is the error of the content. If we can identify the language of the URL pairs, theoretically, we can filter out the monolingual URL pairs.

Table 9. False pairs distribution

Error Pairs	Error Type			
	Pairs of I	Pairs of II	Pairs of III	Pairs of IV
Number	204	40	126	39
Patio	49.88%	9.78%	30.81%	9.53%

(3) URL Analysis

According to the 4460 pairs of URLs in the evaluation, we made an analysis about the site types of the URLs and the pattern distribution. Table 10 shows the distribution of different site types and their precisions.

Table 10. Distribution of different site types

Result	gov.hk	edu.hk	org.hk
TRUE	2 555	779	696
FALSE	133	180	96
Total	2 688	959	792
Precision	95.05%	81.23%	87.88%

From the Table 10, we can find that the precision of the governmental websites ranks the first in the three types. It reaches the precision of 95.05% which is absolutely above the total precision of our method. The other two types' precisions are all under 90%. It indicates that during our experiment, the governmental type of the websites will be much more easily found compared with the educational websites and the organizational websites.

5 Conclusion and Future Works

In this paper we have presented a way to mine bilingual webpages with the help of search engine and the patterns replacing. When choosing the high credibility bilingual URL pairing patterns to do the replacement, we can find the corresponding Chinese URL in a fast way. The experiment ultimately collected a total of 153, 683 the English websites of the parallel sites, where there are 88 915 new URLs are determined to exist on the Internet. And the accuracy of actual parallel pages is 90.8%. Though the accuracy is not in accord with our expectations but there is still a big room for improvement.

In the future work, we plan to extract bilingual websites of other website types and search for the webpages of other districts like Taiwan, etc. We will also find the patterns with high credibility of different language pairs to see if the method still works on detecting the parallel websites of other languages.

Acknowledgments. This work is supported by National Natural Science Foundation of China through the grant (No.70903032), Major Projects of National Social Science Fund (13&ZD174), and National Social Science Fund Project (No.14BTQ033).

References

1. Oard, D.W.: Cross-language text retrieval research in the USA. In: Proceedings of the Third DELOS Workshop: Cross-Language Information Retrieval, pp. 7–16 (1997)
2. Brown, P.F., Cocke, J., Pietra, S.A.D., Pietra, V.J.D., Jelinek, F., Lafferty, J.D., Mercer, R.L., Roossin, P.S.: A statistical approach to machine translation. Computational Linguistics 16(2), 79–85 (1990)
3. Resnik, P.: Parallel strands: A preliminary investigation into mining the web for bilingual text. In: Farwell, D., Gerber, L., Hovy, E. (eds.) AMTA 1998. LNCS (LNAI), vol. 1529, pp. 72–82. Springer, Heidelberg (1998)
4. Resnik, P.: Mining the web for bilingual text. In: Proceedings of the 37th Annual Meeting of the Association for Computational Linguistics on Computational Linguistics, pp. 527–534 (1999)
5. Resnik, P., Smith, N.A.: The web as a parallel corpus. Computational Linguistics 29(3), 349–380 (2003)
6. Vicente, I.S., Manterola, I.: PaCo2: A Fully Automated tool for gathering Parallel Corpora from the Web. In: Proceedings of the Eighth International Conference on Language Resources and Evaluation (LREC 2012), pp. 1–6 (2012)

7. Zhang, C.Z., Yao, X.C., Kit, C.Y.: Finding More Bilingual Webpages with High Credibility via Link Analysis. In: Proceedings of the 6th Workshop on Building and Using Comparable Corpora, pp. 138–143 (2013)
8. Ma, X., Liberman, M.Y.: Bits: a method for bilingual text search over the Web. In: Proceedings of MT Summit VII, Singapore, pp. 13–17 (1999)
9. Zhang, Y., Wu, K., Gao, J., Vines, P.: Automatic acquisition of Chinese-English parallel corpus from the web. In: Lalmas, M., MacFarlane, A., Rüger, S.M., Tombros, A., Tsikrika, T., Yavlinsky, A. (eds.) ECIR 2006. LNCS, vol. 3936, pp. 420–431. Springer, Heidelberg (2006)
10. Shi, L., Niu, C., Zhou, M., Gao, J.F.: A DOM tree alignment model for mining parallel data from the web. In: Proceedings of COLING/ACL 2006, Sydney, pp. 489–496 (2006)
11. Miquel, E.-G., Mikel, L.F.: Combining content-based and URL-based heuristics to harvest aligned bitexts from multilingual sites with Bitextor. The Prague Bulletin of Mathematical Linguistics (93), 77–86 (2010)
12. Ling, W., Xiang, G., Dyer, C., Black, A., Trancoso, I.: Microblogs as Parallel Corpora. In: The 51st Annual Meeting of the Association for Computational Linguistics (ACL), pp. 176–186 (2013)
13. Ye, S.N., Lv, Y.J., Huang, Y., Liu, Q.: Automatic parallel sentences extracting from web. Journal of Chinese Information Processing 22(5), 67–73 (2008) (in Chinese)
14. Kit, C.Y., Ng, J.Y.H.: An Intelligent Web Agent to Mine Bilingual Parallel Pages via Automatic Discovery of URL Pairing Patterns. In: Proceedings of Web Intelligence and Intelligent Agent Technology Workshops, pp. 526–529 (2007)
15. Qi, L., Yang, L., Sun, M.S.: A Parallel Pages Mining Approach: Combining URL Patterns and HTML Structures. Journal of Chinese Information Processing 27(3), 91–99 (2013) (in Chinese)

The Chinese-English Contrastive Language Knowledge Base and Its Applications

Xiaojing Bai[1], Christoph Zähner[2], Hongying Zan[3], and Shiwen Yu[4]

[1] Department of Foreign Languages and Literatures, Tsinghua University, Beijing, China
bxj@tsinghua.edu.cn
[2] Language Centre, University of Cambridge, Cambridge, UK
cz201@cam.ac.uk
[3] College of Information Engineering, Zhengzhou University, Zhengzhou, China
iehyzan@zzu.edu.cn
[4] Institute of Computational Linguistics, Peking University, Beijing, China
yusw@pku.edu.cn

Abstract. In this paper, we introduce our ongoing research on a Chinese-English Contrastive Language Knowledge Base, including its architecture, the selection of its entries and the XML-based annotation schemes used. We also report on the progress of annotation. The knowledge base is linguistically motivated, focusing on a wide range of sub-sentential contrasts between Chinese and English. It will offer a new form of bilingual resources for NLP tasks, for use in contrastive linguistic research and translation studies, amongst others. Currently, joint efforts are being made to develop tools for Computer-Assisted Translation and Second Language Acquisition using this knowledge base.

Keywords: Language Knowledge Base, Contrastive Linguistics, Parallel Corpus, Sub-sentential Alignment, Computer-Assisted Translation, Second Language Acquisition.

1 Introduction

Language knowledge bases are collections of linguistic knowledge that facilitate the automatic analysis and generation of natural languages in NLP systems. They are indispensable components of NLP systems, and their quality and scale influence the performance of these systems significantly [1].

Starting with a sentence-aligned parallel corpus [2], the Chinese-English Contrastive Language Knowledge Base (CECLKB) aims to provide formal descriptions of the sub-sentential contrast between Chinese and English: How do the two languages express the same notion? What is the nature of the correpondence between the two expressions representing the same notion? What syntactic and semantic constraints are involved? The sub-sentential contrastive knowledge, originally implicit in the parallel corpus, is made explicit and marked up with XML

M. Sun et al. (Eds.): CCL and NLP-NABD 2014, LNAI 8801, pp. 107–119, 2014.

tags in order to support the processing of natural languages in bilingual or multilingual scenarios.

In this paper, we briefly review related research in Section 2, followed by an overview of CECLKB in Section 3. Section 4 describes our plans for employing CECLKB for Computer-Assisted Translation (CAT) and Second Language Acquisition (SLA). The last section summarises the present stage of our research and looks at plans for more future efforts.

2 Related Research

The construction of a contrastive language knowledge base was first motivated by the employment of new metrics for subsegment-level analysis and the prospect they offer for enhancing Translation Memory (TM) [3]. Compared with sentence-level alignment, sub-sentential alignment of parallel texts provides us with a more fine-grained look at the correspondence between matching expressions in different languages.

Despite the fact that sentences function as the operational unit of most TM systems currently in use, there has long been an assumption that where the complete sentence has not been translated before, the identification of corresponding sub-sentence segments by the TM would be of use to the translator [4]. Bowker and Barlow indicate that linguistic repetition occurs most often at the level of expressions or phrases [5], and Macken expects the second-generation TM systems to provide additional translation suggestions for sub-sentential chunks [6].

In parallel text processing, the alignment of parallel texts occurs either at the sentence level or at other levels including words and expressions, clauses and sentence structures, or even document structures [7]. There have been substantial efforts made on word alignment in projects such as Blinker, Arcade, Plug and GALE [8, 9, 10, 11], with the GALE project working on Chinese-English parallel texts in particular. Other research on Chinese-English alignment focuses on the characteristics of word alignment, distinguishing genuine links (strong or weak) from pseudo links [12], or looks at the alignment of senses between the two languages with the help of WordNet [13].

3 An Overview of the Knowledge Base

CECLKB is a formalized and structured collection of contrastive linguistic knowledge. The design of its architecture, the entries included and the annotation scheme for all entries are based on the anticipated applications of the knowledge base and the findings of relevant linguistic research and translation studies concerned with typical contrasting features of Chinese and English.

As the correspondence between Chinese and English can be found at various levels, CECLKB has entries of contrastive knowledge at the word, phrase, chunk and sentence pattern levels. This entails the alignment of parallel texts at all these levels and contrasts with the alignment in previous research, which mainly worked on the word level.

Each entry in CECLKB contains a Chinese-English sentence pair[1], with one and only one linguistic focus. It focuses on and marks up a specific instance of correspondence between a selected Chinese word, phrase, chunk or sentence pattern and its corresponding expression in English. The markup highlights the syntactic and semantic constraints on the particular instance of correspondence, which adds more dimensions to the cross-language observation than the previous research did. The following is an example of an entry in CECLKB[2].

Example 1

weicheng01.xml

<a id="160" no="1"><s id="50"><NR SR="EX" COMP_SO="T">周经理</NR><VP FCS="T" GF="B"><VV>听</VV><DER>得</DER><VA COMP="DG">开心</VA></VP>, 叫主任回信说：</s></a>

<a id="160" no="1"><s id="80"><S GF="SP" CO="HL"><VP><VBN> Delighted</VBN>
<PP><IN>with</IN><NP><PDT>all</PDT><DT>this</DT></NP></PP></VP></S>, Chou instructed Wang to reply in the following manner: </s></a>

3.1 Architecture of CECLKB

The architecture of CECLKB (Fig.1) shows that there are four types of entries: word entries, phrase entries, chunk entries and sentence pattern entries. We currently work with six sub-categories of word entries and one sub-category for each of the other three types of entries. Subsequently, more sub-categories and entries will be included to enrich the knowledge base and widen its coverage.

The parallel texts in CECLKB include i) Chinese source texts and their English translation, and ii) English source texts and their Chinese translation[3]. This ensures a balanced representation of linguistic phenomena and helps minimize the problems caused by the direction of translation [14]. We start with Chinese (either as the source

---

1 In a sentence-aligned parallel corpus, a sentence pair is a 2-tuple AS=<Si, Ti>, where both Si (in the source language) and Ti (in the target language) consist of a set of one or more sentences, with Si and Ti being corresponding expressions of each other.

2 The parallel corpus that our work is based on consists of parallel texts. There are XML tags in these texts already, marking up the alignment at the text, paragraph and sentence levels. In Example 1, the first line specifies the title of the text, from which the sentence pair is taken. The tags <a> and </a> mark up the aligned sentence pair, the value of the attribute *id* is the same for the corresponding Chinese and English sentences, and the value of the attribute *no* specifies the number of sentences involved. Sentences are marked up with <s> and </s>, and the value of the attribute *id* specifies the sentence's location in the text. The other XML tags are the results of the present research, which will be illustrated in Section 3.3.

3 There are XML tags in the parallel texts, which indicate the direction of translation and are retrievable when needed.

language or the target language) and establish how Chinese words, phrases, chunks or sentence patterns are structured syntactically, what semantic features they have, and how they are expressed in English. The parallel texts selected are mainly novels or essays relating to culture, ensuring that the knowledge base can support applications for a range of general purposes. The size of the parallel corpus is shown in Table 1.

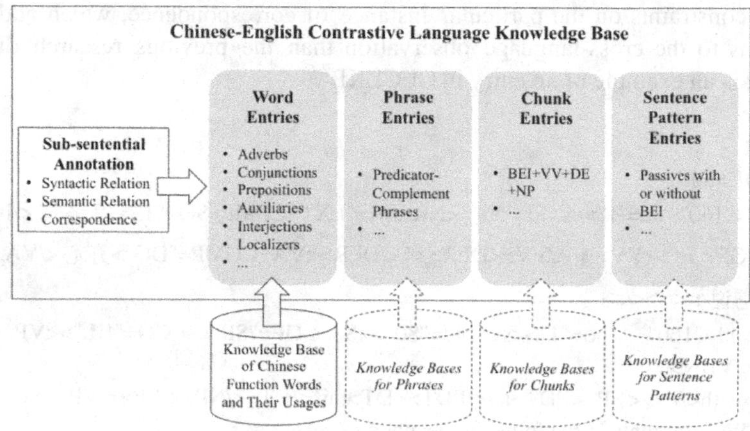

Fig. 1. The Architecture of CECLKB

Table 1. Size of the Parallel Corpus

Translation Direction	Chinese to English	English to Chinese
Total Number of Texts Pairs	250	1221
Total Number of Sentence Pairs	39134	157996
Number of Sentence Pairs from Novels	24929	102774
Number of Sentence Pairs from Essays on Culture	2800	16890

CECLKB is designed to integrate with other existing language knowledge bases, promoting the sharing of formalized linguistic knowledge among different projects. The Chinese Function Word Usage Knowledge Base [15] is the first that has been integrated; it allows the retrieval of linguistic features of Chinese function words directly through CECLKB.

3.2 Entries in CECLKB

Each entry in CECLKB contains a sub-sentential alignment, which exploits parallel texts to obtain fine-grained contrastive knowledge. At present, CECLKB entries focus on: i) adverbs, e.g. 随手 *casually*, ii) predicator-complement phrases, e.g. 吃得很多

ate quite a bit, iii) BEI+VV+DE+NP[4], e.g. 被破获的扒手 *captured pickpocket*, and iv) passives with or without BEI, e.g. 啤酒(被)酿造出来 *the beer was brewed*. Below we set out the rationales behind our selection of entries.

There are far fewer function words than content words in Chinese. A function word, however, usually carries much more weight than a content word does [16]. To begin with, we select adverbs as the focus of word entries, which are usually categorized as function words but do have their own lexical meanings.

Predicator-complement phrases come next. They are one of the most frequently used phrase types in Chinese. They have a wide variety of internal and external formal features, and the semantic links[5] of these complements are complex. Our pilot study showed a rich diversity of corresponding English expressions in parallel texts, a further reason for selecting them as the focus for phrase entries.

A BEI+VV+DE+NN structure represents a typical chunk in CECLKB. A chunk is defined as an ordered sequence of words and word categories, which exhibits special lexical, syntactic or semantic features. These special features are usually well captured by the corresponding English expressions in parallel texts. A chunk may also constitute a phrase of a certain type, such as BEI+VV+DE+NN constituting a complex noun phrase. Classified as a chunk, however, the sequence is seen more as a typical combination of particular words (被 and 的) and word categories (VV and NN) than as an ordinary phrase.

Entries of the fourth type deal with cases where corresponding Chinese and English sentence patterns fail to pair up in parallel texts. With passive constructions we first select the Chinese passives with or without BEI, which supposedly correspond to English passives. The focus of our observation is set on: i) Chinese passives with BEI, which are not expressed by English passives; and ii) Chinese passives without BEI or Chinese non-passives, which are expressed by English passives.

3.3 Annotation Schemes

The way in which linguistic knowledge is annotated reflects the nature of the relevant linguistic phenomena and how the formal descriptions are to be used. The annotations in CECLKB mark up the syntactic, semantic and corresponding relations in each entry, adding additional XML tags to the sentence pairs extracted from the corpus.

---

4 BEI stands for the preposition 被, the most important passive marker in Chinese. DE stands for the auxiliary 的, a structural particle usually placed after an attributive modifier. The chunk BEI+VV+DE+NP, in most circumstances, forms a noun phrase with passive attribute.

5 In a sentence, if constituent A is semantically linked to constituent B, then A is immediately related to B in meaning. In Chinese, there is considerable ambiguity about the semantic link of three kinds of sentence constituents: complements, modifiers (particularly adverbials) and predicates [17]. In Example 1, the complement 开心 *delighted* specifies the feeling of the experiencer 周经理 *Chou* – the subject of the clause, and is therefore semantically linked to 周经理 instead of the predicator 听 *listen*.

When designing the annotation schemes, we mainly consider: i) what tags and attributes are needed to mark up the three relations set out below; ii) whether different tags and attributes are needed for different types of entries; iii) whether the annotation schemes are extensible; and iv) whether the annotations are adaptable for use with a range of applications?

For the convenience of explanation, we begin by defining the three kinds of correspondences (abbreviated as HL, CT and NO respectively) in CECLKB, illustrated by five examples of the adverb 随手 *casually* and its corresponding English expressions.

- HL: Highlighted Correspondence (Examples 2 and 3) is a 2-tuple in a sentence pair, written as HL=<CSeg, ESeg>, where CSeg is the focused Chinese word, phrase, chunk or sentence pattern, and ESeg is an English expression, with CSeg and ESeg being the corresponding expressions of each other.
- CT: Contextual Correspondence (Examples 4 and 5) is also a 2-tuple in a sentence pair, written as CT=<CSeg, ESeg>, where CSeg is the combination of the focused Chinese word, phrase, chunk or sentence pattern and its context, and ESeg is an English expression, with CSeg and ESeg being the corresponding expressions of each other. Further, there is no sub-segment in ESeg, which corresponds, on its own, to the focused Chinese word, phrase, chunk or sentence pattern.
- NO: No Correspondence (Example 6) is assumed when there does not exist an English expression in a sentence pair, which corresponds, in either of the two ways mentioned above, to the focused Chinese word, phrase, chunk or sentence pattern.

Example 2: **随手**翻开第二本的扉页，大叫道："辛楣，你看见这个没有？"
He **casually** opened to the flyleaf of the other book and exclaimed, "Hey, Hsin-mei, did you see this one?"

Example 3: 范博文接过香来，**随手**又丢在地下，看见人堆里有一条缝，他就挤进去了。
Fan Po-wen took one and **immediately** let it drop to the ground, then, seeing a gap in the crowd, he pushed his way in.

Example 4: 马丁一言不发，也没有打什么招呼，就走了出去，悄悄地**随手**关上了门。
Without speaking or giving any kind of salutation, Martin went out, **closing the door** silently **behind him.**

Example 5: 福尔摩斯在他的一张名片背后**随手**写了几个字，扔给雷斯垂德。
Holmes **scribbled** a few words upon the back of one of his visiting cards and threw it over to Lestrade.

Example 6: 我们不打算趁四周无人时**随手**借它一只，就象我爸爸当年干的那个样子，因为那么一来，就会有人在后面追我们。
We warn't going to borrow it when there warn't anybody around, the way pap would do, for that might set people after us.

XML tags and attributes are designed to mark up i) the Chinese segments in focus, ii) the context of the focused segments, and iii) the corresponding expressions of the focused segments in English. For entries of different types or sub-categories, bilingual correpondence may involve a diversity of syntactic and semantic constrains. It is therefore necessary to have XML tags and attributes that apply to all entries and the special ones that apply to some entries only.

We use the Stanford parser for the pre-annotation of syntactic relations and have therefore adopted its inventory of POS and phrasal-category tags [18, 19], supplemented by an inventory of attributes and values (see Appendix for a selected list)[6].

Example 7 in Table 2 illustrates how predicator-complement phrase entries are annotated. The left column of the table shows how the phrase entry is annotated, and the right column zooms in on the three main targets of annotation.

Table 2. A Predicator-Complement Phrase Entry (Example 7)

Stored Annotation	Targets of Annotation
1984-1.xml <a id="22" no="1"> <s id="1"> 玻璃**<NN SR="PT">窗</NN><VP FCS="T" GF="B"><VV COMP_SO="T">关</VV><DER>得</DER><VP COMP="DG"><ADVP><AD>很</AD></ADVP><VP><VA>严实</VA></VP></VP></VP>**，可是朝窗外望一眼，依然觉出外面冷得紧。</s></a> <a id="22" no="1"> <s id="1"> Outside, even through the **<ADJP GF="ATM" CO="HL"><VBN>shut</VBN></ADJP>** window-pane, the world looked cold. </s></a>	• **Chinese segment in focus** <VP FCS="T" GF="B"> <VV COMP_SO="T">关</VV> <DER>得</DER> <VP COMP="DG"> <ADVP><AD>很</AD></ADVP> <VP><VA>严实</VA></VP> </VP> </VP> • **Context of the focused segment** <NN SR="PT">窗</NN> • **English expression corresponding to the focused segment** <ADJP GF="ATM" CO="HL"> <VBN>shut</VBN> </ADJP>

In syntactic annotation we mark up:

- the focused Chinese phrase (关得严实), its syntactic structure and its grammatical function in the clause by i) tagging the POS of each word constituent and the syntactic tree of the phrase, and ii) adding the attribute *FCS* (its value being "T" to signal a focused phrase) and the attribute *GF* (its value being the code of the grammatical function) to the phrasal-category tag of the phrase;

---

6 There are detailed annotation schemes for different categories and sub-categories of entries. For the sake of brevity, we only introduce attributes and values related to the examples here.

- the context (窗 *window*, the subject) of the focused phrase, its syntactic structure and its semantic role in the clause by i) tagging its POS or phrasal category, and ii) adding the attribute *SR* (its value being the code of the semantic role) to the POS or phrasal-category tag of the context; and
- the corresponding English expression (*shut*) of the focused phrase, its syntactic structure and its grammatical function in the clause by i) tagging the POS of each word constituent and the syntactic tree of the expression, and ii) adding the attribute *GF* to the phrasal-category tag of the expression.

In semantic annotation we mark up:

- the type of the complement by adding the attribute *COMP* (its value being the code of the complement type) to the phrasal-category tag of the complement; and
- the semantic link of the complement, by adding the attribute *COMP_SO* (its value being "T") to the constituent in the clause that the complement specifies.

In correspondence annotation we mark up:

- the highlighted correspondence, by adding the attribute *CO* (its value being "HL") to the tag of the corresponding English expression;
- the contextual correspondence, by adding the attribute *CO* (its value being "CT") to the tag of the corresponding English expression; and
- the lack of parallelism, by adding the attribute *CO* (its value being "NO") to the tag of the focused Chinese phrase.

3.4 Progress of Annotation

Human annotators following a strict set of guidelines annotate the corresponding texts, with the support of annotation tools. The annotators are researchers, graduate students and trained undergraduates. They have a background in linguistics and are native speakers of Chinese, who speak English. The guidelines consist of the general principles of annotation and the detailed rules, suggestions and samples for different categories and sub-categories of entries. Annotations are checked for adherence to guidelines and consistency by two chief annotators. New rules and samples are added to the guidelines when annotators encounter examples not yet covered.

At the present stage, the tools we use are the Stanford parser[7] (for syntactic pre-processing) and the UAM CorpusTool[8] (for markup). An annotation tool is being developed, which will integrate the automatic pre-processing with the human markup process. It will also assist XML validation, tree display and quantitative analysis. Once implemented, we expect to make the tool available to other projects.

For the pilot annotation covering all four major entry types, 4000 sentence pairs have been extracted from the parallel corpus. We have completed the second round of annotation for 100 entries in the adverb sub-category and 100 entries in the

[7] `http://nlp.stanford.edu/software/lex-parser.shtml`
[8] `http://www.wagsoft.com/CorpusTool/`

predicator-complement sub-category. In the first round, we also completed the annotation for 230 entries in the BEI+VV+DE+NP sub-category.

4 Applications in CAT and SLA

The complexity of language makes it extremely demanding to process natural languages automatically and precisely. This being the case, we have designed the contrastive language knowledge base as a collection of well-understood and formally described facts about language, which extend the human intelligence using CAT and SLA tools rather than attempting to substitute it.

4.1 CECLKB and TM Tools in CAT

The success of TM is a question of its usefulness, that is to what extent can translations extracted from a TM tool be of use to a human translator [4]. The needs of translators vary when they search for contrastive linguistic knowledge. The TM tool that we are designing incorporates CECLKB and is therefore able to allow translators to highlight certain types of entries, which will then be given more weight when the TM tool extracts previous translations.

Take the Chinese adverb 随手 as an example. The Contemporary Chinese Dictionary [20] gives the following information about this word, which includes a bilingual definition and a contextual translation:

- 顺手 sth. done at sb.'s convenience; without extra effort; sth. that can be done handily along with sth. else: 出门时请～关门。*Please shut the door as you leave.*

With the support of CECLKB, a TM tool can amongst other things provide the following:

- ways of expressing this adverb in English when it is found in different contexts (see Examples 2 to 6), and particularly, how this adverb is expressed in contextual correspondences (see Examples 4 and 5), something which is usually not available in bilingual dictionaries; and
- probabilistic rules based on the formal descriptions, to assist the translator with his choices and decisions in the process of translation.

We are suggesting that a translator "borrows", but not necessarily "follows", these probabilistic rules. Information obtained from the analysis of tags, attributes and their values may offer additional choices to the translator. For instance, in CECLKB the adverb entries of 随手 exhibit the bilingual correspondence as follows[9]:

---

9 In Fig. 2, CE stands for the sentence pairs with Chinese as the source language and English as the target language, while EC stands for the sentence pairs with English as the source language and Chinese as the target language.

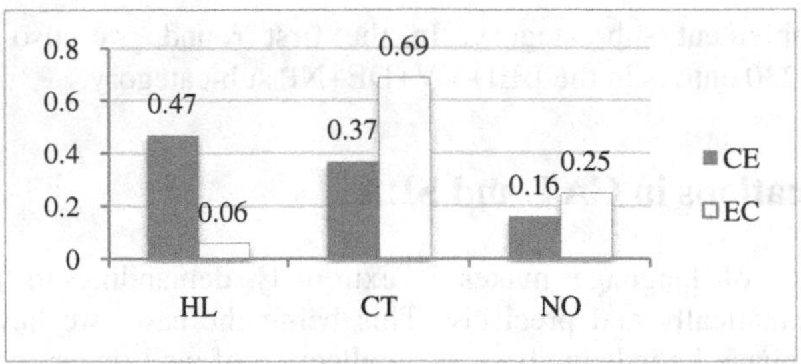

Fig. 2. Bilingual Correspondence in the Adverb Entries of 随手

As the annotation is still going on, the sample currently available for analysis is quite small[10]. It can be seen, however, that in the CE sentence pairs, the meanings of 随手 are more often expressed by corresponding English adverbs, such as *immediately*, *casually*, *idly*, etc. In contrast, the EC sentence pairs give us more English verbs, such as *scribble*, *jam*, *shove*, *snatch*, *toss*, etc., which describe not only the action but also the manner in which the action is carried out. This is just one example, but there will be much more contrastive linguistic knowledge that a translator can obtain from CECLKB through TM tools.

4.2 CECLKB and Language Tools in SLA

While acquiring a new language the learner needs to understand the range of subtle semantic, stylistic and rhetorical meanings associated with any new expression she encounters. The learner also needs to understand the range of expressions available to her when voicing her own ideas and feelings.

For instance, with the predicator-complement phrases (see Example 7), an SLA learner of Chinese needs to learn that these phrases describe events and that they express a sense of degree or the potential of the events. Specifically, she must understand that (窗)关得严实 *(window) be shut firmly* is different from (窗)关得上 *(window) can be shut* in that the former indicates how tight the window is shut (the degree of the event), while the latter indicates if the window can be closed (the potential of the event). Further, she needs to know that (窗)关得严实 is also different from (窗)做得结实 *(window) be solidly built*. The complement 严实 *firm(ly)* elaborates on the action 关 *shut*, while the complement 结实 *solid(ly)* comments on the state of 窗 *window*. This kind of information is available in CECLKB, with the types of complements and their semantic links annotated for all predicator-complement phrases.

The learner not only learns to use a predicator-complement phrase to describe an event and its degree or potential, she also needs to know how to use and structure the phrase. Table 3 shows how the annotated 100 predicator-complement phrases function grammatically: 81 of them acting as the predicates in subject-predicate constructions, e.g. 窗关得严实. Further, it shows that 11 phrases with potential

[10] In Fig. 2, only 19 CE sentence pairs and 36 EC sentence pairs are observed.

complements, e.g. 看得见(整个房间) *could command (the whole room)*, act as the predicators in predicator-object constructions, while phrases with degree complements are not found used in this way. See Appendix for the details of the tags for grammatical functions.

Table 3. Predicator-Complement Phrases: Grammatical Functions vs. Complement Types

Grammatical Functions	Degree Complements	Potential Complements
A	0	1
B	73	8
C	0	11
D	1	0
G	1	0
K	5	0

There are other ways in which the annotations can be exploited in SLA learning scenarios. The SLA language tool we are developing helps non-native Chinese learners improve their reading skills. An understanding of function words, phrases, chunks and sentence patterns plays an important role in developing a level of proficiency in reading Chinese texts. With pre-designed learning scenarios, training data can be retrieved automatically and dynamically from the knowledge base.

5 Conclusion

It is our expectation that a contrastive knowledge base with its collection of rich, in-depth and formalized knowledge about two (or more) languages will be of significant use to NLP technology. CECLKB is linguistically motivated and can provide dynamic and diversified language assistance for CAT and SLA applications. It achieves this by i) including four different types of knowledge entries, ii) selecting diversified sub-categories of knowledge entries with special linguistic focuses, iii) describing the bilingual and sub-sentential contrast from three perspectives in general, and iv) specifying annotations typically applying to some sub-categories only. Further efforts will focus on the annotation of more data, the statistical analysis of the annotated data, the revision of annotation guidelines, the development of the annotation tool and the building of related CAT and SLA tools.

We are considering making part of the knowledge base available to NLP, SLA and other relevant research once a significant part of it is completed and validated. Our current development of an SLA demonstrator will make a small portion of the knowledge base accessible online.

Acknowledgements. This paper is supported by the National Key Basic Research Program of China 2014CB340504, the National Social Science Fund of China 14BYY096, and the Philosophy and Social Science Fund of the Ministry of Education of China 12JHQ046.

References

1. Yu, S., Duan, H., Zhu, X., Zhang, H.: The Construction and Utilization of a Comprehensive Language Knowledge-base. Journal of Chinese Information Processing 18(5), 1–10 (2004)
2. Bai, X., Chang, B., Zhan, W.: The Construction of a Large-scale Chinese-English Parallel Corpus. In: Huang, H. (ed.) Recent Development in Machine Translation Studies - Proceedings of the National Conference on Machine Translation 2002, pp. 124–131. Publishing House of Electronics Industry, Beijing (2002)
3. Benito, D.: Future Trends in Translation Memory. Tradumàtica 7 (2009), `http://www.fti.uab.cat/tradumatica/revista/hemeroteca.htm`, ISSN 1578-7559
4. Simard, M., Langlais, P.: Sub-sentential Exploitation of Translation Memories. In: Proceedings of Machine Translation Summit VIII: Machine Translation in the Information Age, pp. 335–339 (2001)
5. Bowker, L., Barlow, M.: Bilingual Concordancers and Translation Memories: A Comparative Evaluation. In: Proceedings of the Second International Workshop on Language Resources for Translation Work, Research and Training, pp. 70–79 (2004)
6. Macken, L.: Sub-Sentential Alignment of Translational Correspondences. University of Antwerp (2010)
7. Véronis, J. (ed.): Parallel Text Processing – Alignment and Use of Translation Corpora. Kluwer Academic Publishers, The Netherlands (2003)
8. Melamed, D.: Annotation Style Guide for the Blinker Project – Version 1.0.4 (2008), `http://arxiv.org/pdf/cmp-lg/9805004v1.pdf`
9. Véronis, J.: ARCADE: Tagging Guidelines for Word Alignment – Version 1.0 (1998), `http://aune.lpl.univ-aix.fr/projects/arcade/2nd/word/guide/`
10. Merkel, M.: Annotation Style Guide for the PLUG Link Annotator. Linköping University (1999)
11. Linguistic Data Consortium. Guidelines for Chinese-English Word Alignment – Version 4.0 (2009), `http://catalog.ldc.upenn.edu/docs/LDC2012T24/GALE_Chinese_alignment_guidelines_v4.0.pdf`
12. Zhao, H., Liu, Q., Zhang, R., Lv, Y., Sumita, E.: Guidelines for Chinese-English Word Alignment. Journal of Chinese Information Processing 23(3), 65–87 (2009)
13. Bond, F., Wang, S.: Issues in building English-Chinese parallel corpora with WordNets. In: Orav, H., Fellbaum, C., Vossen, P. (eds.) Proceedings of the Seventh Global WordNet Conference (GWC-7), Tartu, Estonia, pp. 391–399 (2014)
14. Johansson, S.: Seeing through Multilingual Corpora: On the Use of Corpora in Contrastive Studies. John Benjamins Publishing, Amsterdam (2007)
15. Zan, H., Zhang, K., Zhu, X., Yu, S.: Research on the Chinese Function Word Usage Knowledge Base. International Journal on Asian Language Processing 21(4), 185–198 (2011)
16. Lu, J., Ma, Z.: Some Comments on the Function Words in Contemporary Chinese. Language & Culture Press, Beijing (1999)
17. Lu, J.: On Semantic Link Analysis. Essays on Linguistics, 1. Beijing Language and Culture University Press, Beijing (1997)
18. Santorini, B.: Part-of-Speech Tagging Guidelines for the Penn Treebank Project (3rd revision) (1990), `http://repository.upenn.edu/cis_reports/570/`

19. Xia, F.: The Part-Of-Speech Tagging Guidelines for the Penn Chinese Treebank (3.0) (2000), `http://repository.upenn.edu/ircs_reports/38/`
20. Institute of Linguistics, Chinese Academy of Social Science. The Contemporary Chinese Dictionary [Chinese-English Edition]. Foreign Language Teaching and Research Press, Beijing (2002)

Appendix. XML Attributes and Their Values - A Selected List

Major Grammatical Functions of Chinese Constituents

A: Subject in Subject-Predicate Construction
B: Predicate in Subject-Predicate Construction
C: Predicator in Predicator-Object Construction
D: Object in Predicator-Object Construction
E: Predicator in Predicator-Complement Construction
F: Complement in Predicator-Complement Construction
G: Attributive in Attributive-Head Construction
H: Head in Attributive-Head Construction
I: Adverbial in Adverbial-Head Construction
J: Head in Adverbial-Head Construction
K: Appendage

Major Grammatical Functions of English Constituents

P: Predicate
PR: Predicator
C: Complement
including:
- S: Subject
- O: Object
- PDC: Predicative Complement
- LCC: Locative Complement
- PPC: Prepositional Complement
- CTC: Catenative Complement
- CLC: Clausal complement
- PC: Complement of Preposition

A: Adjunct
including but not limited to
- ATM: Attributive Modifier
- ETM: External Modifier
- APM: Appositive modifier

SP: Supplement
GP: Gapping
SL: Embedded Constituents

Major Semantic Roles

CS: Causer
AG: Agent
PT: Patient
EX: Experiencer
ST: Stimulus
TH: Theme
RL: Relevant
RG: Range
LC: Location

Types of Complements

PT: Potential
DG: Degree
RS: Result
DR: Direction

Clustering Product Aspects Using Two Effective Aspect Relations for Opinion Mining

Yanyan Zhao[1], Bing Qin[2], and Ting Liu[2]

[1] Department of Media Technology and Art, Harbin Institute of Technology
[2] Department of Computer Science and Technology, Harbin Institute of Technology
{yyzhao,bqin,tliu}@ir.hit.edu.cn

Abstract. Aspect recognition and clustering is important for many sentiment analysis tasks. To date, many algorithms for recognizing product aspects have been explored, however, limited work have been done for clustering the product aspects. In this paper, we focus on the problem of product aspect clustering. Two effective aspect relations: relevant aspect relation and irrelevant aspect relation are proposed to describe the relationships between two aspects. According to these two relations, we can explore many relevant and irrelevant aspects into two different sets as background knowledge to describe each product aspect. Then, a hierarchical clustering algorithm is designed to cluster these aspects into different groups, in which aspect similarity computation is conducted with the relevant aspect set and irrelevant aspect set of each product aspect. Experimental results on camera domain demonstrate that the proposed method performs better than the baseline without using the two aspect relations, and meanwhile proves that the two aspect relations are effective.

Keywords: Sentiment analysis, Product aspect clustering, Social media.

1 Introduction

Social media holds a considerable amount of user-generated content describing the opinions of customers on products and services through reviews, blog, tweets, etc. These reviews are valuable for customers to make purchasing decisions and for companies to guide the business activities. Consequently, the advent of social media has stirred much excitement and provided abundant opportunities for opinion mining and sentiment analysis [12,6,23].

For many opinion mining applications, for example, opinion summarization [19,18] or recommender systems [7,14], recognizing product aspects from the product reviews is usually treated as the first step. Afterwards, we collect relevant sentences and analyze opinions for each product aspect. Thus product aspect recognition is a critical task for opinion mining [13,5,9,10]. There are two subtasks for this task, one is aspect extraction, and the other one is aspect clustering. Aspect extraction aims to extract the entities, which the users write comments

M. Sun et al. (Eds.): CCL and NLP-NABD 2014, LNAI 8801, pp. 120–130, 2014.

on. For example, it can extract the "图像" ("picture" in English) as product aspect from the review "图像很漂亮" ("the picture is great"). On the other hand, aspect clustering aims to cluster the aspects that have the similar meaning into the same groups. For example, the word "图像" ("picture" in English) and "照片" ("photo" in English) express the same meaning, we need to group them.

To date, most of the aspect relevant research work is focusing on the first sub-task including many kinds of methods, such as rule-based [1,3,22,13], supervised [20,4,8], and topic model-based [10,2,15] methods. Unfortunately, just a few work is done on the second sub-task. Due to the importance of the second sub-task, we need to pay more attention to it and this paper is mainly focusing on this sub-task. In the previous work, some researchers used topic model based methods [17,10,16] to cluster domain-specific aspects. However, topic models always jointly modeled topics and sentiment words. Mukherjee et al. [11] used a switch variable trained with Maximum-Entropy to separate topic and sentiment words. Some researchers consider this task as a traditional clustering task, the key part of which is similarity computation. Zhai et al. [21] modeled this task as a semi-supervised learning problem using lexical similarity. However, it needed some manually selected seeds as the input, which are random and accordingly hard to handle or reproduce in the experiments.

In this paper, we propose a simple and effective unsupervised method, which applies two effective aspect relations. Specifically, we treat this task as a typical clustering problem, which mainly emphasizes on the similarity computation. However, the common similarity measures are usually based on literal meaning of two aspects, which is far from enough. To address this issue, we find two interesting phenomena. One is summarized as **relevant aspect phenomenon**. That is to say, *in one sentence, if one aspect contains the other one, the two aspects are relevant and can be grouped into a same cluster.* For example, in the sentence "我今天买了个[人像镜头]，这个[镜头]的分辨率不错啊" ("I bought a [portrait lens], the resolution of the [lens] is perfect"), the phrase "人像镜头" ("portrait lens" in English) and "镜头" ("lens" in English) shows relevant aspect phenomenon. Thus the two aspects can be classified into a same group. The relationship between them is called **relevant aspect relation**.

The other phenomenon is **irrelevant aspect phenomenon**. That is to say, *in one sentence the product aspect is always used in one form instead of using different forms, even though this aspect can be expressed in other forms.* Based on this phenomenon, the aspects appearing in the same sentence can be considered as different aspects if they do not contain each other. Take the following two sentences as an example:

- Sentence 1: 我在电脑上浏览佳能600D的[照片]，感觉[照片]挺不错的，<分辨率>挺高。

  (I browsed the [*pictures*] in the computer, and found the [*pictures*] were perfect and the < *resolution* > was high.)
- Sentence 2: 我在电脑上浏览佳能600D的[照片]，感觉[图像]挺不错的，<分辨率>挺高。

(I browsed the [*pictures*] in the computer, and found the [*photos*] were perfect and the < *resolution* > was high.)

In most cases, if one word must be mentioned multiple times in a sentence, people always use the same word. Thus, the word "照片" ("picture" in English) used in Sentence 1 shows the phenomenon. However, we seldom use different word form to express a same meaning in a same sentence, such as the word "照片" ("picture" in English) and "图像" ("photo" in English) used in Sentence 2. Therefore, in Sentence 1, since the aspect "照片" and aspect "分辨率" do not contain each other, they can be considered as different aspects. That is to say, they belong to different groups. Thus, the relationship between them is called **irrelevant aspect relation**.

According to these two phenomena, for each product aspect, we can collect a relevant aspect set and an irrelevant aspect set from a large corpora respectively. That is to say, we provide two kinds of background knowledge for each aspect. On one hand, the relevant aspect set is to help the given aspect to get the domain synonyms more accurately. On the other hand, the irrelevant aspect set is to help separate this aspect from other irrelevant aspects that do not refer to the same aspect.

Since aspect clustering is a typical clustering problem, a hierarchical clustering method is applied to classify the aspects into different groups based on their relevant aspect sets and irrelevant aspect sets. Several similarity computation methods are used to compute the similarity between two aspects.

We evaluate our framework on the corpus of camera domain as a case study. Experimental results show that the both two kinds of aspect relations achieve significant performance that gains over the baseline clustering method without using these two relations.

The remainder of this paper is organized as follows. Section 2 introduces the two kinds of aspect relations, and constructs the relevant and irrelevant aspect set for each product aspect. Section 3 shows the hierarchical clustering algorithm based on the two aspect relations. Section 4 presents the experiments and results. Finally we conclude this paper in Section 5.

2 Two Effective Aspect Relations

For each aspect, two aspect sets, irrelevant aspect set and relevant aspect set can be built. Figure 1 shows an example consisting of a Chinese review, which is tagged with all the appearing product aspects.

As shown in Figure 1, four kinds of product aspects can be found. Take the aspect "镜头" ("lens" in English) as an example, since "镜头" is the suffix of "光变镜头", "光变镜头" is the relevant aspect of the given aspect "镜头" and can be concluded into the relevant set. On the other hand, "光圈" and "成像效果" are totally different from "镜头" literally, thus they are concluded into the irrelevant set.

镜头采用了专业的施奈德3倍光变镜头，光圈为F2.8－F4.8，
虽然指标并不出众，但是专业的镜头相对来说会给成像效果
带来相当大的助益；
Translated as:
The lens is the professional schneider 3x optical zoom lens,
aperture is between F2.8 and F4.8, although these performance
indicators are not outstanding, the professional lens relatively is
helpful for the image quality.

Fig. 1. An example consisting of a Chinese review, which is tagged with all the appearing product aspects with different colors

Formally, we describe each aspect a as a tuple $< set\_R, set\_IR >$ as follows, where set_R is a set that stores items relevant to a and set_IR is a set that stores items irrelevant to a.

$$a : set\_R[r_1, r_2, ..., r_i, ..., r_n]set\_IR[ir_1, ir_2, ..., ir_j, ..., ir_m]$$

Here, for aspect a, there are two important evidence sets, that is, n relevant aspects and m irrelevant aspects to generate the final aspect clustering.

- **relevant aspect** r_i: aspect a and r_i is relevant, if a and r_i are appearing in the same sentence and contain inclusion relations, e.g., a is the suffix of r_i, and vice versa.
- **irrelevant aspect** ir_j: aspect a and ir_j is irrelevant, if a and ir_j are appearing in the same sentence and do not contain inclusion relation with each other.

As a result, "镜头" in Figure 1 can be expressed as:

镜头: set_R[光变镜头]set_IR[光圈, 成像效果]
(lens: set_R[optical zoom lens]set_IR[aperture, image quality] in English).

Here, "光变镜头" is its relevant aspect, "光圈" and "成像效果" are its irrelevant aspects. Since "镜头" can appear in lots of review sentences, we can accordingly acquire lots of relevant aspect sets and irrelevant aspect sets from a domain-specific corpus. Then a final set_R andset_IR with more aspect elements can be further built.

For example, for the aspect "镜头", 71 relevant aspects and 149 irrelevant aspects can be found from 138 reviews. Based on these background knowledge, we can design new hierarchical clustering algorithms to classify the domain aspects into different groups.

3 Hierarchical Clustering Based on Two Aspect Relations

Since aspect clustering is a typical clustering problem, we can use many kinds of clustering algorithms. In this paper, we take hierarchical clustering algorithm as a case of study. During the process, similarity computation between aspects is the main part. Traditional similarity measures are using the thesaurus dictionaries or just computing the similarity between two aspect literally. However, they are far from sufficient due to a few reasons. First, many aspects are domain words or phrases, which are not included in the traditional thesaurus dictionaries. For example, the aspect "光变镜头" ("optical zoom lens" in English) is not appearing in any dictionaries. Secondly, many aspects are not synonyms in a dictionary, but indicating the same aspect under the given domain.

To alleviate these problems, Section 2 introduces the background knowledge for each aspect, including the relevant aspect sets and the irrelevant aspect sets. That is to say, we can use more knowledge to compute the similarity between two aspects besides their similarity literally.

Accordingly, the similarity computation between two aspects a_i and a_j composes three parts.

- Literal Similarity (LS): Similarity between a_i and a_j literally, which is recorded as $s_1(a_i, a_j)$. In this part, two factors are considered. One is to explore whether these two aspects are synonyms according to a dictionary. The other one is to compute the similarity between a_i and a_j literally. That is to say, we treat each character as an element, and then an aspect can be considered as a vector with characters. Many similarity methods can be used. In this paper we just try the Cosine similarity measurement. Based on these, we conclude this kind of similarity as follows:

$$s_1(a_i, a_j) = \begin{cases} 1 & \text{if } a_i \text{ and } a_j \text{ are synonyms,} \\ \cos(a_i, a_j) & \text{if } a_i \text{ and } a_j \text{ are not synonyms.} \end{cases} \quad (1)$$

- Relevant Set Similarity (RSS): Similarity between the relevant aspect sets of a_i and a_j, which is recorded as $s_2(a_i, a_j)$. This idea is based on such a hypothesis: the relevant aspect sets of two similar aspects that show the background knowledge are similar. Since the relevant background knowledge for each aspect can be considered as a vector. Then this kind of similarity can be converted to compute the similarity between two vectors. The computation procedure is shown as follows.

$$s_2(a_i, a_j) = sim(rel\_vector_i, rel\_vector_j) = \frac{rel\_vector_i \cdot rel\_vector_j}{\parallel rel\_vector_i \parallel \parallel rel\_vector_j \parallel} \quad (2)$$

- IRrelevant Set Similarity (IRSS): Similarity between the irrelevant aspect sets of a_i and a_j, which is recorded as $s_3(a_i, a_j)$. This similarity is computed based on such a hypothesis: if a_i is similar to a_j, it cannot appear in the irrelevant aspect set of a_j. We describe the similarity between a_i and a_j as follows:

$$s_3(a_i, a_j) = \begin{cases} 1 & \text{if } a_i \text{ appears in the irrelevant aspect set of } a_j, \\ 1 & \text{if } a_j \text{ appears in the irrelevant aspect set of } a_i, \\ 0 & \text{else.} \end{cases} \quad (3)$$

More formally, the final similarity between aspects a_i and a_j can be concluded as follows:

$$S_a(a_i, a_j) = \alpha * s_1(a_i, a_j) + \beta * s_2(a_i, a_j) - \gamma * s_3(a_i, a_j), \quad (4)$$

where similarity s_2 reflects the relevant aspect phenomenon and s_3 reflects the irrelevant aspect phenomenon respectively.

Based on this similarity, the hierarchical clustering algorithm is described in Figure 2 in detail.

Hierarchical Clustering Algorithm based on New Similarities

Input: Set of aspects *A*, $A = \{a_1, a_2, ..., a_n\}$,
each aspect is described with *R* and *IR*

Output: Aspect clusters *AC*

1. Suppose each aspect as a cluster, noted as $c_1,...,c_i,..., c_n$
2. Compute the similarity between each pair of clusters
   If the similarity between c_i and c_j is maximum, and greater than Θ:
   Merge c_i and c_j into a new cluster
3. Repeat 2 until the amount of the clusters does not change
4. The final clusters are *AC*

Fig. 2. Hierarchical Clustering Algorithm based on New Similarities

Here, in Step 2, the similarity between two clusters $c_i = \{a_1^i, ..., a_p^i, ..., a_n^i\}$ and $c_j = \{a_1^j, ..., a_q^j, ..., a_m^j\}$ is computed as follows.

$$S_c(c_i, c_j) = \frac{\sum_{p=1}^{n} \sum_{q=1}^{m} S_a(a_p^i, a_q^j)}{n \times m} \quad (5)$$

4 Experiments

4.1 Experimental Setup

Corpus. We conducted the experiments on a Chinese corpus of digital camera domain, which came from the corpora of the Chinese Opinion Analysis Evaluation (COAE). Table 1 describes the corpus in detail.

From 138 reviews, 4,039 aspects are manually found and annotated before reduplication removing, and 1,189 aspects are left after reduplication removing. Besides, each aspect averagely appears about 3.4 times. Therefore, for each aspect, we can collect its two effective aspect relation sets from many sources, because this aspect may appear multiple times in the corpus.

Table 1. Corpus statistics of Digital camera domain

Statistics	
# reviews	138
# aspects (before reduplication removing)	4,039
# aspects (after reduplication removing)	1,189
# single aspects	867
# multiple aspects	322
average # per aspect	4,039 ÷ 1,189 ≈ 3.4

Evaluation. We follow the evaluation metrics of Zhai et al. [21] to evaluate the clusters in this study. The evaluation metrics include two parts: *Entropy* and *Purity*. Given a data set DS, its gold partition is $G = g_1, ..., g_j, ..., g_k$, where k is the given number of clusters. Suppose our method can group DS into k disjoint subsets, that is, $DS = DS_1, ..., DS_i, ..., DS_k$, *Entropy* and *Purity* can be defined as follows.

Entropy: For each resulting cluster DS_i, we can measure its entropy using Equation (6), where $P_i(g_j)$ is the proportion of g_j data points in DS_i. The total entropy of the whole clustering (which considers all clusters) is calculated by Equation (7).

$$entropy(DS_i) = -\sum_{j=1}^{k} P_i(g_j) \log_2 P_i(g_j) \tag{6}$$

$$entropy_{total} = \sum_{i=1}^{k} \frac{|DS_i|}{|DS|} entropy(DS_i) \tag{7}$$

Purity: Purity measures the extent that a cluster contains only data from one gold-partition. The cluster purity is computed with Equation (8). The total purity of the whole clustering (all clusters) is computed with Equation (9).

$$purity(DS_i) = \max_j P_i(g_j) \tag{8}$$

$$purity_{total} = \sum_{i=1}^{k} \frac{|DS_i|}{|DS|} purity(DS_i) \tag{9}$$

Comparative Systems. Similarity computation between aspects is the main part during the clustering procedure. According to the three similarity computation measures between aspects, we designed four comparative systems to show the performance of each similarity measure when clustering.

- Literal Similarity (LS): We compute the similarity between two aspects a_i and a_j literally.
- Relevant Set Similarity (RSS) + LS: We compute the similarity between two aspects a_i and a_j using their relevant aspect sets, on the foundation of the literal similarity.
- IRrelevant Set Similarity (IRSS) + LS: We compute the similarity between two aspects a_i and a_j using their irrelevant aspect sets, on the foundation of the literal similarity.
- RSS + IRSS +LS: We combine the three kinds of similarities between two aspects a_i and a_j.

4.2 Results

Table 2 shows the experimental results of the four comparative systems on product aspect clustering task. Here, **LS** (Literal Similarity) is the baseline system, which is computed without any background knowledge. All the other three systems are based on the baseline system, and computed with different kinds of background knowledge.

Table 2. Comparative results on product aspect clustering

Method	Entropy	Purity
LS (Baseline)	1.53	0.94
LS + RSS	1.39	0.95
LS + IRSS	1.40	0.95
LS + RSS + IRSS	**1.37**	**0.96**

Since we can acquire a relevant aspect set and an irrelevant aspect set to describe each aspect, two kinds of background knowledge can be expanded accordingly.

Compared with the baseline system **LS**, the system **LS+RSS** that adds the relevant aspect set as the new background knowledge can yield better results, with the *Entropy* of 1.39 and the *Purity* of 0.95. This can illustrate that the relevant aspect set is effective in aspect clustering. Specifically, for an aspect a_i, besides the knowledge of a_i's literal meaning, its relevant aspect set expanded from multiple sentence contexts is another good dimension to measure the similarity between two aspects.

Moreover, the system **LS+IRSS** that adds the irrelevant aspect set as the new background knowledge can also yield better results, with the *Entropy* of 1.40 and the *Purity* of 0.95, compared with **LS**. This proves that the irrelevant aspect set can also be treated as another important evidence for aspect clustering. Obviously, if the aspect a_i appears in the irrelevant aspect set of the aspect a_j, a_i and a_j cannot be grouped together. This background knowledge can naturally avoid a part of the situation that a_i and a_j are literally similar, but in fact they do not belong to a same group.

Based on the above, the dimension of relevant aspect similarity (**RSS**) can be considered as a supplement of the literal similarity (**LS**), and the dimension of irrelevant aspect similarity (**IRSS**) can be considered as a filter to reduce some wrong cases. Therefore, the two aspect relations **RSS** and **IRSS** are complementary to each other, we combine them into a new system **LS+RSS+IRSS** based on the baseline **LS**. Table 2 shows that **LS+RSS+IRSS** performs best among all the comparative systems, with the *Entropy* of 1.37 and the *Purity* of 0.96.

5 Conclusion and Future Work

Aspect extraction and aspect clustering are both critical for the applications of sentiment analysis and opinion mining. However, the research on the aspect clustering task is far from enough. In this paper, we propose an easy and effective unsupervised method based on two effective aspect relations, namely, relevant aspect relation and irrelevant aspect relation. These two kinds of relations can expand the background knowledge of each aspect, and improve the performance of the similarity computation between two aspects. Experimental results on camera domain show that our method achieves better performance than the baseline without using the aspect relations, which proves that the two proposed relations are useful. As the future work, in order to capture more background knowledge for each aspect, we will expand them from the Web.

Acknowledgments. We thank the anonymous reviewers for their helpful comments. This work was supported by National Natural Science Foundation of China (NSFC) via grant 61300113, 61133012 and 61273321, and the Ministry of Education Research of Social Sciences Youth funded projects via grant 12YJCZH304.

References

1. Bloom, K., Garg, N., Argamon, S.: Extracting appraisal expressions. In: HLT-NAACL 2007, pp. 308–315 (2007)
2. Branavan, S., Chen, H., Eisenstein, J., Barzilay, R.: Learning document-level semantic properties from free-text annotations. In: Proceedings of ACL 2008: HLT, pp. 263–271 (2008)
3. Hu, M., Liu, B.: Mining and summarizing customer reviews. In: Proceedings of KDD 2004, pp. 168–177 (2004)

4. Jakob, N., Gurevych, I.: Extracting opinion targets in a single- and cross-domain setting with conditional random fields. In: Proceedings of the 2010 Conference on Empirical Methods in Natural Language Processing, EMNLP 2010, pp. 1035–1045. Association for Computational Linguistics, Stroudsburg (2010)
5. Li, S., Wang, R., Zhou, G.: Opinion target extraction using a shallow semantic parsing framework. In: AAAI, pp. 1671–1677 (2012)
6. Liu, B.: Sentiment Analysis and Opinion Mining. Synthesis Lectures on Human Language Technologies. Morgan & Claypool Publishers (2012)
7. Liu, B., Hu, M., Cheng, J.: Opinion observer: analyzing and comparing opinions on the web. In: Proceedings of WWW 2005, pp. 342–351 (2005)
8. Liu, K., Xu, L., Zhao, J.: Opinion target extraction using word-based translation model. In: Proceedings of the 2012 Joint Conference on Empirical Methods in Natural Language Processing and Computational Natural Language Learning, EMNLP-CoNLL 2012, pp. 1346–1356. Association for Computational Linguistics, Stroudsburg (2012)
9. Liu, K., Xu, L., Zhao, J.: Syntactic patterns versus word alignment: Extracting opinion targets from online reviews. In: Proceedings of the 51st Annual Meeting of the Association for Computational Linguistics (vol. 1: Long Papers), pp. 1754–1763. Association for Computational Linguistics, Sofia (2013)
10. Mukherjee, A., Liu, B.: Aspect extraction through semi-supervised modeling. In: Proceedings of the 50th Annual Meeting of the Association for Computational Linguistics (vol. 1: Long Papers), pp. 339–348. Association for Computational Linguistics, Jeju Island (2012)
11. Mukherjee, A., Liu, B.: Modeling review comments. In: Proceedings of the 50th Annual Meeting of the Association for Computational Linguistics (vol. 1: Long Papers), pp. 320–329. Association for Computational Linguistics, Jeju Island (2012), http://www.aclweb.org/anthology/P12-1034
12. Pang, B., Lee, L.: Opinion mining and sentiment analysis. Found. Trends Inf. Retr. 2(1-2), 1–135 (2008)
13. Qiu, G., Liu, B., Bu, J., Chen, C.: Opinion word expansion and target extraction through double propagation. Computational Linguistics 37(1), 9–27 (2011)
14. Reschke, K., Vogel, A., Jurafsky, D.: Generating recommendation dialogs by extracting information from user reviews. In: Proceedings of the 51st Annual Meeting of the Association for Computational Linguistics (vol. 2: Short Papers), pp. 499–504. Association for Computational Linguistics, Sofia (2013), http://www.aclweb.org/anthology/P13-2089
15. Sauper, C., Haghighi, A., Barzilay, R.: Content models with attitude. In: Proceedings of the 49th Annual Meeting of the Association for Computational Linguistics: Human Language Technologies, HLT 2011, vol. 1, pp. 350–358. Association for Computational Linguistics, Stroudsburg (2011)
16. Sauper, C., Haghighi, A., Barzilay, R.: Content models with attitude. In: Proceedings of the 49th Annual Meeting of the Association for Computational Linguistics: Human Language Technologies, pp. 350–358. Association for Computational Linguistics, Portland (2011), http://www.aclweb.org/anthology/P11-1036
17. Titov, I., McDonald, R.: A joint model of text and aspect ratings for sentiment summarization. In: Proceedings of ACL 2008: HLT, pp. 308–316. Association for Computational Linguistics, Columbus (2008)
18. Wei, W., Gulla, J.A.: Sentiment learning on product reviews via sentiment ontology tree. In: ACL, pp. 404–413 (2010)

19. Woodsend, K., Lapata, M.: Multiple aspect summarization using integer linear programming. In: Proceedings of the 2012 Joint Conference on Empirical Methods in Natural Language Processing and Computational Natural Language Learning, pp. 233–243. Association for Computational Linguistics, Jeju Island (2012), http://www.aclweb.org/anthology/D12-1022
20. Yu, J., Zha, Z.J., Wang, M., Chua, T.S.: Aspect ranking: Identifying important product aspects from online consumer reviews. In: Proceedings of the 49th Annual Meeting of the Association for Computational Linguistics: Human Language Technologies, HLT 2011, vol. 1, pp. 1496–1505. Association for Computational Linguistics, Stroudsburg (2011)
21. Zhai, Z., Liu, B., Xu, H., Jia, P.: Clustering product features for opinion mining. In: Proceedings of WSDM, pp. 347–354 (2011)
22. Zhao, Y., Qin, B., Hu, S., Liu, T.: Generalizing syntactic structures for product attribute candidate extraction. In: Human Language Technologies: The 2010 Annual Conference of the North American Chapter of the Association for Computational Linguistics, pp. 377–380. Association for Computational Linguistics, Los Angeles (2010)
23. Zhao, Y., Qin, B., Liu, T.: Sentiment analysis. Journal of Software 21(8), 1834–1848 (2010)

Text Classification with Document Embeddings

Chaochao Huang, Xipeng Qiu, and Xuanjing Huang

[1] Shanghai Key Laboratory of Intelligent Information Processing
[2] School of Computer Science, Fudan University, Shanghai, China
{chaochaohuang12,xpqiu,xjhuang}@fudan.edu.cn

Abstract. Distributed representations have gained a lot of interests in natural language processing community. In this paper, we propose a method to learn document embedding with neural network architecture for text classification task. In our architecture, each document can be represented as a fine-grained representation of different meanings so that the classification can be done more accurately. The results of our experiments show that our method achieve better performances on two popular datasets.

1 Introduction

Text classification is a crucial and well-proven method for organizing the collection of large scale documents, which has been widely used in a lot of tasks in natural language processing or information retrieval, for instance, spam filtering[1, 3, 5],email routing[11] and sentiment analysis[21].

Currently, most of the state-of-the-art text classification methods are based on machine learning algorithms[25], such as decision tree[7, 22], Naive Bayes[15], support vector machine (SVM)[10], and so on.

Since the input of machine learning algorithms must be a fixed-length feature vector, the documents are often represented with vector space model (VSM) [24] (also called bag-of-words(BOW)). Each dimension corresponds to one word, and the dimensionality of the vector is the size of the vocabulary. However, this kind of representation has two disadvantages: (1) the represented vector is often high dimensional and very sparse, which brings a challenge for traditional machine learning algorithm; (2) it ignores the semantics of the words.

Although lots of feature selection methods [27] are proposed, these features are still sparse and not optimum. A great correlation and redundant information exist among these features.

Recently, word embeddings are becoming more and more popular and have shown excellent performance in various natural language processing tasks [17, 2, 6, 19, 9]. Each word is represented by a dense vector and words with similar meanings will be close to each other in the vector space. Distributed representations, which are originally designed for words[23], have also been used to represent phrases sentences[18, 16].

Although word embeddings have been applied to text classification [14, 13], there are two problems when utilizing the word embeddings on text classification.

1. It is still not clear to combine the word embeddings to represent the documents. The documents often have words with various lengths, we cannot use the word

M. Sun et al. (Eds.): CCL and NLP-NABD 2014, LNAI 8801, pp. 131–140, 2014.

embeddings directly to train a classifier. A simple approach is using a weighted average of all the words in the document.
2. Traditional word embeddings are learned by probabilistic language model in a separate step, which are not optimal for text classification task.

In this paper, we propose a method to learn word embeddings directly in text classification task. A document is also represented by a vector, called *document embedding*. Document embeddings can be calculated by the vector representations of its containing words. Our method can handle all words contained in a document and need not reduce the dimensionality of input.

In our method, each document is represented as the combination of the word embeddings of its containing words. Since the word embedding can represent different meanings of each word, the document embedding can also represent different meanings of each document and documents close to each other in the vector space may be of the same topic. The experimental results also proves this hypothesis.

The remaining parts of the paper is arranged as follows: Section 2 surveys related works on text classification. Section 3 describes our architecture and learning algorithms. The experiments will be detailed described in section 4 and finally there will be a conclusion.

2 Related Works

Recently, deep neural networks are so popular and are widely used in lots of domains for the purpose of classification, including text classification. For instance, Restricted Boltzman Machines(RBMs) have been utilized to do the document and image classification[12].

Liu [14] used deep belief network (DBN) to obtain the high level abstraction of input data to model the semantic correlation among words of documents for text classification. However, since he used Restricted Boltzmann Machines (RBM) [8] to obtain the high level abstraction of input data, the dimensionality of the input data need be reduced in advance. Thus, a lot of information may be lost.

Le and Mikolov [13] proposed *Paragraph Vector*, an unsupervised framework that learns continuous distributed vector representations for pieces of texts. The texts can be of variable-length, ranging from sentences to documents. Although paragraph vector can be applied to variable-length pieces of document, it is learned separately before they are used in text classification.

Socher et al. [26] used a more sophisticated approach to combine the word vectors in an order given by a parse tree of a sentence, using matrix-vector operations. However, it has been shown to work for only sentences because it relies on parsing.

3 Neural Network Architecture for Text Classification

According to our hypothesis, a document can be represented as the accumulation of all words it contains. Each word has an exact and unique meaning, which is represented by the different decimals in each element of the word embedding. Similarly, the document's meaning is also represented by each element of its *document embedding*.

3.1 Document Embeddings

The architecture we propose is described in figure 1.

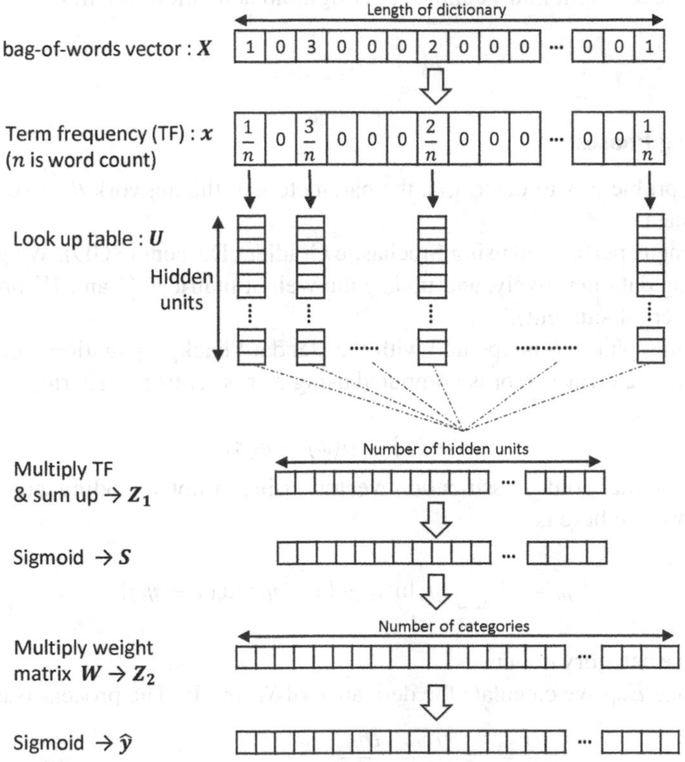

Fig. 1. Neural Network Architecture

A document is a bag-of-words representation $X = \{X_1, X_2, ..., X_n\}$, in which X_i means the ith word shows up X_i times in the document. We first transform X into x by:

$$x_i = X_i / \sum_{X_i \in X} X_i \tag{1}$$

so that the following calculations will not be affected by the length of the document.

U is a look up table of the dictionary. Each column in U is a word embedding. As the description above, a document S is calculated as:

$$Z_1 = Ux \tag{2}$$

$$S = f(Z_1) \tag{3}$$

where Z_1 is a document embedding.

Supposing that $\hat{y}$ is the output from the network, it is computed as follows:

$$Z_2 = WS \tag{4}$$
$$\hat{y} = f(Z_2) \tag{5}$$

where W is the a weight matrix and $f(z)$ is sigmoid activation function:

$$f(z) = \frac{1}{1+e^{-z}} \tag{6}$$

3.2 Training Phases

The training problem is to determine the parameters of the network $\theta = (U, W)$ from the training data.

The training is performed using Stochastic Gradient Descent (SGD). We go through all the training data iteratively, and update the weight matrices U and W online (after processing every document).
At each training phase, θ is updated with the standard backpropagation algorithm and the gradient of the error vector is computed using a cross entropy criterion:

$$error(x) = y(x) - \hat{y}(x) \tag{7}$$

Where $y(x)$ is the gold classification vector, using n-hot encoding and the cross entropy[20] we use here is:

$$E_m = -\sum_{i=1}^{m} [y_i \ln \hat{y}_i + (1 - y_i) \ln (1 - \hat{y}_i)] \tag{8}$$

where m is the category count.

To minimize E_m, we calculate the derivative of W and U. The process is as follows:

$$\begin{aligned}\frac{\partial E_m}{\partial Z_{2j}} &= \frac{\partial E_m}{\partial \hat{y}_j}\frac{\partial \hat{y}_i}{\partial Z_{2j}} \\ &= (-\frac{y_j}{\hat{y}_j} + \frac{1-y_j}{1-\hat{y}_j})\hat{y}_j(1-\hat{y}_j) \\ &= \hat{y}_j - y_j\end{aligned} \tag{9}$$

We assume

$$e_{0j} = \frac{\partial E_m}{\partial Z_{2j}} \tag{10}$$

$$e_{1j} = \frac{\partial E_m}{\partial Z_{1j}} \tag{11}$$

Now that through back propagation we get

$$\begin{aligned}\frac{\partial E_m}{\partial Z_{1i}} &= \sum_{k=1}^{m} \frac{\partial E_m}{\partial Z_{2k}}\frac{\partial Z_{2k}}{\partial S_i}\frac{\partial S_i}{\partial Z_{1i}} \\ &= \sum_{k=1}^{m} e_{0k} W_{ki} S_i (1 - S_i)\end{aligned} \tag{12}$$

Then using chain derivation rule we get

$$\begin{aligned}\frac{\partial E_m}{\partial W_{ij}} &= e_{0i}\frac{\partial Z_{2i}}{\partial W_{ij}} \\ &= (\hat{y}_i - y_i)S_j\end{aligned} \tag{13}$$

$$\begin{aligned}\frac{\partial E_m}{\partial U_{ij}} &= e_{1i}\frac{\partial Z_{1i}}{\partial U_{ij}} \\ &= [\sum_{k=1}^{m} e_{0k}W_{ki}S_i(1-S_i)]x_j \\ &= [\sum_{k=1}^{m}(\hat{y}_k - y_k)W_{ki}S_i(1-S_i)]x_j\end{aligned} \tag{14}$$

Now we can easily find that the weight matrix W between the document vector $d(x)$ and the output layer $y^*(x)$ can be updated as:

$$W^* = W + \alpha\frac{\partial E_m}{\partial W} \tag{15}$$

and the dictionary look up table matrix U can be updated following:

$$U^* = U + \alpha\frac{\partial E_m}{\partial U} \tag{16}$$

where α is the learning rate.

4 Experiments

We evaluate the performance our method by comparing the BOW representation.

4.1 Datasets

We setup our experiments on two datasets: LSHTC and Sogou datasets.

LSHTC This dataset is from the 4th Large Scale Hierarchical Text Classification (LSHTC) Challenge[1]. The challenge is based on a large dataset created from Wikipedia and the document set is multi-class, multi-label and hierarchical though we do not utilize any hierarchical information. Documents here is high dimensional(roughly 1,620,000) and very sparse on each category. The format of each document is like:

12370,306783 1:1 45:3 1982:1 ... 32600:1

[1] http://www.kaggle.com/c/lshtc

which means the document belongs to category 12370 and 30678 at the same time, and the remaining part is the sparse representation in bag-of-words.

In consideration of time efficiency, we choose 100 categories from the dataset that most frequently appear. We only choose the documents which only contain one category in the top 100 categories.

For each category, we choose less than 150 samples for training and less than 10 samples for testing. Finally we get 13113 training documents and 800 testing documents, every document is single-labeled. The categories we choose are shown in table 1.

Table 1. LSHTC Chosen Categories

24177, 285613, 98808, 264962, 167593, 242532, 52954, 300558, 444502, 78249, 237290, 220514, 10721, 337728, 174545, 73518, 24016, 327590, 154064, 374771, 366417, 87241, 73092, 115838, 334220, 169902, 59758, 347803, 364106, 178462, 287120, 14843, 260304, 73462, 23611, 322170, 174425, 167844, 29462, 158599, 299629, 34161, 390974, 228232, 150636, 341276, 36224, 289559, 418360, 323972, 352578, 284433, 383600, 300073, 231746, 60639, 251484, 2830, 183203, 234578, 283823, 161537, 286264, 304661, 93718, 348488, 139391, 397350, 244711, 186125, 419276, 1508, 398319, 428719, 290537, 403132, 395447, 351111, 324660, 13252, 131804, 430081, 24052, 244616, 86836, 393137, 374859, 111772, 206933, 109127, 96443, 228238, 269785, 2903, 272741, 213350, 225356, 174595, 414726, 429208

Sogou Dataset This dataset[2] is all of website news in Chinese and the corpus mainly come from Sohu.com. All the documents' categories are manually labeled and the category count is 10.

Also for time efficiency, we use the mini version of the dataset, which contains 17910 documents on 9 categories. The detail on each category is shown in table 2 We firstly do word segmentation on the whole set and get about 270,000 words in our dictionary. Then we transfer each document into bag-of-words representation just like the above dataset. Finally we got 17,014 training vectors and 896 testing vectors, all are single-labeled.

The overall description of datasets is in table 3.

4.2 Experimental Settings

Firstly, we initialize U and W (described in section 3) with random decimals between -1 and 1. We found that the larger the hidden units count is, the higher the classification accuracy will be, however the memory and time cost will also grow up. So hidden units count is set to 30, balancing the memory cost and the outcome accuracy. Learning rate is dynamic and initialized to 1.0. When $error(x)$ grows up in 10 consecutive training documents, learning rate will decrease by 0.01, vice versa.

[2] http://www.sogou.com/labs/dl/c.html

Table 2. Summary of Sogou Mini Set

Category Number	Category	Train	Test
C000008	Finance	1890	100
C000014	Sports	1891	99
C000024	Military	1890	100
C000023	Culture	1891	99
C000022	Recruitment	1890	100
C000020	Education	1891	99
C000016	Travel	1890	100
C000013	Health	1891	99
C000010	Vehicle	1890	100

Table 3. Overall Description of Datasets

Dataset	Category Count	Train Count	Test Count	Vocabulary Size
LSHTC	100	13113	800	161899
Sogou Mini	9	17014	896	270000

Just as we demonstrate in section 3, the training is performed using Stochastic Gradient Descent (SGD). We go through all the training data iteratively, and update the weight matrices U and W online (after processing every document) until convergence appears. Here we define convergence as $error(x)$ is smaller than 10^{-5} in 10 consecutive training documents.

We evaluate our model in two ways. First, we use the output $\hat{y}$ of our neural network directly as the classification vector and use the index of the largest element as the category number. Second, we replace each point in bag-of-words vector with the corresponding column in U(which is in fact a kind of word embedding), multiplying the TF of the word. Then we use a linear SVM classifier to train and test the new document vectors.

During all the process, we use AMD GPU and its Aparapi[3] to do parallel computing and accelerate the whole process.

4.3 Results

To compare the performance of our representations with BOW, we use the popular LIBSVM[4] as the final classifier. Table 4 and 5 show the results. *NN-15* represents that the dimensionality of document embedding is 15, while *NN-30* represents that the dimensionality of document embedding is 30.

Since our NN architecture can output the class label directly, we also give the results without combining SVM. The evaluations without SVM have a similar accuracy with BOW+SVM when a document is represented by 30 dimensional vector. With combining SVM, our method outperforms BOW+SVM a lot on both the datasets.

[3] `http://developer.amd.com/tools-and-sdks/opencl-zone/opencl-libraries/aparapi/`

Table 4. Comparative results on LSHTC dataset

Method	Micro-P	Macro-P	Macro-R	Macro-F
BOW + SVM	64.50	61.46	64.50	62.95
NN-15	52.12	52.13	47.12	49.50
NN-15 + SVM	62.12	62.12	61.71	61.91
NN-30	53.00	50.39	53.00	51.66
NN-30 + SVM	68.00	62.76	68.00	65.28

Table 5. Comparative results on Sogou dataset

Method	Micro-P	Macro-P	Macro-R	Macro-F
BOW + SVM	91.07	91.17	91.07	91.12
NN-15	90.18	90.17	90.42	90.29
NN-15 + SVM	90.85	90.84	90.94	90.89
NN-30	91.07	91.15	91.06	91.11
NN-30 + SVM	91.52	91.58	91.51	91.54

From the results, we can see that our architecture achieve better performances on both the datasets. This is mainly because we represent each document in a more detailed way comparing with pure bag-of-words representations. And the detailed representations are highly related to the topic of documents. Thus making the classification has a higher accuracy.

We can also find that the experimental results over the two test datasets are quite different. Performance on Sogou is better than that on LSHTC, on all the five methods. That is perhaps due to different data density of the two datasets. We believe that our architecture is more powerful on dense dataset, which has more average documents on each category. Therefore, our method which can generate document embedding to represent a document and do the document classification task is efficient and useful.

5 Related Works

Liu [14] used deep belief network (DBN) for text classification. However, since he used Restricted Boltzmann Machines (RBM) [8] to obtain the high level abstraction of input data, the dimensionality of the input data needs to be reduced in advance. Thus a lot of information may be lost.

Le and Mikolov [13] proposed *Paragraph Vector*, an unsupervised framework that learns continuous distributed vector representations for pieces of texts. The texts can be of variable-length, ranging from sentences to documents. Although paragraph vector can be applied to variable-length pieces of document, it is learned separately before they are used in text classification.

Socher et al. [26] used a more sophisticated approach to combine the word vectors in an order given by a parse tree of a sentence, using matrix-vector operations. However, it has been shown to work for only sentences because it relies on parsing.

6 Conclusion

In this paper, we propose a neural network architecture for text classification. In our architecture, each document is represented by a low dimensional embedding that is similar to word embedding. Experiments show that our embeddings have a higher classification accuracy than BOW vectors.

In future, we will use our method to do the multi-label text classification task. Besides, we will also investigate whether it can increase the performance by increasing the network layers.

Acknowledgments. We would like to thank the anonymous reviewers for their valuable comments. This work was funded by NSFC (No.61003091) and Science and Technology Commission of Shanghai Municipality (14ZR1403200).

References

[1] Androutsopoulos, I., Koutsias, J., Chandrinos, K.V., Paliouras, G., Spyropoulos, C.D.: An evaluation of naive bayesian anti-spam filtering. arXiv preprint cs/0006013 (2000)

[2] Bengio, Y., Schwenk, H., Senécal, J.S., Morin, F., Gauvain, J.L.: Neural probabilistic language models. In: Holmes, D.E., Jain, L.C. (eds.) Innovations in Machine Learning. STUDFUZZ, vol. 194, pp. 137–186. Springer, Heidelberg (2006)

[3] Carvalho, V.R., Cohen, W.W.: On the collective classification of email speech acts. In: Proceedings of the 28th Annual International ACM SIGIR Conference on Research and Development in Information Retrieval, pp. 345–352. ACM (2005)

[4] Chang, C.C., Lin, C.J.: Libsvm: a library for support vector machines. ACM Transactions on Intelligent Systems and Technology (TIST) 2(3), 27 (2011)

[5] Cohen, W.W.: Learning rules that classify e-mail. In: AAAI Spring Symposium on Machine Learning in Information Access, California, vol. 18, p. 25 (1996)

[6] Collobert, R., Weston, J., Bottou, L., Karlen, M., Kavukcuoglu, K., Kuksa, P.: Natural language processing (almost) from scratch. The Journal of Machine Learning Research 12, 2493–2537 (2011)

[7] Dumais, S., Platt, J., Heckerman, D., Sahami, M.: Inductive learning algorithms and representations for text categorization. In: Proceedings of the Seventh International Conference on Information and Knowledge Management, pp. 148–155. ACM (1998)

[8] Hinton, G.E., Salakhutdinov, R.R.: Reducing the dimensionality of data with neural networks. Science 313(5786), 504–507 (2006)

[9] Huang, E.H., Socher, R., Manning, C.D., Ng, A.Y.: Improving word representations via global context and multiple word prototypes. In: Proceedings of the 50th Annual Meeting of the Association for Computational Linguistics: Long Papers-vol. 1, pp. 873–882. Association for Computational Linguistics (2012)

[10] Joachims, T.: Text categorization with support vector machines: Learning with many relevant features. Springer (1998)

[11] Khosravi, H., Wilks, Y.: Routing email automatically by purpose not topic. Natural Language Engineering 5(3), 237–250 (1999)

[12] Larochelle, H., Bengio, Y.: Classification using discriminative restricted boltzmann machines. In: Proceedings of the 25th International Conference on Machine Learning, pp. 536–543. ACM (2008)

[13] Le, Q.V., Mikolov, T.: Distributed representations of sentences and documents. arXiv preprint arXiv:1405.4053 (2014)
[14] Liu, T.: A novel text classification approach based on deep belief network. In: Wong, K.W., Mendis, B.S.U., Bouzerdoum, A. (eds.) ICONIP 2010, Part I. LNCS, vol. 6443, pp. 314–321. Springer, Heidelberg (2010)
[15] McCallum, A., Nigam, K., et al.: A comparison of event models for naive bayes text classification. In: AAAI 1998 Workshop on Learning for Text Categorization, vol. 752, pp. 41–48. Citeseer (1998)
[16] Mikolov, T., Sutskever, I., Chen, K., Corrado, G.S., Dean, J.: Distributed representations of words and phrases and their compositionality. In: Advances in Neural Information Processing Systems, pp. 3111–3119 (2013)
[17] Mikolov, T., Yih, W.T., Zweig, G.: Linguistic regularities in continuous space word representations. In: Proceedings of NAACL-HLT, pp. 746–751 (2013)
[18] Mitchell, J., Lapata, M.: Composition in distributional models of semantics. Cognitive Science 34(8), 1388–1429 (2010)
[19] Mnih, A., Hinton, G.E.: A scalable hierarchical distributed language model. In: NIPS, pp. 1081–1088 (2008)
[20] Nasr, G.E., Badr, E., Joun, C.: Cross entropy error function in neural networks: Forecasting gasoline demand. In: FLAIRS Conference, pp. 381–384 (2002)
[21] Pang, B., Lee, L.: Opinion mining and sentiment analysis. Foundations and Trends in Information Retrieval 2(1-2), 1–135 (2008)
[22] Quinlan, J.R.: Induction of decision trees. Machine Learning 1(1), 81–106 (1986)
[23] Rumelhart, D.E., Hinton, G.E., Williams, R.J.: Learning representations by back-propagating errors. MIT Press, Cambridge (1988)
[24] Salton, G., Wong, A., Yang, C.: A vector space model for automatic indexing. Communications of the ACM 18(11), 613–620 (1975)
[25] Sebastiani, F.: Machine learning in automated text categorization. ACM Computing Surveys 34(1), 1–47 (2002)
[26] Socher, R., Lin, C.C., Ng, A.Y., Manning, C.D.: Parsing Natural Scenes and Natural Language with Recursive Neural Networks. In: Proceedings of the 26th International Conference on Machine Learning, ICML (2011)
[27] Yang, Y., Pedersen, J.: A comparative study on feature selection in text categorization. In: Proc. of Int. Conf. on Mach. Learn. (ICML), vol. 97 (1997)

Reasoning Over Relations Based on Chinese Knowledge Bases

Guoliang Ji, Yinghua Zhang, Hongwei Hao, and Jun Zhao

Institute of Automation, Chinese Academy of Sciences
{jiguoliang2013,yinghua.zhang,hongwei.hao}@ia.ac.cn,
jzhao@nlpr.ia.ac.cn

Abstract. Knowledge bases are useful resource for many applications, but reasoning new relationships between new entities based on them is difficult because they often lack the knowledge of new relations and entities. In this paper, we introduce the novel Neural Tensor Network (NTN)[1] model to reason new facts based on Chinese knowledge bases. We represent entities as an average of their constituting word or character vectors, which share the statistical strength between entities, such as 荔枝巢蛾 and 荔枝异形小卷蛾. The NTN model uses a tensor network to replace a standard neural layer, which strengthen the interaction of two entity vectors in a simple and efficient way. In experiments, we compare the NTN and several other models, the results show that all models' performance can be improved when word vectors are pre-trained from an unsupervised large corpora and character vectors don't have this advantage. The NTN model outperforms others and reachs high classification accuracy 91.1% and 89.6% when using pre-trained word vectors and random character vectors, respectively. Therefore, when Chinese word segmentation is a difficult task, initialization with random character vectors is a feasible choice.

Keywords: knowledge bases, reason, Neural Tensor Network, word representations, character representations.

1 Introduction

With the advent of the era of big data, a lot of information stored in the form of structured data has been built in knowledge bases which are multi-relational graph data whose nodes represent entities and edges corresponds to relations [2]. Relations in knowledge bases are always be denote by triples in the form of (entity, relation, entity). Recently, knowledge bases are extremely useful resource for many nature natural language processing tasks such as coreference resolution, information retrieval, recommendation systems and social networks. However, the entities and relationships that exist in knowledge bases are always incompleteness for users due to various practical reasons. Hence, learning new facts based on the knowledge bases is a necessary way to improve them.

Much work(probability graph model and inductive logic programming and Markov Logic Network et al.) has focused on extending existing knowledge bases

M. Sun et al. (Eds.): CCL and NLP-NABD 2014, LNAI 8801, pp. 141–150, 2014.

using pattern or classifiers applied to large text corpora[1]. However, not all knowledge is recorded by text, especially common sense which is obvious to people. For example, given the fact (荔枝巢蛾 门 节肢动物门), a person can infer the new fact (荔枝异形小卷蛾 门 节肢动物门) without needing to find any textual evidence. Therefore, learning new relations(triples) based on knowledge bases has been increasingly popular. Nickle et al.(2011 and 2013)[3, 4] introduced a tensor factorization method for learning on multi-relation data. Mukherjee et al.(2013)[2] used a matrix tri-factorization approach to extracting new facts in knowledge bases. Recently, Socher et al.(2013)[1] applied a neural tensor network to reasoing common sense, which is the base of our work.

In this paper, we introduce the neural tensor networks (NTN)[1] to accomplish common sense reasoning with the facts that exist in Chinese knowledge bases. This network model can accurately predict the additional relationships among entities that are not exist in knowledge bases. We represent every entity as a vector. For sharing statistical strength among the entities that contain similar substrings, we represent each entity as the average of its word or character vectors whose initial value are pre-trained with a neural network language model based on an unsupervised large scale corpora or are sampled from a zero mean Gaussian distribution. Each relation corresponds to a group of parameters of neural tensor networks. The entities and relationships can interact well through the neural tensor networks.

The main contribution of this paper is to apply the NTN model to reason new facts based on Chinese bases. The paper is organized as follows. Section 2 and section 3 introduce some related work and the Neural Tensor Network model , repectively. Section 4 discuss how to use the NTN model to reason on Chinese knowledge bases. Section 5 reports parameters' setting and results of experiments. Section 6 we summarize our contribute and consider the further work directions.

2 Related Work

This work mainly involves two areas of NLP research: semantic vector spaces and deep learning.

Semantic Vector Spaces. Neural language models (Bengio et al.2003; Mnih and Hinon,2007; Collobert and Westion,2008; Schwenk and Gauvain,2002; Emami et al.,2003) have been shown to be very powerful at language modeling, a task where models are asked to accurately predict the next word given previously seen words[5]. By using distributed representations of words which model words' similarity, most of these models addresses the data sparseness problem that n-gram models encounter when large contexts are used. Collobert and Weston(2008) used a neural language model to compute scores $g(s)$ and $g(s^w)$ of the n-gram s and s^w, where s^w is s with the last word replaced by word w, and a ranking-loss training object to make g(s)to be larger than $g(s^w)$ by a margin of 1 for any other word w in the vocabulary. This model have showed increased performance and the word embedding produced by it have been used in many literatures. Huang and Socher(2013) added global information of documents to the neural language model of Collobert & Weston and produced multiple word prototypes. Our Chinese word and character vectors come from Huang and Socher's language model.

Deep Learning. The neural tensor network is related to several neural network models in deep learning literature. Ranzato and Hinton introduced a factored 3-way Restricted Boltzmann Machine which is also parameterized by a tensor[1]. D.Yu and L.Deng introduce a model with tensor layers for speech recognition[1]. Socher and Chen[1] introduced the neural tensor network for reasoning for knowledge bases completion, and they developed a recursive version of this model for sentiment analysis. Bowman[5] trained a recursive neural tensor networks model on a new corpus of constructed examples of logical reasoning in short sentences and the result is promising to capture logical reasoning. Nickle[3] introduced a tensor factorizaton method for multi-relational learning, where a knowledge base was regarded as a three dimensional tensor.

3 Neural Tensor Network Model

This section introduces the neural tensor network to reason relationships among entities by learning vector representations for them. As shown in Fig. 1(part I),each triple described as (e_1, R, e_2), where $e_i(i = 1, 2), R$ represent entities and relationship respectively, corresponds a tensor network whose inputs are $e_i(i = 1, 2)$. The model obtains a high confidence if they are in that relationship and a low one otherwise. The following are three sections: (i)model structure, (ii)training objective, (iii)classify relation triples.

3.1 Model Structure

In this model, we introduce the NTN model structure. First, we define a set of parameters indexed by R for each relation's scoring function and let e_1, e_2 be the vector representations of two entities. Then the Neural Tensor Network (NTN) computes the score of a given triple (e_1, R, e_2) through a bilinear tensor layer which relates two entity vectors across multiple dimensions.

$$score(e_1, R, e_2) = U_R^T f(e_1^T T_R^{[1:k]} e_2 + W_R \begin{bmatrix} e_1 \\ e_2 \end{bmatrix} + b_R) \qquad (1)$$

where $f = tanh$ or $f = sigmoid$ that often be used in neural network models, $T_R^{[1:k]} \in R^{d \times d \times k}$ is a tensor and the bilinear product $e_1^T T_R^{[1:k]} e_2$ results in a vector $h \in R^k$, where each entry is computed by one slice $i = 1, \ldots, k$ of the tensor: $h_i = e_1^T T_R^{[1:k]} e_2$ [1]. The parameters $U_R \in R^k$, $W_R \in R^{k \times 2d}$ and $b_R \in R^k$ are the form of standard neural network. The main advantage of this model is that it can relate the two inputs multiplicatively, which incorporates the interaction of the two inputs efficiently.

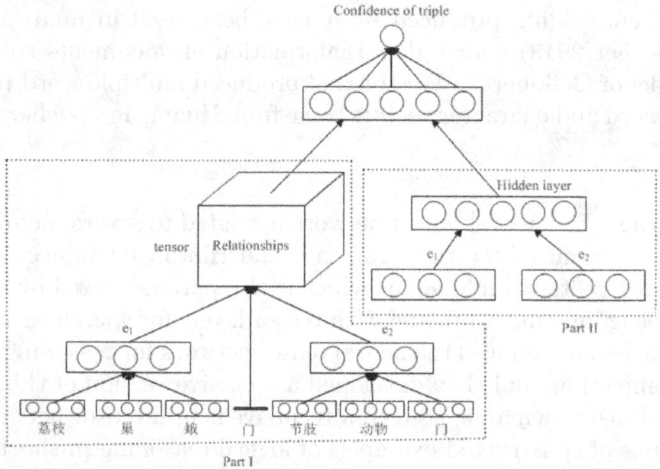

Fig. 1. Overview of the Neural Tensor Network model. Part(I) is a tensor network which enforce the interaction between two entities, part(II) is a standard neural network layer. We train the word vectors and predict whether a triple is true or not according to it's confidence.

3.2 Training Objective

In the training set, each triple denoted by $T^{(i)} = (e_1^i, R^{(i)}, e_2^i)$ should receive a higher confidence than a triple whose second entity is replaced with a random entity. Provided that there are N_R many different relations which are indexed by $R^{(i)}$ $(i = 1, \ldots, N_R)$. Each relation corresponds to a set of neural tensor net parameters. We call the triple with a random entity negative sample and represent it with $T_c^{(i)} = \left(e_1^{(i)}, R^{(i)}, e_c\right)$, ,where e_c was randomly sampled from the set of all entities. We denote the set of all relationships' NTN parameters by $\Omega = U, T, W, b, L$, where U, T, W, b are model parameters and L is word vectors. We minimize the following objective:

$$J = \sum_{i=1}^{N} \sum_{c=1}^{C} max\left(0, 1 - score\left(T^{(i)}\right) + score\left(T_c^{(i)}\right)\right) + \lambda \left\|\Omega\right\|_2^2 \qquad (2)$$

Where N is the total number of triples in the training set. We score the positive relation triple higher than its negative one up to a margin of 1[1]. In order to enhance the learning ability of the NTN model, for each positive triple we sample C random negative triples. We use the L_2 weight regularization for all neural tensor network parameters whose weighted hyper parameter is λ.

3.3 Classify Relation Triples

The goal is to predict the likely truth in the form of triples (e_1, R, e_2) according to their scores in the testing data. We should find a threshold t_R for every relation such that if $score(e_1, R, e_2) \geq t_R$, the triple is correct, otherwise it does not. Hence, we need to create a valid set to decide the thresholds and a testing set to evaluate the model.

4 Reasoning on Chinese Knowledge Bases

Before reasoning with Neural Tensor Network, we also need to do word segmentation for entities existing in Chinese knowledge bases. However, in our Chinese knowledge bases, entities are always phrases which are difficult to segment correctly. Therefore, we consider two kinds of Chinese word segmentation: word and character.

4.1 Word and Character Representations

We represent Chinese word and character as continuous vectors. We explore two settings. In the first setting we simply initialize each word(character) vector $x \in R^n$ by sampling it from a zero mean Gaussian distribution: $x \sim N(0, \sigma^2)$. In the second setting, we pre-train the word (character) vectors with an unsupervised neural language model(Huang and Socher,2013). Fig. 2 shows the model. It makes use of local and global context to pre-train the word(character) vectors. These word(character) vectors are then stacked into a word embedding matrix $L \in R^{|V| \times n}$, where V represents the size of vocabulary and n is the dimension of vectors. These vectors will be revised to capture certain semantic during learning process.

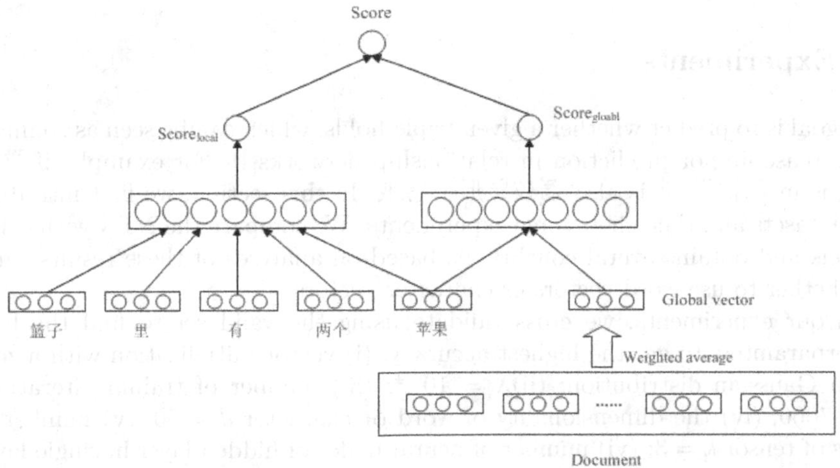

Fig. 2. An overview of the neural language model. The model makes use of local and global context to learn word representations based on large scale unsupervised corpora.

In both cases, each word(character) has an associated vocabulary index k into the embedding matrix which we use to retrieve the word's (character's) vector representation. Mathematically, if we want to get the *k-th* word's(character's) vector of the vocabulary, we only need to use a binary vector which is zero in all positions except at the *k-th* index,

$$x_i = b_k^T L \tag{3}$$

4.2 Entity Representation

Previous work[6–8] assigned a single vector representation to each entity of the knowledge base, which does not allow the sharing of statistical strength between the words describing each entity[1]. We represent each word(character) as a d-dimensional vector and compute an entity vector as the composition of its word(character) vectors. For example, entity 荔枝巢蛾 is consist of words 荔枝, 巢 and 蛾, or is consist of character 荔, 枝, 巢, and 蛾. In this task, we represent the entity vector by averaging its word or character vectors. For example,

$$v_{荔枝巢蛾} = \frac{1}{3}(v_{荔枝} + v_{巢} + v_{蛾}) \tag{4}$$

or

$$v_{荔枝巢蛾} = \frac{1}{4}(v_{荔} + v_{枝} + v_{巢} + v_{蛾}) \tag{5}$$

As word or character is the smallest unit, we train the model on the word's and character's level. The training err derivatives are also back-propagated to these vectors.

5 Experiments

Our goal is to predict whether a given triple holds, which can be seen as common sense reasoning or prediction in relationship networks[1]. For example, if 荔枝巢蛾 is in 动物界, it is also 荔枝异形小卷蛾. In this section, we first introduce the datasets and then show some experiments. We compare the NTN with other models and obtain several conclusions based on analyses of these results, such as whether to use word vectors or character vectors.

In our experiments, we cross validate using the valid set to find the best hyperparamters to get the highest accuracy. (i) vector initialization with a zero mean Gaussian distribution; (ii)$\lambda = 10^{-4}$; (iii) number of training iterations $T = 7000$; (iv) the dimensionality of word or character $d = 50$; (v) number of slices of tensor $k = 3$; (vi) number of neural nodes of hidden layer in single layer model $h = 200$.

We develop all code with Python and use theano to compute the derivatives of all parameters. Theano is a Python library that allows you to define, optimize, and evaluate mathematical expressions involving multi-dimensional arrays efficiently[10].It can be used for doing efficient symbolic differentiation, even for function with many inputs[10]. The NTN model is trained by taking derivatives with respect to all the above parameters. We use minibatched CG and L-BFGS algorithm for optimization which converges to a local optimum of our objective function.

5.1 Date Sets

Table.1 shows the statistics of the databases. In this task, we construct two datasets named AniPla and Diet sampled from Baidu Encyclopedia infobox. All data stored in the form of (e_1, R, e_2). In AniPla, the first entities are animal's and plant's names, the second entities are the qualities of animals and plants, for example,(龙猫 目 啮齿目) and (竹叶青 种 茶叶). In total, there are 12881 unique entities in 12 different relations. We use 28110 triples for training and 7030 triples for testing. The valid set has 7026 triples for compute the thresholds $t_R\,(R = 1, 2, \ldots, 12)$ for all relations. As Diet, the first entities are food's names, the second entities are the qualities of food, for example, (清蒸鱼 主要食材 鱼) and (香菇面 工艺 煮). In total, there are 23547 unique entities in 8 different relations. We use 27000 triples for training and 6000 triples for testing. The valid set has 6000 triples for compute the thresholds $t_R\,(R = 1, 2, \ldots, 8)$ for all relations. We do word segmentation for AniPla and Diet by manual handling and software, respectively.

Table 1. The statistics of datasets

#Dateset	#Relation	#Entity	#Train	#Valid	#Test
AniPla	12	12881	28110	7026	7030
Diet	8	23547	27000	6000	6000

5.2 Results

This section we compare the results of NTN and other models with different initialize methods of word(character) representations. The Tensor Factorization model[3] dosen't need to use word or character vectors. Table.2 and Table.3 show the resulting accuracy of each model.

Table 2. AniPla: Accuracy of models

Model	Wrod vectors(%)		Character vectors(%)	
	Random	Pre-trained	Random	Pre-trained
Single Layer model	80.5	84.6	85.2	82.1
Neural Tensor network	89.3	**91.1**	**89.6**	87.7
Tensor Factorization model	88.6			

Table 3. Diet: Accuracy of models

Model	Wrod vectors(%)		Character vectors(%)	
	Random	Pre-trained	Random	Pre-trained
Single Layer model	71.3	74.0	75.0	70.1
Neural Tensor network	73.3	**75.3**	**75.9**	73.2
Tensor Factorization model	75.1			

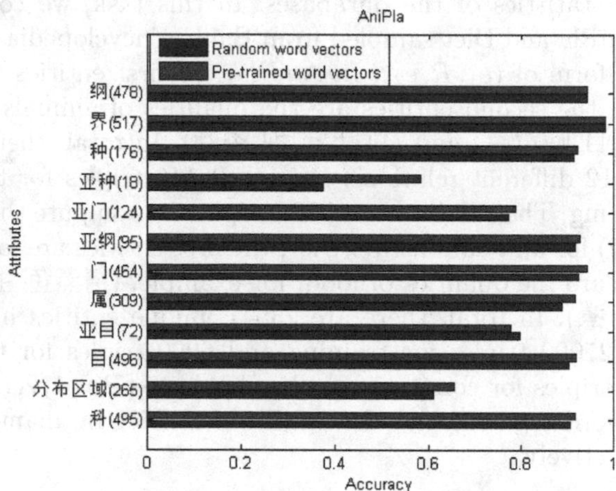

Fig. 3. Comparison of accuracy of diffierernt relations(AniPla). The number in the bracket represents the size of samples in the test set.

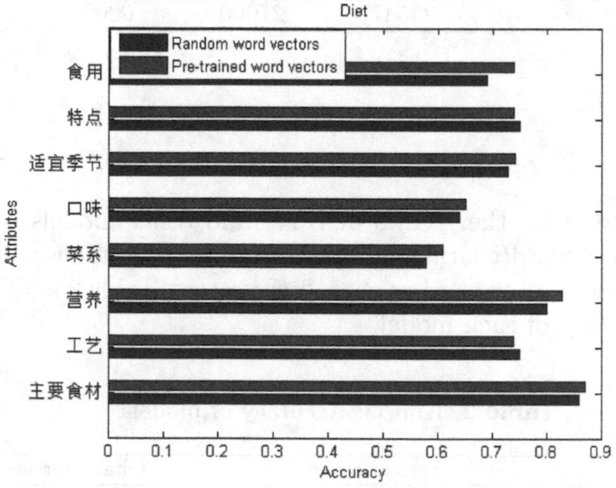

Fig. 4. Comparison of accuracy of differernt relations(Diet)

Table.2 shows that models obtain higher accuracy with pre-trained word vectors than with random vectors. In Table.3, pre-trained word vectors don't have any advantages than random vectors. We can conclude that software can't do word segmentation for entities perfectly.

First, we analyze the influence of word and character initializations. Table.2 reports the accuracy of each model. With unsupervised word vectors' initialization, the single layer and NTN models can reach high classification accuracy: 84.6% and 91.1% on the dataset respectively. However, with random initialization, they both obtain a lower accuracy. It shows that the models have improved accuracy with initialization from pre-trained word vectors. In Fig. 4, the red bar is longer than the blue bar among most relations that also confirms it. By contrast, pre-trained character vectors don't have significantly advantage than random vectors. This phenomenon shows that Chinese semantics are expressed through words, not characters.

We now compare the accuracy of different models. All the data in Table.2 and Table.3shows that the NTN model is more power than other models. Even with character vector and random initialization, the NTN model can achieve accuracy 89.6%, which shows that when Chinese word segmentation is a hard task (the entities in many Chinese datasets are always phrases which are difficult to segment), the NTN model with character vectors from random initialization is a feasible strategy.

Fig. 3 and Fig. 4 shows the accuracy among different relation types. Here we use the NTN model to evaluation. The accuracy varies among different relations. In AniPla, the accuracy rangs from 38.7% to 96.2% and the two most difficult relations are 分布区域 and 亚种. In Diet, the accuracy rangs from 61.0% to 87.1% and the two most difficult relations are 口味 and 菜系. According to Fig. 3 and Fig. 4, we can see the Diet is more difficult to reason than AniPla.

6 Conclusion

We introduce the Neural Tensor Network for common sense reasoning based on existing Chinese knowledge bases. This model constructs a tensor to enhance the interaction between entities in an efficient way and obtains a high prediction accuracy by training word vectors whose initial value come from a unsupervised large corpora. The future work is to improve these ideas to achieve higher accuracy and apply the NTN model to complete knowledge bases.

References

1. Socher, R., Chen, D., Manning, C.D., Ng, Y.: Reasoning With Neural Tensor Networks for Knowledge Base Completion. In: Advances in Neural Information Processing Systems 26 (2013)
2. Mukherjee, T., Pande, V., Kok, S.: Extracting New Facts in Knowledge Bases:-A matrix trifactorization approach. In: ICML Workshop on Structured Learning: Inferring Graphs from Structured and Unstructured Inputs (2013)

3. Nickel, M., Tresp, V., Chen, Kriegel, H.P.: A Three-Way Model for Collective Learning on Multi-Relational Data. In: Proceedings of the 28th International Conference on Machine Learning (2011)
4. Nickel, M., Tresp, V.: Logstic Tensor Factorization for Multi-Relational Data. In: Proceedings of the 30th International Conference on Machine Learning (2013)
5. Huang, E.H., Socher, R., Manning, C.D., Ng, Y.: Improving Word Representations via Global Context and Multiple Word Prototypes. In: Annual Meeting of the Association for Computational Linguistics, ACL (2012)
6. Bordes, A., Weston, J., Collobert, R., Bengio, Y.: Learning structured embeddings of knowledge bases. In: AAAI (2011)
7. Jenatton, R., Le Roux, N., Bordes, A., Obozinski, G.: A latent factor model for highly multi-relational data. In: NIPS (2012)
8. Bordes, A., Glorot, X., Weston, J., Bengio, Y.: Joint Learning of Words and Meaning Representations for Open-Text Semantic Parsing. In: AISTATS (2012)
9. Bowman, S.R.: Can recursive neural tensor networks learn logical reasoning? In: International Conference on Learning Representations (2013)
10. Deep Learning Tutorials, `http://deeplearning.net/tutorial/`
11. Bergstra, J., Breuleux, O., Bastien, F., Lamblin, P., Pascanu, R., Desjardins, G., Turian, J., Warde-Farley, D., Bengio, Y.: Theano: A CPU and GPU Math Expression Compiler. In: Proceedings of the Python for Scientific Computing Conference, SciPy (2010)
12. May, P., Ehrlich, H.-C., Steinke, T.: ZIB Structure Prediction Pipeline: Composing a Complex Biological Workflow Through Web Services. In: Nagel, W.E., Walter, W.V., Lehner, W. (eds.) Euro-Par 2006. LNCS, vol. 4128, pp. 1148–1158. Springer, Heidelberg (2006)
13. Foster, I., Kesselman, C.: The Grid: Blueprint for a New Computing Infrastructure. Morgan Kaufmann, San Francisco (1999)
14. Foster, I., Kesselman, C., Nick, J., Tuecke, S.: The Physiology of the Grid: an Open Grid Services Architecture for Distributed Systems Integration. Technical report, Global Grid Forum (2002)

Distant Supervision for Relation Extraction via Sparse Representation

Daojian Zeng[1], Siwei Lai[1], Xuepeng Wang[1], Kang Liu[1], Jun Zhao[1], and Xueqiang Lv[2]

[1] National Laboratory of Pattern Recognition
Institute of Automation, Chinese Academy of Sciences
{djzeng,swlai,xpwang,kliu,jzhao}@nlpr.ia.ac.cn

[2] Beijing Key Laboratory of Internet Culture and Digital Dissemination Research
Beijing Information Science & Technology University
lxq@bistu.edu.cn

Abstract. In relation extraction, *distant supervision* is proposed to automatically generate a large amount of labeled data. *Distant supervision* heuristically aligns the given knowledge base to free text and consider the alignment as labeled data. This procedure is effective to get training data. However, this heuristically label procedure is confronted with wrong labels. Thus, the extracted features are noisy and cause poor extraction performance. In this paper, we exploit the sparse representation to address the noise feature problem. Given a new test feature vector, we first compute its sparse linear combination of all the training features. To reduce the influence of noise features, a noise term is adopted in the procedure of finding the sparse solution. Then, the residuals to each class are computed. Finally, we classify the test sample by assigning it to the object class that has minimal residual. Experimental results demonstrate that the noise term is effective to noise features and our approach significantly outperforms the state-of-the-art methods.

1 Introduction

Relation extraction refers to the task of predicting semantic relations between entities expressed in text, e.g. to detect an */business/company/founders* relation between the company *WhatsApp* and the person *Jan Koum* from the following text: *WhatsApp Inc. was founded in 2009 by Americans Brian Acton and Jan Koum (also the CEO), both former employees of Yahoo.* Most approaches to relation extraction use supervised paradigm, which achieve high precision and recall [1,20,22]. Unfortunately, fully supervised methods are limited by the availability of training data and cannot satisfy the demands of extracting thousands of relations with explosion of Web text.

Although it lacks of off-the-shelf explicitly labeled data, an abundance of knowledge bases exist, such as DBpedia[1], YAGO[2] and Freebase[3]. To address the

[1] http://dbpedia.org/

[2] http://www.mpi-inf.mpg.de/yago-naga/yago/

[3] http://www.freebase.com

M. Sun et al. (Eds.): CCL and NLP-NABD 2014, LNAI 8801, pp. 151–162, 2014.

issue of lacking a large amount of labeled data, a particularly attractive approach to relation extraction is based on *distant supervision* [12]. The *distant supervision* assumes that if two entities participate in a relation of a known knowledge base, all of the sentences that mention these two entities express that relation in some way. Thus, *distant supervision* heuristically align the given knowledge base to free text and consider the alignment as labeled data. An example accounting for the training instances generated through *distant supervision* is illustrated in Figure 1. The entity pairs $\langle Apple, SteveJobs \rangle$ participate in a known Freebase relation. The relation mentions 1 and 2 are selected as training instances. In succession, we usually extract diverse lexical and syntactic features from all of the mentions and combine them into a richer feature vector [12], which subsequently fed to a classifier. This procedure is effective to get training examlpes. However, it is confronted with noise features. For instance, the mention 2 does not express the corresponding relation, but selected as an training instances as well in Figure 1. Therefore, features extracted from this mention are noisy. This analogous case is widespread in relation extraction based on *distant supervision*.

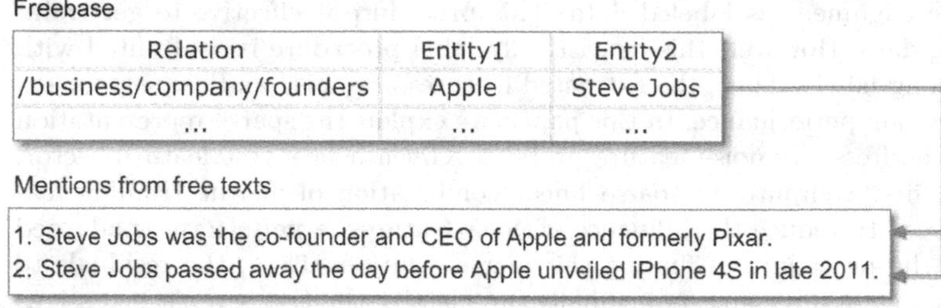

Fig. 1. Training instances generated through distant supervision

In this paper, we exploit the sparse representation to address the noise feature problem mentioned above. The rationale of this method is that if sufficient training samples are available from each class, it will be possible to represent the test samples as a linear combination of just those training samples from the same class [18]. In relation extraction, given a new test feature vector, we first compute its sparse representation of all the features extracted from training samples. It may not be possible to express the test instance exactly as a sparse superposition of the training samples due to the noise features. To reduce the influence of noise feature, a noise term is adopted in the procedure of finding the sparse solution. Then, the residuals to each class are computed. Finally, we classify the test sample by assigning it to the object class that has minimal residual. To the best of our knowledge, this work is the first trial to apply this technique on relation extraction based on *distant supervision*. It is not at all clear that the sparse representation should have relevance to the noise features. Nevertheless, our experiments demonstrate that the sparse representation can be quite effective to alleviate the noise feature problem. Moreover, our noise-tolerant approaches significantly outperform the state-of-the-art methods.

The remainder of this paper is organized as follows. Section 2 reviews previous works in the area of relation extraction. Section 3 gives a detailed description of relation extraction via sparse representation. The experimental results are presented in Section 4. Finally, there is a conclusion in Section 5.

2 Related Work

Relation extraction is an important topics in Natural Language Processing (NLP). Many approaches have been explored for relation extraction, such as bootstrapping, unsupervised relation discovery and supervised method. Researchers have proposed various features to identify the relations between two entities by using different methods.

In bootstrapping and unsupervised paradigms, contextual features are used. The Distributional Hypothesis [6] theory indicates that words occur in the same context tend to have similar meanings. Accordingly, it is assumed that the entity pairs occurring in similar context tend to have similar relations. Hasegawa *et al.* [7] adopted a hierarchical clustering method to cluster the contexts of entity pairs and simply selected the most frequent words in the contexts to represent the relation that held between the entities. Chen *et al.* [3] proposed a novel unsupervised method based on model order selection and discriminative label identification to deal with this problem.

In the supervised paradigm, relation extraction is usually considered as a multi classification problem and researchers concentrate on extracting more complex features. Generally, these methods can be categorized into two types: feature-based and kernel-based. In feature-based methods, a diverse set of strategies have been exploited to convert the classification clues in structures such as sequences, parse trees into feature vectors [11,15]. Feature-based methods suffer from the problem of selecting a suitable feature-set when converting the structured representation into feature vectors. Kernel methods provide a natural alternative to exploit rich representation of the input classification clues like syntactic parse trees, etc. Kernel methods allow the usage of a large set of features without explicitly extracting them. So far, various kernels have been proposed to solve relation extraction, such as convolution tree kernel [13], subsequence kernel [1] and dependency tree kernel [2].

The methods mentioned above, however, suffered from lacking of a large amount of labeled data for training. To address this problem, Mintz *et al.* [12] adopted Freebase, a large-scale knowledge base which contains billions of relation instances, to distantly supervise Wikipedia corpus. The *distant supervision* paradigm selected the sentences that matched the facts in knowledge base as positive examples. As mentioned in section 1, this training data generating algorithm sometimes exposed to wrong label problem and brought noise labeled data. To address the shortcoming, Riedel *et al.* [14] and Hoffmann *et al.* [8] cast the relaxed *distant supervision* assumption as multi-instance learning. In addition, Surdeanu *et al.*[16] proposed a novel approach to multi-instance multi-label learning for relation extraction, which can model all of the sentences in texts and all of the labels in knowledge bases. Takamatsu *et al.* [17] pointed out the relaxed assumption would fail and proposed a novel generative model to model the heuristic labeling process in order to reduce the wrong labels. Zhang *et al.* [21] analyzed some critical factors in *distant supervision* which have great impact on the accuracy to improve the performance. These previous studies mainly pay attention to errors generated in the procedure of *distant supervision.* In contrast, our work alternatively resolves the noise features and exploit the sparse representation to solve the problem.

3 Methodology

In this paper, we apply sparse representation with convex optimization for *distant supervision* relation extraction. Sparse representations are representations that account for most or all of the information of a signal with a linear combination of a small number of elementary signals called atoms [9]. Often, the atoms are chosen from an over-complete dictionary. This technology has been successfully applied on many active research areas, such as computer vision [19] and speech signal processing [10]. Our models for relation extraction are based on the theoretic framework proposed by Wright *et al.* [19], which reveals that occlusion and corruption in face recognition can be handled uniformly and robustly within the sparse representation classification framework. In distant supervision relation extraction, the noise features are analogous to the occlusion and corruption in face recognition. The feature vectors of all the train instances are selected as the dictionary and the classifier enhances the robustness to noise feature by adopting noise term in the procedure of finding the sparse solution.

3.1 Problem Statement

The problem in *distant supervision* relation extraction is to use labeled training samples from k distinct classes to correctly determine the class to which a new test sample belongs. The distant supervision assumption is that if two entities participate in a relation, all of the sentences that mention these two entities might express that relation. To leverage the information from different mentions, the features for identical tuples from different sentences are usually combined, creating a richer feature vector [12]. Let $\mathbf{v} \in \mathbb{R}^m$ denote the richer feature vector. The given n_i training samples from the ith class can be represented as the columns of a matrix $\mathbf{A}_i = [\mathbf{v}_{i,1}, \mathbf{v}_{i,2}, \cdots, \mathbf{v}_{i,n_i}] \in \mathbb{R}^{m \times n_i}$. The entire training set is denoted as the concatenation of the n training samples of all k classes: $\mathbf{A} = [\mathbf{A}_1, \mathbf{A}_2, \cdots, \mathbf{A}_k] \in \mathbb{R}^{m \times n}$ $(n = \sum_{i=1}^{k} n_i)$. The *distant supervision* relation extraction is formulated as given matrix $\mathbf{A}$ to determine the class to which the richer feature vector $\mathbf{y} \in \mathbb{R}^m$ of a test sample belongs.

3.2 Sparse Linear Combination

So far, a variety of statistical, generative and discriminative methods have been proposed for exploiting the structure of the matrix $\mathbf{A}$ for classification. One particularly simple and effective method is to consider the samples from a single class as a linear combination of the subspace. In relation extraction, we select the training examples as the subspace. Given sufficient training samples of the i-th class, $\mathbf{A}_i = [\mathbf{v}_{i,1}, \mathbf{v}_{i,2}, \cdots, \mathbf{v}_{i,n_i}] \in \mathbb{R}^{m \times n_i}$, a test sample $\mathbf{y} \in \mathbb{R}^m$ can be represented as follows:

$$\mathbf{y} = \mathbf{v}_{i,1}w_{i,1} + \mathbf{v}_{i,2}w_{i,2} + \cdots + \mathbf{v}_{i,n_i}w_{i,n_i}, \tag{1}$$

where $w_{i,j} \in \mathbb{R}$ is the weight for the j-th training sample $\mathbf{v}_{i,j}$ associated with class i.

The class of the test sample $\mathbf{y}$ is unknown before the linear combination. Therefore, we select the matrix $\mathbf{A}$ of all the training samples as a dictionary and the test sample is further represented as a sparse linear combination of matrix $\mathbf{A}$.

$$\mathbf{y} = \mathbf{A}\mathbf{w} \in \mathbb{R}^m, \tag{2}$$

where $\mathbf{w} = [0, \cdots, 0, w_{i,1}, w_{i,2}, \cdots, w_{i,n_i}, 0, \cdots, 0] \in \mathbb{R}^n$ is the weight for all of the training samples and the entries are zero except for those associated with the i-th class.

As the entries of the vector $\mathbf{w}$ encode the proportion of the test sample, the relation extraction is converted to get optimal $\mathbf{w}$ in equation (2) when given $\mathbf{y}$ and $\mathbf{A}$. Obviously, this equation is overdetermined when $m >$ n and we can get its unique solution. In relation extraction, various syntactic and semantic features are usually exploited and the feature dimension is very high. In addition, $\mathbf{y} = \mathbf{A}\mathbf{w}$ may not be perfectly satisfied in the presence of noise features. Thus, equation is underdetermined and the solution $\mathbf{w}$ is not unique. At first glance, it seems impossible to get the solution of w in this case. However, we can get the following observations: a valid test sample $\mathbf{y}$ can be represented using only the training samples from the same class. This representation is naturally sparse if the number of the relation classes is reasonably large. Thus, to get the optimal $\mathbf{w}$, we transform the problem to find the sparsest solution to $\mathbf{y} = \mathbf{A}\mathbf{w}$, solving the following optimization problem:

$$\hat{\mathbf{w}} = \arg\min \|\mathbf{w}\|_0 \qquad \textit{subject to} \quad \mathbf{A}\mathbf{w} = \mathbf{y}, \tag{3}$$

where $\|\cdot\|$ denotes the ℓ^0-norm, which means to find the solution vector that has zero entries as much as possible. However, this ℓ^0-minimization problem is NP-hard and difficult even to get an approximate solution. Recent work in the sparse representation prove that if the solution w is sparse enough, ℓ^0-norm can be replaced by ℓ^1-norm [5]. We further transform the problem to ℓ^1-minimization problem:

$$\hat{\mathbf{w}} = \arg\min \|\mathbf{w}\|_1 \qquad \textit{subject to} \quad \mathbf{A}\mathbf{w} = \mathbf{y}, \tag{4}$$

This is a convex optimization problem and can be solved in polynomial time by standard linear programming methods [4].

3.3 Dealing with Noise Features

In the above section, we assumed that the test feature vectors are exactly represented as a sparse linear combination of all the training feature vectors. Since the features are noisy in *distant supervision*, the exact representation is not reasonable and we cannot assume that $\mathbf{Aw}$ is known with arbitrary precision. To tolerate the noise entries in the feature vector, a noise term is adopted in the procedure of finding the sparse solution and the equation (2) is modified to explicitly model the noise as follows:

$$\mathbf{y} = \mathbf{Aw} + \mathbf{e}, \tag{5}$$

where $\mathbf{e} \in \mathbb{R}^m$ is the added noise term. There are mainly two approach to solve the feature noise in equation (5). On the one hand, $\mathbf{e}$ is considered as a term with bounded energy $\|\mathbf{e}\|_2 < \varepsilon$. This model is called **N**oise **T**erm as **B**ounded **E**nergy(**NTBE**). Therefore, the sparse solution $\mathbf{w}$ is then approximately recovered by solving the following convex optimization problem:

$$\hat{\mathbf{w}} = \arg\min \|\mathbf{w}\|_1 \qquad \textit{subject to} \quad \|\mathbf{Aw} - \mathbf{y}\|_2 \leqslant \varepsilon. \tag{6}$$

Similarly, this convex optimization problem can be efficiently solved. The optimal solution subjects to the constraint that the energy of the reconstruction error of $\mathbf{y}$ is no bigger than ε.

On the other hand, $\mathbf{e}$ is considered as an error vector, some entries of which are nonzero. This model is called **N**oise **T**erm as **E**rror **V**ector (**NTEV**). The noise features may affect any entry of the feature vector and may be arbitrarily large in magnitude. In this model, the noise features are represented as a linear combination of error basis and handled uniformly through sparse representation. Then, equation (5) is replaced as:

$$\mathbf{y} = \mathbf{Aw} + \mathbf{e} = [\mathbf{A}, \mathbf{I}] \begin{bmatrix} \mathbf{w} \\ \mathbf{e} \end{bmatrix} = \mathbf{A}'\mathbf{w}' \tag{7}$$

where the matrix $\mathbf{A}$ and sparse weight w are respectively extended to $\mathbf{A}' = [\mathbf{A}, \mathbf{I}] \in \mathbb{R}^{m \times (n+m)}$ and $\mathbf{w}' = \begin{bmatrix} \mathbf{w} \\ \mathbf{e} \end{bmatrix} \in \mathbb{R}^{n+m}$. Compared to the first approach, this method can explicitly model the location of feature corruption. The nonzero entries of $\mathbf{e}$ indicate corrupted dimensions of the feature vector. Apparently, equation (8) is underdetermined and does not have a unique solution for $\mathbf{w}'$. Similarly to equation (4), we attempt to get the the sparsest solution $\mathbf{w}'$ from solving the following extended constrained ℓ^1 minimization problem:

$$\hat{\mathbf{w}'} = \arg\min \|\mathbf{w}'\|_1 \qquad \textit{subject to} \quad \mathbf{A}'\mathbf{w}' = \mathbf{y}. \tag{8}$$

3.4 Relation Classification

This section introduces how to get class label of test samples based on the results of sparse representation. Given a new test sample vector $\mathbf{y}$, we first compute its sparse representation $\hat{\mathbf{w}}$ via equation (6) or (8). Ideally, the entries in the estimate $\hat{\mathbf{w}}$ will be zero except for the entries that associated with the target class. However, the feature noise and modeling error may lead to small nonzero entries for multiple classes. To resovle this problem, it usually classifies $\mathbf{y}$ based on how well the coefficients associated with all of the training samples of each class reproduce $\hat{\mathbf{y}}_i$. The test sample is classified according to the reconstruction error between $\mathbf{y}$ and its approximations.

For class i, $\tau_i(\mathbf{w})$ represents a new vector whose only nonzero entries are the entries in $\mathbf{w}$ that are associated with class i. We can approximately reproduce $\mathbf{y}$ in class i as $\hat{\mathbf{y}}_i = \mathbf{A}\tau_i(\hat{\mathbf{w}})$. Then the classifier assign $\mathbf{y}$ to the class that minimizes the residual between $\mathbf{y}$ and $\hat{\mathbf{y}}_i$. If we use **NTBE** to model the noise, we can predict the relation class as follows:

$$\arg\min_i r_i(\mathbf{y}) = \|\mathbf{y} - \hat{\mathbf{y}}_i\|_2 = \|\mathbf{y} - A\tau_i(\hat{\mathbf{w}})\|_2 \tag{9}$$

If use **NTEV** to model the noise, we approximately get $\hat{\mathbf{w}'} = \begin{bmatrix} \hat{\mathbf{w}} \\ \hat{\mathbf{e}} \end{bmatrix}$. $\hat{\mathbf{e}}$ represents the estimated noise of the test sample feature vector $\mathbf{y}$ and $\mathbf{y} - \hat{\mathbf{e}}$ recovers the clean feature vector. To get the class label, we slightly modify the residual $r_i(\mathbf{y})$ and compute as follows:

$$\arg\min_i r_i(\mathbf{y}) = \|\mathbf{y} - \hat{\mathbf{y}}_i\|_2 = \|\mathbf{y} - \hat{\mathbf{e}} - A\tau_i(\hat{\mathbf{w}})\|_2 \tag{10}$$

Furthermore, the residual is interpreted as a conditional probability by applying a softmax operation:

$$p(i|\mathbf{y}, \mathbf{A}) = \frac{e^{1-r_i(\mathbf{y})}}{\sum_{m=1}^{k} e^{1-r_m(\mathbf{y})}} \tag{11}$$

4 Experiments

To evaluate the performance of our proposed approach, we conduct three sets of experiments. The first is to test **NTBE** with different noise term ε, to gain some understanding of how the choice of noise term impacts upon the performance. In the second set of experiments, we make comparison of the performance among our method and other three kinds of landmark methods [12,8,16] using held-out evaluation. As the held-out evaluation is confronted with false negative problem, the goal of the third one is to evaluate the extracted results manually.

4.1 Dataset and Experiment Settings

Dataset: We select a real world dataset[4], NYT'10, to evaluate our method. The dataset was developed by Riedel *et al.* [14] and also used by Hoffmann *et al.* [8]. In the dataset, Freebase was used as the *distant supervision* source and the New York Times (NYT) was selected as the text corpus. Four categories of Freebase relations are used, including "people", "business", "person" and "location". The

[4] `http://iesl.cs.umass.edu/riedel/ecml/`

NYT data contains over 1.8 million articles written and published between January 1, 1987 and June 19, 2007. The Freebase relations were divided into two parts, one for training and one for testing. The former is aligned to the years 2005-2006 of the NYT corpus, the latter to the year 2007. As we need negative examples for training, this dataset generally pick 10% of the entity pairs that appear in the same sentence but are not related according to Freebase. Moreover, three kinds of features, namely, lexical, syntactic and named entity tag features, were extracted from relation mentions. The statistics about the dataset is presented in Table 1. There are 51 relationships and an *NA* class.

Table 1. Statistics about the NYT'10 dataset

# of relation labels	# of training examples	# of NA training examples	# of testing examples	# of NA testing examples	# of features
51	4,700	63,596	1,950	94,917	1,071,684

Experiment Settings: As the number of *NA* training examples is too large, we randomly choose 1% *NA* training examples as the negative examples in the following experiments. Table 1 presents that the number of features exceeds one million. Using all of this features will lead to the very high dimension of feature vector and data sparsity. To control the feature sparsity degree, Surdeanu *et al.* [16] released the source code[5] to reproduce their experiments and use a threshold θ to filter the features that appears less than θ times. They set $\theta = 5$ in the original code by default. To guarantee the fair comparison for all of the methods, we follow their settings and adopt the same way to filter the features in our experiments. In the sparse representation-based relation extraction, the main problem is to solve the ℓ^1-minimization problem. In this paper, we use SPGL1[6] to solve this problem and set the parameters as default.

4.2 The Effect of Noise Term

In the **NTBE** model, an extra input parameter ε is needed. This parameter determines the tolerance to the noise features. The optimal value of ε varies with different datasets. In this part, we experimentally study the effect of the noise term ε in our proposed method. Since there is no development dataset in NYT'10, we tuned the noise term ε by trying different value via five-fold cross-validation. Figure 2 illustrates the curves of F1 score for each fold. $\varepsilon = 0$ means that the test feature vector are exactly represent as a sparse linear combination of all the training feature vectors. From Figure 2, we can observe a phenomenon that the performance gradually increases as the error energy ε increases before reaching the optimum. However, it sharply decreases if we continue increasing the optimal error energy. We get the optimal results when $\varepsilon = 0.3$. An intuitive

[5] `http://nlp.stanford.edu/software/mimlre.shtml`

[6] `http://www.cs.ubc.ca/~mpf/spgl1/`

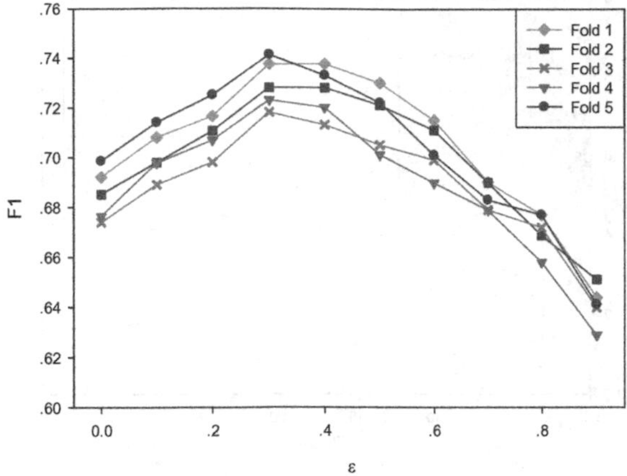

Fig. 2. Five-fold cross validation for the error energy ε

explanation can be accounted for this phenomenon: The feature vector contains much noise when the error energy is very small and the model tends to be overfitting. Whereas the feature vector is likely to lose principal information and the model tends to be underfitting when the error energy is excessively large.

4.3 Held-out Evaluation

In the held-out evaluation, half of the Freebase relations were divided for testing. The relation instances discovered from testing articles were automatically compared with those in Freebase. Held-out evaluation gives a rough measure of precision without requiring expensive human evaluation. To get the final performance of our proposed method, we select three approaches as competitors to be compared with our method in Figure 3. *Mintz* represents the baseline distant supervision model for relation extraction proposed by Mintz *et al.* [12]. *MultiR* is a state-of-the-art multi instance learning system proposed by Hoffmann *et al.* [8]. *MIML* indicates the multi-instance multi-label learning system [16], which jointly models all of the instances of a pair of entities in text and all of their labels. We compare these three approached with our proposed sparse representation based methods. In *NTBE*, the error energy is set to the optimal value $\varepsilon = 0.3$. For *MultiR* and *MIML*, we used the authors' implementation. We re-implemented Mintz's algorithm.

From Figure 3, we have the following observations. *NTBE* outperforms the state-of-the-art over the whole precision-recall curve. *NTEV* achieves the best results except that the recall is between 0.12 and 0.17. The precision-recall curve of *NTEV* has a sharp decline when the recall is about 0.12. The reason for this phenomenon is that the number of *NA* testing examples is far more than the number of testing examples. By analyzing the results, we find that a large number of the *NA* testing examples have conditional probabilities greater than the testing

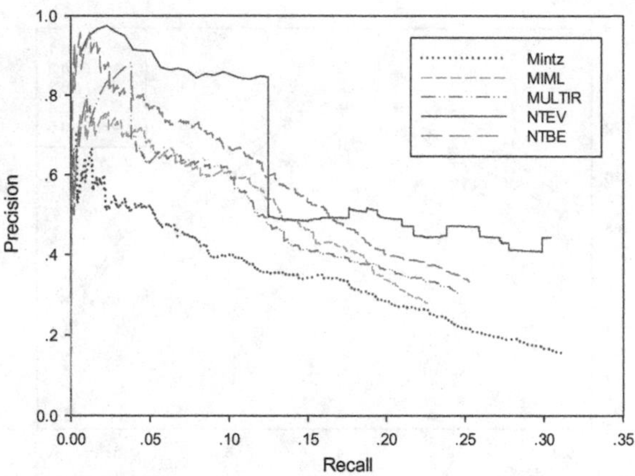

Fig. 3. Precision and recall for the held out evaluation

examples. The precision will declines gradually while the recall rate remains unchange. Therefore, there has been a sharp decline in the precision-recall curve. The similar phenomenon can be observed in *MultiR* when the recall rate is about 0.03. In the held out evaluation, we compare newly discovered relation instances to the held out Freebase. As the incompleteness of Freebase, held out evaluation suffers from false negatives and the precision is underestimated. We address this problem through manual evaluation in the next section.

4.4 Manual Evaluation

For the manual evaluation, we choose those entity pairs which at least one participating entity is not in Freebase. Since the number of the relation instances expressed in the test data is unknown, we cannot calculate recall in this case. Alternatively, we calculate the precision of the Top-N extracted relation instances. Table 2 presents the manually evaluated precisions for the Top-100, Top-200, Top-500, from which we can see that both of our methods outperform all of the compared methods. *NTEV* achieves the best performance. We also perform one-tailed t-test ($p \leqslant 0.05$) which demonstrates that our method significantly outperforms all of the baselines.

Table 2. Precision of the Top-100, Top-200, Top-500 for manual evaluation

Top-N	Mintz	MultiR	MIML	NTBE	NTEV
Top-100	0.77	0.83	0.88	0.89	**0.91**
Top-200	0.71	0.74	0.81	0.82	**0.85**
Top-500	0.55	0.59	0.63	0.68	**0.72**
Average	0.676	0.720	0.773	0.796	**0.826**

5 Conclusion

The *distant supervision* assumes that every sentence that mentions two related entities in a knowledge base express the corresponding relation. The *distant supervision* assumption can fail, which results in noise feature problem and causes poor extraction performance. In this paper, we exploit sparse representation for *distant supervision* relation extraction. To tolerance the noise features, a noise term is adopted in our model. Two models, **NTBE** and **NTEV**, are adopted to model the noise. Experiment results demonstrate that the sparse representation is quite effective to alleviate the noise feature problem.

Acknowledgments. This work was supported by the National Natural Science Foundation of China (No.61202329, 61272332, 61333018), CCF-Tencent Open Research Fund and the Opening Project of Beijing Key Laboratory of Internet Culture and Digital Dissemination Research(ICDD201301). We thank the anonymous reviewers for their insightful comments.

References

1. Bunescu, R., Mooney, R.: Subsequence kernels for relation extraction. In: Advances in Neural Information Processing Systems 18, p. 171 (2006)
2. Bunescu, R.C., Mooney, R.J.: A shortest path dependency kernel for relation extraction. In: Proceedings of the Conference on Human Language Technology and Empirical Methods in Natural Language Processing, pp. 724–731 (2005)
3. Chen, J., Ji, D., Tan, C.L., Niu, Z.: Unsupervised feature selection for relation extraction. In: Proceedings of IJCNLP (2005)
4. Chen, S.S., Donoho, D.L., Saunders, M.A.: Atomic decomposition by basis pursuit. SIAM Rev. 43(1), 129–159 (2001)
5. Donoho, D.L.: For most large underdetermined systems of linear equations the minimal ℓ1-norm solution is also the sparsest solution. Comm. Pure and Applied Math. 59, 797–829 (2006)
6. Harris, Z.: Distributional structure. Word 10(23), 146–162 (1954)
7. Hasegawa, T., Sekine, S., Grishman, R.: Discovering relations among named entities from large corpora. In: Proceedings of the 42nd Annual Meeting on Association for Computational Linguistics (2004)
8. Hoffmann, R., Zhang, C., Ling, X., Zettlemoyer, L., Weld, D.S.: Knowledge-based weak supervision for information extraction of overlapping relations. In: Proceedings of the 49th Annual Meeting of the Association for Computational Linguistics: Human Language Technologies, vol. 1, pp. 541–550 (2011)
9. Huang, K., Aviyente, S.: Sparse representation for signal classification. In: Schölkopf, B., Platt, J., Hoffman, T. (eds.) Advances in Neural Information Processing Systems 19, pp. 609–616 (2006)
10. Jafari, M.G., Plumbley, M.D.: Fast dictionary learning for sparse representations of speech signals. J. Sel. Topics Signal Processing 5(5), 1025–1031 (2011)
11. Kambhatla, N.: Combining lexical, syntactic, and semantic features with maximum entropy models for extracting relations. In: Proceedings of the ACL 2004 on Interactive Poster and Demonstration Sessions (2004)

12. Mintz, M., Bills, S., Snow, R., Jurafsky, D.: Distant supervision for relation extraction without labeled data. In: Proceedings of the Joint Conference of the 47th Annual Meeting of the ACL and the 4th International Joint Conference on Natural Language Processing of the AFNLP, vol. 2, pp. 1003–1011 (2009)
13. Qian, L., Zhou, G., Kong, F., Zhu, Q., Qian, P.: Exploiting constituent dependencies for tree kernel-based semantic relation extraction. In: Proceedings of the 22nd International Conference on Computational Linguistics, pp. 697–704 (August 2008)
14. Riedel, S., Yao, L., McCallum, A.: Modeling relations and their mentions without labeled text. In: Balcázar, J.L., Bonchi, F., Gionis, A., Sebag, M. (eds.) ECML PKDD 2010, Part III. LNCS, vol. 6323, pp. 148–163. Springer, Heidelberg (2010)
15. Suchanek, F.M., Ifrim, G., Weikum, G.: Combining linguistic and statistical analysis to extract relations from web documents. In: Proceedings of the 12th ACM SIGKDD International Conference on Knowledge Discovery and Data Mining, pp. 712–717 (2006)
16. Surdeanu, M., Tibshirani, J., Nallapati, R., Manning, C.D.: Multi-instance multi-label learning for relation extraction. In: Proceedings of the 2012 Joint Conference on Empirical Methods in Natural Language Processing and Computational Natural Language Learning, pp. 455–465 (2012)
17. Takamatsu, S., Sato, I., Nakagawa, H.: Reducing wrong labels in distant supervision for relation extraction. In: Proceedings of the 50th Annual Meeting of the Association for Computational Linguistics: Long Papers, vol. 1, pp. 721–729 (2012)
18. Wright, J., Yang, A., Ganesh, A., Sastry, S., Ma, Y.: Robust face recognition via sparse representation. IEEE Transactions on Pattern Analysis and Machine Intelligence 31(2), 210–227 (2009)
19. Wright, J., Ma, Y., Mairal, J., Sapiro, G., Huang, T.S., Yan, S.: Sparse representation for computer vision and pattern recognition. Proceedings of the IEEE 98(6), 1031–1044 (2010)
20. Zelenko, D., Aone, C., Richardella, A.: Kernel methods for relation extraction. The Journal of Machine Learning Research 3, 1083–1106 (2003)
21. Zhang, X., Zhang, J., Zeng, J., Yan, J., Chen, Z., Sui, Z.: Towards accurate distant supervision for relational facts extraction. In: Proceedings of the 51st Annual Meeting of the Association for Computational Linguistics, pp. 810–815 (2013)
22. Zhou, G., Jian, S., Jie, Z., Min, Z.: Exploring various knowledge in relation extraction. In: Proceedings of the 43rd Annual Meeting on Association for Computational Linguistics, pp. 427–434 (2005)

Learning the Distinctive Pattern Space Features for Relation Extraction

Daojian Zeng[1], Yubo Chen[1], Kang Liu[1], Jun Zhao[1], and Xueqiang Lv[2]

[1] National Laboratory of Pattern Recognition
Institute of Automation, Chinese Academy of Sciences
{djzeng,yubo.chen,kliu,jzhao}@nlpr.ia.ac.cn
[2] Beijing Key Laboratory of Internet Culture and Digital Dissemination Research
Beijing Information Science & Technology University
lxq@bistu.edu.cn

Abstract. Recently, Distant Supervision (DS) is used to automatically generate training data for relation extraction. As the vast redundancy of information on the web, multiple sentences corresponding to a fact may be achieved. In this paper, we propose pattern space features to leverage data redundancy. Each dimension of pattern space feature vector corresponds to a basis pattern and the vector value is the similarity of entity pairs' patterns to basis patterns. To achieve distinctive basis patterns, a pattern selection procedure is adopted to filter out noisy patterns. In addition, since too specific patterns will increase the number of basis patterns, we propose a novel pattern extraction method that can avoid extracting too specific patterns while maintaining pattern distinctiveness. To demonstrate the effectiveness of the proposed features, we conduct the experiments on a real world data set with 6 different relation types. Experimental results demonstrate that pattern space features significantly outperform State-of-the-art.

1 Introduction

There are huge amount of unstructured texts on the web, which constitute a huge and rapidly growing information repository. However, these kinds of unstructured textual information is only human readable, which hinders people from developing more compelling applications. So, there is an urgent need to automatically convert unstructured information into structured data which can be understood by machines.

As one way to extract structural information, relation extraction is to predict semantic relations between entities from texts [3]. Generally, the task of relation extraction can be defined as follows: given two entities e_1 and e_2 in the corresponding text T, we aim to identify the relation between these two entities based on diverse lexical, syntactic and semantic information.

As the vast redundancy of information on the web (e.g., A facts may state several times in different ways within multiple sentences), a natural avenue for our research is to infer semantic relations by considering the multiple sentences

M. Sun et al. (Eds.): CCL and NLP-NABD 2014, LNAI 8801, pp. 163–174, 2014.

that contain the entity pairs. Taking the entity pair ⟨*Fanboys*, *Kyle Newman*⟩ in the following two sentences as an example:

1. *He is also known for his role in [Kyle Newman] 's film [Fanboys].*
2. *The award was presented by [Fanboys] director [Kyle Newman].*

The first sentence provides evidence not only for *directed_by* but also *written_by* and *produced_by*. Similarly, we cannot infer the relation *directed_by* only from the second sentence (e.g. *"[Google privacy] director [Alma Whitten] is stepping down after a tough three-year tenure"*). However, we can deduce the relation between *Fanboys* and *Kyle Newman* convincingly in combination with these two sentences.

As far as I am aware, there are two published studies leveraging the redundancy of information for relation extraction [11,4]. Mintz et al. [11] inferred the relations by simply concatenating the multiple sentences that contain the entity pairs via a supervised machine learning paradigm. However, this method resulted in the poor performance due to the high dimensionality of the extracted lexical features. For instance, the dimension of feature vector exceed one million in MultiR[1]. To solve the high dimensionality of the feature vector, Bollegala et al. [4] proposed relation dual representation and entity pairs are represented as the distribution over patterns. However, this method has two main shortcomings. First, there may be noisy patterns, which will have a serious impact on the final features. Second, this feature representation may cause the *null pattern* problem when using a supervised paradigm. For example, "*X* work as *Y*" is one of the patterns constituting the pattern space while "*X* serve as *Y*" is not in the space.

In this paper, we proposed pattern space features to remedy the two defects mentioned above. Pattern space features are represented as the distribution over selected basis patterns. To address the noisy patterns, we first extract lexical-syntactic patterns that connect to the given entity pairs from all of the matched sentences and entity pairs. Next, the patterns with low distinctiveness are filtered out based on Discriminative Category Matching (DCM) theory [8] and the preserved patterns constitute basis patterns. Finally, different from Bollegala et al. [4] proposed method, each vector value of pattern space features is the similarity of entity pairs' patterns to basis patterns calculated by a shortest dependency path kernel function rather than the occurrence counts. Thus, the *null pattern* problem is avoided.

In summary, the contribution of this paper can be concluded as follows.

- We propose pattern space features to identify relation between two entities. Pattern space features can leverage various kinds of features from multiple sentences.
- To extract distinctive basis patterns, we propose a novel pattern extraction approach and use DCM theory to filter out noisy and ambiguous patterns.
- To solve *null pattern* problem, we define a shortest dependency path kernel function to measure the similarity between two patterns.

[1] `http://www.cs.washington.edu/ai/raphaelh/mr/`

2 Related Work

Relation extraction is important topics in information extraction. Many approaches have been explored in relation extraction, including bootstrapping, unsupervised relation discover and supervised classification.

Bootstrapping methods for relation extraction are attractive because they first only need a very small number of seed instances or patterns [1,5]. Then, new patterns are extracted for subsequent iterations until convergence. The quality of the extracted relations depends heavily upon the initial seeds. In general, the resulting patterns often suffer from semantic drift and low precision.

The second scheme is purely unsupervised relation extraction. The Distributional Hypothesis [9] theory indicates that words occur in the same context tend to have similar meanings. Accordingly, it is assumed that the entity pairs occur in similar context tend to have similar relations. In general, unsupervised relation extraction methods use contextual features to represent relation of entity pairs in large amounts of corpus, and then cluster these features to classify these entity pairs. Finally, the words between two entities are simplified to produce relation-strings. Hasegawa et al. [10] adopted a hierarchical clustering method to cluster the contexts of entity pairs and simply select the most frequent words in the contexts to represent the relation that holds between the entities. Rosenfeld et al. [14] and Bollegala et al. [4] proposed relation dual representation in which the entity pairs were represented as the distribution over pattern space. The entity pairs are clustered in the entity pair vs. pattern matrix to identify semantic relations. Unsupervised approach can use very large amounts of data and extract very large number of relation instances, but do not output canonicalized relations and need to do relation mapping for further usage.

In the supervised paradigm, relation extraction is considered as a classification problem and researchers have done much work on how to automatically derive feature to represent the relation between two entities. Generally, the methods can be categorized into two types: feature-based and kernel-based. In feature-based method, a diverse set of strategies have been exploited to convert the extraction clues in structures such as sequences, parse trees to feature vectors for use by classifiers [15]. Feature-based method suffers from the problem of selecting a suitable feature-set. Kernel methods provide a natural alternative to exploit rich representation of the input extraction clues like syntactic parse trees etc. Kernel methods allow the use of a large set of features without the need to extract them explicitly. So far various kernels have been proposed to solve relation extraction problem, such as convolution tree kernel [12], subsequence kernel [6] and dependency tree kernel [7]. The methods mentioned above, however, suffered from lacking of a large amount of labeled data for training. Mintz et al. [11] proposed DS to address this problem. The DS paradigm selects the sentences that match the facts in knowledge base as positive examples. DS algorithm sometimes exposes to wrong label problem and brings noisy labeled data. To address the shortcoming of DS, Riedel et al. [13] cast the relaxed DS assumption as multi-instance learning. Supervised paradigm has been demonstrated to be effective for relation detection and yields relatively high performance. In this paper, we

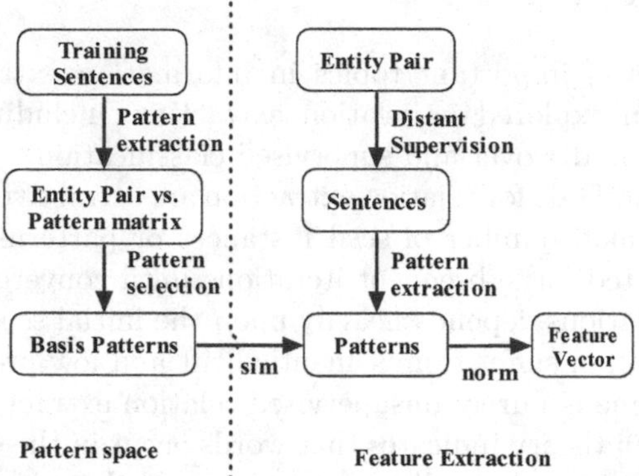

Fig. 1. The flow chart of pattern space feature extraction

also employ supervised paradigm and DS is adopted to automatically generate training data. The wrong label problem in DS is ignored and beyond the scope of this paper. As discussed in section 1, it is very important to leverage information from multiple sentences. In this paper, we propose pattern space features to extract relation from multiple sentences based on relation duality and compare our feature with Mintz et al. [11] and Bollegala et al. [4] proposed feature in the experiment section.

3 Pattern Space Feature Extraction

3.1 Feature Generation Framework

In relation extraction task, our goal is to identify relation between two entities. The key problem is to pick up appropriate feature vector to represent relation of entity pairs, with a suitable measure of distance between vectors. The feature vector must be chosen in such a way that entity pairs have similar relation would be close to each other, and conversely, entity pairs involved in distinct relation would be far apart.

The flow chart of pattern space feature extraction is shown in Figure 1. It mainly includes two parts: *Pattern space* and *Feature extraction*. In the *Pattern space* part, our main goal is to acquire basis patterns. Firstly, we extract raw patterns from the training sentences. Furthermore, the entity pairs and entire patterns form a matrix in which each row represents an entity pairs and each column stands for a unique pattern based on relation duality. Finally, we use pattern selection method to filter out noisy pattern, and the basis patterns are achieved. The entire basis patterns span pattern space for generating feature. In the *Feature extraction* part, it usually provides us with an entity pair. Then, we can get its corresponding patterns through DS and pattern extraction. To extract pattern space features, we calculate the similarity among the corresponding patterns and basis patterns. The pattern space feature vector is created with each dimension corresponding to a basis pattern and the vector value is the similarity calculated above. Finally, the pattern space feature vector is further normalized by its length.

3.2 Pattern Space Features Explanation

Relational duality was formally put forward by Bollegala et al. in 2010, which means that a relation could be represented extensionally and intensionally. An extensional definition of a relation is to list the entity pairs containing such relation. On the other hand, a relation could be defined by specifying the patterns that express such relation. For example, consider the relation *directed_by* between a film and a person. The extensional definition the relation of *directed_by* enumerates the entity pairs hold this relation. (e.g. (*Bwana Devil, Arch Oboler*), (*Das Boot, Wolfgang Petersen*), etc.) Words occurring in the same context tend to have similar meanings through the Distributional Hypothesis theory [9]. In relation extraction, it is reasonable to assume that the entity pairs occurring in similar patterns tend to have similar relations. Accordingly, the intensional definition the relation of *directed_by* needs to specify the lexical or syntactic patterns belongs to this relation such as "X is a film directed by Y", "X is suspense-thriller film from director Y", etc.

As the dual representation of semantic relation mentioned above, we can represent the dual property as a matrix with entity pairs in the rows and patterns in the columns. The matrix cell value is the occurrence counts of entity pair in the pattern space. In previous works [4,2], each row serves as a feature vector for an entity pair. Each dimension of the vector corresponds to a pattern and the vector value is the pattern occurrence counts of entity pair. Although entity pairs with similar relation would be close to each other through such representation, there are mainly two challenges. First, there may be noisy patterns in the patterns space and the sparsity in feature vector is severe. Second, the variation of patterns are more severe than word tokens, the space spanned by patterns from training samples is not a complete space. The patterns extracted from the test instance may not exist in pattern space and cause *null pattern* problem. The severity of the problem will depend upon numerous factors such as the amount of the train instances as well as the similarity between the train and test instances. With the amount the training instances increasing, the number of patterns will further increase. The severity of the *null pattern* problem will be less, but not completely non-existent. In addition, it will aggravate the sparsity in feature vector.

Hence, to address the *null pattern* problem mentioned above, we design a kernel function to compute the similarity between two patterns in the pattern space feature extraction framework. The matrix cell value is then replaced by the similarity and each row acts as the feature vector. Furthermore, we use DCM [8] theory to rank the patterns of each relation. Then, the patterns with low distinctiveness are filtered out (See section 3.4). The preserved patterns constitute basis patterns, which span the pattern space. An entity pair is represented as a vector and each dimension is the weight in the pattern space. This feature representation allows us to compute the similarity of two entity pairs by comparing the distribution over pattern space.

3.3 Pattern Extraction

The proposed feature generation algorithm regards the distribution of a particular entity pair over the space spanned by patterns as feature vector. Patterns play a key role in the feature extraction framework. Consequently, the pattern extraction module is crucial to the success of this approach. Too many patterns will cause the dimension of feature vector to be too large. It is not suitable to extract context pattern due to the wide variation of surface text. Fortunately, the syntactic structures of the sentence and the grammatical relations enable us to reduce the variation. Besides, syntactic features are indeed useful in relation extraction, especially when two entities are nearby in the dependency structure but distant in terms of words [11].

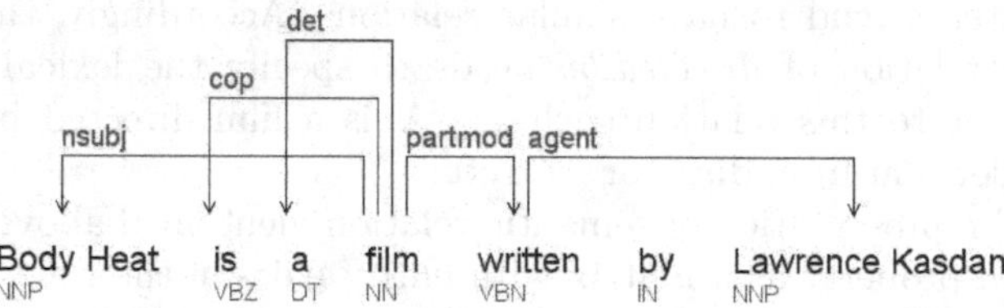

Fig. 2. The dependency tree of "[Body Heat] is a film written by [Lawrence Kasdan]"

Following the idea in literature [7], we assume that the shortest dependency path tracing from entity 1 through the dependency tree to entity 2 gives a concrete syntactic structure expressing the relation between entity-pairs. For a given sentence, we first obtain its dependency tree using Stanford Parser[2]. Then, these dependencies form a directed graph, $\langle V, E \rangle$, where each word is a vertex in V, and E is the set of word-word dependencies, as shown in Figure 2. Then, we get the shortest connecting path between the given entity pair on the dependency graph to represent the relation. To avoid extracting too specific patterns, the lexical words in the shortest path are usually replaced with POS tags. However, the lexical form of verb is particularly important in relation extraction. For example, when the wildcard is replaced by different verb, the following pattern indicates distinct relationship(e.g. *written* vs. *written_by*, *directed* vs. *directed_by*, etc.).

$$\mathbf{X} \xleftarrow{nsubj} NN \xrightarrow{partmod} * \xrightarrow{agent} \mathbf{Y}$$

Hence, the lexical form of verb in the dependency path, which is distinctive to relations, is preserved in order to trade off data sparseness and pattern distinctiveness. According to the above analysis, the pattern extracted from Figure 2 is as follows:

[2] `http://nlp.stanford.edu/software/lex-parser.shtml`

$$\mathbf{X} \xleftarrow{nsubj} NN \xrightarrow{partmod} written \xrightarrow{agent} \mathbf{Y}$$

In order to compute the similarity between two patterns, we design a simple kernel function amounts to calculating the number of common features of two patterns, which is, to some extent, inspired by a shortest path dependency kernel proposed in paper [7]. If $p_x = x_1 x_2 \cdots x_m$ and $p_y = y_1 y_2 \cdots y_n$ are two patterns, where x_i and y_i denotes the set of tokens corresponding to position i of the patterns. The similarity of two patterns is computed as in Equation 1.

$$sim\left(p_x, p_y\right) = \begin{cases} 0, & m \neq n \\ \sum\limits_{i=1}^{n} t(x_i, y_i)/n, & m = n \end{cases} \tag{1}$$

Where $t(x_i, y_i) = 1$ if x_i equals y_i, else $t(x_i, y_i) = 0$. To better explain the definition of similarity function, let us consider the following sentence: "*In 2005, she appeared as flight attendant Claire Colburn alongside Orlando Bloom, in [Elizabethtown], a movie written and directed by [Cameron Crowe]* ". The corresponding pattern is:

$$\mathbf{X} \xrightarrow{appos} NN \xrightarrow{partmod} written \xrightarrow{agent} \mathbf{Y}$$

Then, this pattern is represented as a sequence set $p_1 = [x_1\ x_2\ x_3\ x_4\ x_5]$, where x_1 = "*appos*", x_2 = "*NN*", x_3 = "*partmod*", x_4 = "*directed*", and x_5 = "*agent*". Similarly, the pattern extracted from Figure 2 is represented as $p_2 = [y_1\ y_2\ y_3\ y_4\ y_5]$, where y_1 = "*nsubj*", y_2 = "*NN*", y_3 = "*partmod*", y_4 = "*written*", and y_5 = "*agent*". Based on the formula from Equation 1, the similarity between p_1 and p_2 is computed as $sim(p_1, p_2) = 4/5 = 0.8$.

3.4 Pattern Selection

The number of patterns in the pattern space is the final dimension of feature vector. Excessive number of patterns not only led to high computation cost but also feature sparsity. In the pattern space feature extraction paradigm mentioned above, the feature quality relies entirely on the distinctiveness of patterns. Filtering out noisy patterns is a matter of paramount importance.

In this paper, the DCM [8] theory is adopted to guide us select patterns and each relation type is analogy to a category in document collections. The approach proposed here for selecting patterns is based on two assumptions. The first is that patterns shared by majority of entity pairs in a relation are vital important for this relation. In other words, patterns that appear frequently within a relation category should be critical in term of classification, while patterns that shared only by few entity pairs are either less commonly used or provide implicit evidence of a relation. Following paper [2], to capture this property we define pattern significance, $Sig_{i,R}$, to weight pattern p_i within relation R.

$$Sig_{i,R} = \frac{\log_2\left(N_{i,R} + 1\right)}{\log_2\left(N_R + 1\right)} \tag{2}$$

Where $N_{i,R}$ is the number of pattern p_i in the cluster of relation R. N_R is the total number of patterns in Relation R.

The second assumption is that patterns shared by more than one relation category may be ambiguous and express different amounts of evidence to different relations. Patterns appear in more relations, more ambiguous it is. Similarly, we define the following Equation to capture the clarity of pattern p_i.

$$C_i = \begin{cases} \log_2 \frac{n * \max\limits_{j \in \{1 \cdots n\}} \{Sig_{i,R_j}\}}{\sum_{j=1}^{n} Sig_{i,R_j}} * \frac{1}{\log_2 n}, & n > 1 \\ 1, & n = 1 \end{cases} \quad (3)$$

Where n is the number of relation clusters that p_i belongs to. If a pattern p_i only appear in one relation cluster, its clarity C_i achieve the maximum value 1.

Following the theory of DCM, the weight of pattern p_i within relation R, $W_{i,R}$, is defined as follows:

$$W_{i,R} = \frac{Sig_{i,R}^2 * C_i^2}{\sqrt{Sig_{i,R}^2 + C_i^2}} * \sqrt{2} \quad (4)$$

To filter out noisy patterns, we trade off significance and clarity to get the weight of patterns in a relation category following Equation 4. We remove the patterns with the weight less than θ through all of the relation category.

4 Experiments

We set up experiments to answer the following questions: (i) Does the proposed features improve the accuracy in comparison with the State-of-the-art? (ii) How does the pattern selection procedure affect the performance of system.

4.1 DataSet

Manually labeling training data is a time-consuming and labor intensive task. In this paper, DS is adopted to automatically generate the training data. We employ Wikipedia[3] as the target corpus and Freebase as the knowledge base.

In order to obtain the training data using DS, previous works usually abide by the following steps. First, the named entity recognition (NER) tagger segments textual data into sentences and finds entity mentions in the corpus. Then, the entity pairs are associated with Freebase RDF triples. If the entity pairs appear in Freebase, the relevant sentences are selected as positive examples. This data generating procedure is simple and straightforward. However, it is inefficiency especially when processing large corpus. In this paper, we firstly use Lucene[4] to index the Freebase Wikipedia Extraction (WEX)[5]. Then, we extract Freebase

[3] http://www.wikipedia.org/

[4] http://lucene.apache.org/

[5] http://wiki.freebase.com/wiki/WEX

RDF triples and query index with *subject+object* to find relevant sentences. Third, the sentences are filtered except in accordance with the following two conditions: (i) The maximum length of a sentence is L tokens. (ii) The gaps of entity pairs should not exceed G tokens. Finally, since classes with very few training instances are hard to learn, the relations with labeled samples exceed N are selected as our experimental data.

4.2 Experimental Settings

According to the definition in section 1, relation extraction can be seen as a multi-class classification problem and the task of relation extraction is to identify certain predefined relationship between two entities. Note that there might not exist any semantic relationship between the two entities.

In this paper, we mainly focus on the entity pairs contain some relationships. Because we do not attempt to filter out entity pairs with no relationships, all of the entity pairs generated in section 4.1 have certain relationship. The sentence length greatly influences dependency parse results and the smaller the gaps of two entities is, the more likely that they have some relations. In the following experiments, we fix the maximum length of a sentence $L = 40$ and the maximum gaps of entity pairs $G = 15$. We pay attention to the relations with labeled samples exceed 2000. For each relation, we randomly select 1000 examples as the training instances and 1000 example as test instances. Finally, six mostly frequently mentioned relations are preserved. These include, for example, *written_by*, *produced_by*, *place_of_birth*, *profession*, *directed_by* and *nationality*.

After selecting dataset, we then use method proposed in section 3 to extract feature vectors. Each feature vector is assigned a relational label according to the relation that exists between the two entities. Finally, we train a multi-class classifier to learn a classification model to classify all of the relation types. For simplicity, we usually use logistic regression as our classifier.

To evaluate the performance of proposed feature, the test instances automatically generated by DS are regarded as a gold standard. Once all the test instances have been classified, they can be ranked by confidence score and the precision@N is used to evaluate the topmost results by the classification model.

4.3 Our Proposed Feature vs. State-of-the-art

In DS relation extraction, multiple sentences corresponding to an entity pair may be achieved. How to leverage information from multiple sentences is crucial for the final performance especially when it is not sufficient to deduce the relationship between two entities only from one sentence. Mintz et al. [11] simply combine feature extracted from different sentences as a richer feature vector to deal with this problem. Besides, Bollegala et al. [4] proposed relation dual representation and entity pairs are represented as the distribution over patterns. Then, entity pairs are clustered to identify sematic relations. To evaluate the performance of this paper proposed feature, we select Mintz et al. [11] and

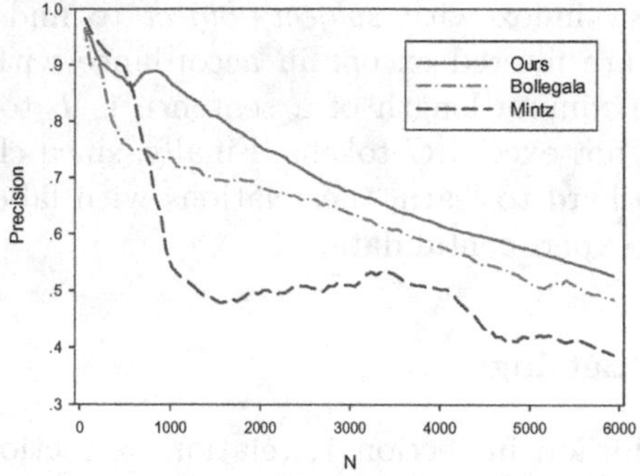

Fig. 3. The precision@N curve of six relation types

Bollegala et al. [4] proposed feature and as competitors to compare with pattern space features.

The precision@N results are presented in Figure 3, *Ours* is the feature proposed in this paper and we select the best DCM selection threshold $\theta = 0.2$ (See section 4.4). In addition, we simply use L2-regularized multi-class logistic regression[6] as classifier for all of these features. From Figure 3, we can have the following observation: (i) *Mintz* proposed feature achieves relatively high precision with a small N and encounters a sharp decline in the precision when N is greater than 900. (ii) *Ours* achieves about 13% improvement over *Mintz* and 4% improvement over *Bollegala* at precision@6000. In the dataset, about 9.5% of the test instances encounter *null pattern* problem when using *Bollegala*. Pattern space features have made a better solution of the *null pattern* problem. *Ours* achieves the best result, which demonstrates the effectiveness of pattern space features.

4.4 The Effect of Pattern Selection

The number of patterns in the pattern space is the final dimension of feature vector. Excessive number of patterns not only leads to high computational cost but also feature sparsity. In this paper, we developed a pattern selection procedure to find the typical and discriminative patterns based on DCM. We experimentally study the effect of pattern selection procedure. First, we study the impact of DCM threshold value on the number of patterns. Figure 4 presents the changing curve of the pattern number along with DCM threshold θ. We can see that the pattern number suffers a sharp decline when the threshold between 0.1 and 0.2. Next, we investigate the effect of DCM threshold value on the average precision of various relation types. Figure 5 presents the precision of six types against the threshold θ. *Mean* represents the mean average precision of six relation types. We can see that the precision reaches the maximum value when the threshold

[6] `http://www.csie.ntu.edu.tw/~cjlin/liblinear/`

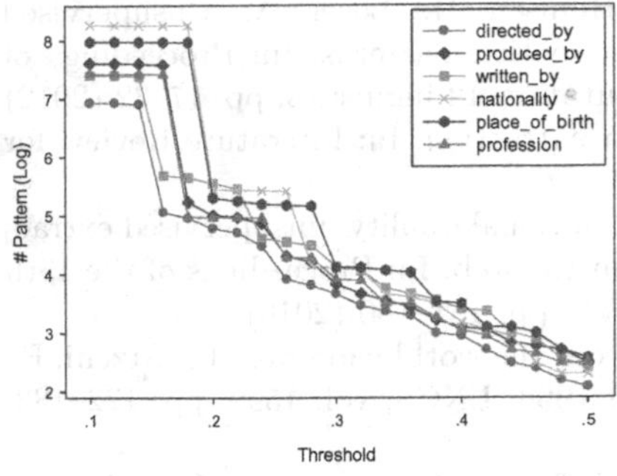

Fig. 4. The sensitivity of pattern number against DCM threshold

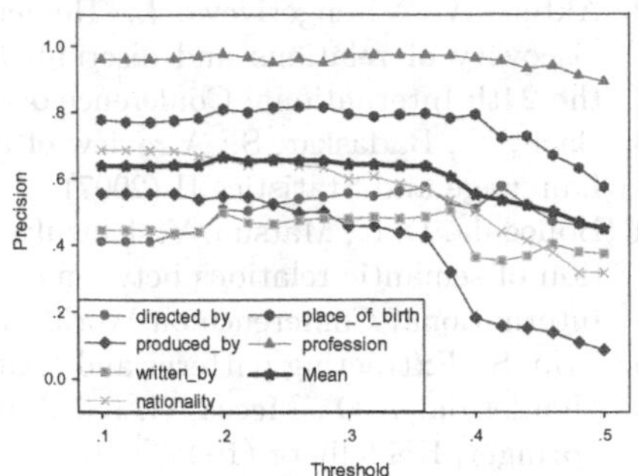

Fig. 5. The effect of varying the DCM threshold

is set $\theta = 0.2$, which is the best parameter that used in the above experiments. At the same time, there is no significant difference about the number of the patterns belonging to each relation type. Consequently, the mean average precision reaches the maximum value is reasonable. It is apparent that the pattern selection algorithm can select distinctive basis patterns and greatly reduce the dimensionality of feature vector while maintaining the high precision.

5 Conclusion

We proposed pattern space features for relation extraction. Pattern space features can leverage information from multiple sentences to deduce the relations between two entities. Each dimension of pattern space feature vector corresponds to a basis pattern. For two pattern space feature vectors to match, all of their dimensions no longer need to match exactly due to pattern similarity function. Furthermore, to avoid noisy patterns, we devised a pattern selection procedure to filter out patterns with low distinctiveness. Experimental results demonstrate that the proposed feature significantly outperforms State-of-the-art. The proposed pattern filtering procedure are effective for the improvement of precision.

Acknowledgments. This work was supported by the National Natural Science Foundation of China (No.61202329, 61272332, 61333018), CCF-Tencent Open Research Fund and the Opening Project of Beijing Key Laboratory of Internet Culture and Digital Dissemination Research(ICDD201301). We thank the anonymous reviewers for their insightful comments.

References

1. Agichtein, E., Gravano, L.: Snowball: extracting relations from large plain-text collections. In: Proceedings of the Fifth ACM Conference on Digital Libraries, pp. 85–94 (2000)

2. Akbik, A., Visengeriyeva, L., Herger, P., Hemsen, H., Löser, A.: Unsupervised discovery of relations and discriminative extraction patterns. In: Proceedings of the 24th International Conference on Computational Linguistics, pp. 17–32 (2012)
3. Bach, N., Badaskar, S.: A review of relation extraction. In: Literature Review for Language and Statistics II (2007)
4. Bollegala, D.T., Matsuo, Y., Ishizuka, M.: Relational duality: unsupervised extraction of semantic relations between entities on the web. In: Proceedings of the 19th International Conference on World Wide Web, pp. 151–160 (2010)
5. Brin, S.: Extracting patterns and relations from the world wide web. In: Atzeni, P., Mendelzon, A.O., Mecca, G. (eds.) WebDB 1998. LNCS, vol. 1590, pp. 172–183. Springer, Heidelberg (1999)
6. Bunescu, R., Mooney, R.: Subsequence kernels for relation extraction. In: Advances in Neural Information Processing Systems 18, p. 171 (2006)
7. Bunescu, R.C., Mooney, R.J.: A shortest path dependency kernel for relation extraction. In: Proceedings of the Conference on Human Language Technology and Empirical Methods in Natural Language Processing, pp. 724–731 (2005)
8. Fung, G.P.C., Yu, J.X., Lu, H.: Discriminative category matching: Efficient text classification for huge document collections. In: Proceedings of the 2002 IEEE International Conference on Data Mining, ICDM 2002, pp. 187–194 (2002)
9. Harris, Z.: Distributional structure. Word 10(23), 146–162 (1954)
10. Hasegawa, T., Sekine, S., Grishman, R.: Discovering relations among named entities from large corpora. In: Proceedings of the 42nd Annual Meeting on Association for Computational Linguistics (2004)
11. Mintz, M., Bills, S., Snow, R., Jurafsky, D.: Distant supervision for relation extraction without labeled data. In: Proceedings of the Joint Conference of the 47th Annual Meeting of the ACL and the 4th International Joint Conference on Natural Language Processing of the AFNLP, vol. 2, pp. 1003–1011 (2009)
12. Qian, L., Zhou, G., Kong, F., Zhu, Q., Qian, P.: Exploiting constituent dependencies for tree kernel-based semantic relation extraction. In: Proceedings of the 22nd International Conference on Computational Linguistics, pp. 697–704 (2008)
13. Riedel, S., Yao, L., McCallum, A.: Modeling relations and their mentions without labeled text. In: Balcázar, J.L., Bonchi, F., Gionis, A., Sebag, M. (eds.) ECML PKDD 2010, Part III. LNCS, vol. 6323, pp. 148–163. Springer, Heidelberg (2010)
14. Rosenfeld, B., Feldman, R.: Clustering for unsupervised relation identification. In: Proceedings of the Sixteenth ACM Conference on Information and Knowledge Management, pp. 411–418 (2007)
15. Suchanek, F.M., Ifrim, G., Weikum, G.: Combining linguistic and statistical analysis to extract relations from web documents. In: Proceedings of the 12th ACM SIGKDD International Conference on Knowledge Discovery and Data Mining, pp. 712–717 (2006)

An Investigation on Statistical Machine Translation with Neural Language Models

Yinggong Zhao, Shujian Huang, Huadong Chen, and Jiajun Chen

State Key Laboratory for Novel Software Technology,
Nanjing University, Nanjing 210046, China
{zhaoyg,huangsj,chenhd,chenjj}@nlp.nju.edu.cn

Abstract. Recent work has shown the effectiveness of neural probabilistic language models(NPLMs) in statistical machine translation(SMT) through both reranking the n-best outputs and direct decoding. However there are still some issues remained for application of NPLMs. In this paper we further investigate through detailed experiments and extension of state-of-art NPLMs. Our experiments on large-scale datasets show that our final setting, i.e., decoding with conventional n-gram LMs plus un-normalized feedforward NPLMs extended with word clusters could significantly improve the translation performance by up to averaged 1.1 BLEU on four test datasets, while decoding time is acceptable. And results also show that current NPLMs, including feedforward and RNN still cannot simply replace n-gram LMs for SMT.

Keywords: statistical machine translation, neural probabilistic language model, recurrent neural network, feedforward neural network.

1 Introduction

Language model is the key component of SMT system as it ensures the fluency of the translation output. For a long period, n-gram LMs, which model over discrete representations of words have been the dominant form. However data sparsity always be an obstacle of such model as the size of training data cannot meet the increasing of parameters under the one-hot representation.

To address this issue, Bengio et al. [2] proposed distributed word representations, in which each word is represented as a dense vector in a low-dimensional feature space(compared to conventional one-hot representation), modelling over which they propose a feed-forward NPLM. During training, the NPLM learns both a distributed representation for each word in the vocabulary and a probability distribution for n-grams over words representations. Furthermore, Mikolov et al. [12] introduced recurrent structure into neural network that can capture all previous words as context. Further experiments show that NPLMs can rival or even surpass traditional n-gram LMs [14,11] evaluated in terms of perplexity.

Although recent work [17,24] have shown that NPLMs can be directly incorporated into SMT system for direct decoding and outperform both baseline and simply re-ranking. There are some questions remained. Firstly, in both works

M. Sun et al. (Eds.): CCL and NLP-NABD 2014, LNAI 8801, pp. 175–186, 2014.

only un-normalized NPLM score are used during decoding. Although such usage could bring improvements, there is no detailed comparison on normalized and un-normalized NPLM for SMT decoding; secondly, current NPLM only train on part of words that occur in corpus and the rest words are simply truncated as <unk>; finally, although NPLMs can improve SMT as supplement, it would be interesting to see whether NPLMs can replace conventional n-gram LMs for SMT or other NLP tasks.

In this work, we try to answer the above questions. We demonstrate that un-normalized NPLM performs same as normalized for SMT, as context score turns to be constant, which means the cost can be heavily reduced during decoding. Then we extend current NPLMs with a simple strategy, i.e., we use word cluster for truncated words during NPLM training, which could further improve MT performance by another 0.2 BLEU on average. Finally, we compare our model with conventional n-gram LM and recurrent neural network(RNNLM) [10]. Results show that traditional n-gram LMs outperform current NPLMs, which means that they still cannot be simply replaced.

The rest of this paper is organized as follows: In section 2 we briefly review the state-of-art NPLMs with feedforward and RNN as examples. Then we present the implementation details on incorporating NPLMs to SMT systems in section 3. Experimental settings are reported in section 4. Then from 5 to 7 we discuss three questions separately. We conclude our work and present future work in section 9.

2 Overview of Neural Probabilistic Language Models

In this section, we briefly review current NPLM models. The basic idea behind NPLMs is to predict probability of word w given context $\mathbf{u}$. There are many types of NPLMs, e.g., feedforward [2], log-bilinear [13], recurrent neural network(RNN for short) [12]. One nice property of NPLMs is that for whatever n-gram input, the model can assign a non-zero score so that no smoothing or back-off is required. In this work, we mainly focus on two typical NPLMs, i.e., feedforward and recurrent.

Similar to n-gram LM, feedforward LM has fixed context size order given, whose architecture could be seen on figure 2. Let n be the order of the language model; let $\mathbf{u}$ range over contexts, i.e., strings of length $(n-1)$, and w range over words. The embeddings of $\mathbf{u}$ is concatenated at input layer and then mapped to output layer through project layer. Two hidden layers can learn non-linear knowledge. Meanwhile, the parameter complexity is $O(|V| + |H| * n)$, while it is $O(|V|^n)$ for n-gram LM.

One obstacle that hampers the application of feedforward NPLM is the heavy calculation caused by repeated summations throughout whole vocabulary under standard maximum likelihood estimation (MLE) in NPLM training. Vaswani et al. [24] combined strategies including rectifier linear units [16], noise contrastive estimation [8] and mini-batch learning for fast training.

Meanwhile, RNNLM (figure 2) is different from feedforward LM. The input layer is composed of a vector $w(t)$ that represents current word w_t and of vector

$s(t-1)$ that represents hidden layer from previous step. After training, the output layer represents $P(w_{t+1}|w_t, s(t-1))$. As RNNLM also faces heavy cost of training as feedforward. Mikolov et al. [12] decomposed $P(w_{t+1}|w_t, s(t-1))$ into $P(w_{t+1}|c_{t+1}, w_t, s(t-1))P(c_{t+1}|w_t, s(t-1))$ so as to reduce complexity from $O(|V|)$ to $O(\sqrt{|V|})$.

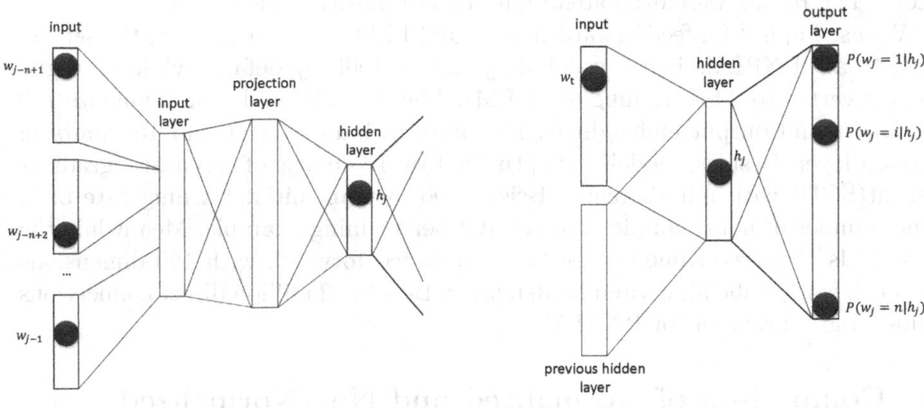

Fig. 1. Architectures of feedforward NPLM

Fig. 2. Architectures of RNNLM

3 Adding NPLMs to MT System

In order to incorporate neural LMs into MT system, we first rerank k-best lists with NPLMs following previous work. As feedforward NPLM scores n-grams, it can also be integrated into decoder just as conventional n-gram models. Different from conventional n-gram LM, for which only performs search for each input query, each time matrix operation is done for NPLMs, which makes caching a necessary. During decoding, we maintain a dictionary for each thread to store the n-grams that have been calculated.

4 Experimental Setting

In this section, we first list the detailed setting for whole experiment. The training data came from the NIST 2012 Chinese-English evaluation task with sentences shorter than 60 words. Phrases were extracted from all training data, while rules with nonterminals were extracted from only the FBIS corpus (LDC2003E14). We ran MERT on the NIST 2003 test data(MT03), while performance is tested from the NIST 2004 to 2008(referred as MT04, MT05, MT06, MT08). Alignments were extract with GIZA++ [19] with refinement from both directions. An in-house hierarchical phrase-based SMT system [5] was used to report main experimental results.

The baselines contained two conventional 5-gram LMs, estimated with modified Kneser-Ney smoothing [4] on the English side of the bitext and the 329M-word Xinhua portion of English Gigaword (LDC2011T07). Against these baselines, we tested systems that included the two conventional LMs as well as two 5-gram NPLMs trained on the same corpus. We trained both the log-linear models and the discriminative rerankers on 1000-best lists with MERT [18]. In order to make the results stable[6], we ran MERT three times and reported the average score. The results were evaluated under case-insensitive NIST BLEU.

We used nplm[1] for feedforward(ff for short) LM training. Following the setting in [24], all ff NPLMs had a vocabulary size of 100k by default while all digits are converted to 0 for training of NPLMs. The NPLMs used dimension size 150 for input and output embeddings, 750 units in hidden layer and 150 units in hidden layer. Besides, model was optimized by 10 epochs of stochastic gradient ascent(SGD) with mini-batches of size 1000 and an initial learning rate of 1. The number of noise samples was set 100 per training example. Meanwhile the RNNLMs[2] followed same setting for data as feedforward, with 150 dimensions for both word embeddings and hidden layer. Besides, 2 million direct connections under 4-gram was set for RNNLM.

5 Comparison of Normalized and Non-Normalized NPLMs for MT

In order to manifest the difference between normalized and unnormalized NPLMs, we run SMT experiments under both types of NPLMs, together with baseline setting that only uses two n-gram LMs. The detailed results could be found in table 1. We see that both re-ranking improves around 0.4 BLEU, while direct decoding can get better results up to over 0.85 BLEU. Besides, normalized NPLMs can achieve only slightly better performance(less than 0.05 BLEU on average)

Table 1. Results for Chinese-English experiments, without (baseline) and with neural LMs for reranking and integrated decoding

setting	mt03(dev)	mt04	mt05	mt06	mt08	test average
baseline	38.17	38.43	37.70	34.25	24.57	33.74
reranking+ff-normalized	38.84	38.62	37.98	35.00	25.08	34.17(+0.43)
reranking+ff-unnormalized	38.73	38.56	37.93	34.98	24.99	34.11(+0.37)
decoding+ff-normalized	38.91	39.45	38.72	34.87	25.27	34.58(+0.84)
decoding+ff-unnormalized	39.14	39.49	38.80	34.87	25.31	34.62(+0.88)
reranking+rnn-normalized-only	38.00	37.99	37.22	34.34	24.42	33.49 (-0.25)
reranking+rnn-unnormalized-only	37.30	36.99	35.89	33.36	23.66	32.48(-1.26)
reranking+rnn-normalized	38.69	38.46	37.85	35.04	25.03	34.09(+0.35)
reranking+rnn-unnormalized	38.61	38.28	37.74	34.84	24.88	33.94(+0.20)

[1] http://nlg.isi.edu/software/nplm/

[2] http://www.fit.vutbr.cz/mikolov/rnnlm/

Table 2. Running time in minutes for MT Chinese-English Evaluation datasets

setting	mt03	mt04	mt05	mt6	mt08	average
baseline	27	50	29	35	25	33.2
decoding+ff-normalized	3355	6563	5352	5691	4816	5155.4(×155.3)
decoding+ff-unnormalized	224	476	251	318	239	301.6(×9.1)
reranking+rnnlm-normalized	153	346	230	273	210	242.4
reranking+rnnlm-unnormalized	59	111	66	85	66	77.4

on re-ranking task, but un-normalized NLPMs outperform on decoding(also less than 0.05 BLEU on average). Obviously, the difference is so tiny that we believe we can use unnormalized NPLM score. Besides, we also collected the decoding time on different datasets presented on table 2. We observed that decoding with normalized NPLM is on average almost 155 times slower than baseline, and 17.1 times slower than with un-normalized NPLMs. The performance difference between normalized and unnormalized NPLMs for SMT may be the context score is a constant. In order to further verify this conclusion, we check the distribution of the context 4-grams for 1000-best output of MT03 using NPLM trained on Gigaword Xinhua portion, with the histogram plotted in figure 3. We could find that it obeys sharp normal distribution with μ -0.0717 and σ 0.3106, which means that the unnormalized NPLM score could be approximately equal to normalized score. Finally we could draw conclusion based on our experiments that unnormalized feedforward NPLM is sufficient for SMT, which is also consistent with the finding of [15].

Although in Section 2 we know that complexity is already reduced to $O(\sqrt{|V|})$ with decomposition, we want to see whether normalization term can be simply thrown away. As RNNLM cannot be incorporated for direct decoding for hierarchical phrase-based system, we check this idea with reranking only. Similarly, in table 2 reranking with unormalized RNNLMs is three times faster than normalized, but with a heavy loss on BLEU performance(see in table 1). For feedforward NPLM, the normalized term is summed over whole vocabulary, while RNNLM sums over only subset of vocabulary for RNNLM. The histogram of normalized term can be found in figure 4.

6 Incorporating Word Clusters for NPLMs

As we know the vocabulary size on large training set is usually quite big, e.g., the vocabulary size is 823.6k for Xinhua portion of Gigaword and 286.3k for target side of training data[3]. As a result, it is impractical to train NPLMs on whole vocabulary. Mentioned in section 4, the size was set 100k by default. We want to verify the effect of vocabulary size on BLEU performance. Without loss of generality, we trained both NPLMs on vocabulary size under 12.5k, 25k, 50k, 100k and 200k on both Gigaword Xinhua and target side of training data.

[3] When counting vocabulary size, all digits are converted to zero for fair comparison.

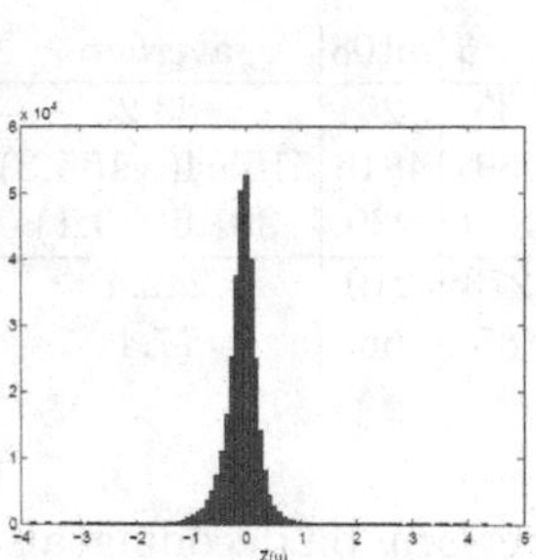

Fig. 3. Histogram of context normalized score of 1000-best of mt03 from feedforward NPLM trained on gigaword

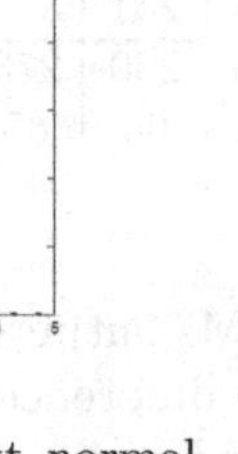

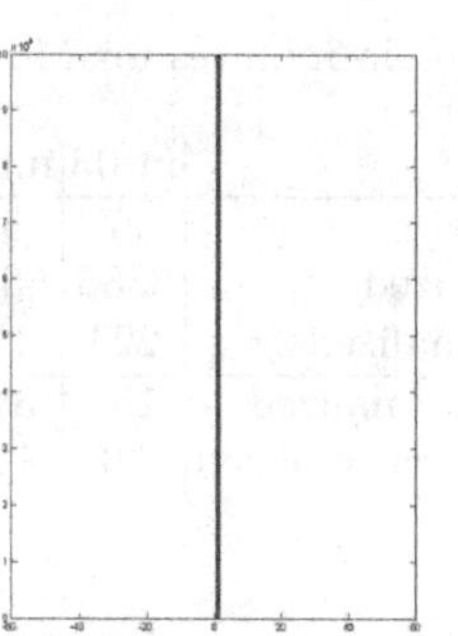

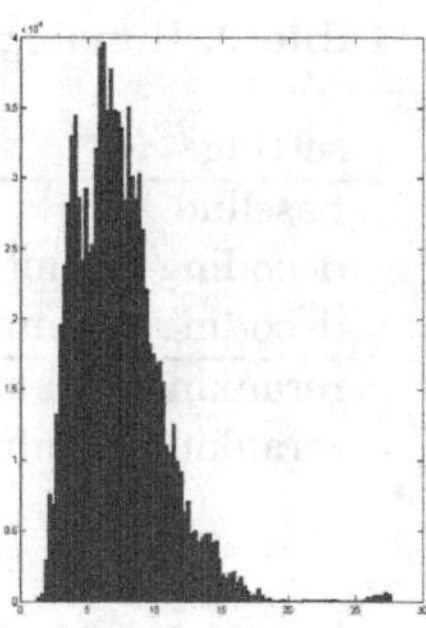

Fig. 4. Histogram of context normalized score of 1000-best of mt03 from RNNLM trained on gigaword, left is classes and right for words

The detailed BLEU results are shown in table 4. We can see that performance steadily improves as vocabulary size increases, while it drops when size turns from 100k to 200k. This means that larger vocabulary size does not mean better MT performance, as NPLMs cannot get precise estimation for low-frequency words. In contrast, things are different on n-gram LMs. In details, we trained two n-gram LMs with vocabulary 100k and got BLEU results of both tuning and test sets, which is shown on second row of table 4. We find that what is opposite to NPLMs, full-vocabulary n-gram LMs brings better performance than restricted vocabulary for SMT. Such results show that NPLM cannot obtain good estimate for low-frequency words.

As mentioned in section 4, all out-of-vocabulary words(OOVs) are replaced by some special like <unk>. Therefore there is no difference between two words A and B given same context if they both belong to OOVs, which means the missing of lot of information. Inspired by [26], who improved SMT with word clusters for both n-gram LMs and TMs, we also adopted word classes trained with mkcls[4] for OOVs. In details, each word not in word list is replaced with unk+word-class-label, while no changes for word within the list. With Fixing the vocabulary size as 100k, we trained different clusters-augmented NPLMs with numbers ranged from 250, 500, 1000 to 2000. The final MT results which are illustrated in table 5 show of NPLM augmented with word clusters can further achieve improvement than decoding with normal NPLMs by nearly 0.3 BLEU when cluster number is larger than 500. The biggest improvement on test dataset(MT05) could reach as high as 1.5 BLEU, which demonstrates that direct decoding with NPLMs plus word clusters achieves higher performance.

[4] code.google.com/p/giza-pp

Table 3. Results for Chinese-English experiments, without neural LM (baseline) and with neural LM for reranking and integrated decoding. For baseline, n-gram LMs are trained with full vocabulary.

setting	mt03(dev)	mt04	mt05	mt06	mt08	test average
Baseline	38.17	38.43	37.70	34.25	24.58	33.74
Decoding(ngram-100k)	37.29	38.08	37.09	33.69	24.40	33.31(-0.43)
Decoding+ff-12.5k	38.68	39.02	38.24	34.60	24.71	34.14(+0.40)
Decoding+ff-25k	38.95	39.17	38.75	34.65	24.73	34.33(+0.59)
Decoding+ff-50k	39.01	39.18	38.73	34.68	25.04	34.41(+0.67)
Decoding+ff-100k	39.14	39.49	38.80	34.87	25.31	34.62(+0.88)
Decoding+ff-200k	39.08	39.37	38.85	34.60	25.10	34.48(+0.74)

Table 4. Results for Chinese-English experiments, without neural LM (baseline) and with neural LM for reranking and integrated decoding. For baseline, n-gram LMs are trained with full vocabulary.

Model	Cutoff	
	Gigaword	NIST
Decoding+ff-12.5k	1043	313
Decoding+ff-25k	279	67
Decoding+ff-50k	75	14
Decoding+ff-100k	17	3
Decoding+ff-200k	6	1

Table 5. Results for Chinese-English experiments, without neural LM (baseline) and with neural LM for reranking and integrated decoding

setting	mt03(dev)	mt04	mt05	mt06	mt08	test average
Baseline	38.17	38.43	37.70	34.25	24.58	33.74
Decoding+ff-100k	39.14	39.49	38.80	34.87	25.31	34.62(+0.88)
Decoding+ff-100k+c100	39.06	39.31	38.63	35.00	25.30	34.56(+0.82)
Decoding+ff-100k+c500	39.40	39.53	38.78	35.60	25.65	34.89(+1.15)
Decoding+ff-100k+c1k	39.40	39.83	39.20	35.00	25.20	34.81(+1.07)
Decoding+ff-100k+c2k	39.17	39.70	39.05	35.10	25.56	34.86(+1.12)

7 Comparison of Different Types of LMs

As direct decoding with NPLMs can bring significant improvements, one important issue is that whether the NPLMs can replace conventional n-gram language model, which was concerned in[20]. Actually, such comparison has been conducted in terms of perplexity, one latest results could be found in [24]. In following sections, we will discuss this question throughout detailed experiments:

First of all, we tried direct decoding with n-gram or NPLM only. As mentioned in section 3, we only compare feedforward NPLM and n-gram. Table 6 shows the performance of decoding only with n-gram LM and NPLM respectively. Overall speaking, decoding with nplm only is averaged 1.3 BLEU lower than n-gram lms, while feedforward NPLMs augmented with word clusters can achieve better performance, with only about 1.0 BLEU point lower on average. Besides, compared with decoding under n-gram LMs vocabulary size 100k, such gap narrows to 0.9 BLEU and 0.6 BLEU separately. Here we can see that feedforward NPLMs still cannot replace n-gram LMs.

Table 6. Results for Chinese-English experiments, with only ngrams and neural LMs seperately

setting	mt03(dev)	mt04	mt05	mt06	mt08	test average
Baseline	38.17	38.43	37.70	34.25	24.58	33.74
Decoding(ngram-100k)	37.29	38.08	37.09	33.69	24.40	33.31(-0.43)
decoding+ff-100k	36.76	37.29	35.70	32.85	23.81	32.41(-1.33)
decoding+ff-100k+c1k	37.15	37.17	36.02	33.35	24.33	32.71(-1.03)

In order to further prove this observation, we experimented on all n-gram, feedforward and RNN LMs on a re-ranking task. We first removed language model features of 1000-best outputs from the baseline system. Then different combinations of LMs were appended to output results for re-ranking. Detailed results can be seen on table 7. We may see that when adding one type LM features, similar performance was achieved on feedforward and ngram LMs, but much lower on RNNLM. Similar result can be observed when combing two LMs. Finally the best results can be achieved using all LM features, with a 0.5 BLEU improvement against baseline.

Table 7. Results for Chinese-English experiments, with only ngrams and neural LMs seperately

setting	mt03(dev)	mt04	mt05	mt06	mt08	test average
hiero-baseline	38.17	38.43	37.70	34.25	24.57	33.74
reranking-no-lm	36.00	35.99	35.11	32.29	23.03	31.61(-1.93)
reranking+ngrams	38.29	38.10	37.58	34.53	24.71	33.73(-0.01)
reranking+ff	38.54	38.16	37.38	34.79	24.62	33.74 (+0.00)
reranking+rnnlm	38.00	37.99	37.22	34.34	24.42	33.49 (-0.25)
reranking+rnnlm+ff	38.73	38.53	37.79	34.93	24.85	34.03 (+0.29)
reranking+ngrams+ff	38.84	38.62	37.98	35.00	25.08	34.17 (+0.43)
reranking+ngrams+rnnlm	38.69	38.46	37.85	35.04	25.03	34.09(+0.35)
reranking+ngram+rnnlm+ff	39.13	38.43	37.95	35.23	25.30	34.23(+0.49)

Table 8. *Number of parameters and storage size for three types of LMs trained on gigaword xinhua portion, with vocabulary size 100k. The order for n-gram and feedforward LMs is 5. All parameter settings are illustrated in section 4.*

Layer	#Parameter
1-gram	100k
2-gram	5.56m
3-gram	8.87m
4-gram	12.58m
5-gram	13.76m

n-gram

Layer	#Parameter
Input Embeddings	100k×150
Input → Hidden 1	600×750
Hidden 1 → Hidden 2	750×150
Output Embeddings	100k×150

Feedforward

Layer	#Parameter
Input Embeedings	100k×150
Prev Hidden → Hidden	150×150
Output Embeddings	100k×150
4-gram direct connections	2m

RNN

Model	n-gram	feedforward	RNN
Size	1.62G	116.6M	114.6M+7.26M

Model Size

7.1 Comparison of LMs

In this section, we investigate the possible reason for the difference of performance three types LMs. We focus on the power of models in terms of parameter space, which is listed in table 8 given same training corpus and vocabulary size. All probability information is hard-encoded in n-gram LMs[5]. In contrast, words are mapped to low-dimensional representations via both input and output embeddings. For RNNLM, the context is composed only one previous word and one hidden vector that contains all previous information(represented as one 150×150 matrix). Meanwhile, in addition to both input and output embeddings, feedforward NPLM also comprises two hidden layers(one 600×750 matrix and one 750×150 matrix). We believe the difference of parameters may cause the low performance of NPLMs on SMT.

8 Related Work

Neural network language models have attracted widespread attentions in recent years due to its property to overcome curse of dimension through learning a low-dimensional distributed word representation. Currently there are two types of NPLMs, i.e., feedforward [2] and RNN [12].

We notice that there are some work that tried to apply NPLMs to MT. Schwenk et al. [21,22] applied feedforward and while Auli et al. [1] and Mikolov [10] investigated RNNLMs. Furthermore Le et al. [9] compared both NPLMs for MT. However, their usage in MT has largely been limited to reranking k-best lists for MT tasks with restricted vocabularies, which could not investigate the role

[5] Besides, bow information is also stored for back-off.

of NPLM for MT in details. Niehues et al. [17] integrated a RBM-based LM directly into a decoder for the first time. The work of Vaswani et al [24] is most related to our work, as they adopted NPLMs for direct decoding on a large-scale MT task, while we try to cover questions that are not covered in their work and further improve the performance.

The problem of normalized NPLM score was first discussed for log-bilinear model [15]. Later on both Niehues et al. [17] and Vaswani et al. [24] adopted unnormalized score for direct decoding, however they did not further investigate normalized score for MT and for other NPLMs(e.g., RNNLM), which were both discussed in this paper.

Word clustering has been used in language modeling for a long period [3]. Weubker et al. [26] improved MT with class-based n-gram LMs. Besides, Wu et al. [25] demonstrated that factored RNNLM with knowledge like POS and stem could outperform conventional RNNLM. However, as words can have more than one POS tag, which need to be inferred for the words in translation rules. Instead we used word cluster for truncated words to train NPLMs and also get further improvements.

Recent progress has shown the power of different NPLMs. We notice that Sundermeyer et al. [23] compared feedforward with RNN LMs on speech recognition task. However there is no systematic comparison of neural models against n-gram LM, which we believe is an important question for MT research.

9 Conclusion

In this work, we discuss several questions that exist in the application of NPLMs for SMT system. First of all, through detailed experiments we show that unnormalized feedforward NPLM is equivalent as normalized for decoding and reranking, while removing softmax can reduce the decoding time to 1/10. However, unnormalized RNNLM cannot replace normalized ones as it uses decomposition of probability. We also show that simply increasing vocabulary size of feedforward NPLMs cannot improve MT performance. Instead, replacing OOVs with cluster of original word can make better estimation of NPLMs and bring another 0.2 BLEU improvement for direct MT decoding. Finally, experiments also show that for MT both types of NPLMs might not simply replace conventional n-gram LM. We hope our findings can benefit the research on NPLMs in SMT.

In future, we will investigate following directions: first of all, we will conduct more experiments with direct decoding with RNNLMs for phrase-based MT system [1], in which way the power of RNNLM can be directly tested; secondly, we will compare the NCE training used in NPLM with self-normalization in neural network joint model(NNJM) [7]; we also plan to incorporate linguistic and domain information into the neural models.

Acknowledgement. This work is supported by the National Natural Science Foundation of China (No. 61223003), Specialized Research Fund for the Doctoral

Program of Higher Education of China(No. 20110091110003) and Graduate Research and Innovation Projects in Jiangsu Province(No. CXZZ12_0058). Shujian Huang is the corresponding author.

References

1. Auli, M., Galley, M., Quirk, C., Zweig, G.: Joint language and translation modeling with recurrent neural networks. In: Proceedings of the 2013 Conference on EMNLP, pp. 1044–1054 (2013)
2. Bengio, Y., Ducharme, R., Vincent, P., Jauvin, C.: A neural probabilistic language model. Journal of Machine Learning Research (2003)
3. Brown, P.F., Desouza, P.V., Mercer, R.L., Pietra, V.J.D., Lai, J.C.: Class-based n-gram models of natural language. Computational Linguistics 18(4), 467–479 (1992)
4. Chen, S.F., Goodman, J.: An empirical study of smoothing techniques for language modeling. Tech. Rep. TR-10-98, Harvard University Center for Research in Computing Technology (1998)
5. Chiang, D.: Hierarchical phrase-based translation. Computational Linguistics 33(2), 201–228 (2007)
6. Clark, J.H., Dyer, C., Lavie, A., Smith, N.A.: Better Hypothesis Testing for Statistical Machine Translation: Controlling for Optimizer Instability. In: Proceedings of the 49th Annual Meeting of the Association for Computational Linguistics: Human Language Technologies, Portland, Oregon, USA, pp. 176–181. Association for Computational Linguistics (June 2011), http://www.aclweb.org/anthology/P11-2031
7. Devlin, J., Zbib, R., Huang, Z., Lamar, T., Schwartz, R., Makhoul, J.: Fast and robust neural network joint models for statistical machine translation. In: Proceedings of the ACL, Association for Computational Linguistics, Baltimore (2014)
8. Gutmann, M., Hyvärinen, A.: Noise-contrastive estimation: A new estimation principle for unnormalized statistical models. In: Proceedings of AISTATS (2010)
9. Le, H.S., Allauzen, A., Yvon, F.: Measuring the influence of long range dependencies with neural network language models. In: Proceedings of the NAACL-HLT 2012 Workshop: Will We Ever Really Replace the N-gram Model? On the Future of Language Modeling for HLT, Montréal, Canada (2012)
10. Mikolov, T.: Statistical Language Models Based on Neural Networks. Ph.D. thesis, Brno University of Technology (2012)
11. Mikolov, T., Deoras, A., Kombrink, S., Burget, L., Černocký, J.H.: Empirical evaluation and combination of advanced language modeling techniques. In: Proceedings of INTERSPEECH, pp. 605–608 (2011)
12. Mikolov, T., Karafiát, M., Burget, L., Černocký, J.H., Khudanpur, S.: Recurrent neural network based language model. In: Proceedings of INTERSPEECH (2010)
13. Mnih, A., Hinton, G.: Three new graphical models for statistical language modelling. In: Proceedings of ICML (2007)
14. Mnih, A., Hinton, G.: A scalable hierarchical distributed language model. In: NIPS (2009)
15. Mnih, A., Teh, Y.W.: A fast and simple algorithm for training neural probabilistic language models. In: Proceedings of the 29th ICML, pp. 1751–1758 (2012)
16. Nair, V., Hinton, G.E.: Rectified linear units improve restricted Boltzmann machines. In: Proceedings of ICML, pp. 807–814 (2010)
17. Niehues, J., Waibel, A.: Continuous space language models using Restricted Boltzmann Machines. In: Proceedings of IWSLT (2012)

18. Och, F.J.: Minimum error rate training in statistical machine translation. In: Proceedings of ACL, pp. 160–167 (2003)
19. Och, F.J., Ney, H.: A systematic comparison of various statistical alignment models. Computational Linguistics 29(1), 19–51 (2003)
20. Ramabhadran, B., Khudanpur, S., Arisoy, E. (eds.): Proceedings of the NAACL-HLT 2012 Workshop: Will We Ever Really Replace the N-gram Model? On the Future of Language Modeling for HLT, Montréal, Canada (June 2012)
21. Schwenk, H.: Continuous space language models. Computer Speech and Language 21, 492–518 (2007)
22. Schwenk, H.: Continuous-space language models for statistical machine translation. Prague Bulletin of Mathematical Linguistics 93, 137–146 (2010)
23. Sundermeyer, M., Oparin, I., Gauvain, J.L., Freiberg, B., Schluter, R., Ney, H.: Comparison of feedforward and recurrent neural network language models. In: Proceedings of ICASSP (2013)
24. Vaswani, A., Zhao, Y., Fossum, V., Chiang, D.: Decoding with large-scale neural language models improves translation. In: Proceedings of the 2013 Conference on EMNLP, pp. 1387–1392.
25. Wu, Y., Lu, X., Yamamoto, H., Matsuda, S., Hori, C., Kashioka, H.: Factored language model based on recurrent neural network. In: Proceedings of COLING 2012, Mumbai, India, pp. 2835–2850 (December 2012)
26. Wuebker, J., Peitz, S., Rietig, F., Ney, H.: Improving statistical machine translation with word class models. In: Proceedings of EMNLP, pp. 1377–1381 (2013)

Using Semantic Structure to Improve Chinese-English Term Translation

Guiping Zhang[1], Ruiqian Liu[1], Na Ye[1], and Haihong Huang[2]

[1] Knowledge Engineering Research Center, Shenyang Aerospace University, Shenyang, China
[2] Chinese COMAC Shanghai Aircraft Design and Research Institute, Shanghai, China
zgp@ge-soft.com, liuruiqian99@163.com,
yena_1@126.com, Huanghaihong@comac.cc

Abstract. This paper introduces a method which aims at translating Chinese terms into English. Our motivation is providing deep semantic-level information for term translation through analyzing the semantic structure of terms. Using the contextual information in the term and the first sememe of each word in HowNet as features, we trained a Support Vector Machine (SVM) model to identify the dependencies among words in a term. Then a Conditional Random Field (CRF) model is trained to mark semantic relations for term dependencies. During translation, the semantic relations within the Chinese terms are identified and three features based on semantic structure are integrated into the phrase-based statistical machine translation system. Experimental results show that the proposed method achieves 1.58 BLEU points improvement in comparison with the baseline system.

Keywords: dependency analysis, semantic analysis, term translation.

1 Introduction

With the rapid development of science and technology, international technical exchanges are more and more frequent. As the carrier of scientific and technological concepts, the translation of technical terms has attracted much attention. It can not only be applied to cross-language information retrieval, but also to bilingual dictionary compilation.

Some researchers use internet or comparable corpora to mine bilingual terms[1, 2]. These methods cannot deal with out-of-vocabulary (OOV) terms, which is the focus of this paper. Previous work on OOV term translation mainly makes use of the characteristics of terms to extract some new features and combine them into the traditional statistical machine translation (SMT) framework. The new features include the character similarity between Japanese and Chinese[3], the part-of-speech (POS) sequence similarity between Chinese and Korean[4], the morphological correspondence between English and Chinese[5], the phonic correspondence between English and Japanese katakana[6].

We can see that current approaches mainly take advantage of bilingual linguistic information to improve term translation accuracy, and the semantic relations within

M. Sun et al. (Eds.): CCL and NLP-NABD 2014, LNAI 8801, pp. 187–199, 2014.

the term are seldom considered. However, such semantic information plays an important role for lexical reordering and word selection in term translation. For example, "雨伞(umbrella) 自动(automatic) 装袋(bagging) 机(machine)" is translated into "automatic umbrella bagging machine" by the NiuTrans SMT system[7]. But if we know that "自动(automatic)" depends on "装袋(bagging)", then the words in the translation should be reordered and adopts the preposition structure as "automatic bagging machine for umbrella". Another example is "切削(cutting) 工具(tool)". This term is translated into "cut tools" by NiuTrans, but through semantic analysis we can see that the semantic relationship between "切削(cutting)" and "工具(tool)" is property-host instead of patient-event. So this term should be translated into "cutting tools".

With the development of machine translation, semantic relations have been used as an additional feature to improve the translation performance[8]. However, there are too many types of semantic relationships in the translation of sentences and it is difficult to define them in a uniform framework. In contrast, the semantic relationship types within terms are much less and more specific. Besides, the head word of a term is always the last word, which also reduced the difficulty of analyzing terms. Therefore the dependency and semantic analysis result of terms can be more accurate than sentences, and the term semantic structure will be helpful for term translation.

In this paper, we propose a Chinese-English term translation method based on the term semantic analysis. First we use words, part of speech (POS) tags, word distances, word contexts and the first sememe of a word in HowNet[9] as features to train a dependency analysis model by SVM. The model is used to identify dependencies embedded inside a term. A CRF model is used afterwards to incorporate the dependencies and acquire the semantic structure of the Chinese term. Next, three semantic-based features (lexical reordering feature, word selection feature and POS selection feature) are extracted and integrated into the phrase-based SMT translation system. Experimental results show that our method is effective.

This paper is organized as follows: in section 2 we give the framework of the Chinese-English term translation system. In section 3 we introduce the Chinese term semantic analysis method. In section 4 the three features based on semantic structure for term translation are described. Experimental results are shown in section 5. Finally, we draw conclusions in section 6.

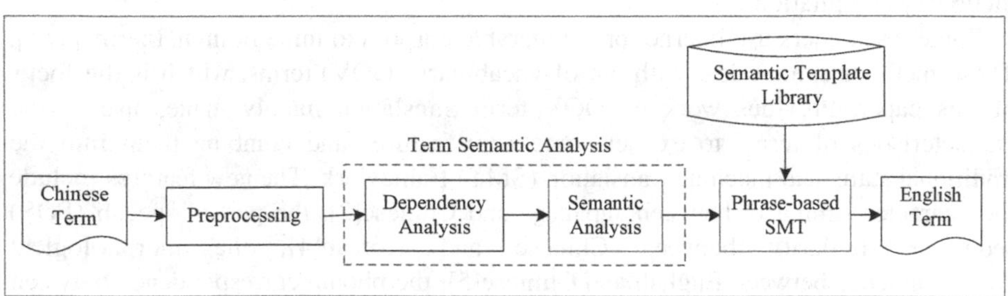

Fig. 1. The framework of the Chinese-English term translation system

2 System Framework

The framework of the Chinese-English term translation system is shown in Figure 1. In the pre-processing stage, Chinese word segmentation and POS tagging are performed. Then the labelled term is input to the term semantic analysis module, which is divided into two parts. Firstly, the dependency analysis module identifies the dependency relationships within the term as shown in figure 2.

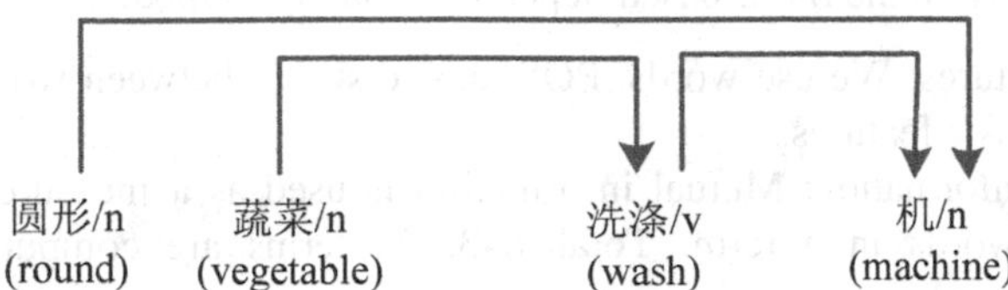

Fig. 2. Term dependency analysis result

Secondly, the semantic analysis module identifies the semantic relationship between each two dependent words as shown in Figure 3.

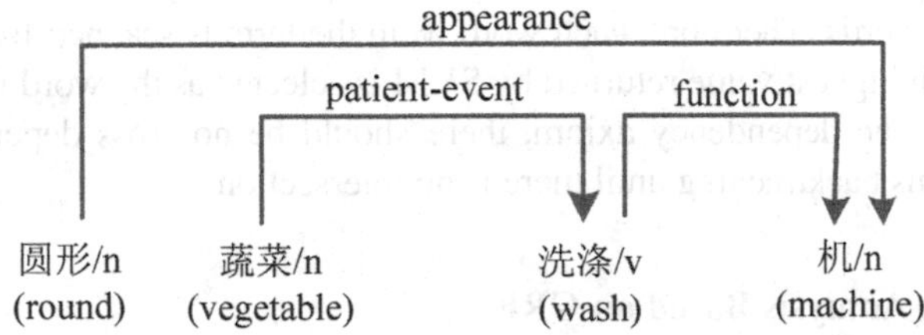

Fig. 3. Term semantic analysis result

After semantic analysis, the term is input to a phrase-based SMT module for translation. On the basis of the semantic structure within the term, three additional features for lexical reordering, word selection and POS selection are extracted through matching the semantic template library. Then the new features are integrated into the SMT model together with the traditional machine translation features to achieve the optimal translation.

3 Term Semantic Analysis

In order to use semantic structure to improve Chinese-English term translation, we should analyze the Chinese terms in semantic level. However, existing dependency analysis tools like Stanford parser[1] do not perform well on Chinese terms. This is because Chinese terms have some special characteristics such as (1) there are many out-

[1] http://nlp.stanford.edu/software/

of-vocabulary words in terms; (2) most terms are noun phrases without head verbs; (3) there is few appropriate corpora designed for terms. Due to the above reasons, a general parser is incapable of dealing those dependencies in a term. In order to solve these problems, we propose a term semantic analysis approach in this paper.

3.1 Dependency Analysis Based on SVM

Through analyzing the characteristics of Chinese terms, we select the following characteristics to train the SVM based dependency analysis model:

(1) Basic features: We use words, POS tags, distance between words and context information as basic features.

(2) Mutual information: Mutual information is used as a measure of correlation degree among words in a term. Total 643,908 terms are computed for mutual information.

(3)The first sememe in HowNet: This feature is generated according to Liu[10], presenting the semantic categories of a word. First sememe of two words can be used to compute their semantic relations.

During dependency analysis, the SVM model is used to analyze each two words in the term and returns a real value. This value indicates the probability that there is dependency between the two words. Therefore, each word w_i in the term is scanned from left to right and the word with highest value returned by SVM is selected as the word that w_i depends on. According to the dependency axiom, there should be no cross dependency, so the algorithm performs backtracking until there is no intersection.

3.2 Semantic Analysis Based on CRF

Through analyzing the characteristics of technical terms, this paper defined 14 types of semantic relationships as shown in Table 1 and two syntactic level relationships which include the structure of "之(of)" and the structure of "与(with)". In order to reflect the semantic relationships between words inside a term, we further divide the relationship type "property-host" into seven subtypes, namely "measurement", "appearance", "situation", "nature", "quantity", "category" and "function".

Table 1. Definition of the semantic relationships

No.	Type	No.	Type
1	Agent-Event	8	Usage
2	Patient-Event	9	Negation
3	Property-Host	10	Name
4	Material-Product	11	Location
5	Overall-Part	12	Continuity
6	Suffix	13	Degree
7	Mode	14	Object

We then choose CRF as our tool to analyze term semantics in this paper. The selected features are shown in table 2.

Table 2. Features for dependency analysis

Feature	Description
WD1	modifier
WD2	modified word
POS1	POS of the modifier
POS2	POS of the modified word
WD1_ATOM	first sememe of the modifier
WD2_ATOM	first sememe of the modified word
PRE_WD	word that modifies the modifier
PRE_POS	POS of the word that modifies the modifier
UN/UNKN	whether the modifier is the head

4 Term Translation Based on Semantic Structure

Traditional statistical machine translation methods use the source-channel model, which is shown in formula 1. It allows an independent modelling of target language model $Pr(e_1^I)$ and translation model $Pr(f_1^J / e_1^I)$.

$$\hat{e}_1^I = \underset{e_1^I}{argmax}\left\{Pr(e_1^I / f_1^J)\right\} \tag{1}$$

$$= \underset{e_1^I}{argmax}\left\{Pr(e_1^I)\cdot Pr(f_1^J / e_1^I)\right\} \tag{2}$$

An alternative to the classical source-channel approach is the direct modeling of the posterior probability $Pr(e_1^I / f_1^J)$. Using a log-linear model[11], we obtain formula 3:

$$Pr\left(e_1^I \mid f_1^J\right) = \exp\left(\sum_{m=1}^{M}\lambda_m h_m\left(e_1^I, f_1^J\right)\right)\cdot Z\left(f_1^J\right) \tag{3}$$

Here, $Z\left(f_1^J\right)$ denotes the appropriate normalization constant. As a decision rule, we obtain formula 4:

$$\hat{e}_1^I = \underset{e_1^I}{\arg\max}\left\{\sum_{m=1}^{M}\lambda_m h_m\left(e_1^I, f_1^J\right)\right\} \tag{4}$$

New features can be added to it freely, so in this paper, we propose three new features based on the semantic structure of the Chinese term to improve the lexical reordering, word selection and POS selection in the term. This section will describe the features in detail.

4.1 Lexical Reordering Feature

This feature aims at modelling the influence of semantic relationships on the order of words within the scope of a phrase. Suppose there is a Chinese phrase *c* and the corresponding English phrase *e*, we calculate the lexical reordering probability between *c* and *e*. This probability is estimated through the semantic relationships of the word pairs. If there are *N* dependent word pairs, then we examine the word alignment and extract the pairs with straight order to construct set R_1 and extract the pairs with inversed order to construct set R_2. And the lexical reordering probability can be computed with formula 5.

$$p_{lex\_od}(c,e) = \begin{cases} \alpha_1 \\ \dfrac{\sum_{i=1}^{|R_1|} p_i(w_1,w_2,r) + \sum_{i=1}^{|R_2|}(1-p_i(w_1,w_2,r)) + \beta(N-|R_1|-|R_2|)}{N} \end{cases} \quad (5)$$

where w_1 and w_2 are the two dependent words, and $p_i(w_1,w_2, r)$ is the probability that w_1 and w_2 has straight order when they have a semantic relationship of *r*. The third component in the numerator refers to the number of words whose dependent word is out of the scope of the current phrase. β is a scaling factor and is empirically set to 0.1. If *c* has only one word, then we set the probability to a constant α_1.

The value of $p_i(w_1,w_2, r)$ is stored in the lexical reordering template as follows:

$$(w_1|w_2)\ \#\ r \qquad\qquad p(w_1, w_2, r)$$

We use maximum likelihood estimation to compute $p(w_1, w_2, r)$ as formula 6 shown.

$$p(w_1,w_2,r) = \frac{c_t(w_1,w_2,r)}{c(w_1,w_2,r)} \quad (6)$$

where $c_t(w_1,w_2,r)$ is the frequency that w_1 and w_2 has straight order, and $c(w_1,w_2,r)$ is the total frequency. Through the formula we get the lexical reordering template as shown in figure 4. If the word pair "储物(w_1)|箱(w_2)" has the semantic relationship of "function", then the corresponding English part of the word pair has the probability of 83.81 percent to be in straight order.

(储物|箱) #function	0.8381
(处理|用) #suffix	0.8333
(底盘|修理) #agent-event	0
(服装|尺) #category	0.1667

Fig. 4. Examples of the lexical reordering template

4.2 Word Selection Feature

This feature aims at modeling the influence of semantic relationships on word selection. Suppose there is a Chinese word pair $(w_1|w_2)$, we calculate the probability of their corresponding translations $(t_1|t_2)$ if they have the semantic relationship of r. The probability is stored in the word selection template as follows:

$$(w_1|w_2)\ \#\ r\ \#\ (t_1/t_2) \qquad\qquad p(w_1, w_2, r)$$

The template shows that if $(w_1|w_2)$ has the semantic relationship r then they have the probability of $p(w_1, w_2, r)$ to be translated to $(t_1|t_2)$. The probability is also computed by maximum likelihood estimation. We give some examples of word selection template in figure 5.

(储物|箱) # function # (storage|box)	0.721
(储物|箱) # agent-event # (for storing|box)	0.653
(服装|尺) # category # (for clothes|spline)	0.75
(服装|尺) # category # (dress|ruler)	0.25

Fig. 5. Examples of the word selection template

According to traditional phrase based statistical machine translation method, the word pair "储物|箱" has higher probability to be translated into "storage|box". However, with the above templates, if we know that the semantic relationship between "储物" and "箱" is "agent-event", then we know that the word pair is more likely to be translated into "for storing|box".

Suppose there is a Chinese phrase c and the corresponding English phrase e, we calculate the word selection probability between c and e. This probability is estimated through the word pairs with semantic relationships. If in the Chinese phrase c, word pair $(w_1|w_2)$ has semantic relationship r, and its candidate English translation is $(t_1|t_2)$ which matches a word selection template, then we use the probability in the template as the translation probability of the word pair. We add all the N probabilities which match a word selection template as the word selection probability of the phrase c. Formula 7 shows the calculation. If c has only one word, then we set the probability to a constant α_2.

$$p_{word\_sl}(c,e) = \begin{cases} \alpha_2 \\ \frac{\sum_{i=1}^{|N|} p(w_1, w_2, r)}{|N|} \end{cases} \tag{7}$$

4.3 POS Selection Feature

Because many words in technical terms do not appear frequently in the corpus, so it may be difficult to match the template if we follow the template style in section 4.2. To solve this data sparseness problem, we use POS sequence instead of the word itself in the POS selection template. Suppose there is a Chinese word pair $(w_1|w_2)$, we calculate the probability of their corresponding POS $(POS_1|POS_2)$ if they have the semantic relationship of r. The probability is stored in the POS selection template as follows:

$(w_1|w_2)$ # r # $(POS_1|POS_2)$ $\quad p(w_1, w_2, r)$

The template shows that if $(w_1|w_2)$ has the semantic relationship r then they have the probability of $p(w_1, w_2, r)$ to be translated to $(POS_1|POS_2)$. The probability is also computed by maximum likelihood estimation. We give some examples of POS selection template in figure 6.

（储物|箱）# function # (JJ|NN)	0.785
（储物|箱）# function # (NN|NN)	0.215
（储物|箱）# agent-event # (IN NN|NN)	1
（处理|水）# patient-event # (VB|NN)	0.5

Fig. 6. Examples of the POS selection template

The POS selection template shows that if "储物|箱" has the semantic relationship of "function" then the probability of its corresponding English POS sequences being "JJ|NN" is 0.785, and "NN|NN" is 0.215.

Suppose in the Chinese phrase c, word pair $(w_1|w_2)$ has semantic relationship r. If the candidate English translation has a POS sequence $(POS_1|POS_2)$ and matches a POS selection template, then we use the probability in the template as the translation probability of the word pair. We add all the N probabilities which match a POS selection template as the POS selection probability of the phrase c. Formula 8 shows the calculation. If c has only one word, then we set the probability to a constant α_3.

$$p_{POS\_sl}(c,e) = \begin{cases} \alpha_3 \\ \frac{\sum_{i=1}^{|N|} p(w_1, w_2, r)}{|N|} \end{cases} \tag{8}$$

This paper used 452,781 Chinese-English terms from the patent titles given by State Patent Office of China to extract the templates. Our trained SVM model and CRF model are applied to perform semantic analysis on these terms. The Stanford postagg[2] is applied for POS tagging and GIZA++ is applied for word alignment.

5 Experimental Results and Analysis

In this section, we describe the experiments which we carried out to test the performance of the improvements presented in the previous sections.

5.1 Data Setup

A. Data Setup for Term Semantic Analysis

Our experiments are carried out on 642,908 terms extracted from patent documents. The term dependency analysis model and the semantic analysis model are trained

[2] http://nlp.stanford.edu/software/

with 3000 manually labelled terms and we choose 238 terms as a testing corpus. Each term has an average length of 5.07 words.

B. Data Setup for Term Translation

Our term translation experiments are carried out on the 451,500 terms mentioned in the above section. Table 3 shows some statistical characteristics of the corpus for term translation.

We use the IRLAS[3] tool to perform Chinese word segmentation. The English terms are tokenized, lowercased and POS tagged by the Stanford tool. The GIZA++ tool is used to perform bilingual word alignment, and NiuTrans is taken as the baseline system.

Table 3. The characteristics of the corpus

		Ch	En
Train	Term pairs	450000	
	Ave length	4.262	4.829
Dev	Term pairs	500	
	Ave length	4.250	4.896
	Perplexity	465.06	439.22
Test	Term pairs	1000	
	Ave length	4.318	4.931
	Perplexity	392.52	378.05

5.2 Results

A. The Result of Semantic Analysis

We build two baseline systems for comparison. In the first system, all words depend on the head word in the term. In the second system, all words depend on the right nearest neighbour. Table 4 gives the performances of the baseline systems and our systems with "basic feature"(system1), "basic feature + mutual information" (system2)and "basic feature + mutual information + first sememe in HowNet" (system3). Word pair accuracy (p_{wpa}) and term accuracy (p_{ta}) are used to evaluate the systems' performances. Word pair accuracy is calculated by formula 9, and term accuracy by formula 10. The results are shown in table 4.

$$p_{wpa} = \frac{c_{wr}}{c_w} \times 100\% \tag{9}$$

[3] http://www.ir.hit.edu.cn

$$p_{ta} = \frac{c_{tr}}{c_t} \times 100\% \tag{10}$$

where c_{wr} is the number of correct arcs, c_w is the total number of arcs, c_{tr} is the number of correct terms and c_t is the total number of terms.

Table 4. The result of dependency and semantic analysis

	Word pair accuracy		Term accuracy
Dependency analysis	baseline1	33.67%	17.84%
	baseline2	71.78%	50.41%
	system1	81.36%	51.51%
	system2	82.55%	55.89%
	system3	***87.85%***	***65.65%***
Semantic analysis	***76.98%***		***59.20%***

It can be seen from the experimental results that the word accuracy of baseline2 is 38.11% higher than baseline1, which indicates that the probability of dependency between nearest words is better than that between a word and its head word. On the other hand, the word accuracy and term accuracy of system2 increase by 1.19% and 4.38% over system1 respectively. Therefore mutual information is a good measure to identify the strength of association between two words. However, due to the large number of unknown words, the effect is not obvious. After adding the feature of first sememe in HowNet, the word pair accuracy and term accuracy have increased 5.3% and 9.76% respectively, which shows that the interdependence between two words highly depends on their semantic. We can also see that the accuracy of word pairs is nearly 80%, and the lexical reordering templates, word selection templates and POS selection templates are extracted on word pair level, which can guarantee the accuracy of the templates.

B. The Result of Term Translation

Firstly, we will determine the values of α_1, α_2 and α_3 mentioned in section 4. Taking the process of deciding the value of α_1 in formula 4-5 as an example, we made experiments with different values of α_1 varying from 0 to 1 on the development set, and the result is shown in figure 7.

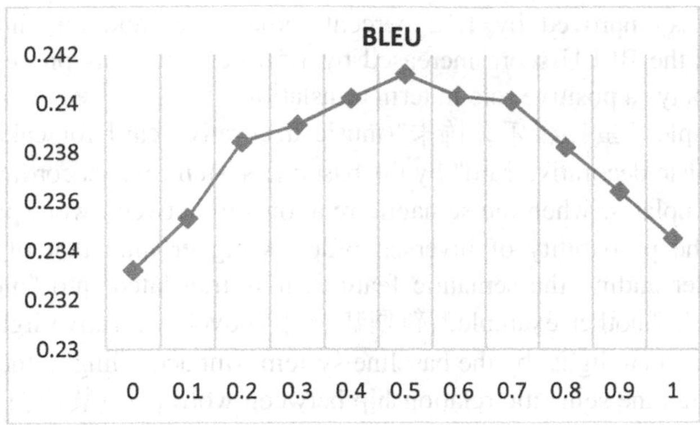

Fig. 7. The BLEU scores with different α

So we set α_1 to 0.5 in the following experiments. The other parameters are decided by the same method. α_2 is set to 0.2, and α_3 is set to 0.5.

To evaluate the performance of Chinese-English term translation, we build six systems: NiuTrans(baseline), "NiuTrans + lexical reordering feature "(system1), "NiuTrans + word selection feature"(system2), "NiuTrans + POS selection feature"(system3), and "NiuTrans + lexical reordering feature + POS selection feature"(system4), and "NiuTrans + lexical reordering feature + word selection feature + POS selection feature"(system5).We use BLEU and NIST for evaluation. Experimental results are shown in table 5. In order to describe the experiment more clearly, we use f_1, f_2 and f_3 to represent the lexical reordering feature, word selection feature and POS selection feature.

Table 5. The result of term translation

	BLEU	NIST
Baseline	0.2324	5.7427
system1(baseline+f_1)	0.2409	5.7823
system2(baseline+f_2)	0.2356	5.7448
system3(baseline+f_3)	0.2400	5.7811
system4(baseline+f_1+f_3)	0.2436	5.7846
system5(baseline+f_1+f_2+f_3)	***0.2482***	***5.7963***

It can be seen from the results that compared with the baseline system, using the lexical reordering feature, the BLEU score increased by 0.85 percent. However, adding the word selection feature makes the BLEU score improved by 0.32 percent. But using the POS selection feature, the BLEU score improves 0.76 percent, because the POS templates are easier to be matched than the word templates. So we add the word selection feature and lexical reordering feature together, and the system performance is improved by 1.12 percent. Finally we add the three features all together, and the BLEU score increased by 1.58 percent. This proves that semantic information plays a positive role in term translation.

For example, "蛋糕音乐装饰卡"(music decorative card for cake) is translated into "cake music decorative card" by the baseline system. But according to the lexical reordering templates, when the semantic relationship between word pair (蛋糕|卡) is "category", the probability of inversed order is higher than that of straight order. Therefore after adding the semantic features it is translated into "music decorative card for cake". Another example, "新型装饰灯"(novel decorative light) is translated into "novel decorate light" by the baseline system. But according to the POS selection templates, when the semantic relationship between word pair (装饰|灯) is "category", the probability of POS sequence "JJ NN" is higher than that of "VB NN", therefore the system after adding semantic features translated it into "novel decorative light".

C. Error Analysis

By analyzing the experimental results of semantic analysis, we find that the main reasons that lead to the errors in semantic analysis are: (1) word segmentation error; (2) many words in terms are quite difficult to understand even for human beings. Moreover, the boundaries between some semantic relationships are not clear.

We also find some reasons that effect the accuracy of term translation: (1) the semantic analysis errors which are produced by the above work; (2) the types of semantic relationships we defined in this paper cannot cover all the internal relationships of terms.

6 Conclusion

In this paper, we presented a Chinese-English term translation method based on semantic structure. We use a SVM model with features of mutual information and the first sememe in Hownet for dependency analysis, and then use a CRF model for semantic analysis. Then we extracted three features on the basis of term semantic structure and integrated them into the phrase-based statistical machine translation framework. Experimental showed the effectiveness of the semantic analysis method as well as the term translation method, which illustrates that the internal semantic structure of terms is important information for term translation.

Acknowledgments. This paper is funded by National Key Technology R&D Program of China (2012BAH14F05).

References

1. Cao, Y., Li, H.: Base noun phrase translation using web data and the EM algorithm. In: Proceedings of the 19th International Conference on Computational Linguistics, vol. 1, pp. 1–7. Association for Computational Linguistics (2002)

2. Fang, G., Yu, H., Nishino, F.: Chinese-English term translation mining based on semantic prediction. In: Proceedings of the COLING/ACL on Main Conference Poster Sessions, pp. 199–206. Association for Computational Linguistics (2006)
3. Wang, J., Zhang, G., Ye, N., Zhou, L.: Research on Japanese-Chinese Term Translation Technique Based on Multi-Features. In: Chinese Conference on Pattern Recognition, CCPR 2009, pp. 1–5. IEEE (2009)
4. Kang, B.K., Chen, Y.R., Chang, B.B., Yu, S.W.: Translating multi word terms into Korean from Chinese documents. In: Proceedings of 2005 IEEE International Conference on Natural Language Processing and Knowledge Engineering, IEEE NLP-KE 2005, pp. 449–454. IEEE (2005)
5. Wu, X., Okazaki, N., Tsunakawa, T., Tsujii, J.I.: Improving English-to-Chinese translation for technical terms using morphological information. In: AMTA 2008. MT at work: Proceedings of the Eighth Conference of the Association for Machine Translation in the Americas, pp. 202–211 (2008)
6. Tsuji, K.: Automatic extraction of translational Japanese-KATAKANA and English word pairs from bilingual corpora. International Journal of Computer Processing of Oriental Languages 15(03), 261–279 (2002)
7. Xiao, T., Zhu, J., Zhang, H., Li, Q.: NiuTrans: an open source toolkit for phrase-based and syntax-based machine translation. In: Proceedings of the ACL 2012 System Demonstrations, pp. 19–24. Association for Computational Linguistics (2012)
8. Beale, S., Nirenburg, S., Mahesh, K.: Semantic analysis in the Mikrokosmos machine translation project. In: Proceedings of the 2nd Symposium on Natural Language Processing, pp. 297–307 (1995)
9. Dong, Z., Dong, Q.: HowNet and the Computation of Meaning, pp. 1–316. World Scientific, Singapore (2006)
10. Liu, Q., Li, S.: Word similarity computing based on How-net. Computational Linguistics and Chinese Language Processing 7(2), 59–76 (2002)
11. Och, F.J., Ney, H.: Discriminative training and maximum entropy models for statistical machine translation. In: Proceedings of the 40th Annual Meeting on Association for Computational Linguistics, pp. 295–302. Association for Computational Linguistics (2002)

Query Expansion for Mining Translation Knowledge from Comparable Data

Lu Xiang[1], Yu Zhou[1], Jie Hao[2], and Dakun Zhang[2]

[1] NLPR, Institute of Automation Chinese Academy of Sciences, Beijing, China
{lu.xiang,yzhou}@nlpr.ia.ac.cn

[2] Toshiba (China) R&D Center
{haojie,zhangdakun}@toshiba.com.cn

Abstract. When mining parallel text from comparable corpora, we confront vast search space since parallel sentence or sub-sentential fragments can be scattered throughout the source and target corpus. To reduce the search space, most previous approaches have tried to use heuristics to mine comparable documents. However, these heuristics are only available in few cases. Instead, we go on a different direction and adopt the cross-language information retrieval (CLIR) framework to find translation candidates directly at sentence level from comparable corpus. What's more, for the sake of better retrieval result, two simple but effective query expansion methods are proposed. Experimental results show that using our query expansion methods can help to improve the recall significantly and obtain candidates of sentence pairs with high quality. Thus, our methods can help to make good preparation for extracting both parallel sentences and fragments subsequently.

Keywords: comparable data, parallel text mining, statistical machine translation, cross-language information retrieval, query expansion.

1 Introduction

The parallel corpora are resources of great importance for many natural language processing tasks, especially for statistical machine translation (SMT), while parallel corpora with high quality is expensive. In order to alleviate the lack of parallel data, many researchers have turned to mine the large amount of available comparable data on Internet. In mining parallel text from comparable data, a great challenge is that the search space is quite vast, which makes it difficult to obtain good parallel resource and the process is too slow to be applied in the practical application.

To reduce the search space, much work [2, 8, 9, 11, 13, 14] utilizes some heuristic information in which they step document alignment first and then only inspect the sentences in the aligned document pairs. However, in many situations, the simple heuristic information such as URL and title are not available which makes document alignment hard to actualize.

In this paper our purpose is to reduce the search space without document-level alignment. We believe it will be much helpful to narrow the search space if we can

M. Sun et al. (Eds.): CCL and NLP-NABD 2014, LNAI 8801, pp. 200–211, 2014.

pre-select part of comparable sentence pairs that most possibly contain parallel text because the size of comparable data is huge. Inspired by this motivation, we resort to the cross-language information retrieval (CLIR) framework to pre-filter the candidates, which indexes the target corpus directly at sentence-level and adopts a search engine to find the sentences in target corpus that are the most likely translations given a source sentence. The best CLIR-returned sentences are kept as candidates.

Some research work [10, 15] has been done on how to use CLIR method for selecting candidate sentences. Among these work, Ştefănescu et al. [15] uses the dictionary-based CLIR framework to select candidates. However, a word usually has several translations, for example, the word "reaction" has 6 meanings as shown in Table 1, and some translations are not right in some specific contexts. We believe it will add extraneous terms to the query and thus will degrade the quality of candidate sentence collection if we just simply use all the dictionary translations. This will definitely affect the parallel text extraction procedure afterwards.

Table 1. An example of ambiguities in a dictionary

Terms	Translation Candidates
reaction	反应；感应；反动；复古；反作用；影响
increase	增加；增长；提高；繁殖；扩大；增添
intensify	加剧；加强；强化；增强；神话

Based on the analysis above, we know that it is inappropriate to use CLIR without any modification. Therefore, this paper presents two query expansion methods for the translation of queries from source language into target language. One is word-level translation and the other one is phrase-level translation. In word-level translation, a bilingual dictionary is utilized to translate the content words in the source sentence. Unlike the work of Ştefănescu et al. [15] that uses all the dictionary translations, we propose a word disambiguation algorithm using beam-search that only uses the monolingual target corpus to select the better word sequence to form the query. In phrase-level translation, a simplified translation model which only uses phrase and lexical translation probability is proposed for the translation. Experiments show that our proposed query expansion methods can not only help to reduce the space efficiently, but also can achieve a better collection of candidate sentence pairs.

The remainder of this paper is organized as follows: Section 2 introduces the related work. Section 3 gives the CLIR framework for candidate sentence generation and describes our two query expansion methods in detail. Section 4 presents the experiments. Finally, we conclude the paper in Section 5.

2 Related Work

Mining parallel text from comparable data has attracted many researchers and much research work has been done on this task. However, it presents many difficulties and one of the greatest obstacles is the vast search space. Much work has been done to prune the search space and all these methods can be classified into two categories: (1) document level pre-filtering, and (2) sentence level pre-filtering.

The general way for document level pre-filtering is to perform document alignment first and then to inspect the sentences in the aligned document pairs only. This road has been taken by many researchers. [2, 3] adopt a bilingual dictionary to compute document similarity for document alignment. [8] uses dictionary-based cross-lingual information retrieval method to get more precise article pairs. [13] implements a hash-based algorithm to directly compute the cross-lingual pairwise similarity to find article pairs. All these methods need to calculate pairwise similarities across the huge bilingual corpora and it's quite computationally intensive. To reduce the computational complexity, most studies fall back to heuristics. [8] just compares news articles published close in time. [11] exploits "inter-wiki" links in Wikipedia to align documents. After document alignment, we can mine parallel resources from the aligned documents.

Since high-quality document-level alignment is difficult to acquire in many situations, some work has tried to pre-select candidate sentence pairs at sentence-level. [12] adopts a beam-search algorithm to extract parallel sentences directly at sentence-level without document alignment. [5, 10] employ a SMT system to translate the source part of comparable corpus and then use the translations as queries to conduct information retrieval to find candidate sentences. However, there are not enough resources between many language pairs to build a SMT system. [15] uses the dictionary-based CLIR framework to generate candidates. But as mentioned before, the serious ambiguity problem existed in a dictionary will affect the performance seriously.

3 Candidate Sentence Generation from Comparable Data

The pipeline of using CLIR framework to generate candidate sentence pairs is shown in Fig. 1. From the figure we can see, all of our processing is directly at the sentence-level. The procedure can be divided into three steps: (1) Building index for the target corpus; (2) Translating the source sentence into target language to form queries; (3) Search for candidate sentence pairs.

3.1 Indexing Target Sentences

To implement our framework, we need to build index for the target corpus first. Splitting the target corpus into sentences and performing a series of basic operations that are similar with the process of Chinese word segmentation or English tokenization and stemming. We use the Java implementation of Lucene[1] to index the target sentences as Lucene documents.

[1] http://lucene.apache.org/

We also compute the length of each sentence. We believe the length information can help us to filter out some non-parallel sentences further because the ratio of the lengths of two sentences that are translations of each other must be within a certain range. Therefore, for each Lucene document, we introduce the following two searchable fields:

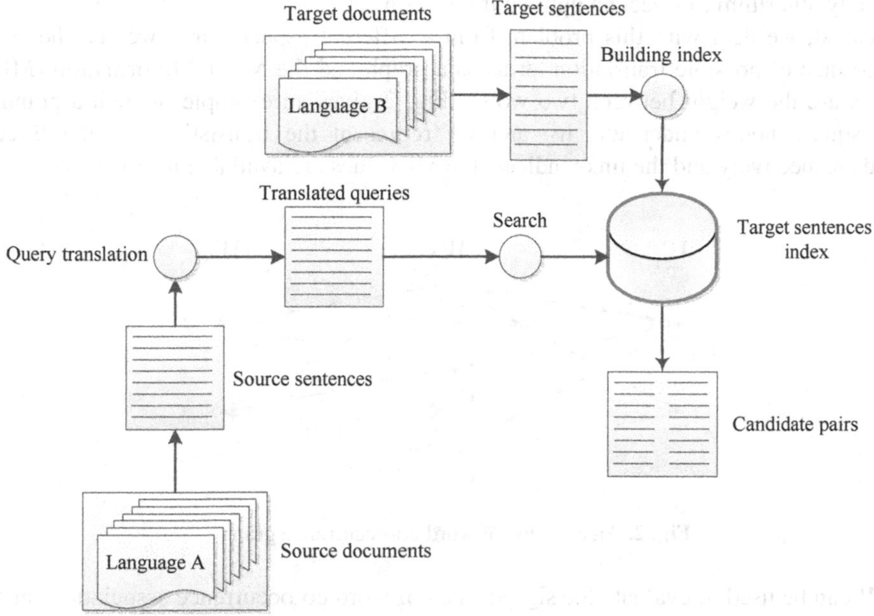

Fig. 1. Our framework to generate candidate sentence pairs

(a) A field storing the target sentence;
(b) A field storing the length of the sentence.

Then we build full-text indexing on these two fields for target sentences. The index structure is extensible and we can add other useful field information easily.

3.2 Generating Query from Source Sentence

After finishing indexing target sentences, our next step is considering how to translate source sentences into target language to generate queries. In our model, for word-level transformation, we adopt a machine-readable bilingual dictionary to translate source sentence into target word by word. And to solve the ambiguity problem mentioned before, we present a beam-search algorithm using nothing more than the monolingual target corpus to select the best translation sequence. For phrase-level transformation, we use a small collection of bilingual corpus to train a simplified translation model for the translation.

3.2.1 Word-level Transformation

To map the information from source sentences into target, the most simple and convenient way is to utilize the bilingual machine readable dictionaries. However, the dictionary translations are usually ambiguous and thus will affect the retrieval results. Much efforts have been done to solve the problem of disambiguation [4, 6, 7] and most of the existing approaches exploit the word co-occurrence patterns and then use a greedy algorithm to select an optimal translation set.

Instead, we deal with this problem from a different aspect. First, we see the co-occurrence of possible translation terms as a graph and the Mutual Information (MI) values are the weight between two words. Fig. 2 gives an example of such a graph. The square nodes under w_1, w_2 and w_3 represent the translations of the three words respectively and the links indicate the MI values are available for the pairs.

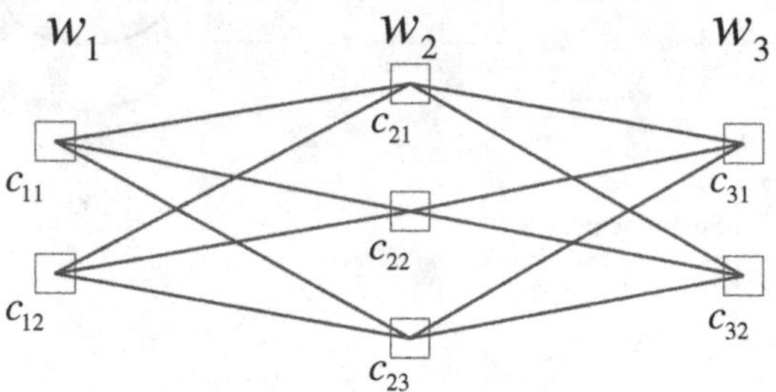

Fig. 2. An example of word co-occurrence graph

MI can be used to evaluate the significance of word co-occurrence associations and is defined as the following formula (1) [1]:

$$\mathrm{MI}(x,y) = \log_2 \frac{p(x,y)}{p(x)\,p(y)} \tag{1}$$

Here, $p(x,y)$ is the co-occurrence probability of x and y within a window size[2]. $p(x)$, $p(y)$ and $p(x,y)$ are the maximum likelihood estimates of the corresponding probabilities.

Given a source sentence S with a set of n content words $\{e_1, e_2, \cdots, e_n\}$ and a set of translation T obtained from the bilingual dictionary, $T(e_i) = \{c_{i1}, c_{i2}, \cdots, c_{im}\}$, we need to select the best translation for each content word to form the final translation set. However, to find such an optimal set will cost large amount of computation. Instead, we treat the problem as the optimal path selection and use a beam search algorithm to search for the B-best path.

Here, we define the path as a set of words $\{t_1, t_2, \cdots, t_n\}$, where $t_i \in T(e_i)$.

[2] In our application, $p(x,y)$ is the co-occurrence probability of x and y within a sentence.

For example, in Fig. 2, w_1 has two translations, denoted as $T(w_1)=\{c_{11},c_{12}\}$. Similarly, we have $T(w_2)=\{c_{21},c_{22},c_{23}\}$ and $T(w_3)=\{c_{31},c_{32}\}$. It is easy to see $\{c_{11},c_{21},c_{31}\}$ and $\{c_{12},c_{21},c_{31}\}$ are possible two paths.

Our optimal algorithm to select path relies on the MI values. The MI values are based on the assumption that the words co-occur in the same query, and their proper corresponding translations are likely to co-occur in the same documents. We think the MI values can reflect the semantic association between words in some degree. On the basis of this idea, our evaluation function of $\text{Path}(t_1,t_2,\cdots,t_n)$ is shown below (2):

$$\text{Score}(\text{Path}) = \sum_{t_i,t_j \in Path, i \neq j} MI(t_i,t_j) \tag{2}$$

The best Path $Path^*$ is defined below (3):

$$Path^* = \arg\max(Score(Path)) \tag{3}$$

We use the beam-search algorithm for the best word translation sequence with the highest path score. The algorithm is given in Fig. 3, where T is a set of translations as mentioned before, and the variable *candidate* represents one of the current path kept in the *candidates*. *T'* is the translation candidates of one word and *c''* is one translation in *T'*. The *agenda* is a sequential list, used to keep all the paths generated at each stage, ordered by the score which is calculated using formula (2). The variable *candidates* is the set of paths that can be used to generate new path, that is the *B*-best path from previous stage. And *B* is the number of paths retrained at each stage. Its value is an important factor to the performance of the algorithm and we set *B* to 128 in our application.

```
function Beam-Search( T,agenda,candidates, B)
  candidates ← T(e1)
  agenda ← CLEAR(agenda)
  for T' in { T(e2), T(e3), ···, T(en)}:
      for candidate in candidates:
          for c'' in T':
              agenda ←ADD(candidate, c'')
      candidates ← TOP-B(agenda,B)
      agenda ← CLEAR(agenda)
```

Fig. 3. The beam-search algorithm

CLEAR empties the agenda and removes all the items from agenda. ADD refers to an operation that add a new translation node to expand the path and TOP-B returns the highest B scoring paths from the agenda.

3.2.2 Phrase-level Transformation

In word-level transformation, the basic unit of translation is a single word. Though our proposed beam-search method to select word sequence can help to discard some error translations, the improvement of performance is limited since we only use the co-occurrence information in the target corpus and the context of the word in the source sentence is not available. However, the context of the word to be translated is helpful for the selection of translation. Thus, we can enlarge the translation unit from word-level to phrase-level to use the context information.

At present, phrase-based SMT model usually consists of three factors: the phrase translation table, the reordering model, and the language model. But in fact, even if the sentence is not smooth or the order of the words is not proper, we can retrieve a satisfied result set if the words given to the search engine are correct. In order to reduce the computational complexity, we propose to use a simplified phrase translation model that only uses the phrase translation table to translate source sentence into target language. Here, four features are used to choose the translation: phrase translation probability $\varphi(f \mid e)$, $\varphi(e \mid f)$ and lexical weighting $\text{lex}(f \mid e)$, $\text{lex}(e \mid f)$. A small bilingual parallel corpus is used to train the translation model.

3.3 Searching for Candidate Sentences

After translating the source sentence into target language, we can obtain a set of target words. A boolean model is used to retrieve the documents and each of the target words is added as a disjunctive query term (the OR operator). In order to narrow the search space and obtain the better result, a range filter is built. This kind of filter makes the search engine only search the subset of sentences in which the ratio of sentence and the source sentence is within a certain range. In our experiments, the range is set as [0.5, 2]. After the query is constructed, we use it to feed the Lucene search engine to get the best *h* hits.

4 Experiments

4.1 Experiments Setup

We want to measure the performance of using our query translation methods for the search engine to find translation candidates. We conduct our experiments on manually created English-Chinese data set. The target corpus, denoted as FBIS&NIST, consists of the Chinese side of FBIS corpus, NIST MT 2003 and NIST MT 2005. We use Lucene to index FBIS&NIST. The English side of NIST MT 2003 (denoted as EN-03) and NIST MT 2005 (denoted as EN-05) are used as the source corpus. Table 2 shows the relevant statistics of the target corpus and source corpus.

Table 2. Statistics of the target and source corpus

	sentences
FBIS&NIST	237,671
EN-03	919
EN-05	1082

Each sentence in the source corpus is used as query and the best *k* hits (target sentences) returned by the search engine are kept as candidates. Ideally, we would like to see the real translations in the candidates so that we can have a chance to extract them in the next steps. To measure the quality of retrieval results, we define recall as follows: Let *G* denote the total sentence number of the source corpus. Each sentence will obtain a set of target sentences as translation candidates and then we will have *G* such retrieval sets. Let *R* denote the number of retrieval sets that contain the real translations. Then

$$\text{Recall} = \frac{R}{G} * 100 \tag{4}$$

The higher recall means more retrieval sets contain the real parallel text which is very important to the following steps.

4.2 Evaluation

We first design experiments to evaluate the efficiency of our proposed two query translation methods. In word-level translation, we use a common English-Chinese dictionary containing 41,814 entries. In phrase-level translation, we adopt the Moses toolkit and FBIS corpus with 235,670 sentence pairs to train the SMT system.

Results are shown in Table 3. Here, in baseline system [15], we use the bilingual dictionary to translate the source sentence and using all the translations as query terms to search for target sentences. Method_1 refers to use the beam-search word sequence selection method and Method_2 refers to use the simplified translation model described in sub-section 3.2.1 and sub-section 3.2.2 respectively.

Table 3. Results of using different query translation method (%)

The number of *k*		**1**	**5**	**10**	**20**	**50**
EN-03	Baseline	59.19	73.12	76.82	81.39	84.54
	Method_1	71.38	79.86	84.76	87.59	89.44
	Method_2	72.79	82.91	86.50	88.46	90.75
EN-05	Baseline	54.89	70.14	73.84	79.02	84.75
	Method_1	65.71	76.61	82.71	85.85	89.27
	Method_2	74.86	84.47	86.78	88.81	91.49

As Table 3 shows, the recall increases with the k increasing. Both on EN-03 and EN-05, our proposed two query translation methods improve the performance significantly compared to the baseline, which proves the effectiveness of our methods. On one hand, our methods can help to achieve a much better quality of candidates which is important to the following parallel text mining steps. On the other hand, even if we only keep the best 10 hits but the baseline keeps the best 50 hits for each sentence, we can obtain the comparable recall. This means the search space can be reduced about 10 times.

We can see that the performance of using the simplified translation model is better than that of using the beam-search word sequence selection method. This is mainly because the beam-search method to select word sequence only uses the co-occurrence information in the target corpus while the translation model uses the context of the word to be translated.

As we know the performance of the translation model is domain-sensitive. In order to make a more comprehensive comparison of every method, we also conduct a cross-domain experiment. We have 1,500 sentence pairs from computer science domain and add the Chinese side into the former built index. The English side, denoted as COM, is used as source corpus to retrieve candidates. The results are shown in Table 4.

Table 4. Cross-domain evaluation result (%)

the number of k		**1**	**5**	**10**	**20**	**50**
COM	Baseline	57.33	71.40	75.40	79.60	85.20
	Method_1	67.66	78.73	82.6	84.66	88.33
	Method_2	35.93	48.80	53.53	58.13	65.20

From Table 4 we can see that our beam-search method improves the performance significantly while the performance of using the translation model decreases a lot. This is because the bilingual dictionary we used is a general dictionary. We believe that the performance can be further promoted if we enlarge the dictionary. However, the translation model is trained on a news domain data and it performs poorly on the other domain which declines the retrieval performance.

Comparing the performance of using different query translation method shown in Table 3 and Table 4, we can conclude that both our proposed beam-search method to select word sequence and the simplified translation model are very helpful to transform source sentence into target language to obtain a better quality of candidate sentence pairs. Better yet, these two methods can be applied to translate queries in different situations according to the resources at hand. If we have in-domain parallel corpus, a translation model can be trained to translate the source sentence into target language. And if we only have bilingual dictionaries, the beam-search method also can help to select a set of good translations to form a better query.

4.3 Further Experiments

To further verify the effectiveness of our method in the real comparable data, we further conduct the experiment on the English-Chinese Wikipedia data. We process the English and Chinese Wikipedia data separately and index the Chinese side using the method described in Section 3.1. For each English sentence, the beam-search method is used to translate it into target and here we only keep the best-1 retrieval result. And then we use the coverage matching score with bilingual dictionary to simply extract the sentence pairs higher than a threshold within the retrieval result set. The statistics of sentence pairs over a certain threshold is shown as Table 5. Here H_i means different experiments under different thresholds.

Table 5. Statistics of sentence pairs over a certain threshold

Threshold	Number of sentence pairs
H_1: ≥ 0.3	372,387
H_2: ≥ 0.4	250,384
H_3: ≥ 0.45	173,615
H_4: ≥ 0.5	132,043

We use the retained sentence pairs as training data to train the SMT system. GIZA++ and grow-diag-and for word alignment, the Moses toolkit with default settings are used to train the System. NIST MT 2003 and NIST MT 2005 are adopted as development set and test set respectively. The SMT evaluation results using different training data are given in Table 6.

Table 6. SMT evaluation results

Training Data	BLEU
H_1	14.32
H_2	16.98
H_3	16.14
H_4	16.56

As Table 6 shows, the BLEU point of using training data H_1 is obviously below than the points of the other three. This is mainly because the threshold of H_1 is 0.3 and it will introduce much noise into the training data. However, the SMT evaluation results can prove the effectiveness of our method from another aspect. Using the CLIR framework, we can build a SMT system from the large comparable corpora.

5 Conclusion and Future Work

In this paper, we propose two simple and effective query translation methods for the CLIR based candidate sentence pre-selection framework: one is the beam-search word sequence selection method and the other one is the phrase-based simplified translation model. In beam-search word sequence selection method, only bilingual dictionary and monolingual target corpus is needed and a beam-search algorithm is adopted to select a set of word translations. In phrase-based translation model, a simplified translation model is trained to translate the source sentence into target language. Experimental results show that our method can help obtain candidate sentence pairs of high quality which is quite important to the following parallel sentence and fragments' extraction. What's more, our methods can contribute current SMT for two folds: (1) It can help build a SMT system from nothing but a small size of bilingual dictionary; (2) It can help enhance the current SMT performance with additional mined translation resources.

In the future work, we will try to study on the method of how to mining parallel text including both sentences and fragments from the obtained candidate sentence pairs.

Acknowledgement. The research work has been partially funded by the Natural Science Foundation of China under Grant No. 61333018 and the Hi-Tech Research and Development Program ("863" Program) of China under Grant No. 2012AA011101, and also the High New Technology Research and Development Program of Xinjiang Uyghur Autonomous Region under Grant No. 201312103 as well.

References

1. Church, K.W., Hanks, P.: Word association norms, mutual information, and lexicography. Computational Linguistics 16(1), 22–29 (1990)
2. Fung, P., Cheung, P.: Mining very non-parallel corpora: Parallel sentence and lexicon extraction vie bootstrapping and EM. In: EMNLP 2004, pp. 57–63 (2004a)
3. Fung, P., Cheung, P.: Multi-level bootstrapping for extracting parallel sentences from a quasi-comparable corpus. In: COLING 2004, pp. 1051–1057 (2004b)
4. Jang, M.-G., Myaeng, S.H., Park, S.Y.: Using Mutual Information to Resolve Query Translation Ambiguities and Query Term Weighting. In: Proceedings of the 37th Annual Meeting of the Association for Computational Linguistics on Computational Linguistics (1999)
5. Liu, C., Liu, Q., Liu, Y., Sun, M.: THUTR: A Translation Retrieval System. In: Proceedings of the 24th International Conference on Computational Linguistics, pp. 321–328
6. Adriani, M.: Using statistical term similarity for sense disambiguation in cross-language information retrieval. Information Retrieval 2(1), 71–82 (2000)
7. Maeda, A., Sadat, F., Yoshikawa, M., Uemura, S.: Query term disambiguation for web cross-language information retrieval using a search engine. In: Proceedings of the Fifth International Workshop on Information Retrieval with Asian Languages, pp. 25–32. ACM (2000)
8. Munteanu, D.S., Marcu, D.: Improving machine translation performance by exploiting non-parallel corpora. Computational Linguistics 31(4), 477–504 (2005)

9. Munteanu, D.S., Marcu, D.: Extracting parallel sub-sentential fragments from nonparallel corpora. In: Proceedings of the 21st International Conference on Computational Linguistics and the 44th Annual Meeting of the Association for Computational Linguistics, Sydney, Australia, pp. 81–88 (2006)
10. Rauf, S., Schwenk, H.: Parallel sentence generation from comparable corpora for improved SMT. Machine Translation 25(4), 341–375 (2011)
11. Smith, J.R., Quirk, C., Toutanova, K.: Extracting parallel sentences from comparable corpora using document level alignment. In: Proceedings of the Human Language Technologies/North American Association for Computational Linguistics, pp. 403–411 (2010)
12. Tillmann, C.: A Beam-Search extraction algorithm for comparable data. In: Proceedings of ACL, pp. 225–228 (2009)
13. Ture, F., Lin, J.: Why not grab a free lunch? Mining large corpora for parallel sentences to improve translation modeling. In: HLT-NAACL, pp. 626–630 (2012)
14. Xiang, L., Zhou, Y., Zong, C.: An Efficient Framework to Extract Parallel Units from Comparable Data. In: Natural Language Processing and Chinese Computing, pp. 151–163 (2013)
15. Ştefănescu, D., Ion, R., Hunsicker, S.: Hybrid parallel sentence mining from comparable corpora. In: Proceedings of the 16th Conference of the European Association for Machine Translation (EAMT 2012), Trento, Italy (2012)

A Comparative Study on Simplified-Traditional Chinese Translation

Xiaoheng Zhang

Department of Chinese and Bilingual Studies, Hong Kong Polytechnic University
ctxzhang@polyu.edu.hk

Abstract. Due to historical reasons, modern Chinese is written in traditional characters and simplified characters, which quite frequently renders text translation between the two scripting systems indispensable. Computer-based simplified-traditional Chinese conversion is available on MS Word, Google Translate and many language tools on the WWW. Their performance has reached very high precision. However, because of the existence of one-to-many relationships between simplified and traditional Chinese characters, there is considerable room for improvement. This paper presents a comparative study of simplified-traditional Chinese translation on MS Word, Google Translate and JFJ, followed by discussion on further development, including improvement of translation accuracy and support to human proofreading.

Keywords: Chinese characters, writing systems, simplified-traditional Chinese translation, one-to-many relationship, computer-aided proofreading.

1 Introduction

Because of historical reasons [3], there are two Hanzi writing systems in China: the standard system of the Mainland is simplified Chinese, while in Taiwan, Hong Kong and Macau, traditional Chinese is the norm. In addition, these two writing systems are widely used internationally. For instance, the BBC Chinese website (http://www.bbc.co.uk/zhongwen/simp/) is presented in both simplified and traditional versions, as shown in Figure 1.

In addition to various documents, the user interfaces of popular software such as MS Windows, MS Office and Google also have their simplified and traditional Chinese versions. That means there is a tremendous demand for translation between the two Chinese writing systems.

Computer tools for simplified-traditional Chinese translation or conversion are widely available (For simplicity purpose, we will normally use the term "translation" in the following). Their performance has reached very high precision. However, because of the existence of one-to-many relationships between simplified and traditional Chinese characters there is no guarantee of 100% correct conversion [4]. For example, character 干 in simplified Chinese corresponds to 乾 (gan1), 幹 (gan4) and 干 (gan1) of different meanings in traditional Chinese, and traditional

M. Sun et al. (Eds.): CCL and NLP-NABD 2014, LNAI 8801, pp. 212–222, 2014.

character 乾 corresponds to 乾 (qian2) and 干 (gan1) of different meanings in simplified Chinese.

In the following sections, we will introduce an experiment of simplified-traditional Chinese translation on three representative tools, make a comparative analysis and provide some ideas for further improvement.

Fig. 1. BBC Chinese website (中文网) with simplified and traditional Chinese versions (简体版，繁體版)

2 The Experiment

Our experiment was focused on simplified-to-traditional Chinese translation, which is more demanding than traditional-to-simplified translation and thus can better reflect the strength of modern technology in this area. A text in simplified Chinese was carefully selected, which was then translated into traditional Chinese on three representative tools.

2.1 Selection of the Testing Text

The testing text selected for the experiment is this year's Government Work Report by Premier Li Keqiang [5], which was presented to the annual meeting of the National People Congress of People's Republic of China in early March. Its original version is in simplified Chinese.

There are at least four reasons for our selection: (a) The government work report is an important document with attention of people all over the world; (b) Its contents cover every aspect of people's life in China; (c) It was a brand new document not likely to have been used to help improve any translation tool before our experiment. (d) The length of the document, 17,670 characters including spaces, is appropriate, because too short text may reveal few translation errors and too long text may require too much human proofreading.

2.2 Selection of Translation Tools

Three representative tools, including Microsoft Word, Google Translate and JFJ, were selected for our experiment on simplified-traditional Chinese translation.

MS Word has long been the most popular word processor in the world. And its Chinese Translation is probably the most popular off-lined tool for simplified-traditional Chinese translation. We used Word 2010, the newest version of the software available in our labs. When started on MS Word, Chinese Translation presents some options for the user to select, as shown in Figure 2.

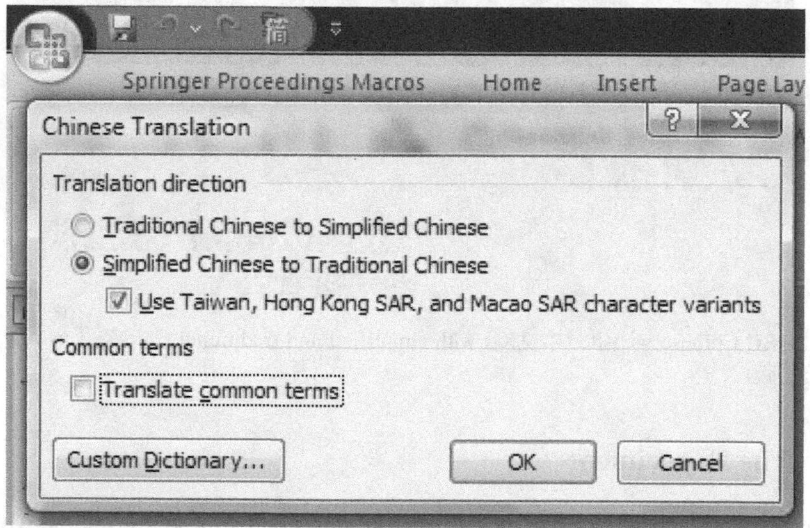

Fig. 2. Option setting on MS Word Chinese Translation

For our experiment, the Translation direction was set on "Simplified Chinese to Traditional Chinese". Normally, simplified-traditional Chinese conversion is performed in a character-to-character mode. For example, simplified 汉字信息处理 (Chinese characters information processing) is converted to 漢字信息處理. MS Word can also translate common terms, in which case the previous translation would become 漢字資訊處理, because in Taiwan and Hong Kong, "information" is more often translated into 資訊 than 信息. Because neither Google Translate nor JFJ support terms translation, this option was set off for a fair comparison among the three tools. (As a matter of fact, MS Word sometimes translates common terms incorrectly. Examples will be presented in Section 4 of this paper.) When button OK is clicked on, MS Word will translate the whole document (or a selected part if it is highlighted beforehand).

Google Translate is an independent tool on the WWW (https://translate.google.com.hk/?hl=en). It is probably the most popular on-lined translation tool. For our experiment, the source language was set to "Chinese (Simplified)" and the target language "Chinese (Traditional)", as shown in Figure 3.

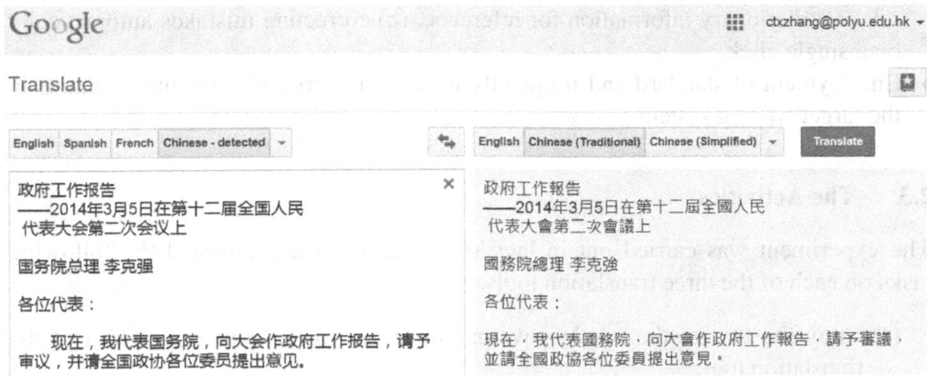

Fig. 3. Google Translate for simplified-traditional Chinese translation

JFJ (acronym of Pinyin Jian-Fan-Jian, or Simplified-Traditional-Simplified) is a small tool developed at Hong Kong Polytechnic University [15, 17]. The version used for the experiment is available on the Web at http://myweb.polyu.edu.hk/~ctxzhang/jfj30/ , as shown in Figure 4.

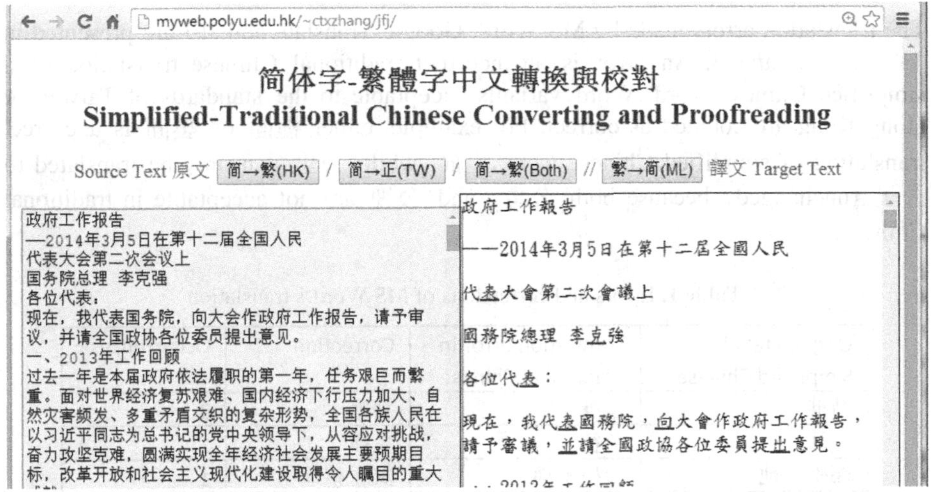

Fig. 4. JFJ simplified to high frequency traditional Chinese characters

The important features of JFJ include:

- Simplified-traditional Chinese bi-directional conversion with 4 options: (a) simplified to Hong Kong traditional Chinese, (b) simplified to Taiwan traditional Chinese, (c) simplified to high frequency traditional Chinese characters, and (d) traditional to simplified Chinese.
- Support for human proofreading by (a) high-lighting all characters with one-to-many relationship between simplified and traditional Chinese, (b) providing

relevant dictionary information for reference, (c) correcting mistakes automatically by a single click.

- Employment of standard and frequently-used characters and punctuation marks in the target writing system.

2.3 The Activities

The experiment was carried out in late March, 2014. We performed the following tasks on each of the three translation tools.

(a) Copy the text of the whole government report to the source text area of the translation tool;
(b) Translate the report from simplified Chinese to traditional Chinese with the tool (by character-to-character conversion, no translation of common terms);
(c) Proofread the translation manually and write down all the errors;
(d) Sort and categorize the errors on a table and calculate the error rates.

3 Experiment Results

The translation errors made by MS Word, Google Translate and JFJ are presented in Tables 1, 2 and 3. An error is an incorrect traditional Chinese translation of a simplified Chinese word. Word variants acceptable to the standards of Taiwan or Hong Kong are counted as correct. For example, either 裡面 or 裏面 is a correct translation of simplified Chinese word 里面, while 公里 can only be translated to 公里 (unchanged), because both 公裏 and 公裡 are not acceptable in traditional Chinese.

Table 1. Errors and corrections of MS Word's translation

Original text in Simplified Chinese	Translation error in Traditional Chinese	Correction	Occurrences
精准	精准	精準	3
免征	免征	免徵	1
深松整地	深松整地	深鬆整地	1
松了绑	松了綁	鬆了綁	1
页岩气	葉岩氣	頁岩氣	1
这只…的手	這只...的手	這隻...的手	2
征地	征地	徵地	1
制售	制售	製售	1
Total:			11
Error rate against all characters in the source text = (11/17670)*100%=0.062%			
Error rate against one-to-many characters = (11/912)*100%=1.206%			

Table 2. Errors and corrections of Google Translate's translation

Original text in Simplified Chinese	Translation error in Traditional Chinese	Correction	Occurrences
遨游太空	遨游太空	遨遊太空	1
备案制	備案製	備案制	1
复制	複制	複製	1
赶超	赶超	趕超	1
公有制	公有製	公有制	3
骨干水源	骨乾水源	骨幹水源	1
旅游近亿人	旅游近億人	旅遊近億人	1
牵一发而动全身	牽一發而動全身	牽一髮而動全身	1
深松整地	深松整地	深鬆整地	1
示范建设	示范建設	示範建設	1
所有制	所有製	所有制	2
体系不健全	體係不健全	體系不健全	1
维护发展中国家共同利益	維護髮展中國家共同利益	維護發展中國家共同利益	1
行政复议	行政復議	行政複議/覆議	1
这只…的手	這只...的手	這隻...的手	2
制度	製度	制度	13
Total			**32**
Error rate against all characters in the source text = (32/17670)*100% = 0.181%			
Error rate against one-to-many characters = (32/912)*100%=3.509%			

Table 3. Errors and corrections of JFJ's translation

Original text in Simplified Chinese	Translation error in Traditional Chinese	Correction	Occurrences
牵一发而动全身	牽一發而動全身	牽一髮而動全身	1
松花江	鬆花江	松花江	1
台风	台風	颱風	1
维护发展中国家共同利益	維護髮展中國家共同利益	維護發展中國家共同利益	1
行政复议	行政復議	行政複議/覆議	1
制售假冒伪劣	制售假冒偽劣	製售假冒偽劣	1
Total:			6
Error rate against all characters in the source text = (6/17670)*100%=0.034%			
Error rate against one-to-many characters =(6/912)*100%=0.658%			

The three tables above contained the combined results of 45 individual experiments made by the author and a class of Chinese native students according to the requirements introduced in Section 2. In other words, the experiment was performed 45 times by different people and the results were then checked and integrated into three tables. That means the data reported here should be very comprehensive and reliable, with all the translation errors made by each tool counted.

The first column of the tables presents all the words and phrases in the original text which have been incorrectly translated by MS Word, Google Translate or JFJ. The second column presents the error translations. Each error is caused by an incorrectly converted character, which is presented with sufficient context to show its incorrect usage and to cause the mistake. For instance, Google can translate 骨干 correctly into骨幹, but would translate 骨干水源 incorrectly into骨乾水源. Hence 骨干水源 and 骨乾水源 appear in the table. The third column presents the corrected expressions in traditional Chinese. And the final column shows the number of times each error occurs in the entire translation text. The rows are sorted by the first column in Putonghua Pinyin order. At the end of the table, there are two error rates: the error rate against all characters in the source text is calculated by dividing the "total number of incorrectly-translated characters" with "total number of characters in the text" before converting into a percentage, the error rate against one-to-many characters is calculated by dividing the "total number of incorrectly-translated characters" with "total number of characters of one-to-many relationship". According to JFJ's report at the end of its translation, there are totally 17,670 characters (including spaces) in the source text, among which 912 have multiple counterparts in traditional Chinese.

The references we used in human proofreading include

— Dictionary of Commonly Used Words in Mainland and Taiwan (Mainland version) [7]
— Dictionary of Commonly Used Words in Mainland and Taiwan (Taiwan version) [8]
— Lexical Items for Fundamental Chinese Learning in Hong Kong [2]
— Revised Edition of the Dictionary of the Chinese National Language [9]
— Academia Sinica Balanced Corpus of Modern Chinese [1]
— Corpus of Modern Chinese by the National Language Commission of China [10]
— Decoding the *Standard List of Commonly-used Chinese Characters* [13].

4 Error Analysis and Solution

Generally speaking, the three tools all performed very well in translating the government work report from simplified Chinese into traditional Chinese. The accuracy of Google Translate is 1-0.181%=99.819%. MS Word performed even better with an accuracy of 1-0.062%=99.938%. And JFJ was the champion with an accuracy of 1-0.034%=99.966%.

4.1 Error Analysis

The distribution of different errors is shown in Table 4.

Table 4. Distribution of different errors made by Word, Google and JFJ

	Word & Google	Word & JFJ	Google & JFJ	Word	Google	JFJ
	深松整地	制售	復議	精准	遨游	鬆花江
	這只...的手		牽一發	免征	備案製	台風
			維護髮展	松了綁	複制	
				葉岩氣	赶超	
				征地	公有製	
					骨乾	
					旅游	
					示范	
					所有製	
					體係	
					製度	
Total	2	1	3	**5**	11	2

Totally the three tools made 24 different errors in their translations, none of which is shared by all the tools. 6 errors were made by two tools, including 3 by Google and JFJ, 2 by Word and Google and 1 by Word and JFJ. 19 errors were made by a single tool, including 11 by Google, 5 by Word and 2 by JFJ. The wide distribution of errors means that the three tools employ quite different approaches in translation, and hence are good representatives of this area of language computing.

The errors listed in the tables are mostly self-evident. We will discuss a few cases which are more interesting or informative. Errors in simplified-traditional Chinese translation normally happen in characters corresponding to more than one counterpart in the target writing system. For example, character 松 in simplified Chinese corresponds to 松 (pine tree) and 鬆 (loose, slack) in traditional Chinese. In the original phrases of 松了绑 and 深松整地, 松 means "to set the hands loose (untied)" and "make the land loose (for farming)", hence should be converted to 鬆 in traditional Chinese. On the other hand, 松花江 is a river's name relevant to the pine tree, hence its correct translation is 松花江.

Simplified Chinese character 只 corresponds to 只 (zhi3) and 隻 (zhi1) in traditional Chinese. When used as a measure word, it should be converted into 隻. So the correct translation of 这只…的手 in traditional Chinese is 這隻…的手, not 這只…的手.

Character 制 also has two counterparts in traditional Chinese, 製 (to make, manufacture) and 制 (system). Word 制售 is the short form of 制造销售, or "to manufacture and sell (products)". 复制 means to make a copy. Hence the character 制 in both cases should be converted to 製. On the other hand, words 备案制, 公有制, 所有制 and 制度 all refer to some systems. Hence their embodied character 制 should remain unchanged in traditional Chinese.

It is surprising that MS Word translates 页岩气 to 葉岩氣, even when the option of "Translate common terms" is turned off. According to Dictionary of Commonly Used Words in Mainland and Taiwan (Taiwan version) [8], the standard translation is

頁岩氣. In fact, none of the many dictionaries we have consulted tells us that the traditional form of simplified 页 can be 葉.

复议 is a less frequently-used word, and few Mainlanders can be confident about its correct translation in traditional Chinese. According to Dictionary of Commonly Used Words in Mainland and Taiwan (Taiwan version) again, the standard counterparts of simplified Chinese 复议 are synonyms 複議 and 覆議, not 復議. And 行政複議 appears in an example sentence of the book.

As for 维护发展中国家共同利益, the computer mistakenly considered 护发 as a word and translated it into 護髮. However the correct word segmentation is 维护/发展/中/国家/共同/利益, where 发展 is a word and should be converted to 發展. 發 and 髮 are different characters in traditional Chinese.

4.2 Error Solution

In this section, we will discuss improvement of the three tools based on further analysis of the errors they made in the experiment.

In the case of MS Word, the function of "Convert common terms" should not be allowed to interfere with translation when the user selects not to use it, such as incorrectly converting 页岩气 to 葉岩氣. On the other hand, the function should be improved. The facts that MS Word would translate 主席缺位期间由副主席代理 to 主席缺位元期間由副主席代理，文件资料 to 檔資料，and 循环经济 to 迴圈經濟 shows that MS Word is not good enough at Chinese words segmentation and is quite confined to the domain of computer science. Word 缺位 in the first example means 职位空缺 or "seat/post vacant". MS Word mistakenly considered character 位 as a word with the meaning of "bit" in information technology, and converted it into 位元. 檔資料 is another strange expression in Chinese. And translating 循环经济 into 迴圈經濟 is not acceptable either, though in computer programming 循环 often means "loop" and can be safely converted to 迴圈 in a Taiwan style. Some people even consider term conversion not worthwhile because of two reasons: loss of original "flavor" of the source text, and introduction of new mistakes [12].

Google Translate made 32 errors in the experiment, as shown in Table 2. Word 制度 appears 33 times in the source document, among which 13 were incorrectly converted to 製度, more than the total number of errors made by MS Word or JFJ. That means there is something seriously wrong. A possible reason is that Google over relies on corpora and statistics MT, and paid insufficient attention to deep and comprehensive linguistic analysis [6]. In the n-gram algorithm, we pre-suppose the appearance of a word to be independent of other words in the context, which is not true in real-world natural languages. Another shortcoming of n-gram is in its implementations, where n is often set to 2 or 3 due to limitation of computing resources. In natural languages, however, the correct analysis of a word often involves a more remotely-located word. For instance, in 放開市場這只"看不見的手"，用好政府這只"看得見的手", the correct translation of 只 is dependent on its modifying relation with noun 手, which is 5 characters away. It seems more reasonable to employ a flexible context length in language analysis, not a fixed bigram or trigram for all cases.

It is surprising that JFJ clearly outperforms the two IT giants in simplified-traditional Chinese translation. And the six errors made by JFJ can be eliminated by better use of contextual information. Let's take 牵一发而动全身 as an example. Simplified Chinese 发 has two counterparts in traditional Chinese: 發 (fa1: develop, grow) and 髮 (fa4: hair). And 一发 is still ambiguous, considering 一發不可收拾, 一發子彈 and 千鈞一髮. However, putting the lengthy 牵一发而动全身 and its correct translation into the conversion dictionary is not cost-effective. And if we do, its variant expressions would not be dealt with as well, including 牽一發動全身 (without 而) and "牽一發, 動全身", etc. We turned to the modern Chinese corpus of the National Language Commission of China [10], and found that 牵一发 appears 12 times, in 牵一发而动全身, 牵一发动全身, "牵一发，动全身" and 牵一发而动全局. In all of these cases, 牵一发 can be safely converted to 牽一髮. That means 牵一发 is a minimum translation segment to unambiguously convert 发 into 髮. It is more cost-effective to put "牵一发-牽一髮" in the computer's conversion dictionary. And the possible appearances of 牵一发而动全国, 牵一发而动全市, 牵一发而动全校 and so on will be covered as well.

5 Conclusion

Simplified-traditional Chinese translation achieved an accuracy of 99% more than a decade ago [11, 14]. The percentage has now been raised to 99.9% and beyond, as shown by our experiments on Google Translate, MS Word and JFJ. Notwithstanding, all of the three tools made more than 5 errors. That means there is substantial space for further progress, as discussed in the previous section.

In another aspect, because of the one-to-many relationships between simplified and traditional Chinese characters and the great complexities of natural languages, there is no guarantee of 100% correct translation in the foreseeable future. As we know, linguistically, every rule leaks; statistically, even the most probable event may not happen. That means human proofreading is needed for machine translation, especially when high quality text output is required [15, 16]. Another lovely feature of JFJ is that it goes on to support human proofreading after automatically translating a text from simplified Chinese into traditional Chinese or vice versa. And this supporting function can be further improved as well. A newly revised version of JFJ taking into account of feedback from our experiment is available for testing on the Web at http://www.acad.polyu.edu.hk/~ctxzhang/jfj/ .

Last but not least, the experiment reported in this article was performed on the single document of Premier Li's government report. To be better representative of modern Chinese language, the testing text will be greatly enriched in our further research, both quantitatively and typologically.

Acknowledgements. The author would like to thank his MA postgraduate students of subject "Modern Chinese Characters and Information Technology" at Hong Kong Polytechnic University for their support in the experiment. He is also very grateful to the three anonymous reviewers, whose informative comments and constructive suggestions played an important role in the revision of the paper.

References

1. Academia Sinica. Academia Sinica Balanced Corpus of Modern Chinese (中央研究院現代漢語語料庫) (1997), http://app.sinica.edu.tw/cgi-bin/kiwi/mkiwi/kiwi.sh?language=1
2. Education Bureau of Hong Kong. Lexical Items for Fundamental Chinese Learning in Hong Kong (香港學校中文學習基礎字詞 (2009), http://www.edbchinese.hk/lexlist/
3. Fu, Y. (傅永和): Fifty Years of Chinese Characters Simplification (汉字简化五十年回顾). Languages of China (中国语文) (6) (2005)
4. Halpern, J., Kerman, J.: The Pitfalls and Complexities of Chinese to Chinese Conversion. Fourteenth International Unicode Conference, Boston (1999)
5. Li, K. (李克强): Government Work Report 2014 (政府工作报告2014) (2014), http://www.gov.cn/guowuyuan/2014-03/05/content_2629550.htm
6. Li, M., Wu, Y., Zeng, Y., Yang, P., Ku, T.: Chinese Characters Conversion System Based on Lookup Table and Language Model. Computational Linguistics and Chinese Language Processing 15(1), 19–36, 19 (2010)
7. Li, X. (李行健, (ed.)): Dictionary of Commonly Used Words in Mainland and Taiwan (两岸常用词典, Mainland version) (2014), http://www.zhonghuayuwen.org/
8. Liu, Z. (劉兆玄, (ed.)): Dictionary of Commonly Used Words in Mainland and Taiwan (兩岸常用詞典, Taiwan version) (2014), http://chinese-linguipedia.org/clk/index.php
9. Ministry of Education. Revised Edition of Dictionary of the Chinese National Language (重編國語辭典修訂本). Ministry of Education, Taipei (1994)
10. National Language Commission of China. Corpus of Modern Chinese (现代汉语语料库) (2010), http://www.cncorpus.org/CCindex.aspx (Consulted on May 31, 2014)
11. Shen, D., Sun, M. (沈达阳，孙茂松): An Intelligent Simplified-Traditional Chinese Conversion System (汉字简繁体智能化转换系统). Chinese Information (中文信息) (6) (1996)
12. Wang, L., Wang, X., Wu, J. (王立军，王晓明 and 吴健): The Correspondence Simplified Characters and Traditional Characters and the Mutual Conversion (简繁对应关系与简繁转换). Journal of Chinese Information Processing (中文信息学报) 27(4) (2013)
13. Wang, N. (王宁): Decoding the *Standard List of Commonly-used Chinese Characters* (《通用规范汉字表》解读). The Commercial Press, Beijing (Chapter 3: Relationship between Simplified and Traditional Chinese Characters 简繁关系) (2013)
14. Xin, C., Sun, Y. (辛春生，孙玉芳): Design and Implementation of Simplified-Traditional Chinese Conversion System (简繁汉字转换系统的设计与实现). Journal of Software (软件学报) (11) (2000)
15. Zhang, X.: A Simplified-Traditional Chinese Conversion Tool with a Supporting Environment for Human Proofreading (一个支持人工校对的中文简繁体转换工具). In: Sun, M., Chen, Q. (孙茂松，陈群秀编 (eds.)) Advances of Computational Linguistics in China 2009-2011 (中国计算语言学研究前沿进展2009-2011), pp. 569 - 575. Tsinghua University Press, Beijing (清华大学出版社) (2011)
16. Zhang, X.: Existing Space for Improvement in Simplified-Traditional Chinese Character Conversion (计算机汉字简繁体转换有待解决的问题). In: Li, X., Zhang, J., Xu, J. (eds.) (李晓琪，张建民，徐娟主编) Digital Teaching of Chinese Language 2012 (数字化汉语教学 2012), pp. 219 - 226. Tsinghua University Press, Beijing (清华大学出版社) (2012)
17. Zhang, X.: Simplified-Traditional Chinese Conversion with Assistance to Human Proofreading. Invited short paper for *Newsletter of the Chinese Language Teachers Association* 37(1), 30 (2013)

Combining Lexical Context with Pseudo-alignment for Bilingual Lexicon Extraction from Comparable Corpora

Bo Li, Qunyan Zhu, Tingting He, and Qianjun Chen

The Center of the National Language Tracing and Research for the Network Media,
National Engineering Research Center for E-Learning,
Network Center of Hubei University,
School of Computer, Central China Normal University, Wuhan, 430079, China
liboccnu@126.com, zhuqunyan@yeah.net,
tthe@mail.ccnu.edu.cn, skysky@hubu.edu.cn

Abstract. Only a few studies have made use of alignment information in bilingual lexicon extraction from comparable corpora, in which comparable corpora are necessarily divided into 1-1 aligned document pairs. They have not been able to show extracted lexicons benefit from the embedding of alignment information. Moreover, strict 1-1 alignments do not exist broadly in comparable corpora. We develop in this paper a language-independent approach to lexicon extraction by combining the classic lexical context with pseudo-alignment information. Experiments on the English-French comparable corpus demonstrate that pseudo-alignment in comparable corpora is an essential feature leading to a significant improvement of standard method of lexicon extraction, a perspective that have never been investigated in a similar way by previous studies.

Keywords: comparable corpora, pseudo-alignment, bilingual lexicon extraction, context-vector

1 Introduction

Bilingual dictionaries are bridges between two different languages and important resources for empirical multilingual natural language processing tasks such as cross-lingual information retrieval (CLIR) [1] and statistical machine translation [13]. With the high-speed development of international communication, the bilingual dictionary demand grows highly accordingly. Hand-coded dictionaries are of high quality, but it is expensive to build and researchers have tried, since the end of the 1980s, to automatically extract bilingual lexicons from parallel corpora [7, 10, 11, 17]. Parallel corpora are however difficult and time consuming to get in several domains and the majority of bilingual collections are comparable and not parallel. Due to their more abundant, less expensive and low cost of acquisition via web, various methods have been previously proposed to extract bilingual lexicons from comparable corpora [3, 4, 5, 6, 8, 12, 15, 19].

Most works in bilingual lexicon extraction follow the assumption that words in translation should have similar context in both languages. Based on this assumption, a

M. Sun et al. (Eds.): CCL and NLP-NABD 2014, LNAI 8801, pp. 223–233, 2014.

standard approach usually builds context vectors for each word of the source and target languages. The candidate translations for a particular word are obtained by comparing the translated source context vector with the target context vector using a general bilingual dictionary [8], and it has been proved to get a good performance in previous works.

In addition to context information, heuristics are often used to improve the general accuracy of the context-vector approach, like orthographic similarities between the source and the target terms [16]. Cognate-based techniques are popular in bilingual term spotting, in particular for specific domains. It can be explained by the large amount of transliteration even in unrelated languages. Also, related languages like Latin languages can share similarities between a term and its translation, like identical lemmas.

As far as we could tell, only a few studies have paid attention to the co-occurrence information between words in aligned documents [14, 18]. Those approaches did not take lexical context into account, resulting in poor performance compared to work in the same vain. Moreover, comparable corpora in those studies were divided into strict 1-1 aligned document pairs which, however, did not exist broadly in comparable corpora. For instance, [14] aimed to enhance the performance of lexicon extraction for those rare words. They did make use of the alignment information in a machine learning manner, which however relied on strictly 1-1 alignments and expensive training process. Moreover, by extracting aligned pairs, they had actually reduced a lot the size of original corpora and suffered from great information loss.

However, factors affecting the meaning of a word are far more than this, let alone the task is dealing with two languages of different cultural background. Besides, due to *polysemy* and *homonymy*, it is hard to identify precise translations of a word according to a single type of feature, a conclusion that can be drawn from poor performance in previous studies [4]. A natural solution to this problem is to resort to comprehensive features, especially those reflecting different aspects of a word. Therefore, in this paper, we propose a comprehensive approach considering the lexical context together with the co-occurrence feature in loose aligned document pairs.

The rest of the paper is organized as follows: Section 2 reviews related works on some popular methods in lexicon extraction from comparable corpora. Section 3 presents the combined model we proposed: we firstly present the method to calculate similarity using context information and then discuss the principle and method to build word co-occurrence. Section 4 shows the experimental setup and evaluation of our method on three groups of corpora. Conclusions will be drawn in section 5.

2 Related Work

Several research works have been done on the task of extracting bilingual lexicon from comparable corpora. Most approaches are based on the same intuitive assumption of word distribution, that is words appear in context of the same form or semantic are attended to be translation pairs. The starting point of the strategy is as follows: for each word w, the context information of w is described in a certain way, such as a vector, and then we can get the translation candidates of w by ranking the context similarity between w and any target word. This method was often been conducted with an existing bilingual resources [6] or parser tool [5].

Existing research works are trying to improve performance through two ways: one is trying to find another way to describe the context which contains more context information; the other is to find a more effective way to measure the similarity between word contexts. Such as [3] defines words in a fixed size of window to be the context, and tests several different models in bilingual lexicon extraction from parallel or comparable corpora in specialized domains. It shows that the combination of multi models significantly improves results, and that the use of the thesaurus UMLS/MeSH is of primary importance. But [5] improves the context information by using dependency parsing. It uses contexts derived from head-words linked by dependency trees instead of the immediate adjacent lexical words. With the deep semantic information, it gains significant improvement compared to approaches solely relying on the lexical context. [6] presents a geometric view on bilingual lexicon extraction from comparable corpora, which can interpret all the context vector approaches in a uniform framework. It uses singular value decomposition (SVD) to map the original context vector to another space in which synonyms dictionary entries are close to each other, while polysemous ones still select different neighbors. The precision is proved to be improved. [12] tries to extract French-Japanese terminologies from comparable corpora, considering both single and multi-word terms. They show the fact that the quality of comparable corpora is more important than the quantity and that this ensures the quality of acquired terminological resources. It also concludes that the quality of co-occurrence vectors can be substantially improved by ensuring domain and discourse comparability of the corpora from which co-occurrences are obtained. [18] introduces a new way to align two document collections in different languages, and test the effectiveness of several combined CLIR approaches based on comparable corpora, dictionary-based query translation, and pseudo-relevance feedback. But it did not take the co-occurrence information of words in document pairs into account. [14] incorporates the lexical context similarity with the co-occurrence model between words in strict aligned documents to extract bilingual lexicons, which mainly tries to solve the problem of data sparseness of rare words. Furthermore, comparable corpora in [14, 18] were divided into strict 1-1 aligned document pairs that do not exist broadly in comparable corpora. In this case, the size of original corpora was greatly reduced while retaining the aligned document pairs, leading to great information loss. In addition, a large volume of training data was needed, which makes the method infeasible in general extraction task.

It has been proved in most previous studies that lexical context is important for bilingual lexicon extraction. The pseudo-alignments in comparable corpora are another feature we deem to be important. We thus plan to combine these two features to form a comprehensive model to extract bilingual lexicon from comparable corpora.

3 The Combination Model

3.1 Lexical Context Similarity

We implemented the context-vector similarity in a way similar to Pascale Fung [9], using context information to extract bilingual lexicon. It assumes that the words in the source and target language are likely to be mutual translations if their context is similar. Based on the assumption, the standard approach builds a context vector respectively for the source and target word. Then the context vector of the source word is translated to the target language, so that we can compare the source context vector with the target context vector and a similarity between them is also calculated. The context vector is built as follows:

For an English word w_e, we collect its context words in the entire English corpus, then a context vector $\overrightarrow{v_e}$ for w_e is built, the dimension of the $\overrightarrow{v_e}$ is the same with the number of entries the lexicon has, the value of the i-th dimension of $\overrightarrow{v_e}$ is W_{ie} :

$$W_{ie} = TF_{ie} \times IDF_i \tag{1}$$

where TF_{ie} represents the number of times the i-th word in the dictionary appears in the context of w_e.

$$IDF_i = \log\frac{maxn}{n_i} + 1 \tag{2}$$

where maxn is the maximum frequency of any word in the corpus, n_i is the total number of occurrences of word w_e in the corpus.

For a French word w_f , we acquire a context word vector $\overrightarrow{v_f}$ in a similar manner as the English word w_e.

Once the context vector of each word has been built, the problem is to measure the similarity between two words. In the cross-language settings, one needs to compare two vectors in different languages, i.e. one vector in the source language needs to be mapped to a vector in the target language. In this paper, $\overrightarrow{\mathrm{v_f}}$ is mapped to $\overrightarrow{\mathrm{v_e}}$ by accumulating the contributions from words in $\overrightarrow{\mathrm{v_f}}$. Here we calculate the contributions by adding up the weights of words in $\overrightarrow{\mathrm{v_f}}$ with the identical translations in $\overrightarrow{\mathrm{v_e}}$. We used the Cosine similarity for context-vector comparisons, which has often been shown to achieve superior results in comparative studies. With the cross-language vector mapping and the cosine formula, the similarity between words w_e and w_f is computed as:

$$S_c(w_e, w_f) = \cos(\overrightarrow{v_e}, \overrightarrow{v_f}) = \frac{<\overrightarrow{v_e}, \overrightarrow{v_f}>}{\sqrt{\sum_{w_e \in \overrightarrow{v_e}} (f(w_e)^2 + (\sum_{w_f \in T_{w_e} \cap \overrightarrow{v_f}} f(w_f))^2)}} \tag{3}$$

where T_{we} is the translation set of w_e in the bilingual dictionary.

3.2 Pseudo-alignment Similarity

According to the characteristics of the comparable corpus, Comparable documents are not strictly parallel, but have overlapping information. Therefore, words occur in a pair of comparable documents tends to have more probability of being translation candidates of each other. So in this work, first, we get a loose alignment between the two corpora, which has great differences with strict 1-1 alignment in other works and it is more suitable for the reality. Then, we propose a quantity which is large if w_e and w_f appear in many document pairs with a high comparability score, and small otherwise.

In order to establish loose alignments among documents, one in fact needs to measure the similarity of each document pair consisting of documents in two languages. We directly use here the measure $\mathrm{M}(\mathrm{C}_e, C_f)$ proposed by [9]. The measure is light-weighted and does not depend on complex resources like the machine translation system. Let us assume we have an English document C_e and a French document C_f, then $\mathrm{M}(\mathrm{C}_e, C_f)$ measures the proportion of the English and French words for which a translation can be found in the document pair, that is:

$$\mathrm{M}(C_e, C_f) = \frac{\sum_{w \in W_e^C \cap D_e^v} \mu(w, W_f^C) + \sum_{w \in W_f^C \cap D_f^v} \mu(w, W_e^C)}{|W_e^C \cap D_e^v| + |W_f^C \cap D_f^v|} \tag{4}$$

where W_e^C (resp. W_f^C) is the set of all words which appear in the English(resp. French) corpus . D_e^V (resp. D_f^V) is the English (resp. French) part of a given, independent bilingual dictionary. μ is a function indicating whether a translation from the translation set T_w of w is found in the French word set, that is:

$$\mu(w, W^C) = \begin{cases} 1 & iff\ T_w \cap W^C \neq \emptyset \\ 0 & else \end{cases} \tag{5}$$

In order to measure the co-occurrence feature of w_e and w_f, first, we define the joint probability of w_e and w_f as (6), which is in direct proportion to the number of comparable document pairs they occur in, that is:

$$\mathrm{p}(w_e, w_f) \propto \sum_{d_e \in D_e, d_f \in D_f} \delta(d_e, d_f) \tag{6}$$

where D_e (resp.D_f) is the set of documents containing word w_e (resp. w_f). $\delta(d_e, d_f)$ is defined as:

$$\delta(d_e, d_f) = \begin{cases} 1 & if(M(d_e, d_f) \geq \eta) \\ 0 & else \end{cases} \tag{7}$$

where η is the threshold to judge the comparability of two corpus or documents. Here we can conclude that the co-occurrence probability of w_e and w_f is in direct proportion to the number of comparable document pairs they occur in. According to equation (6), the marginal probability of w_e is:

$$\mathrm{P}(w_e) = \sum_{w_f \in W_f^C} p(w_e, w_f)$$

$$= \sum_{w_f \in W_f^C} \sum_{d_e \in D_e, d_f \in D_f} \delta(d_e, d_f)$$

$$= \sum_{d_e \in D_e} \sum_{d_f \in D_f^C} |d_f| \cdot \delta(d_e, d_f) \quad (8)$$

where D_f^C is the set of all documents in French corpus. Our corpora is large enough to assume that all d_f in D_f^C have almost the same vocabulary size and all d_e have the same number of comparable counterparts in D_f^C, then $\mathrm{p}(w_e) \propto |D_e|$. Point-wise mutual information (PMI) is a measure of association widely used in information theory and statistics. PMI is first proposed by [2] as equation (9), Here we use the $\mathrm{PMI}(w_e, w_f)$ to judge how relevant the source word w_e is to the target wordw_f:

$$\mathrm{PMI}(w_e, w_f) = \log \frac{p(w_e, w_f)}{p(w_e) \cdot p(w_f)} \quad (9)$$

Then, we proposed a quantity $\varphi(w_e, w_f)$, which is in direct proportion to the PMI of w_e and w_f:

$$\varphi(w_e, w_f) = \frac{\sum_{d_e \in D_e} \sum_{d_f \in D_f} \delta(d_e, d_f)}{|D_e| \cdot |D_f|} \quad (10)$$

which is easy to compute and has the desired property: it is reasonable to measure the co-occurrence feature of w_e and w_f.

The lexical context is a classic feature that has been proved to be efficient in lexicon extraction. The pseudo-alignment in comparable corpora is another feature we deem to be important. Those two features can be combined to form a comprehensive measure and we thus obtain:

$$S_{coo}(w_e, w_f) = S_c(w_e, w_f)(1 + \varphi(w_e, w_f)) \quad (11)$$

This is simply the product of two similarities from different aspects.

4 Experiments and Results

4.1 Experimental Setup

We perform our lexicon extraction on English and French comparable corpora which were used in the multilingual track of CLEF (http://www.clefcampaign.org), including the Los Angeles Times (LAT94, English), Glasgow Herald (GH95, English), Le Monde (MON94, French), SDA French 94(SDA94, French) and SDA French 95(SDA95, French). To gain the diversity of the corpora, two monolingual corpora from the Wikipedia dump[1] were built. English articles are retained below the root category *Society* and French articles are extracted from the *Société* category. A dump contains text, but also some special data and syntax (images, internal links, etc.) which are not interesting for our experiments. We remove all tags in the collection. A stop-word list is used to filter the textual content of the articles. The English corpus

[1] `http://download.wikimedia.org`

consists of 533k documents and the French one consists of 508k documents. Table 1 contains the details about the comparable corpora in which documents containing less than 30 words have been deleted.

Standard preprocessing steps: tokenization, POS-tagging by Tree tagger and lemmatization are performed on all the linguistic resources. We will directly work on lemmatized forms of content words (nouns, verbs, adjectives, adverbs).

Table 1. The size of the corpora

	language	Docs
CLEF corpora	English	165 K
	French	130 K
Wikipedia Corpora	English	368 K
	French	378 K

The seed lexicon used in our experiments is constructed from an online dictionary. It consists of 33k distinct English words and 28k distinct French words, which constitutes 76k translation pairs.

In order to measure the performance of the bilingual lexicon extraction method presented above, we divided the original seed dictionary into 2 parts: 10% of the English words (about 3k words) together with their translations are randomly chosen and used as the evaluation set, the remaining words being used to compute context vectors and similarity between them.

4.2 Experiment Groups

While getting the POS information of the corpus, we divided the entire corpus to three parts which were the three groups of corpora using in the experiments. Then we randomly pick some files from them to do the experiments, documents in each language have the same number. The source and size of the final corpus is listed in Table 2.

Table 2. The source and size of the corpora in the experiments

group	Data	Language	Source	Size
1	CLEF Base corpus	English	GH95	19K
		French	SDA95	19K
2	CLEF Base corpus + CLEF extend corpus	English	GH95, LAT94	46 K
		French	SDA95, MON94,SDA94	46 K
3	CLEF Base corpus+ Wikipedia corpus	English	GH95, Layer less than 4 under Society category,	54 K
		French	SDA95, Layer less than 7 under Société category	54 K

While building the context vector of the source and target corpora, syntactic contexts are considered to be less ambiguous and more sense-sensitive than contexts defined as windows of size N for the reason of no structural damage to a complete sentence. But in our work, the Wikipedia texts are not so standard in grammar because of their voluntary editor. Therefore, we use the period concluding a sentence combined with a context widow of size 10 to define the range of context.

4.3 Results and Analysis

After calculating similarities based on the baseline method and the one developed in this paper, for each word in the test set, we list their French translation candidates which are ranked by the two methods of calculating similarity respectively. In order to test the performance of the words in the evaluation lists, we get the top N ranked translate candidates of each word, then measure the precision rate and recall rate. In addition, several studies have proved that it is easier to find the correct translations for frequent words than for infrequent words, to take this fact into account, we distinguished different frequency ranges to assess the validity of our approach for all frequency ranges, Words with frequency less than 100 are defined as low-frequency words (W_L), while words with frequency larger than 400 are high-frequency words (W_H), and words with frequency in between are medium-frequency words (W_M). The results obtained when using the lexical context information alone (baseline) and the refined combined model proposed in this paper (new) were displayed in Table 3. The relative improvement is further shown in Table 4. Gi' (i=1, 2, 3) stands for the result of group Gi' while using the improved method.

Table 3. Precision and recall rate of two approaches on three groups

	Precision		Recall	
	baseline	new	baseline	New
G1	0.250	0.251	0.106	0.106
G2	0.277	0.293	0.122	0.127
G3	0.325	0.345	0.145	0.153

Table 4. Improvement of presicion for words in different frequcney ranges. G2' and G3' denotes performance of our approach on test group G2 and G3 respectively.

	G2	G3	G2'	> G2	G3'	> G3
W_L	0.167	0.206	0.175	4.8%	0.221	7.3%
W_M	0.338	0.390	0.358	5.9%	0.420	7.7%
W_H	0.561	0.632	0.599	6.8%	0.657	4.0%
All	0.277	0.325	0.293	**5.8%**	0.345	**6.2%**

Table 3 shows the overall results on three groups of test corpora obtained with our approach as well as the baseline method. One can find that performance of lexicon extraction, in terms of both precision and recall, has been enhanced on all groups, although the improvement is more remarkable on G2 and G3. It is a tough task to improve the performance of lexicon extraction when considering target words distributed in all frequency ranges[6, 9], compare to those studies only focusing on words of high frequency [4, 12]. According to the experiment results obtained in previous work for the same task [9], our results here should be considered as important, although the increase in terms of precision is not that much. We also notice from table 3 that the performance does not change much on group G1 with our approach. The reason is that corpora in group G1 are of small size where context information and alignments of high quality do not exist in large scale. We can draw a conclusion out of these results: the size of corpus influences the quality of bilingual lexicons extracted with the method proposed in this paper.

We will give here more comments on translation performance for words distributed in different frequency ranges, since it is much easier to translate words of higher frequency [4, 12]. The improvement on group G1 is not that significant and we only focus on those on groups G2 and G3 and list detailed results in table 4. One could find a consistent improvement for words in all the frequency ranges. When using the improved approach, the precision of low-frequency words is strongly improved from 0.167 to 0.175 (corresponding to a relative increase of 4.8%) on group G2, from 0.206 to 0.221 (corresponding to a relative increase of 7.3%) on group G3. For middle frequency words, the precision is relatively increased by 5.9% on group G2 and 7.7% on group G3. Lastly, for high frequency words, the performance is also significantly improved: from 56.1% to 59.9% (corresponding to a relative increase of 6.8%) on group G2 and from 63.2% to 65.7 % (corresponding to a relative increase of 4%) on group G3. We can thus conclude that our approach performs consistently on all frequency ranges. Especially for those low frequency words of which the performance is rather difficult to improve, our approach has shown a consistent and satisfactory enhancement.

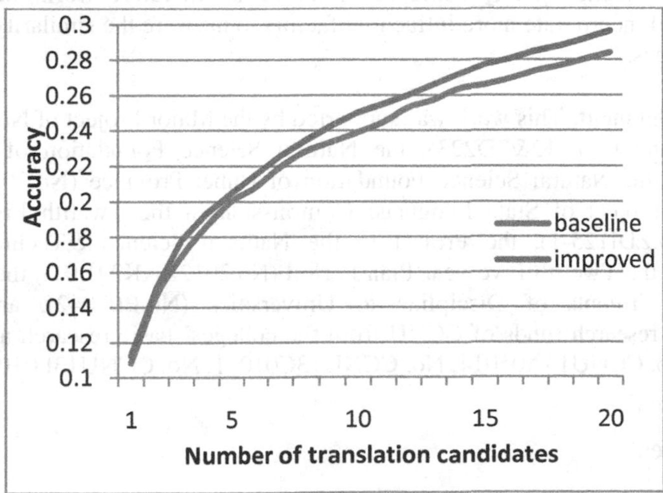

Fig. 1. Comparison of the average precision for the top 1 to 20 candidates with the baseline approach and our improved approach on group G2

The average precision of three groups on different approaches is displayed in Fig 1. From it, one can see that the overall average precision is further improved by 1.3% compared with the baseline. For N from 1 to 20, there is always a significant improvement in the precision and recall rate. The most fastest rising appears in top 1 to top 5, this is mainly because correct translations can be easily found in top 5 with only little random error, with the increase of number of candidates, the accuracy does not increase so sharply means the candidates among top 10 to 20 are usually words relates to the true translations, so one can refine the model eventually to get better precision.

5 Conclusion

We have proposed in this paper a combined model to improve the efficiency of bilingual lexicon extraction from comparable corpora. This model combines the traditional lexical context information with the word co-occurrence in loosely aligned documents to compute the similarity between two words. It has been proved to be effective mainly because the novel model has taken into account various characteristics that could reflect word meaning from a comprehensive perspective. We have first established in our approach loosely aligned document pairs relying on a light-weighted comparability measure proposed in [9]. Contrary to previous studies, the pseudo-alignment in our work does not need to be strictly 1-1 style, which is compliant with the real case in practice. The co-occurrence information of words in aligned documents is then incorporated into the traditional model solely relying on lexical context similarity to form a comprehensive model. Experiments have shown that translation precision can be improved significantly on all test groups, i.e. a relative improvement of 6.2% on group G3 from 32.5% to 34.5%. In addition, we have noticed much more improvement on those corpora of larger size where alignment of higher quality could be found easier. In future work, we will try to discover and incorporate more influential factors to measure the similarity of words in two languages.

Acknowledgement. This work was supported by the Major Project of National Social Science Fund (No. 12&2D223), the Natural Science Foundation of China (No. 61300144), the Natural Science Foundation of Hubei Province (No.2011CDA034), the Major Project of State Language Commission in the Twelfth Five-year Plan Period (No.ZDI125-1), the Project in the National Science &Technology Pillar Program in the Twelfth Five-year Plan Period (No.2012BAK24B01), the Program of Introducing Talents of Discipline to Universities (No.B07042), and the self-determined research funds of CCNU from the colleges' basic research and operation of MOE(No. CCNU13A05014, No. CCNU13C01001, No. CCNU13F010).

References

1. Ballesteros, L., Croft, W.B.: Phrasal translation and query expansion techniques for cross-language information retrieval. In: SIGIR, pp. 84–91 (1997)

2. Church, K.W., Hanks, P.: Word Association Norms, Mutual Information, and Lexicography. Computational Linguistics 16(1), 22–29 (1990)
3. Déjean, H., Gaussier, E., Sadat, F.: An approach based on multilingual thesauri and model combination for bilingual lexicon extraction. In: Proceedings of the 19th International Conference on Computational Linguistics (COLING 2002), Taipei, Taiwan, pp. 218–224 (2002)
4. Fung, P., Yee, L.Y.: An IR approach for translating new words from nonparallel, comparable texts. In: 17th International Conference on Computational Linguistics, Montreal, Quebec, Canada, pp. 414–420 (1998)
5. Garera, N., Callison-Burch, C., Yarowsky, D.: Improving translation lexicon induction from monolingual corpora via dependency contexts and part-of-speech equivalences. In: Proceedings of the 13th Conference on Computational Natural Language Learning, pp. 129–137 (2009)
6. Gaussier, E., Renders, J.-M., Matveeva, I., Goutte, C., Déjean, H.: A geometric view on bilingual lexicon extraction from comparable corpora. In: 42nd Annual Meeting of the Association for Computational Linguistics, Barcelona, Spain, pp. 526–533 (2004)
7. Kay, M., Röscheisen, M.: Text-Translation Alignment. Computational Linguistics 19, 121–142 (1993)
8. Laroche, A., Langlais, P.: Revisiting Context-based Projection Methods for Term translation spotting in Comparable Corpora. In: Proceedings of the 23rd Coling Conference, Beijing, China, pp. 617–625 (2010)
9. Li, B., Gaussier, E.: Improving corpus comparability for bilingual lexicon extraction from comparable corpora. In: Proceedings of the 23rd International Conference on Computational Linguistics (Coling 2010), Beijing (2010)
10. Melamed, I.D.: A portable algorithm for mapping bitext correspondence. In: Proceedings of the 35th Annual Meeting of the ACL (1997)
11. Melamed, I.D.: A word-to-word model of translational equivalence. In: Proceedings of the 35th Conference of the Association for Computational Linguistics (ACL 1997), Madrid, pp. 490–497 (1997)
12. Morin, E., Daille, B., Takeuchi, K., Kageura, K.: Bilingual terminology mining-using brain, not brawn comparable corpora. In: Proceedings of the 45th Annual Meeting of the Association for Computational Linguistics, pp. 664–671 (2007)
13. Och, F.J., Ney, H.: A Systematic Comparison of Various Statistical Alignment Models. Computational Linguistics 29(1), 19–51 (2003)
14. Prochasson, E., Fung, P.: Rare word translation extraction from aligned comparable documents. In: Proceedings of the 49th Annual Meeting of the Association for Computational Linguistics: Human Language Technologies, Portland, Oregon, USA, pp. 1327–1335 (2011)
15. Robitaille, X., Sasaki, Y., Tonoike, M., Sato, S., Utsuro, T.: Compiling French-Japanese terminologies from the web. In: Proceedings of the 11th Conference of the European Chapter of the Association for Computational Linguistics (EACL 2006), Trento, Italy, pp. 225–232 (2006)
16. Shao, L., Ng, H.: Mining New Word Translations from Comparable Corpora. In: Proceedings of the 20th ACL Conference, p. 618 (2004)
17. Chen, S.F.: Aligning sentences in bilingual corpora using lexical information. In: Proceedings of the 31st Annual Meeting of the Association for Computational Linguistics, Columbus, Ohio, pp. 9–16 (1993)
18. Talvensaari, T., Laurikkala, J., Järvelin, K., Juhola, M.: Creating and exploiting a comparable corpus in cross-language information retrieval. TOIS 25(4) (2007)
19. Yu, K., Tsujii, J.: Extracting bilingual dictionary from comparable corpora with dependency heterogeneity. In: Proceedings of HLT-NAACL, Boulder, Colorado, pp. 121–124 (2009)

Chinese-English OOV Term Translation with Web Mining, Multiple Feature Fusion and Supervised Learning

Yun Zhao[1], Qinen Zhu[1], Cheng Jin[1], Yuejie Zhang[1], Xuanjing Huang[1], and Tao Zhang[2]

[1] School of Computer Science
Shanghai Key Laboratory of Intelligent Information Processing,
Fudan University, Shanghai 200433, P.R. China
[2] School of Information Management & Engineering,
Shanghai University of Finance & Economics, Shanghai 200433, P.R. China
{12210240077,13210240131,jc,yjzhang,xjhuang}@fudan.edu.cn,
taozhang@mail.shfeu.edu.cn

Abstract. This paper focuses on the Web-based Chinese-English Out-of-Vocabulary (OOV) term translation pattern, and emphasizes on the translation selection based on multiple feature fusion and the ranking based on Ranking Support Vector Machine (Ranking SVM). By utilizing the SIGHAN2005 corpus for the Chinese Named Entity Recognition (NER) task and selected new terms, the experiments based on different data sources show the consistent results. From the experimental results for combining our model with Chinese-English Cross-Language Information Retrieval (CLIR) on the data sets of TREC, it can be found that the obvious performance improvements for both query translation and CLIR are obtained.

Keywords: Chinese-English OOV Term Translation, Web mining, multiple feature fusion, supervised learning, Ranking SVM.

1 Introduction

In Cross-Language Information Retrieval (CLIR), users' queries are generally composed of short terms, in which there are many Out-of-Vocabulary (OOV) terms like Named Entities (NEs), new words, terminologies [1][5][6][12]. The translation quality of OOV term directly influences the precision of querying multilingual information and OOV term translation has become a challenging issue in CLIR [9][15][17]. With the increasing growth of Web information which includes multilingual hypertext resources with abundant topics, it appears that Web information can mitigate the problem of the restricted OOV term translation accuracy [11][13][18]. However, how to select the correct translations from Web and locate the appropriate translation resources rapidly is still the main goal for OOV term translation [14][16][19]. Hence, finding the effective feature representation and the optimal ranking pattern for translation candidates is the core part for the Web-based OOV term translation.

M. Sun et al. (Eds.): CCL and NLP-NABD 2014, LNAI 8801, pp. 234–246, 2014.

Many researchers have utilized Web search engines to find translation candidates for Chinese-English OOV term translation [8][10][13]. Zhang et al. [25] extracted the translation candidates for OOV query terms from Web in Chinese-English CLIR, and improved the CLIR performance. Zhang et al. [24] searched the translation candidates by using cross-language query expansion and Web, and obtained the Top-1 accuracy of 81.0% in Chinese-English OOV word translation. Fang et al. [4] used semantic prediction and query expansion to get the translation candidates, and acquired the Top-3 accuracy of 82.9% in Chinese-English OOV term translation. Chen et al. [3] used the combination of Web statistics and the vocabulary, and acquired the Top-1 accuracy of 87.6% in Chinese-English OOV word translation. Yang et al. [21] utilized the combination of transliteration, Web mining and ranking based on AdaBoost, and got the Top-5 accuracy of 76.35% for Chinese-English backward transliteration. Yang et al. [22] utilized heuristic Web mining and asymmetric alignment, and got the Top-1 accuracy of 48.71% in Chinese-English organization name translation. Yang et al. [23] combined Web mining and ranking by SVM and Ranking SVM, and obtained the Top-1 accuracy of 65.75% in Chinese-English organization name translation.

Unfortunately, there are still three common problems in Chinese-English OOV term translation based on Web mining. (1) **The noises in English translation candidates cannot be processed appropriately.** Although there does not exist the issue of word segmentation in English key term extraction, many noises may be introduced into the candidates extracted from Web documents. However, such noises are often simply processed, or even without any processing. (2) **The feature information for the evaluation of translation candidates is not enough and comprehensive.** Most methods implement the evaluation for candidates through mining simple local and Boolean features. However, if only a certain Web document that an OOV term appears is explored, the global information contained in the whole Web document set is ignored, and the inconsistency and polysemy of candidates cannot be considered. (3) **The relevance measurement for translation pairs is simple, or the computation cost is too high.** For ranking candidates, most approaches adopt the simple combination computation of feature values, or get assessment based on classification models. The feature weights are determined according to the general induction and suitable for specific fields, and cannot guarantee the accuracy for ranking. The Ranking SVM model can effectively express multiple ranking constraints, and has better universality and applicability [2][20].

To support more precise Chinese-English OOV term translation, we establish a multiple-feature-based translation pattern based on Web mining and Ranking SVM. An English key term extraction mechanism is built on the simplified selection, and then the emphasis is put on the noise filtering. Heuristic rules summarized from translation candidates are used to remove insignificant noises, and Information Entropy is introduced to further discard meaningless substrings. On the other hand, translation candidates are chosen by the fusion of multiple features. The representation forms of local, global and Boolean feature are constructed under the consideration for the characteristics of Chinese/English OOV term and Web information. For the relevance measurement between an OOV term and its translation candidates, the supervised learning based on Ranking SVM is utilized to rank candidates accurately. By utilizing the SIGHAN2005 corpus for the Chinese Named Entity Recognition (NER) task and manually selected new terms in various fields, our model can "*filter*" the most possible translation candidates with better ability. This paper also attempts to apply our model in Chinese-English CLIR. It can be observed from the experimental results on the data sets of TREC that the obvious improvement for query translation is obtained.

2 English Key Term Extraction

In Web mining of OOV term translation, a crucial problem is to select the translation candidates from the returned Web documents, that is, the key term extraction task. The **Initial Extraction** mechanism is first established to extract the initial English key terms from the webpage snippets obtained by using the Chinese OOV term as a query for the search engine. The English fragments segmented by the non-English characters in each snippet are selected. Given the following snippet, "*Naruto wallpapers*", "*Naruto*", "*Two destinys two different fates*" and "*Recognize my existence*" are chosen as the initial key terms.

火影忍者壁纸(Naruto wallpapers)
您的位置：首页 > 火影忍者> 火影忍者壁纸> Naruto ... 火影忍者壁纸： Two destinys two different fates ... 火影忍者壁纸： Recognize my existence ...
www.manmankan.com/wallpaper/1/10/ - 12k - 网页快照 - 类似网页

Obviously, there are a lot of noises among the initial key terms. Therefore, some noise patterns are regarded as **Heuristic Filtering Rules (HFR)** and utilized to remove the noisy strings. (1) If an initial key term appears in the stoplist, then it is removed as a noisy string. The stoplist contains the stopwords with high frequency in common use, which are usually irrelevant with the original OOV term, such as "*Translate this page*" and "*Retrieved from Wikipedia*". (2) If an initial key term begins or ends with a preposition or conjunction, then it is removed as a noisy string. (3) If an initial key term satisfies some filtering patterns, then it is removed as a noisy string. Such patterns are used to select some frequent and obviously incorrect key terms. For example, an initial key term for the OOV term "非洲统一组织 [*Organization of African Unity*]" is "*Fei*1 *zhou*1 *Tong*3 *yi*1 *Zu*3 *zhi*1", which is a unreasonable form composed of both letters and numbers. (4) If multiple initial key terms are same by ignoring the case sensitivity, then the form with the highest frequency is reserved and the others are removed as the noisy strings. For example, for the OOV term "费利克斯[*Felix*]", all the related information for three initial key terms, "*Felix*", "*FELIX*" and "*felix*", must be considered in the subsequent feature selection and computation. (5) For initial key terms with a single word corresponding to the same original OOV term, if a term is a prefix/suffix substring of the other terms, then it is removed as a noisy string.

In the key terms obtained by HFR-based filtering, there are still some redundant substrings, thus the optimization based on **Information Entropy** is proposed to further filter such noises. For a key term x, its entropy is expressed as:

$$H(X) = -\sum_{i=1}^{N} p(x_i)\log_2 p(x_i) \quad (1)$$

where $p(x_i)$ denotes the frequency of x in the ith snippet, and computed as n_i/n, n_i is the occurrence times of x in the ith snippet and n is the total occurrence times of x in the whole snippet set; N is the total snippet number.

Information Entropy can not only represent the amount of information content for key terms, but also the distribution similarity between two key terms in the snippet set. Given two key terms kt_1 and kt_2, kt_1 is a substring of kt_2. If $\lambda H(kt_1)<H(kt_2)$ (the setting for λ is shown in Section 6.2), then $kt1$ is removed as a noisy string. However, if only using Information Entropy to filter substrings, the relations between an OOV term and its key terms cannot be considered. For key terms with low frequency, they often co-occur with some noisy strings. For example, for the OOV term "萨马兰奇 [*Samaranch*]", its correct translation "*Samaranch*" always occurs in the key term "*Juan Antonio Samaranch*". If only determined by using Information Entropy, "*Samaranch*" will be removed. Thus the special feature *P&S_IF* (defined in Section 4), which describes the phonetic and sense relations between an OOV term and its translation candidates, is added to solve this problem. If $(\lambda H(kt_1)<H(kt_2))$ && $(P\&S\_IF(OOVTerm, kt_1)<P\&S\_IF(OOVTerm, kt_2))$, then kt_1 is deleted.

3 Multiple Feature Representation

Local Feature (LF) is constructed based on neighboring tokens and the token itself. There are two types of contextual information to be considered when extracting LFs, namely internal lexical and external contextual information.

(1#) **Term length** (*Len*) – Aims to consider the length of the translation candidate.
(2#) **Phonetic Value** (*PV*) – Aims to investigate the phonetic similarity between an OOV term and its translation candidates. Because the associated syllabification representations can often be found between Chinese and English syllables with fewer ambiguities, the syllabification has become a very effective way in the phonetic feature expression. *PV* means that for measuring the edit distance similarity between the syllabification sequences of an OOV term and its candidates, the corresponding processing is executed according to the specific linguistic rules.

$$PV(S_{OOV}, T_{OOV}) = 1 - \frac{EditDist(S_{OOV}', T_{OOV}')}{Len(S_{OOV}') + Len(T_{OOV}')} \quad (2)$$

where S_{OOV} and T_{OOV} denote the OOV term and its translation candidate respectively, S_{OOV}' and T_{OOV}' are the character strings after the syllabification and removing the vowels, *EditDist*(,) indicates the edit distance between two strings.
(3#) **Length Ratio of OOV Term and Its Translation Candidate** (*LR*) – Aims to explore the composition possibility that the translation candidate can be regarded as the final correct translation for an OOV term. An OOV term and its translation should have the similar length, so the *LR* value is close to 1 as possible. A Chinese term is segmented into significant pieces first, and the number of pieces is taken as its length.

For example, "非典型肺炎[SARS]" is segmented into "非[non]", "典型[typical]" and "肺炎[*pneumonia*]", and its length is 3. For an English term, the number of words is counted as the length. If there is only one word composed of capital letters, its length is defined as the number of letters, e.g., "*SARS*" has the length of 4. Thus the *LR* value of "非典型肺炎[*SARS*]" and its candidate "*SARS*" is 3/4=0.75.

(4#) **Phonetic and Sense Integration Feature** (*P&S_IF*) – Aims to consider the phonetic information and senses of an OOV term and its candidates synthetically. It is set up for multi-word OOV terms. Each constituent can be translated by the phonetic information or senses.

$$P\&S\_IF(S_{OOV}, T_{OOV}) = \frac{LScore(S_{OOV}, T_{OOV}) + PV(S_{OOV}'', T_{OOV}'')}{LScore(S_{OOV}, T_{OOV}) + 1} \tag{3}$$

where *LScore*(,) is the matching word number of non-transliteration words in S_{OOV} and T_{OOV}, while S_{OOV}'' and T_{OOV}'' are the remaining strings of S_{OOV} and T_{OOV} after computing *LScore*. For example, given S_{OOV} "斯堪的纳维亚半岛[Scandinavian Peninsula]" and its TOOV "Scandinavian Peninsula" , the non-transliteration words " 半岛[peninsula]" and "Peninsula" are matched, then LScore(SOOV, TOOV)=1; the PV value between the remaining strings "斯堪的纳维亚[*Scandinavian*]" and "*Scandinavian*" is 0.928, so the final *P&S_IF* value is 1.928/2=0.964.

(5#) **Un-Covered Ratio** (*UCR*) – Aims to explore the ratio of the overlap between an OOV term and the translations of its candidates acquired from Chinese Basic Dictionary (Yang et al. 2009b). It is set up for multi-word OOV terms.

$$UCR(S_{OOV}, T_{OOV}) = 1 - \frac{Len(unTrans)}{Len(S_{OOV})} \tag{4}$$

where *unTrans* is the part in S_{OOV} uncovered by the translation of T_{OOV}. For example, given S_{OOV} "苏伊士运河[Suez Canal]" and its TOOV "Suez Canal", the part in TOOV which can be translated by Basic Dictionary is "Canal" and its translation is " 运河[canal]". Thus the unTrans part in SOOV is "苏伊士[*Suez*]", then the final *UCR* value is 1-3/5=0.4.

Global Feature (GF) is extracted from other occurrences of the same or similar tokens in the Web document set. The common case in the Web-based OOV term translation is that the translation candidates in the previous parts of Web documents often occur with the same or similar forms in the latter parts. The contextual information from the same and other Web documents may be beneficial to determine the final translation. To utilize global information, GFs are built based on the characteristics of Web documents.

(1#) **Global Term Frequency** (*G_Freq*) – Aims to utilize the frequency information that an OOV term and its translation candidates appear in the Web document set. It is always the most important feature and includes four parameters. $\boldsymbol{Freq_{SOOV}}$ denotes the frequency of S_{OOV} in all the returned snippets. $\boldsymbol{TF_{TOOV}}$ indicates the number of T_{OOV}s in all the snippets. $\boldsymbol{DF_{TOOV}}$ represents the number of snippets that contain T_{OOV}. ***CO_Freq*** means the number of snippets that contain both S_{OOV} and T_{OOV}, i.e., co-occurrence frequency.

(2#) **Global Statistical Feature** (*G_SF*) – Aims to explore the statistical measure for the strength of the interdependence between an OOV term and its translation candidates to judge the possibility of a translation candidate being taken as the final correct translation [7].

Chi-Square (χ^2) Feature Value (*CV*) – Aims to evaluate the semantic similarity between S_{OOV} and T_{OOV} by their occurrence in Web documents.

$$CV_{\chi^2}(S_{OOV},T_{OOV})=\frac{N\times(a\times d-b\times c)^2}{(a+b)\times(a+c)\times(b+d)\times(c+d)} \tag{5}$$

where a is the number of snippets with both S_{OOV} and T_{OOV}, b is the number of snippets that contain S_{OOV} but do not contain T_{OOV}, c is the number of snippets that do not contain S_{OOV} but contain T_{OOV}, d is the number of snippets that do not contain neither of S_{OOV} and T_{OOV}, and $N=a+b+c+d$.

Information Gain (*IG*) – Aims to compute the probability that T_{OOV} appears in the snippets with S_{OOV}. The larger *IG* shows that T_{OOV} is a more possible translation for S_{OOV}.

$$IG(S_{OOV},T_{OOV})=a\times\log\frac{a}{(a+b)\times(a+c)}+b\times\log\frac{b}{(a+b)\times(b+d)} \tag{6}$$

Correlation Coefficient (*CC*) – Aims to measure the linear association degree between S_{OOV} and T_{OOV}. It's a variant of *CV*. The larger *CC* value indicates that the relation between S_{OOV} and T_{OOV} is more correlative, and $CC^2=\chi^2$.

$$CC(S_{OOV},T_{OOV})=\frac{\sqrt{N}\times(a\times d-b\times c)}{\sqrt{(a+b)\times(a+c)\times(b+d)\times(c+d)}} \tag{7}$$

Relevance Score (*RS*) – Aims to measure the direct relevance between S_{OOV} and T_{OOV}. It's computed as the ratio between the occurrence probability of T_{OOV} in the snippets with S_{OOV} and that of T_{OOV} in the snippets without S_{OOV}. The larger *RS* indicates that S_{OOV} and T_{OOV} are more relevant.

$$RS(S_{OOV},T_{OOV})=\log\frac{\frac{a}{a+b}+m}{\frac{c}{c+d}+m} \tag{8}$$

where m is used to smooth the *RS* and usually set as 1.

Odds Ratio (*OR*) – Aims to measure the indirect relevance between S_{OOV} and T_{OOV}. The distribution of features on relevant candidates is different from that on irrelevant candidates. The larger *OR* indicates that S_{OOV} and T_{OOV} are more relevant.

$$OR(S_{OOV},T_{OOV})=\frac{\frac{a}{a+b}\times\left(1-\frac{c}{c+d}\right)}{\left(1-\frac{a}{a+b}\right)\times\frac{c}{c+d}} \tag{9}$$

GSS Coefficient (*GSS*) – Aims to measure the relevance between S_{OOV} and T_{OOV}. It is another simplified variant of *CV*. The larger GSS also represents the stronger relevance.

$$GSS(S_{OOV}, T_{OOV}) = a \times d - b \times c \tag{10}$$

(3#) **Pointwise Mutual Information** (*PMI*) – Aims to evaluate the co-occurrence relation between an OOV term and its candidates. If both appear with the higher co-occurrence frequency in the same snippet, they are more relevant.

$$PMI\ (S_{OOV}, T_{OOV}) = \frac{N \times a}{(a+b) \times (a+c)} \tag{11}$$

(4#) **Co-Occurrence Distance** (*CO_Dist*) – Aims to investigate the distance between an OOV term and its candidates in Web documents. This distance is often very closer.

For each snippet that contains both S_{OOV} and T_{OOV}, three positions are considered, that is, the first position that S_{OOV} and T_{OOV} appear (*p*1), the second position (*p*2) and the last one (*p*3). For example, in the following snippet, S_{OOV} is "亚洲开发银行[*Asian Development Bank*, *ADB*]" and T_{OOV} is "*Asian Development Bank*".

> 亚洲开发银行- MBA智库百科
> 2010年6月9日 ... 亚洲开发银行（Asian Development Bank, ADB）亚洲开发银行网站网址：
> http://www.adb.org/亚洲开发银行（Asian Development Bank, ADB，以下简称亚 ...
> wiki.mbalib.com/wiki/**亚洲开发银行** - 网页快照 - 类似结果

$p1_{SOOV}$=0, $p2_{SOOV}$=29, $p3_{SOOV}$=159; $p1_{TOOV}$=36, $p2_{TOOV}$=101, $p3_{TOOV}$=101

The position is indexed from 0. Then the nearest position pair $p2_{SOOV}$ and $p1_{TOOV}$ can be found for this example. The distance *Dist* between S_{OOV} and T_{OOV} is:

$$Dist(S_{OOV}, T_{OOV}) = \begin{cases} pi_{S_{OOV}} - pj_{T_{OOV}} - Len(T_{OOV}), & pi_{S_{OOV}} > pj_{T_{OOV}} \\ pj_{T_{OOV}} - pi_{S_{OOV}} - Len(S_{OOV}), & pi_{S_{OOV}} < pj_{T_{OOV}} \end{cases} \tag{12}$$

Given the example above, *Dist*=$p2_{SOOV}$-$p1_{TOOV}$-6=36-29-6 =1, S_{OOV} and T_{OOV} are a left bracket '(' apart. Thus the average distance *CO-Dist* in the snippet set is:

$$CO\_Dist(S_{OOV}, T_{OOV}) = AVG\_Dist(S_{OOV}, T_{OOV}) = \frac{Sum(Dist)}{CO\_Freq(S_{OOV}, T_{OOV})} \tag{13}$$

where *Sum*( ) is the sum of *Dist* in each snippet.

(5#) **Rank Value** (*RV*) – Aims to consider the rank for translation candidates in the Web document set. It includes six parameters. ***Top_Rank*** (*T_Rank*) is the rank of the snippet that first contains T_{OOV} and given by the search engine. ***Average_Rank*** (*A_Rank*) is the average position of T_{OOV} in the returned snippets.

$$A\_Rank(T_{OOV}) = \frac{Sum(Rank)}{DF_{T_{OOV}}(T_{OOV})} \tag{14}$$

where *Sum*( ) denotes the rank sum of each snippet. ***Simple_Rank*** (*S_Rank*) is computed as $S\_Rank(T_{OOV}) = TF_{TOOV}(T_{OOV}) * Len(T_{OOV})$, for investigating the impact of the frequency and length of T_{OOV} on ranking. ***R_Rank*** is utilized as a comparison basis.

$$R\_Rank(T_{OOV}) = \beta \times \frac{|T_{OOV}|}{MAX\_WL} + (1-\beta) \times \frac{TF_{T_{OOV}}(T_{OOV})}{Freq_{S_{OOV}}(S_{OOV})} \tag{15}$$

where β is set as 0.25 empirically, $|T_{OOV}|$ is the length of T_{OOV}, and *MAX_WL* denotes the maximum length of candidates. ***DF_Rank*** (*D_Rank*) is similar to *S_Rank*, and $D\_Rank(T_{OOV})=DF_{TOOV}(T_{OOV})*Len(T_{OOV})$. ***TF_Rank*** is computed as $TF\_Rank(T_{OOV})= TF_{TOOV}(T_{OOV})$, which aims at investigating the impact of the frequency of T_{OOV}.
(6#) **Similarity of Context Vector** (*SCV*) – Aims to evaluate the distribution similarity between an OOV term and its candidates in the snippet set. The OOV term S_{OOV} and its candidate T_{OOV} are first represented as two context vectors, $CV_{SOOV}=(ts_1, \ldots, ts_i, \ldots, ts_N)$ and $CV_{TOOV}=(tt_1, \ldots, tt_i, \ldots, tt_N)$, ts_i and tt_i denote the number of S_{OOV}s and T_{OOV}s in the ith snippet respectively. Thus the *SCV* can be computed as:

$$SCV(S_{OOV}, T_{OOV}) = \cos(CV_{S_{OOV}}, CV_{T_{OOV}}) = \frac{\sum_{i=1}^{N}(ts_i \times tt_i)}{\sqrt{\sum_{i=1}^{N}(ts_i)^2} \times \sqrt{\sum_{i=1}^{N}(tt_i)^2}} \tag{16}$$

Boolean Feature (BF) is a binary feature and equivalent to a heuristic rule designed for the particular relations between an OOV term and its translation candidates. BFs are used to explore the different occurrence forms with higher possibility for the candidates in Web documents. (1#) **Position Distance with OOV Term** (*PD_S*$_{OOV}$) – If T_{OOV} occurs close to S_{OOV} (within 10 characters), this feature is set as 1. (2#) **Neighbor Relation with OOV Term** (*NR_S*$_{OOV}$) – If T_{OOV} occurs prior or next to S_{OOV}, this feature is set as 1. (3#) **Bracket Neighbor Relation with OOV Term** (*BNR_S*$_{OOV}$) – If T_{OOV} locates prior or next to S_{OOV} and occurs with the form "T_{OOV} (S_{OOV})" or "S_{OOV} (T_{OOV})", this feature is set as 1. (4#) **Special Mark Word** (*SMW*) – Within a certain co-occurrence distance (less than 10 characters) between an OOV term and its candidates, if there is such a term like "全称[full name]", "叫[be named as]", "译为[be translated as …]" or "(或/又)称为[(*or/also*) *be called as* …]", or their English translation terms and so on, this feature is set as 1. (5#) **Capitalized First Letter** (*CFL*) – If T_{OOV} begins with a capitalized letter, this feature is set as 1.

4 Ranking Based on Ranking SVM

For the OOV term translation based on Web mining, another difficulty is how to evaluate the relevance between an OOV term and its translation candidates, that is, how to rank all the translation candidates from "*best*" to "*worst*".

The candidate ranking can be regarded as a binary classification problem. However, usually only highly related fragments of OOV terms can be found, rather than their correct translations. Instead of regarding the candidate ranking as binary classification, it is solved as an Ordinal Regression problem. Ranking SVM maps different objects into a certain kind of order relation. The key is modeling the judgements for user's preferences, and then the constraint relations for ranking can be derived.

For a S_{OOV}, if there are two translation candidates T_{OOVi} and T_{OOVj}, the preference judgement can be formulated as $T_{OOVi} >_{SOOV} T_{OOVj}$. Thus more training samples are constructed, which contain multiple constraint features. The judgement can be transformed into the feature function as:

$$f(S_{OOV}, T_{OOV\,i}, w) >_{S_{OOV}} f(S_{OOV}, T_{OOV\,j}, w) \tag{17}$$

where w is a parameter and represented as a vector $\{w_1, \ldots, w_i, \ldots, w_n\}$. This function can also be expressed as:

$$f(S_{OOV}, T_{OOV}, w) = \sum_{k=1}^{p} w_k LF_k(S_{OOV}, T_{OOV}) + \sum_{l=p+1}^{q} w_l GF_l(S_{OOV}, T_{OOV}) + \sum_{m=q+1}^{n} w_m BF_m(S_{OOV}, T_{OOV}) \tag{18}$$

where $LF_k(\ ,\ )$, $GF_l(\ ,\ )$ and $BF_m(\ ,\ )$ are the local, global and Boolean feature representation respectively. These three kinds of feature representation can be incorporated as a whole and represented as a feature function family with the multi-dimensional feature vector in Formula (19).

$$f(S_{OOV}, T_{OOV}, w) = w \cdot h(S_{OOV}, T_{OOV}) \tag{19}$$

Thus the relevance for each feature vector x (translation candidate) containing a group of features can be evaluated.

5 Experiment and Analysis

4,170 NEs are selected from the Chinese NER corpus in SIGHAN2005. The test set contains 310 Person Names (PRNs), 324 Location Names (LCNs) and 252 Organization Names (OGNs), and the remaining is taken as the training set. 300 Chinese new terms chosen randomly from 9 categories (movie name, book title, brand name, terminology, idiom, rare animal name and NE), are used to investigate the generalization ability of our model. *Top-N-Inclusion-Rate* is defined as the percentage of the OOV terms whose correct translations could be found in the first N translation candidates.

To verify the effectiveness for multiple feature fusion, the test on the feature combination for our model is implemented. As shown in Table 1, the highest *Top*-1-*Inclusion-Rate* of 88.8889% can be acquired by using all the features. It can be seen from Table 1 that the most important features are *P&S_IF*, *NR_*S_{OOV}, *BNR_*S_{OOV} and *UCR*. As for the frequency feature, its contribution is limited, because many candidates with higher *P&S_IF* values are the terms with low frequency. However, when training based on only the features that are beneficial to the whole performance, the best translation accuracy is 85.8024%, which is worse than that by combining all the features. Multiple feature fusion can indeed improve the translation accuracy.

Table 1. Results for feature combination

Feature				*Top-1-Inclusion Rate*	Reduction
All Features				88.8889%	—
Numerical Feature	*Local Numerical Feature*	*-Len*		88.8889%	0.0%
		-PV		84.8765%	-4.01234%
		-LR		88.8889%	0.0%
		-P&S_IF		81.1728%	-7.7160%
		-UCR		84.2592%	-4.6296%
	Global Numerical Feature	*Global Frequency*	*-TF_{TOOV}*	88.8889%	0.0%
			-DF_{TOOV}	90.1234%	+1.2345%
			-CO_Freq	89.1975%	+0.3086%
		-CV		88.8889%	0.0%
		-IG		84.5679%	-4.3210%
		-CC		88.8889%	0.0%
		-RS		85.1852%	-3.7037%
		-OR		89.8148%	+0.9259%
		-GSS		88.8889%	0.0%
		-PMI		89.8148%	+0.9259%
		-CO_Dist		87.0370%	-1.8518%
		RV	*-T_Rank*	88.2716%	-0.6172%
			-A_Rank	89.8148%	+0.9259%
		-SCV		89.5062%	+0.6173%
Boolean Feature		*-PD_S_{OOV}*		88.2716%	-0.6173%
		-NR_S_{OOV}		83.6419%	-5.2469%
		-BNR_S_{OOV}		83.9506%	-4.9383%
		-SMW		88.8889%	0.0%
		-CFL		89.1975%	+0.3086%

Yang et al. [23] is very similar to our approach, we accomplished this method on the same data set to make a contrast, as shown in Table 2. It can be concluded that the ranking based on the supervised learning outperforms the existing conventional strategies, Ranking SVM is better than SVM for ranking, and our approach is superior to Yang et al.'s. Meanwhile, the best performance is obtained for PRNs. It shows that our model is sensitive to the category and the popularity of OOV term.

Table 2. Performance comparison results

Method	Ranking Pattern	Category	*Top-1*	*Top-2*	*Top-3*
Our Model	***based on SVM (Multiple Features)***	***PRN***	88.70%	97.09%	99.35%
		LCN	76.23%	93.82%	96.91%
		OGN	76.58%	92.06%	96.42%
		All	**80.69%**	**94.46%**	**97.62%**
	based on Ranking SVM (Multiple Features)	***PRN***	92.58%	97.74%	99.03%
		LCN	87.34%	95.37%	98.14%
		OGN	84.52%	95.23%	97.22%
		All	**88.89%**	**96.16%**	**98.19%**
Yang *et al.* [23]	***based on SVM (TF_{TOOV}+LR+UCR+CFL)***	***OGN* (Only)**	53.96%	76.98%	88.49%
	based on Ranking SVM (TF_{TOOV}+ LR+UCR+CFL)	***OGN* (Only)**	62.69%	83.33%	88.49%

Another test for the other kinds of Chinese OOV term is performed on the selected new terms and the consistent results can be observed in Table 3.

Table 3. Results for Chinese OOV new terms

Top-N-Inclusion-Rate	*Top-1*	*Top-3*	*Top-5*	*Top-7*	*Top-9*
Chinese OOV New Terms	74.66%	90.33%	94.33%	95.00%	96.00%

Four CLIR runs are carried out on the Chinese topic set and English corpus from TREC-9. (1) *C-E_LongCLIR*1 – using Long Query (LQ, terms in both title and description fields) and the Dictionary-Based Translation (DBT); (2) *C-E_LongCLIR*2 – using LQ, DBT and our model; (3) *C-E_ShortCLIR*1 – using Short Query (SQ, only terms in the title field) and DBT; (4) *C-E_ShortCLIR*2 – using SQ, DBT and our model. The Precision-Recall curves and Median Average Precision (MAP) are shown in Fig. 1. It can be seen from Fig. 1 that the best run is *C-E_LongCLIR*2, and its results exceed those of *C-E_LongCLIR*1. By adopting both query translation based on bilingual dictionary and OOV term translation, Chinese-English CLIR for long query has gained the significant retrieval performance improvement. The same conclusion can be obtained for the other two runs *C-E_ShortCLIR*1 and *C-E_ShortCLIR*2.

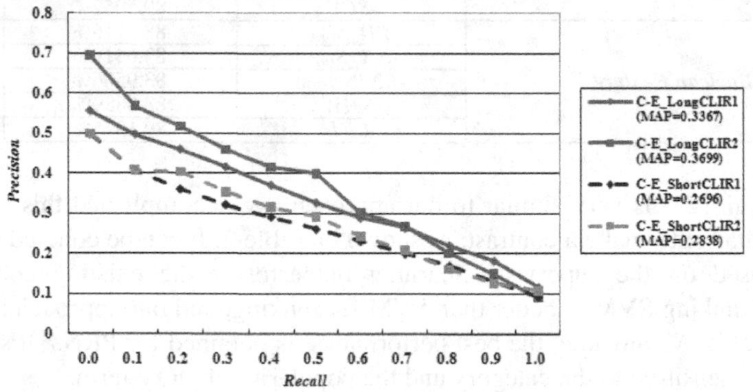

Fig. 1. Results for Chinese-English CLIR combining our model

Through analyzing the results, it can be found that the translation quality is highly related to the following aspects. (1) **The translation results are associated with the search engine used, especially for some specific OOV terms.** For example, given an OOV term "经济法制化", the mining result based on Google in China is "to manage economic affairs according to 1aw", which is more reasonable than "Economic law" acquired by Bing. (2) Some terms are idioms, conventional and political terminologies with Chinese characteristics, and cannot be translated literally. For example, "党群关系[*party masses relationship*]" should be translated into "*party masses relationship*", rather than "*ties between the party*" given by Google Translate. (3) **The proposed model is sensitive to the notability degree of OOV term.** This phenomenon is the main reason why there is an obvious difference among the translation performance for PRN, LCN and OGN. (4) **There are some particular and inherent noises in the extracted translation candidates.** For example, a candidate for the Chinese OOV term "广东人民出版社[*Guangdong People's Publishing House*]" is "*Guangdong ren min chu ban she*". (5) **Word Sense**

Disambiguation (WSD) should be added to improve the translation performance. Although most of OOV terms have a unique sense definition, there are still a few OOV terms with sense ambiguity, e.g., "东北大学[*Northeastern University* or *Tohoku University*]".

6 Conclusions

Traditional OOV term translation methods concern two aspects, that is, transliteration and sense translation. However, more and more Chinese OOV terms cannot be measured by phonetic or meaning information separately. Our proposed model improves the acquirement ability for Chinese-English OOV term translation through Web mining, and solves the translation pair selection and evaluation in a novel way by fusing multiple features and introducing the supervised learning based on Ranking SVM. Our future research will focus on applying the key techniques on statistical machine learning, alignment of sentence and phoneme, and WSD into Chinese-English OOV term translation.

Acknowledgments. This work is supported by National Science & Technology Pillar Program of China (No. 2012BAH59F04), National Natural Science Fund of China (No. 61170095; No. 71171126), and Shanghai Municipal R&D Foundation (No. 12dz1500203, 12511505300). Cheng Jin is the corresponding author.

References

1. Al-Onaizan, Y., Knight, K.: Translating Named Entities using Monolingual and Bilingual Resources. In: Proceedings of ACL 2002, pp. 400–408 (2002)
2. Cao, Y.B., Xu, J., Liu, T.Y., Li, H., Huang, Y.L., Hon, H.W.: Adapting Ranking-SVM to Document Retrieval. In: Proceedings of SIGIR 2006, pp. 186–193 (2006)
3. Chen, C., Chen, H.H.: A High-Accurate Chinese-English NE Backward Translation System Combining Both Lexical Information and Web Statistics. In: Proceedings of COLING-ACL 2006, pp. 81–88 (2006)
4. Fang, G.L., Yu, H., Nishino, F.: Chinese-English Term Translation Mining based on Semantic Prediction. In: Proceedings of COLING-ACL 2006, pp. 199–206 (2006)
5. Ge, Y.D., Hong, Y., Yao, J.M., Zhu, Q.M.: Improving Web-Based OOV Translation Mining for Query Translation. In: Cheng, P.-J., Kan, M.-Y., Lam, W., Nakov, P. (eds.) AIRS 2010. LNCS, vol. 6458, pp. 576–587. Springer, Heidelberg (2010)
6. Hu, R., Chen, W., Bai, P., Lu, Y., Chen, Z., Yang, Q.: Web Query Translation via Web Log Mining. In: Proceedings of SIGIR 2008, pp. 749–750 (2008)
7. Huang, S., Chen, Z., Yu, Y., Ma, W.Y.: Multitype Features Coselection for Web Document Clustering. IEEE Transactions on Knowledge and Data Engineering 18(4), 448–459 (2006)
8. Jiang, L., Zhou, M., Chien, L.F., Niu, C.: Named Entity Translation with Web Mining and Transliteration. In: Proceedings of IJCAI 2007, pp. 1629–1634 (2007)
9. Joachimes, T.: Optimizing Search Engines using Click through Data. In: Proceedings of SIGKDD 2002, pp. 133–142 (2002)

10. Lee, C.J., Chang, J.S., Jang, J.R.: Alignment of Bilingual Named Entities in Parallel Corpora Using Statistical Models and Multiple Knowledge Sources. ACM Transactions on Asian Language Processing 5(2), 121–145 (2006)
11. Lu, W.H., Chien, L.F.: Translation of Web Queries using Anchor Text Mining. ACM Transactions on Asian Language Information Processing 1(2), 159–172 (2002)
12. Lu, W.H., Chien, L.F.: Anchor Text Mining for Translation of Web Queries: A Transitive Translation Approach. ACM Transactions on Information Systems 22(2), 242–269 (2004)
13. Ren, F.L., Zhu, M.H., Wang, H.Z., Zhu, J.B.: Chinese-English Organization Name Translation Based on Correlative Expansion. In: Proceedings of the 2009 Named Entities Workshop, ACL-IJCNLP 2009, pp. 143–151 (2009)
14. Shao, L., Ng, H.T.: Mining New Word Translations from Comparable Corpora. In: Proceedings of COLING 2004, pp. 618–624 (2004)
15. Shi, L.: Mining OOV Translations from Mixed-Language Web Pages for Cross Language Information Retrieval. In: Gurrin, C., He, Y., Kazai, G., Kruschwitz, U., Little, S., Roelleke, T., Rüger, S., van Rijsbergen, K. (eds.) ECIR 2010. LNCS, vol. 5993, pp. 471–482. Springer, Heidelberg (2010)
16. Sproat, R., Tao, T., Zhai, C.X.: Named Entity Transliteration with Comparable Corpora. In: Proceedings of COLING-ACL, pp. 73–80 (2006)
17. Virga, P., Khudanpur, S.: Transliteration of Proper Names in Cross-Language Applications. In: Proceedings of SIGIR 2003, pp. 365–366 (2003)
18. Wang, J.H., Teng, J.W., Cheng, P.J., Lu, W.H., Chien, L.F.: Translating Unknown Cross-Lingual Queries in Digital Libraries using a Web-based Approach. In: Proceedings of JCDL 2004, pp. 108–116 (2004)
19. Wu, J.C., Chang, J.S.: Learning to Find English to Chinese Transliterations on the Web. In: Proceedings of EMNLP-CoNLL 2007, pp. 996–1004 (2007)
20. Xu, J., Cao, Y.B., Li, H., Zhao, M.: Ranking Definitions with Supervised Learning Methods. In: Proceedings of WWW 2005, pp. 811–819 (2005)
21. Yang, F., Zhao, J., Zou, B., Liu, K.: Chinese-English Backward Transliteration Assisted with Mining Monolingual Web Pages. In: Proceedings of ACL 2008, pp. 541–549 (2008)
22. Yang, F., Zhao, J., Liu, K.: A Chinese-English Organization Name Translation System Using Heuristic Web Mining and Asymmetric Alignment. In: Proceedings of ACL-AFNLP 2009, pp. 387–395 (2009a)
23. Yang, M., Shi, Z., Li, S., Zhao, T., Qi, H.: Ranking vs. Classification: a Case Study in Mining Organization Name Translation from Snippets. In: Proceedings of IALP 2009, pp. 308–313 (2009b)
24. Zhang, Y., Huang, F., Vogel, S.: Mining Translations of OOV Terms from the Web through Cross-Lingual Query Expansion. In: Proceedings of SIGIR 2005, pp. 669–670 (2005)
25. Zhang, Y., Vines, P.: Using the Web for Automated Translation Extraction in Cross-Language Information Retrieval. In: Proceedings of SIGIR 2004, pp. 162–169 (2004)

A Universal Phrase Tagset for Multilingual Treebanks

Aaron Li-Feng Han[1,2], Derek F. Wong[1], Lidia S. Chao[1], Yi Lu[1], Liangye He[1], and Liang Tian[1]

[1] NLP[2]CT lab, Department of CIS, University of Macau
[2] ILLC, University of Amsterdam
{Hanlifengaaron,takamachi660,wutianshui0515, tianliang0123}@gmail.com, {derekfw,lidiasc}@umac.mo

Abstract. Many syntactic treebanks and parser toolkits are developed in the past twenty years, including dependency structure parsers and phrase structure parsers. For the phrase structure parsers, they usually utilize different phrase tagsets for different languages, which results in an inconvenience when conducting the multilingual research. This paper designs a refined universal phrase tagset that contains 9 commonly used phrase categories. Furthermore, the mapping covers 25 constituent treebanks and 21 languages. The experiments show that the universal phrase tagset can generally reduce the costs in the parsing models and even improve the parsing accuracy.

Keywords: Universal phrase tagset, Phrase tagset mapping, Multilingual treebanks, Parsing.

1 Introduction

In the past twenty years, many treebanks were developed, such as the Chinese treebank [1][2], English treebank [3][4], German treebank [5], French treebank [6], and Portuguese treebank [7][8], etc. There are mainly two types of parsing structure, dependency structure and phrase structure. For the phrase structure treebanks, to capture the characteristics of specific languages, they tend to design different phrase tagsets. The phrase categories span from ten to twenty or even more. This is indeed helpful in the syntax analysis of the special in-cased language. However, the different phrase tagsets also make inconvenience for the multilingual research. To facilitate the further research of multilingual tasks, this paper designs a refined universal phrase tagset using 9 common phrase categories. The mappings between the phrase tagsets from the existing phrase structure treebanks and the universal phrase tagset are conducted, which covers 25 treebanks and 21 languages.

To evaluate the designed universal phrase tagset and the phrase tagset mapping works, the parsing experiments are conducted for intrinsic analysis on the available corpora, including Penn Chinese treebank (CTB-7) from Linguistic Data Consortium (LDC)[1] for Chinese, the Wall Street Journal (WSJ) Treebank from LDC for English,

[1] https://www.ldc.upenn.edu/

M. Sun et al. (Eds.): CCL and NLP-NABD 2014, LNAI 8801, pp. 247–258, 2014.

Floresta[2]-bosque Treebank for Portuguese, Euro-Fr[3] corpus for French, and Negra[4] Treebank [5] for German.

2 Proposed Universal Phrase Tagset

The universal phrase tagset is designed to include Noun phrase (NP), Verbal phrase (VP), Adjectival phrase (AJP), Adverbial phrase (AVP), Prepositional phrase (PP), sentence or sub-sentence (S), Conjunction phrase (CONJP), Coordinated phrase (COP), and others (X) for covering the list marker, interjection, URL, etc.

The refined phrase tagset mapped from 25 existing treebanks to the universal phrase categories is detailed in Table 1. Most of the mapping is easily understood except for some special cases. For instance, the Chinese phrase tag DNP (phrase formed by *something+associative 的*) is mapped into AJP because it specifies the adjective phrase. The Chinese phrase tag DVP (*something+DEV 地*) is mapped into AVP due to that the character "地" specifies an adverbial phrase in Chinese.

3 Parsing Experiments

To validate the effectiveness of the universal phrase tagset, we conduct the evaluation on the parsing task. We first construct the parsing models based on original treebanks, training and testing. Then, the experiment is repeated by replacing the treebanks with ones annotated with the universal phrasal tags. The parsing experiments are conducted on the treebanks covering Chinese (CN), English (EN), Portuguese (PT), French (FR), and German (DE).

The experiments are based on the Berkeley parser [9], which focuses on learning probabilistic context-free grammars (PCFGs) to assign a sequence of words the most likely parse tree, and introduces the hierarchical latent variable grammars to automatically learn a broad coverage grammar starting from a simple initial one. The generated grammar is refined by hierarchical splitting, merging and smoothing. The Berkeley parser generally gains the best testing result using the 6th smoothed grammar [10]. For a broad analysis of the experiments, we tune the parameters to learn the refined grammar by 7 times of splitting, merging and smoothing except 8 times for French treebank. The experiments are conducted on a server with the configuration stated in Table 2. The evaluation criteria include the cost of training time (hours), size of the generated grammar (MB), and the parsing scores, i.e., Labeled Precision (LPre), Labeled Recall (LRec), the harmonic mean of precision and recall (F1), and exact match (Ex).

---

[2] http://www.linguateca.pt/floresta

[3] http://www.statmt.org/europarl/

[4] http://www.coli.uni-saarland.de/projects/sfb378/negra-corpus/

Table 1. The Mappings between the Universal Phrase Tagset and that of the Existing Treebanks

Universal Phrase Tag	English PennTreebank I [3]	English PennTreebank II [4]	Chinese PennTreebank [11]	Portuguese Floresta Treebank [7]	FrenchTreebank [6]	Japanese Treebank Tüba-J/S [12]
NP	NP, WHNP	NP, NAC, NX, QP, WHNP	NP, CLP, QP, LCP, WHNP	Np	NP	NPper, NPloc, NPtmp, NP, NP.foc
VP	VP	VP	VP, VCD, VCP, VNV, VPT, VRD, VSB	Vp	VN, VP, VPpart, VPinf	VP.foc, VP, VPcnd, VPfin
AJP	ADJP	ADJP, WHADJP	ADJP, DP, DNP	ap, adjp	AP	AP.foc, AP, APcnd
AVP	ADVP, WHADVP	ADVP, WHAVP, PRT, WHADVP	ADVP, DVP	advp	AdP	ADVP.foc, ADVP
PP	PP, WHPP	PP, WHPP	PP	Pp	PP	PP, PP.foc, PPnom, PPgen, PPacc
S	S, SBAR, SBARQ, SINV, SQ	S, SBAR, SBARQ, SINV, SQ, PRN, FRAG, RRC	IP, CP, PRN, FRAG, INC	fcl, icl, acl, cu, x, sq	SENT, Ssub, Sint, Srel, S	S, SS
CONJP		CONJP				
COP					COORD	
X	X	X, INTJ, LST, UCP	LST, FLR, DFL, INTJ, URL, X, UCP			ITJ, GR, err

Universal Phrase Tag	Danish Arboretum Treebank [38]	German NegraTreebank [5]	Spanish UAM Treebank [13]	Hungarian Szeged Treebank [39]	Spanish Treebank [14]	Swedish Talbanken05 [15]
NP	Np	NP, CNP, MPN, NM	HOUR, NP, QP, SCORE, TITLE	NP, QP	NP, MPN, MTC	CNP, NP
VP	vp, acl	VP, CVP, VZ, CVZ	VP	VP, INF_, INF0	SVC	CVP, VP
AJP	Ajp	AP, AA, CAP, MTA	ADJP	ADJP	AP	AP, CAP,
AVP	Dvp	AVP, CAVP	ADVP, PRED-COMPL	ADVP, PA_, PA0	AVP	AVP, CAVP,
PP	pp	PP, CAC, CPP, CCP	PP	PP	PP, MTP	CPP, PP
S	fcl, icl	S, CS, CH, DL, PSEUDO	CL, S	S	S, INC	CS, S
CONJP	cp			C0		
COP		CO		CP	CS, CNP, CPP, CAP, CAVP, CAC, CCP, CO	CONJP, CXP
X	par	ISU, QL		FP, XP		NAC, XP

Table 1. (*continued*)

Universal Phrase Tag	Arabic PENN Treebank [16]	Korean Penn Treebank [17][18]	Estonian Arborest Treebank [40]	Icelandic IcePaHC Treebank [19]	Italian ISST Treebank [20][21]	Portuguese Tycho Brahe Treebank [22]
NP	NP, NX, QP, WHNP	NP	AN>, <AN, NN>, <NN,	NP, QP, WNP	SN	NP, NP-ACC, NP-DAT, NP-GEN, NP-SBJ, IP-SMC, NP-LFD, NP-ADV, NP-VOC, NP-PRN
VP	VP	VP	VN>, <VN, INF_N>, <INF_N	VP	IBAR	VB, VB-P
AJP	ADJP, WHADJP	ADJP, DANP		ADJP, ADJP-SPR	SA	ADJP, ADJP-SPR
AVP	ADVP, WHADVP	ADVP, ADCP	AD>, <AD	ADVP, ADVP-DIR, ADVP-LOC, ADVP-TMP, RP	SAVV	ADVP, WADVP
PP	PP, WHPP			PP, WPP, PP-BY, PP-PRN	SP, SPD, SPDA	PP, PP-ACC, PP-SBJ, PP-LFD, PP-PRN, PP-LOC
S	S, SBAR, SBARQ, SQ	S			F, SV2, SV3, SV5, FAC, FS, FINT, F2	RRC, CP, CP-REL, IP-MAT, IP-INF, IP-SUB, CP-ADV, CP-THT
CONJP	CONJP, NAC			CONJP	CP, COMPC	CONJP
COP			PN>, <PN		FC, COORD	
X	PRN, PRT, FRAG, INTJ, X, UCP	INTJ, PRN, X, LST, XP	<P, P>, <Q, Q>	LATIN	FP, COMPT, COMPIN	
Universal Phrase Tag	Hindi-Urdu Treebank [23]	Catalan AnCora Treebank [24]; [25]	Swedish Treebank [41]	Vietnamese Treebank [26]	Thai CG Treebank [27]	Hebrew [28]
NP	NP, NP-P, NP-NST, SC-A, SC-P, NP-P-Pred	sn	NP	NP, WHNP, QP	np, num, spnum	NP-gn-(H)
VP	VP, VP-Pred, V'	gv	VP	VP		PREDP, VP, VP-MD, VP-INF
AJP	AP, AP-Pred	sa	AP	AP, WHAP		ADJP-gn-(H)
AVP	DegP	sadv, neg	AVP	RP, WHRP		ADVP
PP		sp	PP	PP, WHPP	pp	PP
S		S, S*, S.NF.C, S.NF.A, S.NF.P, S.F.C, S.F.AComp, S.F.AConc, S.F.Acons, S.F.Acond, S.F.R,	ROOT, S	S, SQ, SBAR	s, ws, root	FRAG, FRAGQ, S, SBAR, SQ
CONJP		conj.subord, coord				
COP	CCP, XP-CC					
X	CP	interjeccio, morfema.verbal, morf.pron	XP	XP, YP, MDP		INTJ, PRN

Table 2. The Hardware Configuration

Memory	144 GB
CPU	Intel (R) Xeon (R) E5649 @ 2.53GHz (6 Cores)
Operating System	Ubuntu 64-bit

$$LPre = \frac{|\#correct\ constituent\ in\ guessed\ tree|}{|\#total\ constituent\ in\ guessed\ tree|} \quad (1)$$

$$LRec = \frac{|\#correct\ constituent\ in\ guessed\ tree|}{|\#total\ constituent\ in\ correct\ tree|} \quad (2)$$

$$F_1 = \frac{2 \times LPre \times LRec}{LPre + LRec} \quad (3)$$

$$Ex = \frac{|\#complete\ correct\ guessed\ tree|}{|\#total\ guessed\ tree|} \quad (4)$$

3.1 Parsing of Chinese

For Chinese, we use the Penn Chinese Treebank (CTB-7) [1] [2]. We adopt the standard splitting criteria for the training and testing data. The training documents contain CTB-7 files 0-to-2082, the development documents contain files 2083-to-2242, and the testing documents are files 2243-to-2447.

Table 3. The Parsing Results and Evaluation Scores on CTB-7

Grammar	Training cost		Evaluation score			
	Grammar (MB)	Training time	Precision	Recall	F1	Ex
Uni-gr-1	1.03	1m+54s	70.17	64.21	67.06	11.56
Ori-gr-1	1.16	1m+43s	73.57	68.31	**70.84**	**13.31**
Uni-gr-2	1.33	9m	76.78	72.24	74.44	12.98
Ori-gr-2	1.59	8m+29s	78.46	73.33	**75.81**	**14.5**
Uni-gr-3	1.97	24m+33s	81.37	76.7	78.97	18.7
Ori-gr-3	2.58	24m+28s	81.71	77.35	**79.47**	**19.57**
Uni-gr-4	3.39	1h+12m+19s	83.48	79.28	81.33	20.91
Ori-gr-4	5.01	1h+21m+4s	84.08	80.48	**82.24**	**21.37**
Uni-gr-5	6.97	4h+32m+26s	85.12	81.7	**83.37**	**23.03**
Ori-gr-5	11.08	17h+54m+53s	85.06	81.71	83.35	22.75
Uni-gr-6	15.54	16h+26m+24s	85.55	82.78	**84.15**	**24.68**
Ori-gr-6	27.26	23h+48m+1s	85.18	82.48	83.81	24.64
Uni-gr-7	34.53	56h+15m+16s	85.58	83.24	**84.4**	**25.33**
Ori-gr-7	65.55	94h+47m+18s	84.99	83.01	83.99	24.73

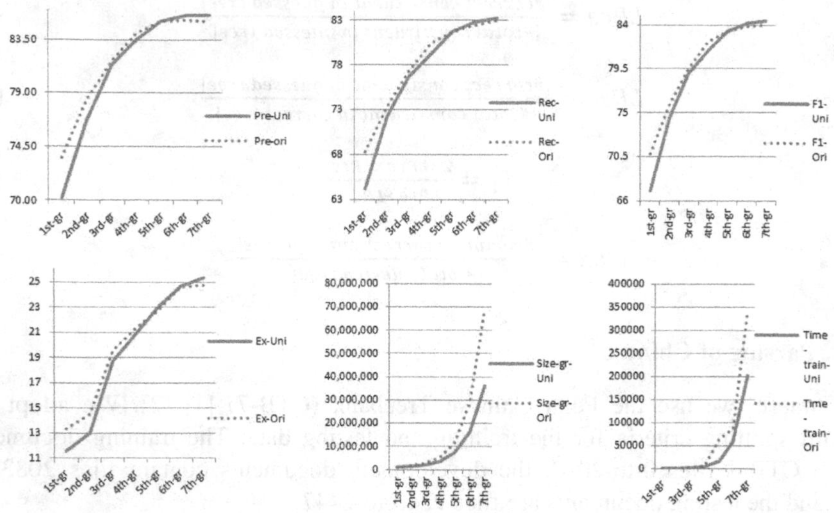

Fig. 1. Comparisons of Parsing Results of Chinese

We draw the corresponding learning curves in Figure 1 with byte and second for size and time. In Table 3, "Uni-gr-n" and "Ori-gr-n" mean the *n*th grammar using the universal and original tags respectively. The experiment shows that the testing scores of precision, recall and F1 are gradually higher using the refined grammars on universal phrase tagset than the scores using the original treebank tags, even though the beginning scores are lower from the first smoothed grammar. The exact match score using the universal phrase tagset also exceeds the corresponding score using original tagset after the 5th smoothed grammar. The highest precision, recall, F1 and exact scores are **85.58** (85.06), **83.24** (83.01), **84.4** (83.99), and **25.33** (24.73) respectively by using the universal phrase tagset (original phrase tags).

Furthermore, the training cost of the universal phrase tagset including the grammar size and the training time is much less than that of the original one especially for the latterly refined grammars. The grammar size (65.55 MB) and training time (94.79 hours) using the original tagset almost doubles that (**34.53 MB** & **56.25 hours**) of the universal one for the learning of 7th refined grammar.

3.2 Parsing of English

For English, we use the Wall Street Journal treebank from the LDC. The WSJ section 2-to-21 corpora are for training, section 22 for developing, and section 23 for testing [29]. The learning curves of EN for training cost and testing scores are shown in Figure 2. The experiment results on EN are similar to that on CN. The highest testing scores of precision, recall, and F1 are **91.45** (91.25), **91.19** (91.11) and **91.32** (91.18) respectively on universal phrase tags (and original phrase tagset). It takes **38.67** (51.64) hours and **30.72** (47.00) MB of memory during the training process for the 7th refined grammar respectively on universal (original) tagset.

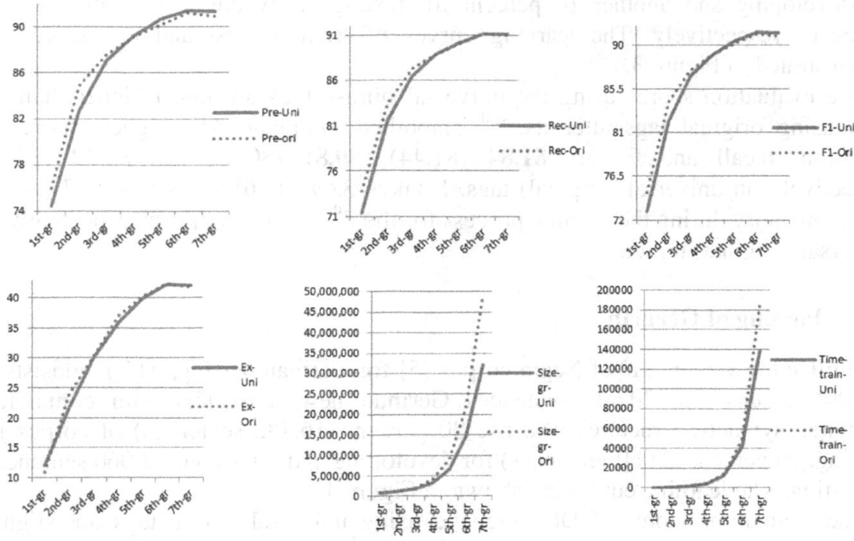

Fig. 2. Comparisons of Parsing Results of English

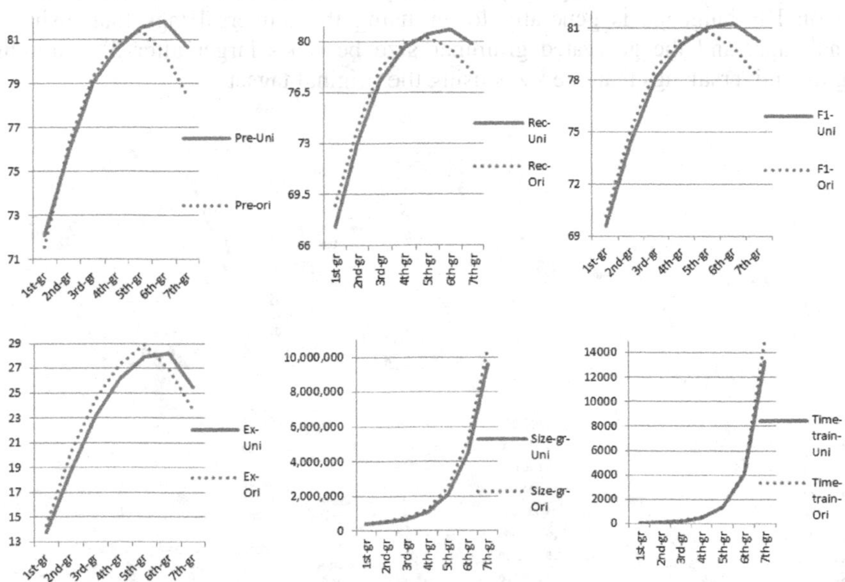

Fig. 3. Comparisons of Parsing Results of Portuguese

3.3 Parsing of Portuguese

The Bosque treebank is a subset of Floresta Virgem corpora [7] [8] with a size of 162,484 lexical units. We utilize 80 percent of the sentences for training, 10 percent for developing and another 10 percent for testing. They are 7393, 939, and 957 sentences respectively. The learning curves of training cost and test scores are demonstrated in Figure 3.

The evaluation scores using the universal phrase tags are much higher than the ones using original tags after the 5th smoothed grammar. The highest scores of precision, recall and F1 are **81.84** (81.44), **80.81** (80.27) and **81.32** (80.85) respectively on universal (original) tags. It takes **3.69** (4.16) hours and **9.17** (10.02) MB of memory during the training process for the 7th refined grammar respectively on universal (original) tagset.

3.4 Parsing of German

We utilize the version 2.0 of Negra corpus [5] for German parsing, which consists of 355,096 tokens and 20,602 sentences German newspaper text with completely annotated syntactic structures. We use 80 percent (16,482 sentences) of corpus for training, 10 percent (2,060 sentences) for developing and 10 percent (2,060 sentences) for testing. The learning curves are shown in Figure 4.

The evaluation scores of DE language using universal phrase tags are slightly higher than the ones using original tags. The highest scores of precision, recall, F1 are **81.35** (81.23), **81.03** (81.02), and **81.19** (81.12) respectively on universal (original) tags. Different from the wining of synthetically F1 score, the exact matched sentence score on DE language is generally lower using the universal tags than using the original tags, and the generated grammar size becomes larger after 5th smoothing using the universal tags than the sizes using the original tagset.

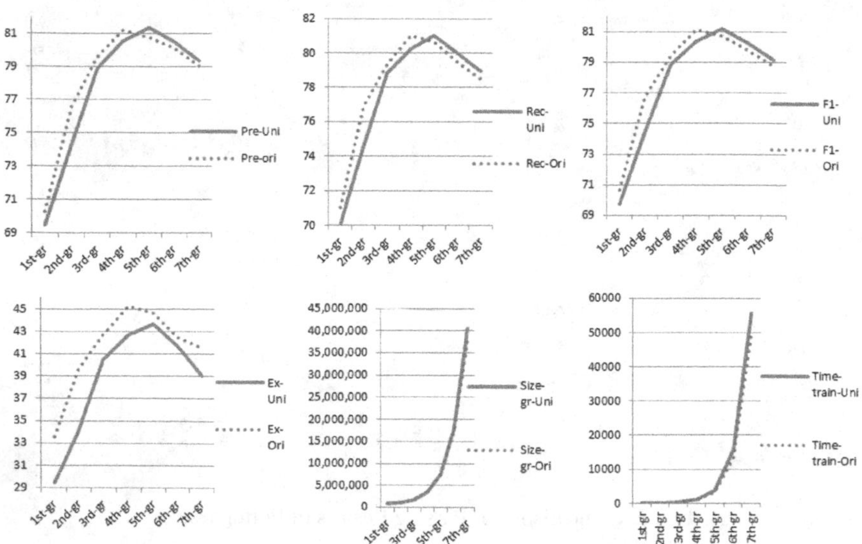

Fig. 4. Comparisons of Parsing Results of German

3.5 Parsing of French

Different with previous standard language treebanks, which are available by license agreement for research or commercial purpose, to generate a usable and reliable French treebank corpus, we first extract 20,000 French sentences from Europarl corpora that are from the proceedings of the European Parliament. Then, we parse the French plain text using the Berkeley French grammar "fra_sm5.gr" [10] with the parsing accuracy around 0.80. The parsed Euro-Fr corpus is used for the training stage.

For the developing and testing corpora, we use the WMT12 and WMT13 French plain text from the international workshop of statistical machine translation by SIGMT[5]. They contain 3,003 and 3,000 sentences respectively, which are parsed by the same parser. The experiment results of learning curves are shown in Figure 5. The evaluation results of FR show that the comprehensive F1 score using the universal tagset can also finally win the one using the original tagset, even though the exact match score is lower as the DE language. Similarly, the training cost using the universal tagset is much less. The highest precision, recall, and F1 scores are **80.49** (80.34), 80.93 (**80.96**), and **80.71** (80.64) respectively using universal (original) tagset.

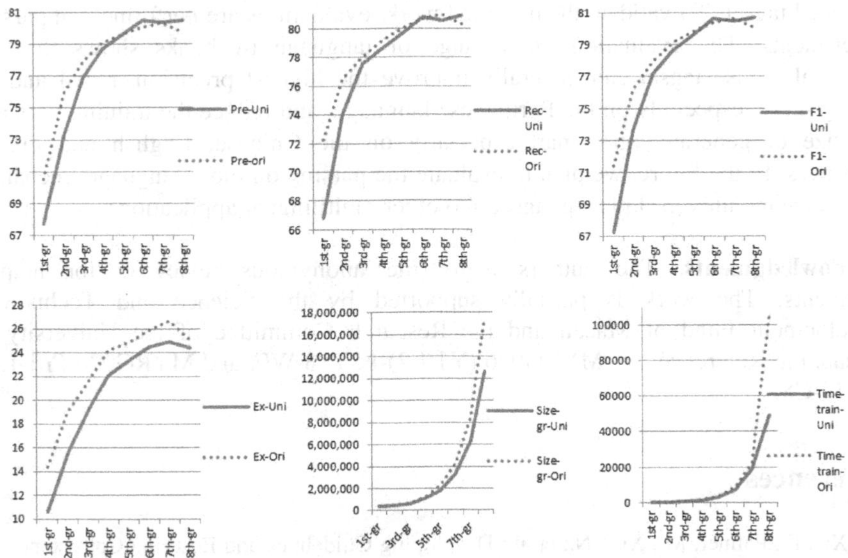

Fig. 5. Comparisons of Parsing Results of French

It takes **13.66** (28.91) hours and **12.07** (16.66) MB of memory during the training process for the 8th refined grammar respectively on universal (original) tagset.

[5] http://www.sigmt.org/

4 Related Work

Han et al. [30] proposed a universal phrase tagset and designed the mapping between the universal tagset and the ones of French and English Treebank. However, we extended the tagset mapping into 25 existing treebanks coving 21 languages; furthermore, we evaluated the effectiveness of the designed tagset mapping by parsing experiments on five available treebanks in this work. Other related work about phrase structures include [31], [32], and [33]. Naseem et al. [36] employed some manually specified universal dependency rules for grammar induction and achieved improvement in dependency parsing. McDonald et al. [37] designed a universal annotation approach for dependency treebanks. Rambow et al. [34] conducted a research about parallel syntactic annotation for multiple languages. Petrov et al. [35] developed a universal part-of-speech (PoS) tagset containing 12 commonly used PoS tags.

5 Conclusion

To facilitate the future researches in multilingual tasks, we have designed a refined universal phrase tagset and the tagset mapping from existing 25 treebanks into the universal tagset. To validate the designed work, evaluations are performed on parsing experiments. The evaluation on a range of language treebanks shows that the universal phrase tagset can generally improve the highest precision, recall and F1 testing score, especially on the Portuguese language, and reduce the training time and the size of generated grammar, especially on the Chinese, English and French languages. In the future, we plan to evaluate the parsing on more language treebanks, and utilize the universal phrase tagset into other multilingual applications.

Acknowledgments. The authors thank the anonymous reviewers for helpful comments. The work is partially supported by the Science and Technology Development Fund of Macau and the Research Committee of the University of Macau, the Reference No. MYRG076 (Y1-L2)-FST13-WF, and MYRG070 (Y1-L2)-FST12-CS.

References

1. Xia, F., Palmer, M., Xue, N., et al.: Developing Guidelines and Ensuring Consistency for Chinese Text Annotation. In: Proceedings of LREC (2000)
2. Xue, N., Xia, F., Chiou, F.-D., Palmer, M.: The Penn Chinese TreeBank: Phrase Structure Annotation of a Large Corpus. Natural Language Engineering 11(2), 207–238 (2005)
3. Marcus, M.P., Marcinkiewicz, M.A., Santorini, B.: Building a large annotated corpus of English: the penn treebank. Comput. Linguist. 19(2), 313–330 (1993)
4. Bies, A., Ferguson, M., Katz, K., MacIntyre, R.: Bracketing Guidelines for Treebank II Style Penn Treebank Project. Technical paper (1995)

5. Skut, W., Krenn, B., Brants, T., Uszkoreit, H.: An annotation scheme for free word order languages. In: Conference on ANLP (1997)
6. Abeillé, A., Clément, L., Toussenel, F.: Building a Treebank for French. Building and Using Parsed Corpora. Kluwer Academic Publishers (2003)
7. Afonso, S., Bick, E., Haber, R., Santos, D.: Floresta sintá(c)tica: a treebank for Portuguese. In: Proceedings of LREC 2002, pp. 1698–1703 (2002)
8. Freitas, C., Rocha, P., Bick, E.: Floresta Sintá(c)tica: Bigger, Thicker and Easier. In: Computational Processing of the Portuguese Language Conference (2008)
9. Petrov, S., Klein, D.: Improved Inference for Unlexicalized Parsing. NAACL (2007)
10. Petrov, S.: Coarse-to-Fine Natural Language Processing. PHD thesis (2009)
11. Xue, N., Jiang, Z.: Addendum to the Chinese Treebank Bracketing Guidelines (CTB7.0). Technical paper. University of Pennsylvania (2010)
12. Kawata, Y., Bartels, J.: Stylebook for the Japanese Treebank in VERBMOBIL. University Tubingen, Report 240 (2000)
13. Moreno, A., López, S., Alcántara, M.: Spanish Tree Bank: Specifications, Version 5. Technical paper (1999)
14. Volk, M.: Spanish Expansion of a Parallel Treebank. Technical paper (2009)
15. Nivre, J., Nilsson, J., Hall, J.: Talbanken05: A Swedish Treebank with Phrase Structure and Dependency Annotation. In: Proceedings of LREC (2006)
16. Bies, A., Maamouri, M.: Penn Arabic Treebank Guidelines. Technical report (2003)
17. Han, C.-H., Han, N.-R., Ko, E.-S.: Bracketing Guidelines for Penn Korean TreeBank. Technical Report, IRCS-01-10 (2001)
18. Han, C.-H., Han, N.-R., Ko, E.-S., Yi, H., Palmer, M.: Penn Korean Treebank: Development and Evaluation. In: Proceedings of PACLIC (2002)
19. Wallenberg, J.C., Ingason, A.K., Sigurðsson, E.F., Rögnvaldsson, E.: Icelandic Parsed Historical Corpus (IcePaHC). Version 0.9. Technical report (2011)
20. Montemagni, S., Barsotti, F., Battista, M., et al.: The Italian Syntactic-Semantic Treebank: Architecture, Annotation, Tools and Evaluation. In: Proceedings of the COLING Workshop on Linguistically Interpreted Corpora, pp. 18–27 (2000)
21. Montemagni, S., Barsotti, F., Battista, M., et al.: Building the Italian Syntactic-Semantic Treebank. In: Abeillé, A. (ed.) Building and using Parsed Corpora. Language and Speech series, ch. 11, pp. 189–210. Kluwer, Dordrecht (2003)
22. Galves, C., Faria, P.: Tycho Brahe Parsed Corpus of Historical Portuguese. Technical (2010)
23. Bhatt, R., Farudi, A., Rambow, O.: Hindi-Urdu Phrase Structure Annotation Guidelines. Technical Paper (2012)
24. Civit, M., Martí, M.A.: Building cast3lb: A Spanish treebank. Research on Language & Computation 2(4), 549–574 (2004)
25. Taulé, M., Martí, M.A., Recasens, M.: AnCora: Multilevel Annotated Corpora for Catalan and Spanish. In: Proceedings of LREC 2008, Marrakech, Morocco (2008)
26. Nguyen, P.-T., Vu, X.-L., et al.: Building a large syntactically-annotated corpus of Vietnamese. In: Lingu. Annotation Workshop, pp. 182–185 (2009)
27. Ruangrajitpakorn, T., Trakultaweekoon, K., Supnithi, T.: A syntactic resource for thai. 2009. CG treebank. In: Workshop on Asian Language Resources, pp. 96–101 (2009)
28. Sima'an, K., Itai, A., Winter, Y., Altman, A., Nativ, N.: Building a tree-bank of modern Hebrew text. Journal Traitement Automatique des Langues. Special Issue on Natural Language Processing and Corpus Linguistics 42(2), 347–380 (2001)
29. Petrov, S., Barrett, L., Thibaux, R., Klein, D.: Learning Accurate, Compact, and Interpretable Tree Annotation. In: COLING and 44th ACL, pp. 433–440 (2006)

30. Han, A.L.-F., Wong, D.F., Chao, L.S., He, L., Li, S., Zhu, L.: Phrase Tagset Mapping for French and English Treebanks and Its Application in Machine Translation Evaluation. In: Gurevych, I., Biemann, C., Zesch, T. (eds.) GSCL 2013. LNCS, vol. 8105, pp. 119–131. Springer, Heidelberg (2013)
31. Van Valin, R.D., Lapolla, R.J.: Syntax, Structure, Meaning and Function. Cambridge University Press (2002)
32. Carnie, A.: Syntax: A Generative Introduction (Introducing Linguistics). Blackwell Publishing (2002)
33. Newmeyer, F.J.: Possible and Probable Languages: A Generative Perspective on Linguistic Typology. Oxford University Press (2005)
34. Rambow, O., Dorr, B., Farwell, D., et al.: Parallel syntactic annotation of multiple languages. In: Proceedings of LREC (2006)
35. Petrov, S., Das, D., McDonald, R.: A Universal Part-of-Speech Tagset. In: Proceedings of the Eighth LREC (2012)
36. Naseem, T., Chen, H., Barzilay, R., Johnson, M.: Using universal linguistic knowledge to guide grammar induction. In: Proc. of EMNLP (2010)
37. McDonald, R., Nivre, J., Quirmbach-Brundage, Y., et al.: Universal Dependency Annotation for Multilingual Parsing. In: Proceedings of ACL (2013)
38. Danish Arboretum corpus. Arboretum: A syntactic tree corpus of Danish, `http://corp.hum.sdu.dk/arboretum.html` (accessed December 2013)
39. Hungarian Szeged Treebank. Szeged Treebank 2.0: A Hungarian natural language database with detailed syntactic analysis. Hungarian linguistics at the University of Szeged
40. Bick, E., Uibo, H., Muischnek, K.: Preliminary experiments for a CG-based syntactic tree corpus of Estonian, `http://corp.hum.sdu.dk/tgrepeye_est.html` (accessed December 2013)
41. Swedish Treebank Syntactic Annotation. Swedish Treebank. Online project, `http://stp.lingfil.uu.se/~nivre/swedish_treebank/` (accessed March 2014)

Co-occurrence Degree Based Word Alignment: A Case Study on Uyghur-Chinese

Chenggang Mi[1,2], Yating Yang[1], Xi Zhou[1], Xiao Li[1], and Turghun Osman[1]

[1] Xinjiang Technical Institute of Physics & Chemistry of Chinese Academy of Sciences
Urumqi, Xinjiang 830011, China
[2] University of Chinese Academy of Sciences
Beijing, 100049, China
michenggang@gmail.com, {yangyt,zhouxi,xiaoli}@ms.xjb.ac.cn, turghunjan@sina.com

Abstract. Most widely used word alignment models are based on word co-occurrence counts in parallel corpus. However, the data sparseness during training of the word alignment model makes word co-occurrence counts of Uyghur-Chinese parallel corpus cannot indicate associations between source and target words effectively. In this paper, we propose a Uyghur-Chinese word alignment method based on word co-occurrence degree to alleviate the data sparseness problem. Our approach combine the co-occurrence counts and the fuzzy co-occurrence weights as word co-occurrence degree, fuzzy co-occurrence weights can be obtained by searching for fuzzy co-occurrence word pairs and computing differences of length between current Uyghur word and other Uyghur words in fuzzy co-occurrence word pairs. Experiment shows that with the co-occurrence degree based word alignment model, the performance of Uyghur-Chinese word alignment result is outperform the baseline word alignment model, the quality of Uyghur-Chinese machine translation also improved.

Keywords: Uyghur-Chinese word alignment, co-occurrence degree, co-occurrence count, agglutinative language, data sparseness.

1 Introduction

Statistical machine translation (SMT) [1] is one of the most popular machine translation frameworks where translations are generated on the basis of statistical models whose parameters are derived from the analysis of bilingual parallel corpora. The statistical machine translation technologies have been extended from word-based model to phrase-based model, and nowadays, as the advent of strong stochastic parsers, syntax-based models are also built [2]. Due to lack of syntax-annotated bilingual parallel corpora, syntax-based models are mainly used in research. Hierarchical phrase-based translation [3] combines the strengths of phrase-based and syntax-based translation, which take phrases as units for translation and synchronous context-free grammars as rules. Phrase-based and hierarchical-based models are often used in recent

M. Sun et al. (Eds.): CCL and NLP-NABD 2014, LNAI 8801, pp. 259–268, 2014.

days. The translation model training, parameters tuning and decoding are all based on the output of word alignment model. To some extent, the performance of word alignment model affects the quality of statistical machine translation.

Research on machine translation between minority languages and Chinese like Uyghur-Chinese machine translation is still at preliminary stage. Because of low-resource and word forming distinctions between Uyghur and Chinese [4], we cannot get a desired translation performance with traditional word alignment models.

In this paper, we propose a co-occurrence degree based Uyghur-Chinese word alignment method to alleviate the data sparseness problem during models training, which combines co-occurrence counts and fuzzy co-occurrence weights to train word alignment models. Experiments show that our method outperforms traditional word alignment models both in Uyghur-Chinese word alignment and Uyghur-Chinese machine translation.

2 Related Research

The original work of bilingual word alignment IBM models 1-5 were proposed by Brown et.al, which described a series of five statistical models of the translation process and gave algorithms for estimating the parameters (Expectation-Maximum algorithm (EM) [5]) of these models given a set of pairs of sentences that were translations of each other. In 1996, Vogel presented the HMM-based word alignment model [6], which made the alignment probabilities dependent on the differences in the alignment positions rather than on the absolute positions. Liu et.al proposed a log-linear model for word alignment [7], which treats all knowledge sources as feature functions; Liang's work focused on word alignment agreement [8].

For solving data sparseness during models training, Tiedemann et.al [9] proposed a clue-based word alignment method, which added several features like string similarities between source language words and target language words into the training of word alignment models, performance of word alignment model and quality of machine translation were both improved. The method proposed by Tiedemann et.al only performed well on cognate languages, but for language pairs like Uyghur-Chinese, the improvement of word alignment performance is not significantly.

The model proposed in this paper based previous works, we extend theirs methods in a situation that source language and target language are not cognate languages (Uyghur and Chinese) and the data sparseness problem is relatively serious. In our method, we replace the traditional word co-occurrence counts with word co-occurrence degree in word alignment model; the word co-occurrence degree consists of co-occurrence counts and fuzzy co-occurrence weights.

3 Uyghur-Chinese Word Alignment

Chinese is one part of Sino-Tibetan language family, and Uyghur belongs to Altaic language family. Because of differences among language families, Chinese and

Uyghur have some significant distinctions in word forming and syntactic structure. In this part, we first introduce features of Uyghur language, and then we compare with Chinese and describe problems which exist in Uyghur-Chinese word alignment.

3.1 Features of Uyghur Language

Uyghur is an agglutinative language [10], which is a type of synthetic language with morphology that primarily uses agglutination: words are formed by joining phonetically unchangeable suffix morphemes to the stem. In agglutinative languages, each suffix is a bound morpheme for one unit of meaning, instead of morphological modifications with internal changes of the root of the word, or changes in stress or tone. The syntax structure of Uyghur is S (Subject)-O (Object)-V (Verb), which is significantly different with Chinese (S-V-O). We give some examples about the Uyghur words forming and syntax structure as follows:

Uyghur word forming examples:

我的包(My bag)： سومكا (*stem*) + م (*suffix0*) -> سومكام

您的书(Your book)： كىتاب (*stem*) + ىڭىز (*suffix0*) -> كىتابىڭىز

Uyghur syntax structure examples:

我不吃饭。(I don't want to eat.) مەن (**Subject**) تاماق (**Object**) يېمەيمەن (**Verb**)

3.2 Data Sparseness in Uyghur-Chinese Word Alignment

Due to rare of Uyghur-Chinese parallel corpora, there exist data sparseness problems during training of Uyghur-Chinese word alignment models.

We train word alignment models based on bilingual parallel corpora. Compared with English-Chinese and English-French, Uyghur-Chinese parallel corpora are relatively rare. Additionally, due to the word forming of Uyghur, a stem in Uyghur may derive several Uyghur words; we cannot expect a Uyghur-Chinese dictionary or Uyghur-Chinese bilingual corpora can collect every word that a certain stem can forming. Therefore, data sparseness will occur during training of Uyghur-Chinese word alignment model, which affects the performance of word alignment model, even the quality of Uyghur-Chinese machine translation.

In this paper, we try to alleviate the data sparseness problem in Uyghur-Chinese word alignment models training.

4 Co-occurrence Degree Based Uyghur-Chinese Word Alignment

Most word alignment models like IBM Model 1-5, HMM are trained based on word co-occurrence information which is obtained by counting word co-occurrence in parallel texts. When a certain Uyghur-Chinese word pair appeared in Uyghur-Chinese parallel corpora, the co-occurrence count of this word pair increased. Due to shortage of Uyghur-Chinese parallel texts, data sparseness may occur during word alignment models training. For fully use of Uyghur-Chinese parallel texts, we propose a co-occurrence degree based word alignment method to replace traditional word co-occurrence counts based methods.

4.1 Word Co-occurrence Degree

Definition of Word Co-occurrence Degree

We obtain Uyghur-Chinese word co-occurrence degree by combine word co-occurrence counts and fuzzy co-occurrence weights. The word co-occurrence counts can be gotten as a common way-number of times a certain Uyghur-Chinese word appeared in corpora; we compute fuzzy co-occurrence weights as summing up length of Uyghur words that have the same stem, meanwhile there exist same Chinese word(s) in Chinese sentences.

Computation of Co-occurrence Degree in Uyghur-Chinese Word Alignment

The co-occurrence degree can be computed as:

$$Score_{co-degree} = Score_{co-counts} + Score_{co-fuzzy} \tag{1}$$

In (1), $Score_{co-counts}$ is the count of word co-occurrence, and $\mathrm{Score}_{\mathrm{co-fuzzy}}$ is the fuzzy co-occurrence weight.

Measure the Word Co-occurrence Counts.

As the traditional way, we simply get the word co-occurrence counts by counting number of times a certain Uyghur-Chinese word pair appeared in Uyghur-Chinese parallel corpora:

$$Score_{co-counts} = n \tag{2}$$

n is the number a certain word pair appeared in Uyghur-Chinese bilingual corpora.

Measure the Fuzzy Word Co-occurrence Weights.

Uyghur words are formed by joining phonetically unchangeable suffix morphemes to a certain stem. We compute the fuzzy word co-occurrence weights of a Uyghur-Chinese word pair based on bilingual corpora. In this paper, we suppose that if a word in current Uyghur sentence has the same stem with word in another Uyghur sentence, meanwhile, there are same Chinese words in Chinese sentences which aligned to above two Uyghur sentences; we consider these two Uyghur-Chinese word pairs are reference word aligned. These kinds of alignments are measured by fuzzy co-occurrence weights, which can be obtained as following two parts.

1) **Searching for Fuzzy Aligned Word Pairs**

Suppose we have three aligned Uyghur-Chinese sentence pairs: (**SENT-UYG1**, **SENT-CHN1**) and (**SENT-UYG2**, **SENT-CHN2**), words of these sentences distribute as follows:

SENT-UYG1: $W_{SentU11}, W_{SentU12}, W_{SentU13}, \cdots, W_{SentU1(k-2)}, W_{SentU1(k-1)}, W_{SentU1k}$
SENT-CHN1: $W_{SentC11}, W_{SentC12}, W_{SentC13}, \cdots, W_{SentC1(l-2)}, W_{SentC1(l-1)}, W_{SentC1l}$
SENT-UYG2: $W_{SentU21}, W_{SentU22}, W_{SentU23}, \cdots, W_{SentU2(h-2)}, W_{SentU2(h-1)}, W_{SentU2h}$
SENT-CHN2: $W_{SentC21}, W_{SentC22}, W_{SentC23}, \cdots, W_{SentC2(n-2)}, W_{SentC2(n-1)}, W_{SentC2n}$
SENT-UYG3: $W_{SentU31}, W_{SentU32}, W_{SentU33}, \cdots, W_{SentU3(p-2)}, W_{SentU3(p-1)}, W_{SentU3p}$
SENT-CHN3: $W_{SentC31}, W_{SentC32}, W_{SentC33}, \cdots, W_{SentC3(q-2)}, W_{SentC3(q-1)}, W_{SentC3q}$

$W_{SentXij}$ is the *j*th word in *i*th sentence (X: U for Uyghur sentence, C for Chinese sentence).*k, l ,h, n, p, q* are length of the 1st Uyghur sentence, length of 1st Chinese sentence, length of 2nd Uyghur sentence, length of 2nd Chinese sentence, length of 3rd Uyghur sentence and length of 3rd Chinese sentence, respectively. If a Uyghur word $W_{SentU1j}$ $(0 \leq \mathrm{j} \leq \mathrm{k}-1)$ in SENT-UYG1 have the same stem with a Uyghur word $W_{SentU2i}$ $(0 \leq \mathrm{i} \leq \mathrm{h}-1)$ in SENT-UYG2 and a Uyghur word $W_{SentU3r}$ $(0 \leq \mathrm{r} \leq \mathrm{p}-1)$ in SENT-UYG3, $W_{SentU2i}$ and $W_{SentU3r}$ are same words; meanwhile, there exist a same Chinese word $W_{SentC1g}$ $(0 \leq \mathrm{g} \leq \mathrm{l}-1)$ in SENT-CHN1, SENT-CHN2 and SENT-CHN3, the word pair <$W_{SentU1i}, W_{SentC1g}$> can be considered as fuzzy aligned in sentence pair SENT-UYG1 and SENT-CHN1.

2) **Computation of Fuzzy Co-occurrence Weights**

According to method described in **1)**, with the help of Uyghur-Chinese dictionary, we first collect all fuzzy co-occurrence pairs for current word pair. Then, we obtain the fuzzy co-occurrence weights of current word pair as combine differences of length between current Uyghur word and other Uyghur words in fuzzy aligned word pairs which obtain from **1)**:

$$Score_{co-fuzzy} = \sum_{i=1}^{k} \frac{|L_{uyg(cur)} - |L_{uyg(i)} - L_{uyg(cur)}||}{\max\{L_{uyg(i)}, L_{uyg(cur)}\}}, \quad 1 \leq i \leq k \tag{3}$$

We obtain the fuzzy co-occurrence word pair <*uyg(i), chn(cur)*> according to the method described in 1). *k* is the number of fuzzy co-occurrence word pairs, $L_{uyg(i)}$ is the length of Uyghur word in ith word pair, $L_{uyg(cur)}$ is the length of current Uyghur word.

4.2 Combine the Word Co-occurrence Degree into Word Alignment Models

IBM models are traditionally trained based on word co-occurrence counts; IBM model 1 is the first and important model to collect lexical information for following models, which can be indicated as follows:

$$p(e,a|f) = \frac{\varepsilon}{(l_f+1)^{l_e}} \prod_{j=1}^{l_e} t(e_j|f_{a(j)}), 1 \le j \le l_e. \quad (4)$$

l_f and l_e are the length of source language sentence (Uyghur) and target language sentence (Chinese), respectively; *a* is the word alignment function, *a: j->i* means source word f_i is align with target word e_j; *t(e|f)* is the translation probability of source word *f* and target word *e*. When training the IBM model 1, *t(e|f)* can be computed based on word co-occurrence counts:

$$t(e|f) = \frac{Score_{co-counts(e,f)}}{Score_{counts(f)}} \quad (5)$$

$Score_{co-counts(e,f)}$ is the word co-occurrence counts of source word f and target word **e** in bilingual parallel corpora, $Score_{counts(f)}$ is the number of times source word **f** appeared in corpora.In this paper, we replace *t(e|f)* (which based on Uyghur-Chinese word co-occurrence counts) with *t'(e|f)* (which based on Uyghur-Chinese word co-occurrence degree), and *t'(e|f)* can be computed as follows:

$$t'(e|f) = \frac{Score_{co-counts(e,f)} + Score_{co-fuzzy(e,f)}}{Score_{counts(f)}} \quad (6)$$

5 Experiments

5.1 Set Up

We use GIZA++[1] which implements IBM models and HMM as the baseline in word alignment experiments and evaluates word alignment results by P_r (Recall), P_p(Precision) and *AER* (Alignment Error Rate). *A* indicates a set of word alignment results and *S* is a set of sure alignments in reference alignments. In the traditional way, the computation of *AER* requires gold alignments annotated as "sure" or "possible", in this paper, we don't distinguish them. Therefore, we can compute AER as:

[1] `https://code.google.com/p/giza-pp/`

$$P_r = \frac{|A \cap S|}{|S|}, \ P_p = \frac{|A \cap S|}{|A|}, \ AER = 1 - \frac{2P_rP_p}{P_r + P_p} \tag{7}$$

We extract 200 sentence pairs from CWMT 2013 Uyghur-Chinese corpora (which collected from news reports and government documents) as the word alignment validate set, and annotated alignment associations by hands. For Uyghur-Chinese machine translation experiments, we use the CWMT 2013 corpora as training set and tune set, and select 1500 sentence pairs as the test set, Table 1.

Table 1. Statistics of corpora used in Uyghur-Chinese machine translation

Corpora	Size(pair)
Training set	109,895
Tune set	700
Test set	1,500

We use Moses[2] [11] as machine translation system and SRILM[3] [12] as language modeling tool. The results of Uyghur-Chinese machine translation are evaluated by BLEU [13].

5.2 Experiments

Uyghur-Chinese Word Alignment Experiments

We use the GIZA++ as the baseline in word alignment experiments. Uyghur-Chinese sentence pairs in word alignment validate set were preprocessed by methods described in 5.3.1. Then, we search for fuzzy aligned word pairs in bilingual corpus, and obtain co-occurrence degree as introduce in 4.1. The co-occurrence counts are replaced with co-occurrence degree in GIZA++. We take the co-occurrence degree as input in training of IBM Model 1. The performance of Uyghur-Chinese word alignment is evaluated by Recall, Precision and AER, respectively.

Uyghur-Chinese Machine Translation Experiments

In Uyghur-Chinese machine translation experiments, we take the results by co-occurrence counts based word alignment model and co-occurrence degree based word alignment model as inputs of model training of Moses, respectively. Parameters of machine translation tools are set as follows: the language model is 5-gram; the maximum length of phrases (rules) is 11. We evaluate the quality of Uyghur-Chinese machine translation by the script multi-bleu.perl which included in Moses.

[2] http://www.statmt.org/moses/

[3] http://www.speech.sri.com/projects/srilm/download.html

5.3 Analysis of Results

Table 2 and Table 3 are the experiment results of Uyghur-Chinese word alignment and Uyghur-Chinese machine translation, respectively.

Table 2. Evaluation on Uyghur-Chinese word alignment. GBaseline is the baseline (GIZA++) for word alignment experiments; GStemmer is the baseline (GIZA++) with an Uyghur Stemmer; and GCo-degree is the co-occurrence degree-based word alignment model which is described in this paper.

Evaluation (%)	Word Alignment Models		
	GBaseline	GStemmer	GCo-degree
Recall (R)	86.32	**87.69(+1.37)**	87.45(+1.13)
Precision (P)	80.40	82.33(+1.93)	**82.79(+2.39)**
AER	16.75	15.07(-1.68)	**14.94(-1.81)**

Through comparing with three different word alignment methods (in Table 2), recall (R) of the stem based method (GStemmer) achieved highest improvement (1.37%), which may because the Uyghur words stemming reduce the data sparseness, to some extent; but its improvement of precision (P) (1.93%) cannot outperform co-occurrence degree based method (GCo-degree) (2.39%), one possible reason is that the stem based method missing some important information of Uyghur words. The AER of co-occurrence degree based method (GCo-degree) achieved lowest among three methods (14.94%). Notice that the decrease of AER between the stem based method (GStemmer) and co-occurrence degree based method (GCo-degree) is not very significantly ((-1.68)-(-1.81) = 0.13), which means two methods both enhancing associations between source words (Uyghur words) and target words (Chinese words) that related with each other.

Table 3. Evaluation on Uyghur-Chinese machine translation. GBaseline is the baseline (GIZA++) for word alignment experiments; GStemmer is the baseline (GIZA++) with an Uyghur Stemmer; and GCo-degree is the co-occurrence degree-based word alignment model which is described in this paper. (**PB** is short for the Phrase-Based Translation Model, and **HPB** is short for the Hierarchical Phrase-Based Translation Model)

TM(BLEU)	Word Alignment Models		
	GBaseline	GStemmer	GCo-degree
PB(test set)	38.63	39.72(+1.09)	39.75(+1.12)
HPB(test set)	39.00	40.57(+1.57)	**40.59(+1.59)**
PB (tune set)	31.69	33.40(+1.71)	33.60(+1.91)
HPB(tune set)	32.43	34.78(+2.35)	**35.00(+2.57)**

In Table 3, we compare performances of Uyghur-Chinese machine translation under different word alignment methods in test set and tune set. The stem based method (GStemmer) and the co-occurrence degree based method (GCo-degree) are both outperform the baseline (GBaseline) in Uyghur-Chinese machine translation. And the performance of co-occurrence degree based method (GCo-degree) achieved higher than stem based method (GStemmer), the most important reason is that the stem based method missing some information in Uyghur, and quality of stem based machine translation also rely on the performance of stemmers. Because of local reordering and generalization abilities, hierarchical phrase-based models outperform phrase based models. Although there are some different ideas about relationship between AER and BLEU in statistical machine translation, we validate some researchers' opinions that the BLEU of Uyghur-Chinese machine translation is related with the precision of Uyghur-Chinese word alignment: with the increase of precision of word alignment by our method, the improvement of Uyghur-Chinese machine translation performance increases correspondingly. This may because the precision of word alignment partly decide the alignment of translated words in Uyghur-Chinese bilingual corpora.

6 Conclusion and Future Work

In this paper, we propose a word co-occurrence degree based method for Uyghur-Chinese word alignment in SMT, which is different from traditional co-occurrence counts based word alignment methods. We obtain the word co-occurrence degree by combine word co-occurrence counts and fuzzy co-occurrence weights. Experimental results show that with the method we present in this article, data sparseness in Uyghur-Chinese word alignment is alleviated effectively; comparing with stem based word alignment method, our approach maintain the integrity of Uyghur words. Performance of co-occurrence degree based word alignment model is significantly outperforming the word co-occurrence counts based method and stem based word alignment method; quality of Uyghur-Chinese machine translation also improved by our method. For future work, we will further investigate relationships between Chinese word segmentation and Uyghur-Chinese word alignment; we also plan to test our approach in other domains and on other language pairs.

Acknowledgements. This work is supported by the Strategic Priority Research Program of the Chinese Academy of Sciences (Grant No. XDA06030400), West Light Foundation of Chinese Academy of Sciences (Grant No. LHXZ201301 XBBS201216), the Xinjiang High-Tech Industrialization Project (Grant No. 201412101) and Young Creative Sci-Tech Talents Cultivation Project of Xinjiang Uyghur Autonomous Region (Grant No. 2013731021).

References

1. Brown, P.E., Pietra, S.A.D., Pietra, V.J.D., Mercer, R.L.: The mathematics of statistical machine translation: Parameter estimation. Computational Linguistics 19(2), 263–311 (1993)
2. Kenji, Y., Kevin, K.: A syntax-based statistical translation model. In: Proceedings of the 39th Annual Meeting on Association for Computational Linguistics, pp. 523–530. Association for Computational Linguistics, Stroudsburg (2001)
3. David, C.: Hierarchical Phrase-Based Translation. Computational Linguistics 33(2), 201–228 (2007)
4. Gulila, A., Mijit, A.: Research on Uyghur Word Segmentation. Journal of Chinese Information Processing 18(6), 61–65 (2004)
5. Dempster, A., Laird, N., Rubin: Maximum-likelihood from incomplete data via the EM algorithm. Journal of The Royal Statistical Society, Series B 39(1), 1–38 (1977)
6. Vogel, S., Ney, H., Tillmann, C.: Hmm-based word alignment in statistical translation. In: Proceedings of the 16th Conference on Computational Linguistics, pp. 836–841. Association for Computational Linguistics (1996)
7. Yang, L., Qun, L., Shouxun, L.: Log-linear Models for Word Alignment. In: Proceedings of the 43rd Annual Meeting on Association for Computational Linguistics, Ann Arbor, USA, pp. 459–466. Association for Computational Linguistics (June 2005)
8. Percy, L., Dan, K., Michael, J.: Agreement-Based Learning. In: Proceedings of Advances in Neural Information Processing Systems (2008)
9. Jörg, T.: Combining clues for word alignment. In: Proceedings of the Tenth Conference on European Chapter of the Association for Computational Linguistics, vol. 1, pp. 339–346. Association for Computational Linguistics, Stroudsburg (2003)
10. Aykiz, K., Kaysar, K., Turgun, I.: Morphological Analysis of Uyghur Noun for Natural Language Information Processing. Journal of Chinese Information Processing 20(3), 43–48 (2006)
11. Philipp, K., Hieu, H., Alexandra, B., Chris, C.B., Marcello, F., Nicola, B., Brooke, C., Wade, S., Christine, M., Richard, Z., Chris, D., Ondrej, B., Alexandra, C., Evan, H.: Moses: Open Source Toolkit for Statistical Machine Translation. In: Proceedings of ACL, Demonstration Session, Prague, Czech Republic. Association for Computational Linguistics (2007)
12. Andreas, S.: SRILM – an extensible language modeling toolkit. In: Proceedings of ICSLP, vol. 2, pp. 901–904 (2002)
13. Kishore, P., Salim, R., Todd, W., Weijing, Z.: BLEU: a Method for Automatic Evaluation of Machine Translation. In: Proceedings of ACL, Philadelphia, USA, pp. 311–318 (2002)

Calculation Analysis on Consonant and Character for Corpus Study of Gesar Epic "HorLing"

Duo La[1] and Tashi Gyal[2,*]

[1] Northwest University for Nationalities, Lanzhou,Gansu, China, 730030
[2] Tibet University, Lhasa, Tibet, China, 850000
Duola67@126.com, zzxx.77@163.com

Abstract. We made an econometric analysis on consonants and characters after the establishment of Gesar epic classic version HorLing corpus. Firstly, we set up a 2-million-consonants corpus for further verification and comparison of the character frequency of HorLing. Secondly, we established the theory of Tibetan consonants combination rules and Tibetan theory consonants and wish the Tibetan theory consonants coverage on HorLing. By the analysis, we not only understood the status of the Gesar epic consonants and characters, but also clarified the application of Tibetan consonants and characters in the real life.

Keywords: Gesar, Tibetan corpus, consonant and characters.

1 Introduction

It is well known that HorLing is the classic version of Gesar epic and the body of the epic. Gesar is the world's longest epic and "living epic". It is still widely talked and sung so far. In spoken and written Tibetan language and dialect differences, it's between spoken and written language. It broke through each dialect barriers and became a universal language. It is important to study the language, which have a restricted view for a nation's way of thinking and attitude of observing.

This paper makes the following contributions: 1) make a qualitative calculation research on vowel sounds; 2) calculate Tibetan theory characters by rule description and software generation; 3) compare with the consonant and characters of Gesar epic, which helps master the language system of the epic; 4) provide a reference data for Tibetan language research and Tibetan information processing. Therefore, it is a very meaningful experiment.

2 Vowels and Frequency in HorLing

In ISO/IEC10646 "Tibetan coding Basic Collection" (hereinafter referred to as the "Basic Collection"), the Tibetan is coded according to the dynamic superposition

* Corresponding author.

M. Sun et al. (Eds.): CCL and NLP-NABD 2014, LNAI 8801, pp. 269–278, 2014.

characteristic of Tibetan. It involves Tibetan consonant and component. There are 192 Code bits in Basic Collection, occupying 0F00-0FBF area, 168 coding consonants and components, 24 vacant codes. In Unicode3.0 released in September 1999, 34 Tibetan components and symbols were supplemented. No Tibetan consonant was supplemented in Unicode4.0, but Tibetan coding space extends to OFFF and contains total 256 code bits [1].

According to the consonant, component and symbol in basic collection, we surveyed their distribution and frequency in Gesar epic. In Gesar "HorLing", the consonant, component and symbol occurs 1387431 times and 68 types. There are 3 kinds of symbol appearing in Horling, e.g., "༄", "༅", "༈". The first two are one, but separated in the code. Each of them appears 21 times. The third one is initiative symbol and appears once. There are three punctuations, i.e., syllables, full stop and comma. Among them, syllables occurs the most, i.e., 329814 times and 23.7716% of the HorLing total consonants. Full stop follows, appearing 30145 times and 2.1727%. The third is comma, a total of 12602 times and accounted for 0.9083%.

In addition to the symbols and punctuation, we also investigated four Tibetan vowels contained in "HorLing". The frequencies of four vowels are all shown in Tibetan except vowel "a", which is implied and from which we can understand the cause and focus of Tibetan voice. In the four vowels, vowel "o" appears 63368 times , i.e., the highest frequency, accounted for 6.2442% of corpus amount (except the above punctuation, which occurs 1014827 times consonant and component). Vowel "I" follows, appearing 56968 times and accounted for 5.6136% of total corpus. The next is vowel "u", appearing 48105 times and 4.7402% of total corpus. Vowel "e" is the final one, appearing 46441 times and 4.5762% of the total corpus.

In accordance with the order of traditional grammar, the order should be "i u e o". But from the viewpoint of frequency, the order is naturally "o i u e". The last vowel is adjusted to become the first one. In addition to the above four symbols, we've seen double-layer vowel "o" appearing 22 times, accounted for 0.0022%. The appearance of the vowel "o" is originally from a calling word "ཀེ་སྭཽ་སྭཽ".It does not belong to the Sanskrit, but just be used Sanskrit transcription in writing, as "ཀེ་བསོ་བསོ" in some versions.

In addition, reversed written vowel "I" appears once. It is not a form of ancient Tibetan's reversed written vowels, but the transcription of Sanskrit words by searching. In the sixth chapter of the first part of HorLing, ChaoTong pretended to be King Gesar, and provoked in the front of the tribe Hore camp. There is a sentence in the lyrics"ཛམ་ཚན་འདི་ལ་ཚ་མོ་ཡོད།། ཛོན་པ་འཛམ་བུ་བྲྀཀྵ་ཤིང་ཡིན།།"[2]. The reversed written vowels combinations are the name of the tree of life in South ZhanBu continent, which are loanwords and derived from Sanskrit. They are occasionally used in the Tibetan text, but rarely in spoken Tibetan. It also suggests that Gesar epic language exists between spoken language and text, or Gesar epic language is an organic combination of text and spoken language. At the same time, the reversed written vowel is not ancient Tibetan, which means Gesar epic language is the common language and does not contain a lasted synchronic language. It may be one of the reasons for epic "Gesar" as the only "living epic".

3 The Consonant and Component and Their Frequency in Horling

The top ten are "ས་ག་ད་ར་མ་བ་ང་ན་ལ་འ" except individual punctuation and vowel in Horling. "ས"appears 84921 times, the highest frequency, accounted for 8.3680% of the corpus amount (the corpus contains 1014827 times of consonant and component except syllables and punctuations); "ག"appears 72025 and accounts for 7.0973% of the total amount of corpus. To be sure, the frequency of "ག" does not include "ག"as a root when combined by ko can and dok can. Frequency of root of "ག" statistic separately (the following consonant acing as other similar function are the same). "ད" appears 69418 times, accounted for 6.8404% of the total. "ར" 63281 times, 6.2356%; "མ" 48392 times, 4.7685%; "བ" 48320 times, 4.7614%; "ང" 46583 times, 4.5902%; "ན" 45724 times, 4.5056%; "ལ" 40112 times, 3.9526%; At the end of the "འ", a total of 37850 times, close to 40000, accounted for 3.7297%.

Fortunately, if we adjust these 10 characters according to the order of traditional grammar, the result is very surprising. The traditional order of the ten words is "ག་ང་ད་ན་བ་མ་འ་ར་ལ་ས", which is just the ten latter root of Tibetan character. Therefore, how could the latter root be high frequency consonant in consonant and component, and what is its primary cause? We will deeply discuss that later combined with character status.

Syllable, full stop and four vowels, 10 latter root, a total of 16 high-frequency consonants and punctuation, and then is the superimposed consonants and other letters. The highest frequency is the first two of the four dok can in Tibetan, i.e. ya and ra, The frequency of "ྱ"and "ྲ", "ྱ" are of 29717 times, 2.9283%; frequency of "ྲ" appear 20773 times, accounted for 2.0469%, the frequency of which is below 20000 and more than 30000. The frequency of the third dok can is"ླ", accounted for 0.8404%, significantly lower than the first two, less than 1%. Even so, "ླ" is not only dok can, and sometimes acts as root of other ko can, such as "ཟླ". The fourth dok can " ྭ"only appear 649 times, accounted for 0.0640%, which ranked 51 in frequency of 62 consonants and components.

In addition, "ར་ལ་ས" has three ko can in Tibetan. Unfortunately, due to not taking traditional way for encoding, but making dok can as a key coding, statistics on frequency of the three ko can cannot adopt the same method, which had to be observed in the part of discussion of character. However, this encoding way provided us an opportunity to research ko can combination roots. There are 16 ko can roots. 3 roots are more than 8000 high frequency, respectively is "ྒ", "ླ", "ྟ". Among them, frequency of " ྒ" is 10831 times, 1.0673%; frequency of "ྟ" is 8020 times, accounting for 0.7903%. "ླ" has talked about as ko can, here is mainly aimed at its root function, these three characters could act as common root for three ko can.

In conclusion, there are 1387431 times of consonants, components and punctuation in "HorLing" of "Gesar" epic. There are 62 types of consonants and components except six punctuation, covering 1014827 consonants and components. We could see that only 6 consonants appear in 15 vowel consonants of Horling according to Basic collection. In addition to once Sanskrit reversed written vowel, the rest can be considered to be Tibetan vowels, coverage of 100%. Appeared in the top 10 are 10 latter roots in the scope of letters. They represent not only latter roots, but appear as roots and act as latter root. The other five could also act as previous root. "ར་ལ་ས" could be used as ko can, but they cannot used as ko can roots. The diversity of the role makes them stand out in more than 1 million consonants and become a top ten high frequency consonants. More impressive is that the cumulative frequency of these 10 consonants and 4 vowels achieved 76.0236%. That is to say, 1014827 consonants in the full text of Horling except syllables and punctuation, 76% of the 14 consonants were repeated and composed in the various roles.

The highest level of the art is not to make the simple things complicated, but to describe the complicated things by the most simple and fluent language, as is not only the art and science. If this view is correct, we could say that the epic of "Gesar" is a perfect combination of art and science. We could also make this question, of course, the characteristics of the phonetic writing is to realize complex expression by a few letter combinations. There is no doubt that it should be acknowledged. What make us surprising is that 30 letters of alphabet writing should only use 10 of them and reached 76% of expression. This work is a miracle.

In 168 coded consonants version of "Basic collection", there has 77 consonant characters [3], including Tibetan single consonant, 49 dok can root character, 28 Sanskrit consonant character and dok can characters. In the epic Gesar, statistics of consonant and components of "HorLing". There are 49 pureTibetan characters except seven vowels and six Sanskrit characters. It shows that in the level of consonant and component, "Gesar" epic" HorLing" covers 100% of the modern Tibetan consonant and component, effectively prove "HorLing" has important value as a template for Tibetan language research.

4 About the Character

Tibetan has 206 basic character in traditional grammar (ལུས་ཀྱི་ཡི་གེ)[4] if "body" understood as character, the statistics might not consider other factors. But the basic character is put forward, which gives us a consideration and evolves "character" .For the attention of the "character" and put forward again of this concept due to the rise of Tibetan information technology, the problem of character were raised at the beginning of encoding for Tibetan.

In terms of Chinese characters, a word can be classified as a character, such as 6763 Chinese characters were collected in GB 2312, including 3755 primary/first-level Chinese characters, 3008 secondary characters, which basicly meet the requirements of regular users of computer processing of Chinese characters, and its coverage to mainland China 99.75% of Chinese characters operating frequency. From which we can see that every word is a syllable unit, at the same time it is a character.

5 The Theory about Tibetan Character

For the Tibetan language, there is a big difference between characters, a syllable is not necessarily a character, a word at the same time sometimes could be a syllable. As mentioned above, a Tibetan syllable is consists of seven parts at most . Although it also like Chinese is just one syllable, but not take it as a character. In fact, Tibetan cannot include previous root, latter root and plus latter root as character , just calculate single character and vowel, and vertical superposition (ko can,dok can).

We need to know how many character in Tibetan, how many characters in voluminous ancient books and the epic? Three categories and 33 ko can in Tibetan, four categories and 40, four vowels, 30 roots, these combined according to the rules of word groups referred to as lus kyi yi e,namely,body word or character.

In order to study Tibetan character, according to the theory of Tibetan voice, we made a rule description and generated in program. In this way,

there are 454 Tibetan characters in the generating program. Including the translation of words: ཙྭ་ཀྵ་ཞྭ, the three actually belong to the category of Sanskrit long vowels. In addition, five new words namely ཟྭ་ཟྭི་ཟྭུ་ཟྭེ་ཟྭོ and 39 DunHuang[5][6] literature and stone ancient Tibetan: ཀྱི་གྱི་འི་ཡི་ཁྱི་ཁི་དྲ་སྱི་གྱི་ཅེ་ཆེ་ཐྱེ་ཏྱེ་ཐྱེ་ཉ་སྨྲ་སྨོ་ཙེ་ཛེ་གྲ་སྲ་ར་ཏྭ་ས་ཟླ་སྲ་སྤྲ་སྤྲུ་ས་ཙེ་ཞི་ཙེ་ད་སྐ་ཆེ་ཞྲེ་ཛ་ཟྭ Among them, the "ཛ" character pronunciation should be "ja",it is a person’s name, suspected that the strokes weren’t connect well when sketching,

"ཀྱུ" written like "ཛ", actually should be "ཀྱུ". In this way, the total number of Tibetan character should be 498. Of course, there are also some superposition of latter root and plus latter root in the DunHuang literature and ancient Tibetan stone tablets, this part actually are superposed according to the need of writing space at that time. Ultimately, they are still latter root and plus latter root, it will not have any change in voice except Non-standard writing .The 498 Tibetan character, like 400 no-tone basic Chinese syllable, which could be regarded as the foundation of the Tibetan voice systems or basic voice.

But we need to know, if only count the modern Tibetan characters, then minus three Sanskrit reversed character "ཙྭ་ཀྵ་ཞྭ" in the 454 characters ,and add five new character "ཟྭ་ཟྭི་ཟྭུ་ཟྭེ་ཟྭོ" [7]. In this way, the number of simple modern Tibetan character should be 456.

6 Character and Frequency of HorLing

As the world’s longest epic "Gesar" ,how many basic voice used when talking and singing, or how many characters for recording in Horling Part one and two? If we could make this clear, then we could understand the reality of the Tibetan voice system probably.Based on this understanding, we counted the number of characters of "HorLing"part one and two, there are altogether 445 characters.

Among them , there are 34 Sanskrit, it respectively is ཐཱ་བྷཱ་ཀཱ་ཊི་ཁྟ་ཊ་ཋེ་ཌཱུ་ཌྷི་ཌ་ཎ་ཏེ་ཐཾ་ནཱ་ནྲྀ་ཕཾ་ཕཱི་ཐྲ་པཱ་པུཾ་བཱ་མཱ་ཛ་ར་ཤ་ཤ་ཥུ་ཥོ་ཧྲ་ཧྲུ་ཨོཾ་ཀྵ , so pure Tibetan left 411.There are no five new words in the epic, three translation character and the reversed-written vowel ancient Tibetan character, and appear some Sanskrit categories, but the frequency of the Sanskrit is very low, just appear while reciting om mani padme hung and ali's four great rivers, and several animal and plant names such as "water lotus", "lion"etc. 34 Sanskrit and frequency table (table 1) as follows:

Table 1. Frequency table of the Sanskrit and frequency

No.	character	times	frequency	No.	character	times	frequency	Amount
1	ཕྚ	142	0.0205	18	ཀྵྀ	2	0.0003	693356
2	ཤྲཱི	30	0.0043	19	ཊཱ	1	0.0001	693356
3	ཤྲ	22	0.0032	20	ཥ	1	0.0001	693356
4	ཎྜ	17	0.0025	21	ཛ	1	0.0001	693356
5	ཧཱུྃ	13	0.0019	22	ཙ	1	0.0001	693356
6	ཏྲི	12	0.0017	23	ཀྵི	1	0.0001	693356
7	ཊ	7	0.0010	24	ཀྵ	1	0.0001	693356
8	ཀྵ	6	0.0009	25	ཎ	1	0.0001	693356
9	ཌ	5	0.0007	26	སྭ	1	0.0001	693356
10	ཨོཾ	5	0.0007	27	ཊི	1	0.0001	693356
11	ཀྱ	5	0.0007	28	ཊྲ	1	0.0001	693356
12	ཛ	4	0.0006	29	ཧཾ	1	0.0001	693356
13	ཛྷ	3	0.0004	30	ཀྵཿ	1	0.0001	693356
14	ཧྲཱུྃ	2	0.0003	31	པུ	1	0.0001	693356
15	ཊཾ	2	0.0003	32	ཛྫ	1	0.0001	693356
16	ཏཾ	2	0.0003	33	ཤྲཱི	1	0.0001	693356
17	ཛྲ	2	0.0003	34	ཤུ	1	0.0001	693356

(Note: not including in the total number of syllable point)

As you can see, in 34 Sanskrit character, a total of 17 character appear twice or more, the rest is only appear one time. The highest frequency in Sanskrit is "ཕྚ", a total of 142 times, in fact the character and its combination are both "ཕ་ཏུར", it is a character with different form of "དཔའ་རྩལ (hero)".

We already know that the number of modern Tibetan character is 456, which appear 411 times in "HorLing", there are still 45 Tibetan character does not appear, and sill 40 characters did not appear in the epic except 5 new character "ཛ་ཛེ་ཛྲ་ཛེ་ཛོ". 411 Horling character accounted for 90.1316% in modern Tibetan characters, there are nearly 10% of the them has not been covered. If some high-frequency character did not appear, then typicality of the HorLing language will be questioned. Therefore, we need to know which character does not appear, and the function of those does not appear.Through comparison and selection, we found that the 40 characters are: "ཀྱ་ཀྲེ་ཀླེ་ཤཀ་སྐྲི་སྨུ་ཀེ་སྣེ་ཤྐ་སྨྲུ་ངི་འེ་ཛ་ཛྲུ་ཏ྄་ཏྲ྄་ཏི་ཏེ་ཏོ་ཧྲེ་ཞུ་ཟ་ཟེ་ཏྲུ་སྟྲ་སྟྲོ་ཟི་ཟླུ་ཞ་ཞེ་ཚེ་ཕ་ཕི་ཚྭ་ཚྲེ་ཚྲྱེ་ཚྲོ་ཞེ་ཞོ་ཟླུ", in general, the 40 characters are not commonly used, and even some could be called "death character", never used, such as "ཀླེ"[8].

The interpretation to meaning item of each character and function of character building,we query to the 30 text file of "reference corpus", total size is 4.11 MB, 2.15 million characters. In which 32 words never appear; the highest frequency appear 99 characters, belongs to the ancient Tibetan "མྱི (people)", following is 6 times, 3 times, one time.

It shows that the 40 character is not commonly used, most of them never appear in the 2 million corpus. The ancient Tibetan accounted for the proportion , in addition to the individual character, most is uncommon character. Therefore, it is reasonable that they did not appear in HorLing , because the characteristics of HorLing language is very popular, a universal language.

About the new character "ཧྥ་ཧྥི་ཧྥུ་ཧྥེ་ཧྥོ" does not appear in "HorLing". For the five new character, there are two statements. One is the five characters are new combination according to the need of translation after liberation, to translate some"f"consonant such as "Leifeng", "plane" and "Mei lanfang" should adpot five characters; Another is that these five characters has been used in the period of the fifth dalai lama (the early qing dynasty). Anyway, the characters might be created lately from the situation of non-appear in Holing corpus.There is no this kind of pronunciation in the folk oral Tibetan. Moreover, so far, there hasn't local characters formed by these characters except translation need, related basic voice replaced with pa and pha, no"f"consonants or initials words.

We already know that 411 characters in"HorLing"accounted for 90.1316% of modern Tibetan characters, also include some Sanskrit common used characters, to a certain extent, it reflect the reality of the usage of Tibetan. It is inevitable that some Sanskrit exists in Tibetan regularly ,therefore, it is necessary to taken into account of the part of the reversed written Sanskrit while coding for Tibetan . In the real life level, it also reflects the Tibetan is a universal buddhist nation and it has the very deep influence as the birthplace of Buddhism.

The top ten high frequency character are "ས་ག་ད་ང་ན་མ་ར་བ་ལ་འ" in the epic, we are very familiar with these ten characters. The top 10 in statistical consonants are "ས་ག་ད་ར་མ་བ་ང་ན་ལ་འ", it is different in order compared with characters. Actually, they are just ten latter roots if we reorder these ten characters,that is, "ག་ང་ད་ན་བ་མ་འ་ར་ལ་ས།".

We know that the total frequency the character is 693356 times, the cumulative frequency of top 10 character is 391069 times, 56.4023% of the total number of characters. Detailed in the following table (table 2) :

Table 2. frequency of top 10 characters list

No.	character	times	Frequency (%)	cumulative times	cumulative frequency (%)	Amount
1	ས	53669	7.7405	53669	7.7405	693356
2	ག	48251	6.9591	101920	14.6995	693356
3	ད	46848	6.7567	148768	21.4562	693356
4	ང	44149	6.3674	192917	27.8237	693356
5	ན	44031	6.3504	236948	34.1741	693356
6	མ	34726	5.0084	271674	39.1825	693356
7	ར	34056	4.9118	305730	44.0942	693356
8	བ	31894	4.5999	337624	48.6942	693356
9	ལ	27888	4.0222	365512	52.7164	693356
10	འ	25557	3.6860	391069	56.4023	693356

In characters, it is still a"ས" in the first place, the second and third places are "ག" and "ད" same as characters statistics layout, and then change on the ordinal, but on the whole, still the 10characters.

In the top 100chracters, mainly is function word, such as five the auxiliary case are in the top 50. They are, "འི" ranks 12th, appear 10408 times, frequency is 1.5011%; "ཡི " in the 18th, 5054 times, the frequency is 0.7289%; "གྱི" in the 33th, 3171 times, frequency is 0.4573%; "གི" in the 44th, 2568 times, frequency is 0.3704%; "ཀྱི" is 46th, 2417 times, frequency is 0.3486%. The frequency of ordering shows that it is obvious for the adhesion phenomenon(function word cohere with national word) of the case.

The cumulative frequency of the first 100 characters is up to 625379 words, accounted for 89.94% of total corpus, the lowest frequency is 945 times. The 100 characters appear 1033 times except the end of the last three characters. So they can be called thousand-times character.

From the number of 101to 200, character root has taken main status. The highest frequency of this phase is 935 times, the lowest is 265 times of the 200th character. Which is relatively balanced, unlike the frequency of the first 100 characters, the first appeared 53669 times, and 100th appear 945 times, they are differ more than 52000 times.

The cumulative frequency of the first 200 characters is up to 675826 times, accounted for 97.47% of the total number. From the number of 101 to 200, mostly is superposition character, followed by consonant and vowel, illustrate the major component of Tibetan alphabet combination in this frequency. The character without superposition and vowel is only one "ཛ", its number is 107, still in the first place, appear 872 times, frequency is 0.1258%.

The frequency and distribution of 447 characters shows that the reflects the usage and distribution of Tibetan characters in epic, on the other hand it also reflects a general situation of the entire Tibetan character. All 447 characters including Sanskrit, there are 29 of which frequency is only once, 10 of which frequency is 2, seven of which frequency is 3, five of which frequency is 4, three of which frequency is 6, only one of which frequency is 7, two of which frequency is 8, there of which frequency is 9, two of which frequency is 10, there of which frequency is 11, there of which frequency is 12, there of which frequency is 13.As you can see from these frequency, 2-3characters distributed for each level in low-frequency ones equably. Throughout the 447 characters, there are 115 characters which frequency are below 30.The rest 33 Sanskrit except "ཀྵ" are mixed In this frequency channel. It can be seen that the character of this frequency channel is not "uncommon character".

7 Conclusion

"HorLing", commonly known as "HorLing wars "or" the war of HorLing", mainly describes the war events between tribe of Hore and Ling, shows the changes of the Tibetan tribal society. Mr Qian mintz wrote in his article: "HorLing wars is a historical picture scroll of Tibetan hero's grand, majestic and grand, it is permeated with enthusiasm upward, positive enterprising and fight passion. This is very similar to the Iliad"[9] He also asserts that "Tibetan HorLing wars is the Chinese nation's "Iliad""[10].

It is earlier to study of A Dream of Red Mansions by corpus method, which inspired us for the first time to study Gesar epic by establishing Tibetan tagging corpus. Though the study we not only get the number of Tibetan theory character, but also verified the frequency of character in the practical application, and classified the characters. Moreover, we verified the 40 low-frequency characters in a larger range (2 million characters) the verification of the corpus to further confirm the reliability of the frequency of characters in "HorLing", it makes sense.

Acknowledgements. This research project was financially supported by the National Natural Science Foundation of China (NSFC)(No. 61262053) and The ministry of education philosophy and social sciences research project for major project(No. 13JZD028), the National Natural Science Foundation of China (NSFC)(No. 61163043).

References

1. Jiang, D., Long, C.J.: Study on Tibetan character, pp. 88–89. Social Sciences Academic Press (August 2010)
2. Mintz, Q.: HorLing wars, the Iliad. Foreign Literature, 125–251 (1986)
3. Jiang, D., Long, C.J.: Study on Tibetan character, pp. 77–78. Social Sciences Academic Press (August 2010)
4. Caidanxiarong: The Tibetan language grammar, pp. 25–26. Qinghai Minorities Press (1998)
5. Luo, B. (ed.): Tubo Medical Literature Essential, pp. 127–300. Ethnic Publishing House (2002)

6. Chenjian, Wangyao (eds.): Duanghuang Manuscript Tibetan Literature, pp. 12–321. Ethnic Publishing House (1983)
7. Compiled by Tso, T., et al.: Atomic Physics (Tibetan-Chinese Languages), pp. 7–29. Gansu Ethnic Publishing House (2005)
8. Compiled by Tsutrin, Z.N.: Ancient Tibetan Dictionary, pp. 15–16. Ethnic Publishing House (1997)
9. Mintz, Q.: HorLing wars, the Iliad. Foreign Literature, 103–105 (1986)
10. Mintz, Q.: HorLing wars, the Iliad. Foreign Literature, 114–120 (1986)

Sentence Level Paraphrase Recognition Based on Different Characteristics Combination

Maoyuan Zhang, Hong Zhang, Deyu Wu, and Xiaohang Pan

Central China Normal University, Computer Science Department,
Luoyu Road. 152, Wuhan, China
{zhangmyccnu,panxiaohang_love}@126.com, qjzhanghong@gmail.com,
wdy158@sohu.com

Abstract. This paper has proposed a novel method based on different characteristics combination to do paraphrase recognition. We employ different measurements to weigh the lexical part and syntactic part due to that the different part of sentence makes distinguishing contribution to the sentence semantic during the task of paraphrase recognition. Our experiment is conducted by parsing the pair sentences of MSRPC first, then followed by adopting differentiated weights to calculate the power of different parts of the sentence.Through this method, we have obtained the outperform precision and average F value result compared with the previous approaches.

Keywords: Pattern Recognition, Sentence Characteristic, Lexical, Syntactic.

1 Introduction

The concept of paraphrasing is generally defined on the basis of the principle of semantic equivalence: A paraphrase is an alternative surface form in the same language expressing the same semantic content as the original form. Paraphrase recognition is aimed to classify the object sentence pair positive paraphrase or not.Paraphrases recognition has attracted global intellectuals devoting their efforts because of its wide range of applications in Query Expansion, Information Extraction, Machine Translation and so forth [1].Consider the following examples, paraphrased from MRSPC sources:

S1: Special, sensitive light sensors pick up the telltale glow, he said.
S2: A sensitive light detector then looks for the telltale blue glow.

Forward methods like surface string similarity and vector model method will fail in recognize this positive paraphrase as they ignored the synonyms of words as well as the structure which represent the meaning of sentence. This paper concentrates on introducing a novel data-driving method to recognize sentence level paraphrase. Sentence's part-of-speech labels as well its parsing tree are being employed to discovery deep semantic relations of sentence pair. Our work is divided into two phases. Firstly, POS-tagging and syntactic analysis are done on

M. Sun et al. (Eds.): CCL and NLP-NABD 2014, LNAI 8801, pp. 279–289, 2014.

the sentence pair to obtain kernel information of the semantic role and parsing tree structure. Secondly, adopt train data to construct a two hierarchical Model based on kernel information of semantic role and parsing tree structure extracted from the first phase. Then test data is employed to recognize paraphrase relationship of the sentence pair. We do deep semantic mining and construct the hierarchical model to do the sentence level paraphrase recognition which does not employed by previous methods .we take the distinguish into consideration and they indeed achieve encourage result. The rest of the paper is organized as follows. A survey of related works is conducted in Section 2, then the definition of semantic level difference method and its algorithm are proposed in Section 3. Section 4 introduces the experiment details and the progress of the method, with detailed analysis of the result. Finally we conclude the paper in Section 5 with a guideline of the future work.

2 Related Works

Sentence level paraphrase recognition is aimed to judge whether two sentences express the same meaning or not. Previous methods can be classified into followed categories due to their different viewpoints. These are the method based on surface string similarity, operated on syntactic or semantic, Machine Learning Method, method employs co-reference or text entailment, and method combine information from different levels.

Surface string similarity approaches which use string edit distance, number of common words, and combination of several string similarity measures to recognize paraphrase[2].This method just considered the surface feature without semantic information of string so that it can not deal with the synonym in sentences. Vector Space Model for semantics is another popular method combine the vector of single word and its cosine similarity to recognize paraphrase[4,5].Vector Space Model employed bag-of-words model but ignored the syntactic relations to calculate the similarity of the two original sentences.

Part researchers employed syntactic similarity based on syntax level to compute the similarity of the dependency trees to detection paraphrase, this method neglected basic lexical similarity's contribution to the task[6,7,8,9].

There are several approaches use Machine Learning to do the recognize job. They trained a classifier using training data to classify unseen pairs paraphrase or not by examining their inherited features[10,11,12,18]. The point is to select proper restraint of the object sentences. Other researchers had put forward the opinion that co-reference resolution could be employed to solve paraphrase recognition to some extend. more practical work is needed to examine the theory's efficiency [3,13].

Sentence level paraphrase recognition can be treated as the extended synonym detection for sentence pair. So the principal work is to seek appropriate characteristics and set fit constraints[19] on those characteristics to measure two sentences indicating the approximately same meaning or not. Generally components of sentence are from lexical and syntactic aspects, different lexical parts or syntactic parts do distinguishing contribution on the semantic point.Take this into account, we combine the POS part with syntactic relationships to meet the approval of the paraphrase standard.

Consider the forward methods' strengths and weaknesses, we utilize machine learning process to treat the lexical and syntactic features of the sentence to do paraphrase recognition and get our improvement. The learning process provide us the chance to know the internal rules of the paraphrase and the proper environment to adjust our method. Our method employ the advantages of machine learning and avoid the unilateral feature of surface string similarity and vector space model approaches.

3 Our Method and Idea

3.1 Approach Overview

As introduced forward, we use machine learning which employ the two different levels of a sentence, one is the lexical level, the other the syntactic level, which correspond to the POS-phase and Syntactic-phase respectively, to do sentence level paraphrase recognition. Figure 1 describes the whole process of our approach. The POS-phase: Do sentence POS-tag job to obtain the sentence lexical analysis, then to calculate the object sentence pair's similarity on lexical level. The main idea is based on the premise that paraphrase sentences consists of the same or similarity concepts, so the Noun part, the Verb part and the Adjective part of sentence should reach a certain level of similarity.

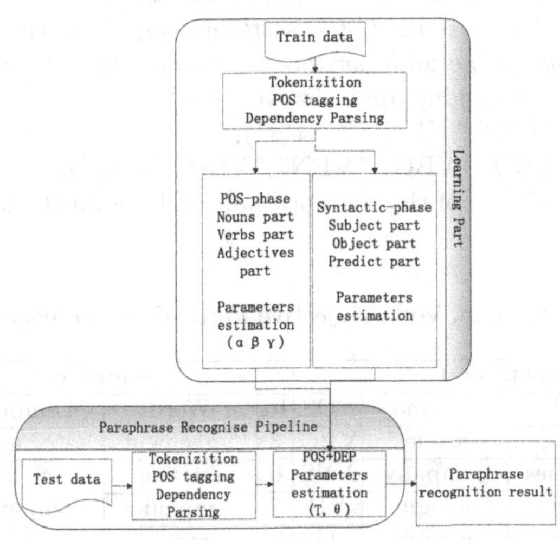

Fig. 1. Overview of our approach

The Syntactic-phase: Do dependency parsing on the sentence, and obtain the object sentence pair's similarity on syntactic level. The core part of sentence is consisted of the subject, object and the predict connects the above two.Similarity of this phase is to extract the subject, object and the predict part of the object sentence pair and setting proper constraints on them to identify paraphrase.

With the forward two-phase, we can get a hierarchical model consist of POS-phase and the Syntactic-phase to recognize paraphrase. The model can give a similarity score of the sentence pair to compared with the threshold, which is obtained from the training data.Sentence pair will be identified as positive paraphrase if the final result over the threshold, otherwise the negative.

3.2 Calculating Lexical and Syntactic Similarity

As described forward, the lexical level contribution on paraphrase recognition is based on POS-tagging result. The nouns shoulder the responsibility to express the static part of the sentence, the verbs part represent the action, while the adjective part describes how the verbs affects the nouns or the degree of the change. Those three parts take the dominate state to determine the similarity of the sentence pair.Furthermore, those three parts also have different degrees of effect on determine the paraphrase positive or not. So we first employ POS-tagging tools to obtain the part of speech result .Here, We take a sentence pair for example.
Sentence pair(Sentence 1, Sentence 2)
Sentence 1 :The settling companies would also assign their possible claims against the underwriters to the investor plaintiffs, he added.
Sentence 2 :Under the agreement, the settling companies will also assign their potential claims against the underwriters to the investors, he added.
According to the POS-tagging analysis, we take
Noun parts("NN","NNP","NNS","NNPS"),
Verb parts("VB","VBD","VBG","VBN","VBP","VBZ"),
and Adjective parts("JJ") of the sentence pair and obtain the following Table 1.

Table 1. Noun, Verb, Adjective Parts of the sentence pair

sentence 1				sentence 2			
Id	Word	Lemma	POS	Id	Word	Lemma	POS
2	settling	settle	VBG	3	agreement	agreement	NN
3	companies	company	NNS	6	settling	settle	VBG
6	assign	assign	VB	7	companies	company	NNS
8	possible	possible	JJ	10	assign	assign	VB
9	claims	claim	NNS	12	potential	potential	JJ
12	underwriters	underwriter	NNS	13	claims	claim	NNS
15	investor	investor	NN	16	underwriters	underwriter	NNS
16	plaintiffs	plaintiff	NNS	19	investors	investor	NNS
19	added	add	VBD	22	added	add	VBD

On lexical level similarity, We calculate the Noun, Verb, Adjective similarity respectively with Formula (1),(2),(3),then adopt the Noun, Verb, Adjective parts of the sentence pair to calculate the POS similarity.

$$Noun_{sim}\left(S_1,S_2\right)=\frac{\left(Noun_{s1}\right)\cap\left(Noun_{s2}\right)}{\left(Noun_{s1}\right)\cup\left(Noun_{s2}\right)} \tag{1}$$

$Noun_{s1}$ is composed of the nouns("NN","NNP","NNS","NNPS") of sentence 1, $Noun_{s2}$ of sentence2. We employ WordNet[20] to search the similar word of the nouns to help calculate the common part $Noun_{s1} \cap Noun_{s2}$, then the $Noun_{s1}$,$Noun_{s2}$ union to get the $Noun_{s1} \cup Noun_{s2}$ part.

$$Verb_{sim}\left(S_1,S_2\right)=\frac{\left(Verb_{s1}\right)\cap\left(Verb_{s2}\right)}{\left(Verb_{s1}\right)\cup\left(Verb_{s2}\right)} \tag{2}$$

Same as the noun parts, Verb parts include "VB","VBD","VBG", "VBN","VBP","VBZ".

$$Adj_{sim}\left(S_1,S_2\right)=\frac{\left(Adj_{s1}\right)\cap\left(Adj_{s2}\right)}{\left(Adj_{s1}\right)\cup\left(Adj_{s2}\right)} \tag{3}$$

Adjective parts("JJ") also do the same computation as the forward noun parts.

$$Pos_{sim}\left(S_1,S_2\right)=\alpha\times Noun_{sim}+\beta\times Verb_{sim}+\gamma\times Adj_{sim} \tag{4}$$

Then the POS similarity is derived from the three parts shown with Formula(4), α,β,γ are the coefficients of each part, here To normalization, the result value between 0 and 1, $\alpha+\beta+\gamma=1$. The number of each coefficient will represent the distinguishing power of itself to POS similarity. The value of these parameters will be detailed in the experiments part.

Then we will settle the recognition work combine Dependency phase.A crucial fact about dependency grammars is that the subject and object part play the vital role relative to other parts in determining the meaning of the sentence. The subject part holds the responsibility to illustrate the kernel concept of the sentence, while the object part indicates the variation of the kernel concept. Those two parts consist the backbone of one sentence. Here, we make use of the dependency relationship to weigh the similarity degree of a sentence pair. we first employ dependency parser to get the dependency relationships.Still take the forward sentence pair(Sentence 1, Sentence 2) for example. The pair's dependency relationships are shown in Table 2. From the dependency parser result ,we obtain the subject parts(nsubj, nsubjpass, xsubj) and object parts(dobj, iobj) as the kernel part of the sentence which expresses the semantic of the sentence. Consider the two parts' role , we endow them the same proportion in computation dependency similarity. The dependency similarity process is described as follows.Formula(5),(6),(7) give the detail calculation.

$$Subj_{sim}\left(S_1,S_2\right)=I(subj_{s1},subj_{s2}) \tag{5}$$

Table 2. Dependency relationships of sentence pair

sentence 1	sentence 2
det(companies-3,The-1)	det(agreement-3,the-2)
amod(companies-3,settling-2)	prep-under(added-22,agreement-3)
nsubj(assign-6,companies-3)	det(companies-7,the-5)
aux(assign-6,would-4)	amod(companies-7,settling-6)
advmod(assign-6,also-5)	nsubj(assign-10,companies-7)
ccomp(added-19,assign-6)	aux(assign-10,will-8)
poss(claims-9,their-7)	advmod(assign-10,also-9)
amod(claims-9,possible-8)	parataxis(added-22,assign-10)
dobj(assign-6,claims-9)	poss(claims-13,their-11)
det(underwriters-12,the-11)	amod(claims-13, potential-12)
prep-against(assign-6,underwriters-12)	dobj(assign-10,claims-13)
det(plaintiffs-16,the-14)	det(underwriters-16,the-15)
nn(plaintiffs-16,investor-15)	prep-against(assign-10,underwriters-16)
prep-to(assign-6,plaintiffs-16)	det(investors-19,the-18)
nsubj(added-19,he-18)	prep-to(assign-10,investors-19)
	nsubj(added-19, he-18)

$$Obj_{sim}\,(S_1,S_2) = I(obj_{s1}, obj_{s2}) \tag{6}$$

$$Dep_{sim}\,(S_1,S_2) = 0.5 \times Subj_{sim} + 0.5 \times Obj_{sim} \tag{7}$$

The $Subj_{sim}$ and the Obj_{sim} compose the Dep_{sim}, $Subj_{sim}$ represents the contribution of the subject parts, and the Obj_{sim} delegates the object parts. We employ the Resnik method[14] to measure the Obj_{sim} and the Obj_{sim} shown as follows.

$$\begin{cases} Res_{sim}\,(C_1,C_2) = IC(C_1,C_2) \\ IC\,(C_1,C_2) = \max[-\log p(c)] \qquad c \in S(C_1,C_2) \\ freq(c) = \sum[count(n)] \qquad n \in words(c) \\ p(c) = \frac{freq(c)}{N} \end{cases} \tag{8}$$

Resnik method is a measure of semantic similarity in an is-a taxonomy, based on the notion of information content,it gives the similarity score of two concept C_1, C_2, $S(C_1,C_2)$ is the common ancestor nodes. $words(c)$ represents the number of words in c branch, N is number of words of whole tree which the the c in. Here we use the upper formula to compute $Subj_{sim}$ and Obj_{sim}. As referred forward, subject parts include nsubj, nsubjpass, xsubj part, and the information content of $subj_{s1}$,$subj_{s2}$ is computed from the words they contain, $subj_{s1}$ is the subject parts of sentence s1, $subj_{s2}$ is that of s2. For example, nsubj(assign-6,companies-3), nsubj(added-19,he-18) composes the $subj_{s1}$ of s1 , nsubj(assign-10 , companies-7), nsubj(added-22,he-21) creates the $subj_{s2}$. We get the average $IC(assign, assign), IC(companies, companies)$ to express $IC(subj_{s1}, subj_{s2})$. Similarly, the Obj_{sim} is achieved by the same compute process with $Subj_{sim}$. Object parts include iobj, dobj part.

As proposed forward, paraphrase's similarity is based on lexical level similarity and the dependency similarity, which described by POS similarity and DEP similarity. So we get the combination of the two aspects to weigh a sentence pair's similarity. The followed Formula(9) illustrates our combination.

$$PR_{sim}\,(S_1,S_2) = \theta \times Subj_{sim} + (1-\theta) \times Obj_{sim} \tag{9}$$

Where PR similarity represents the sentence pair's final similarity score, θ is the parameter, we can get the best PR_{sim} by adjust θ with train data. From the details of the method described forward ,we give the algorithm in Figure 2.

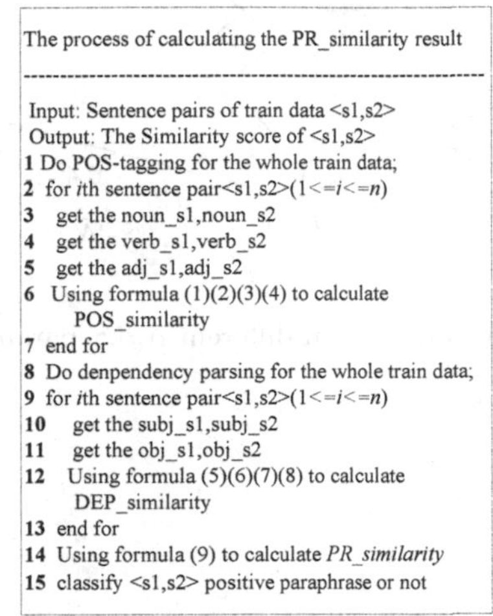

```
The process of calculating the PR_similarity result
--------------------------------------------------------------
Input: Sentence pairs of train data <s1,s2>
Output: The Similarity score of <s1,s2>
Do POS-tagging for the whole train data;
for ith sentence pair<s1,s2>(1<=i<=n)
  get the noun_s1,noun_s2
  get the verb_s1,verb_s2
  get the adj_s1,adj_s2
  Using formula (1)(2)(3)(4) to calculate
    POS_similarity
end for
Do denpendency parsing for the whole train data;
for ith sentence pair<s1,s2>(1<=i<=n)
  get the subj_s1,subj_s2
  get the obj_s1,obj_s2
  Using formula (5)(6)(7)(8) to calculate
    DEP_similarity
end for
Using formula (9) to calculate PR_similarity
classify <s1,s2> positive paraphrase or not
```

Fig. 2. The process of calculating the PR similarity result

4 Experiment and Results

In the experiment we employ Microsoft Research Paraphrase Recognition Corpus[15] to test our method. The MRPRC is made up with 5801 pair sentences which is divided into train data(4077 pair sentences) and test data(1726 pair sentences). The data is unbalanced in that 67words in POS-similarity part and DEP-similarity part both have been expanded with WordNet. The value of the α,β,γ is from 0 to 1 ,and α is bigger than β and γ. We use the train data to adjust the three parameters to achieve the state of art result. Figure 3 describes the variation of the POS_{sim} under different parameters combination, and we get the combination that $\alpha = 0.45$,$\beta = 0.35$,$\gamma = 0.2$ to achieve the best result of POS_{sim}. With the result of the POS_{sim} and Dep_{sim} of the training data, we go on training the θ in PR_{sim} to get the proper threshold to maximize the precision, and set the $\theta = 0.40$. Figure 4 shows 's effect on precision.

The training part of the MSRPC was used to find the classification threshold for the similarity score which maximized accuracy. Strict definition of paraphrase

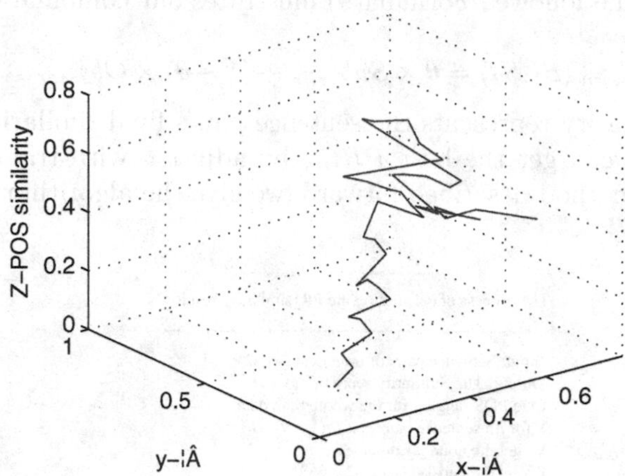

Fig. 3. POS similarity variation on different α,β,γ parameters combination

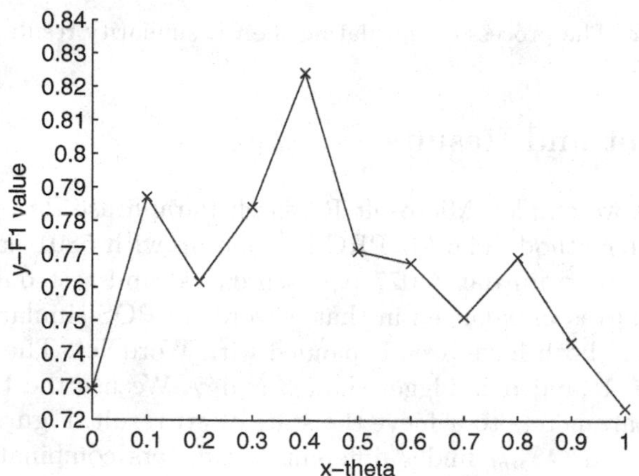

Fig. 4. Precision variation on different θ

requires the object sentence pair have identical meanings, but the creator of the corpus[11] found that this standard will limit the paraphrase to identical string copies of the each other, so they relaxed the paraphrase from'full bidirectional entailment' to 'mostly bidirectional entailments'. The key message of the guidelines for the annotators of the corpus stated that a paraphrase sentence pairs should describe the same event and contain the same important information .We finally adopted the training data with our method to get the appropriate threshold 0.30. The sentence pair would be recognized as true when the PR similarity of the test data over the threshold, otherwise the false . By setting the parameters, we adopt test data to get the experiment result. Here we use the general evaluation measure: accuracy, precision, recall, and F measure. Those are defined as follows.

$$\begin{cases} accuracy = \frac{TP+TN}{TP+TN+FP+FN} \\ precision = \frac{TP}{TP+FP} \\ recall = \frac{TP}{TP+FN} \\ F = \frac{2\times precision \times recall}{precision+recall} \end{cases}$$

where TP are true positives, TN are true negatives, FN are false negatives and FP are false positives.

Table 3. Noun, Verb, Adjective Parts of the sentence pair

Method	accuracy	precision	recall	F-measure
POSDEP	**72.5**	**76.2**	**90.7**	**82.8**
Malakasiotis	**76.2**	79.4	86.8	82.9
Das and Smith	76.1	**79.6**	86.1	82.9
Wan	75.6	77.0	90.0	**83.0**
Finch	75.0	76.6	89.8	82.7
Qiu	72.0	72.5	**93.4**	81.6
Zhang	71.9	74.3	88.2	80.7
Mihalcea	71.5	72.3	92.5	81.2
Vector-based	65.4	71.6	79.5	75.3
random	51.3	68.3	50.0	57.8

Results of semantic similarity of paraphrase based on MSRPC corpus are shown in Table 3.Our method(POS+DEP) result lays on top line, and previous approach results are down the Table 3. The distinguish level similarity approach outperforms both baselines for all three of the similarity measures used in these experiments. It can also be seen that, our result outperforms the previously reported methods in terms of precision and the accuracy is on the average level. From the Table 3, we find that the accuracy part is lower than the recent previous method, we suppose the followed factors may have negative effects on it.As we adopted Stanford POS Tagger to do part of speech work, and Stanford Parser to obtain the dependency relationships. The best resulting accuracy for the tagger is 96.86% overall, and 86.91% on previously unseen words [16], meanwhile the Parser owns the precision 86.32%[17].Because our work based on POS-tagging and Dependency parsing, those two procedures' precision can definitely have effect on the performance of paraphrase recognition, in the future, we will take those factors into account to improve our current method.

5 Conclusion and Future Work

This paper proposed a novel hierarchical model based on lexical and syntactic level to do paraphrase recognition. We used two aspects, the POS-tagging and syntactical structure to construct the model and obtain the effective results. The POS-tagging gives the lexical level semantic similarity and syntactical structure shows the work of dependency similarity on paraphrase recognition, each aspect use WordNet to do semantic expansion in finding similarity. The outcome of evaluation experiments shows that this method outperforms the previous similar approaches. Our semantic level difference method in paraphrase recognition indicates the following viewpoints: (1)The Nouns, Verbs and adjectives shoulder the primary responsibility in lexical level semantic level paraphrase recognition. Nouns describes the entities and verbs illustrate the variation of the entities, adjectives describe the degree of the variation.(2) The subject parts and the object parts in dependency structure of a sentence pair, play vital role in sentence pair paraphrase recognition.(3) Both lexical level semantic and syntactic structure have respective effect on the paraphrase recognition, we adopt linear combination of the two to do paraphrase recognition is valid. The two-hierarchical model method can be apply to the task such as sentence translation, query expansion, question answering etc. Future work will be focus on deep mining of paraphrase constrains besides those put forward in this paper, and solutions will be researched to avoid the problem described in the experiment analysis part.

Acknowledgments. This work was supported by the National Natural Science Foundation of China (No. 61003192), the Major Research Plan of National Natural Science Foundation of China (No. 90920005).

References

1. Clough, P., et al.: MEasuring TExt Reuse. In: Proceedings of the 40th Anniversary Meeting for the Association for Computational Linguistics, Pennsylvania, PA, pp. 152–159 (2002)
2. Barzilay, R., Lee, L.: Learn to paraphrase, An Unsupervised Approach Using Multiple-Sequence Alignment. In: Proceedings of HLT-NAACL, pp. 16–23 (2003)
3. Malakasiotis, P., Androutsopoulos, I.: Learning Textual Entailment using SVMs and String Similarity Measures. In: Proceedings of the ACL-PASCAL Workshop on Textual Entailment and Paraphrasing, 45th Annual Meeting of the Association for Computational Linguistics, Prague, Czech Republic, pp. 42–47 (2007)

4. Fernando, S., Stevenson, M.: A Semantic Similarity Approach to Paraphrase Detection. Computational Linguistics (2008)
5. Erk, K., Pado, S.: Paraphrase assessment in structured vector space Exploring parameters and datasets. In: Proceeding of the 2nd European Conference on Computational Learning Theory, Athens, Greece, pp. 57–65 (2009)
6. Wan, S., et al.: Using dependency-based features to take the para-farce out of paraphrase. In: Proceedings of the 2006 Australasian Language Technology Workshop, pp. 131–138 (2006)
7. Qiu, L., Kan, M., Chua, T.: Paraphrase recognition via dissimilarity significance classification. In: EMNLP 2006 Association for Computational Linguistics, Sydney, pp. 18–26 (2006)
8. Socher, R., et al.: Dynamic Pooling and Unfolding Recursive Auto encoders for Paraphrase Detection. In: Conference of Neural Information Processing Systems Foundation (2011)
9. Lintean, M., Rus, V.: Paraphrase Identification Using Weighted Dependencies and Word Semantics. In: Proceedings of the Twenty-Second International FLAIRS Conference, Sanibel Island, Florida, USA, pp. 260–265. Association for the Advancement of Artificial Intelligence, Sundial Beach (2009)
10. Pang, B., Knight, K., Marcu, D.: Syntax-based alignment of multiple translations, Extracting Paraphrases and Generating New Sentences. In: Proceedings of HLT-NAACL, pp. 102–109 (2003)
11. Dolan, W.B., Brockett, C.: Automatically Constructing a Corpus of Sentential Paraphrases. In: Proceeding of the 3rd International Workshop on Paraphrase, Jeju island, Korea, pp. 9–16 (2005)
12. Zhang, Y., Patrick, J.: Paraphrase identification by text canonicalization. In: Proceedings of the Australasian Language Technology Workshop, Sydney, Australia, pp. 160–166 (2005)
13. Recasens, M., Vila, M.: On Paraphrase and Coreference. Computational Linguistics 36(4), 639–647 (2010)
14. Resnik, P.: Using Information Content to Evaluate Semantic Similarity in a Taxonomy. In: International Joint Conference on AI, pp. 448–453 (1995)
15. Dolan, B., Quirk, C., Brockett, C.: Unsupervised Construction of Large Paraphrase Corpora, Exploiting Massively Parallel News Sources. In: Proceeding of the 20th International Conference on Computational Linguistics, Geneva, Switzerland, pp. 350–356 (2004)
16. Toutanova, K., Manning, C.D.: Enriching the Knowledge Sources Used in a Maximum Entropy Part-of-Speech Tagger. In: Proceedings of the Joint SIGDAT Conference on Empirical Methods in Natural Language Processing and Very Large Corpora, pp. 63–70 (2000)
17. Klein, D., Manning, C.D.: Accurate Unlexicalized Parsing. In: Proceedings of the 41st Meeting of the Association for Computational Linguistics, pp. 423–430 (2003)
18. Malakasiotis, P.: Paraphrase Recognition Using Machine Learning to Combine Similarity Measures. In: Proceedings of the ACL-IJCNLP 2009 Student Research Workshop, Suntec, Singapore, pp. 27–35 (2009)
19. Callison-Burch, C.: Syntactic Constraints on Paraphrases Extracted from Parallel Corpora. In: Proceeding EMNLP 2008 Proceedings of the Conference on Empirical Methods in Natural Language Processing, Stroudsburg, PA, USA, pp. 196–205 (2008)
20. Fellbaum, C.: WordNet: An Electronic Lexical Database. MIT Press (1998)

Learning Tag Relevance by Context Analysis for Social Image Retrieval

Yong Cheng[1], Wenhui Mao[1], Cheng Jin[1], Yuejie Zhang[1], Xuanjing Huang[1], and Tao Zhang[2]

[1] School of Computer Science, Shanghai Key Laboratory of Intelligent Information Processing, Fudan University, Shanghai 200433, P.R. China

[2] School of Information Management & Engineering, Shanghai University of Finance & Economics, Shanghai 200433, P.R. China

{13110240027,13210240099,jc,yjzhang,xjhuang}@fudan.edu.cn, taozhang@mail.shfeu.edu.cn

Abstract. Tags associated with images significantly promote the development of social image retrieval. However, these user-annotated tags suffer the problems of noise and inconsistency, which limits the role they play in image retrieval. In this paper, we build a novel model to learn the tag relevance based on the context analysis for each tag. In our model, we firstly consider the user tagging habits and use a multi-model association network to capture the tag-tag relationship and tag-image relationship, and then accomplish the random-walk over the tag graph for each image to refine the tag relevance. Different from the earlier research work related to tag ranking, our contributions focuse on the globally-comparable tag relevance measure (i.e., can be compared across different images) and better tag relevance learning model by detailed context analysis for each tag. Our experiments on the public data from *Flickr* have obtained very positive results.

Keywords: Tag Relevance, Context Analysis, Tag Ranking, Image Retrieval.

1 Introduction

With the rapid growth of Internet and mobile devices, users are able to share social images more easily than before, and this leads to massive social images that are available online. Therefore, how to retrieval social images more efficiently and accurately has been an important research topic [1]. At present, the existing social image retrieval technology can be classified two categories, that is, content-based and annotation-based [2, 3]. Compare to the content-based approach, the annotation-based social image retrieval can supply better retrieval performance and more convenient user interface. However, this approach needs a lot of human-effort to annotate the images, which limits the application because of the high cost.

More recently, with the development of Web, there are some image sharing websites like *Flickr*, which allow users to upload images with some associated tags and these social tags can help solve the high-cost problem in annotation-based social image retrieval to some extent [4, 5]. Nevertheless, compared with the standard image

M. Sun et al. (Eds.): CCL and NLP-NABD 2014, LNAI 8801, pp. 290–301, 2014.

annotations, the social image tags has some specific features and problems: 1) tagging accuracy, because the annotators are not experts, so inevitably there exists irrelevant tag, weakly-relevant tag, misspelling tags and so on. Fig. 1-*A* shows a social image of tiger with the associated tag set, obviously the tag "*tiger*" is the most relevant tag for this image, next "*wild*", and the other tags are either weakly relevant or irrelevant at all; 2) tag length and content, which means for the similar images, the length of tag sets and tag content may be very different. For example, when comparing Fig. 1-*A* with Fig. 1-*B*, we can see although these two images are similar, both the lengths and contents of these two tag sets are dissimilar. These characteristics make it difficult to apply traditional text retrieval model to image retrieval based on social tags. It can be also observed from Fig. 1 that for the query "*tiger*", if we utilize the classical tf-idf as the retrieval model, the final rank list will be <C, B, A>, which means for all the social image tag sets with "*tiger*", the less tags the image contains, the better rank the social image has, obviously this doesn't meet the actual situation. For example, although Fig. 1-*C* has the least tags, it is the least relevant image for "*tiger*".

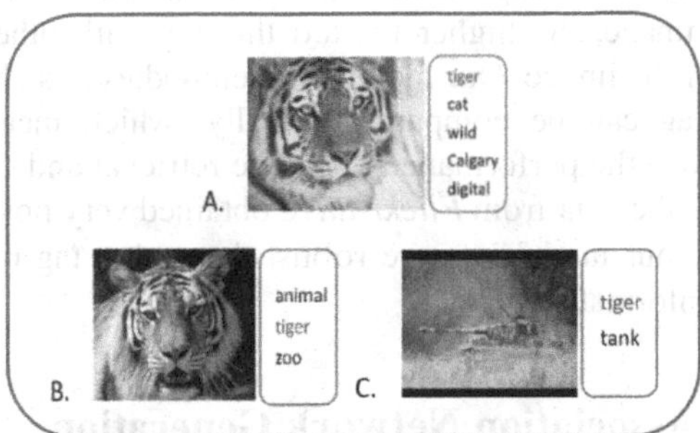

Fig. 1. An instantiation of social images from *Flickr*

To solve all these problems above, the researchers have done a lot of related research work. Overall, these work mainly concerns with two aspects of tag set revise and tag ranking. Tag set revise contains tag enrichment and tag refinement, for example, Qian *et al.* built a graph for each image with its initial tags, and implemented the tag enrichment by a graph-cut approach [6]; and Xu *et al.* proposed to do tag refinement from the perspective of topic modeling and presented a graphical model called regularized Latent Dirichlet Allocation to exploit both the statistics of tags and visual affinities of images in the corpus [7]. Xia *et al.* and Sang *et al.* use concept ontology and user information to do the tag refinement [8, 9]. However, these approaches have the disadvantages that the noisy information may be introduced to tag set or remove useful information from tag set. And for tag ranking, which means rank the tag according their relevance to the image, for example, [10] is the first paper aiming to attack the tag ranking problem, they estimated initial relevance scores through probability density estimation, and then refined the initial scores by performing a random walk algorithm over a tag similarity graph. Zhuang *et al.* proposed a novel two-view learning approach to compute the tag relevance using both textual and visual contents of social images, and they mapped the learning into an optimization task and presented an efficient algorithm to solve it [11]. Xiao *et al.* also used both semantic and visual information to get the tag-tag similarity matrix, and then discovered the significance of each tag [12]. The existing tag ranking methods focused on the inner ranking in the tag sets, while for social image retrieval the emphasis should be put on the global comparison for the same query tag in different image tag sets. These methods only used rough ranking information for image retrieval. Obviously they ignored some useful information which can be used to improve retrieval performance.

Based on these observations above, a novel scheme is developed in this paper for facilitating social image retrieval by learning the relevance of the image tags. In our approach, a multi-model association network is constructed to model the relationship between tags; then we build a context-analysis model to compute the tag relevance and finally refine it using an approximate random-walk algorithm. Our scheme significantly differs from other work in:

1. our approach assume that a tag has high relevance when it has close relationship with other tags in the same image, and we make this assumption from the inspiration of the user tagging process for social images, generally users are less likely to tag two close-related tags as noises simultaneously, in other words, if user chose a tag for an image, the higher related this tag with other tags, the higher relevance this tag for the image. Our model well embodies this characteristic.
2. The relevance of tag can be compared globally, which means we use richer information to improve the performance of image retrieval and our experiments on a large number of public data from *Flickr* have obtained very positive results.
3. For multi-tag query, our model is more robust than other tag ranking approaches using only ranking information.

2 Multimodal Association Network Generation

For tags in the same tag set of a social image, the tag relevance is determined by the related context, that is, the relationship between a tag and the other tags in the same tag set and the relationship between a tag and the associated image. For the tag-tag inter-related relationship, we consider two aspects of the co-occurrence frequency and the visual similarity, because if two tags often co-occur in the same image tag set, or the visual feature of two tags are similar, we may infer the relationship between these two tags is close. For the tag-image inter-related relationship, we consider the visual similarity between the tag and the associated image. Thus a multi-model association network is utilized as an important knowledge source for tag relevance measurement.

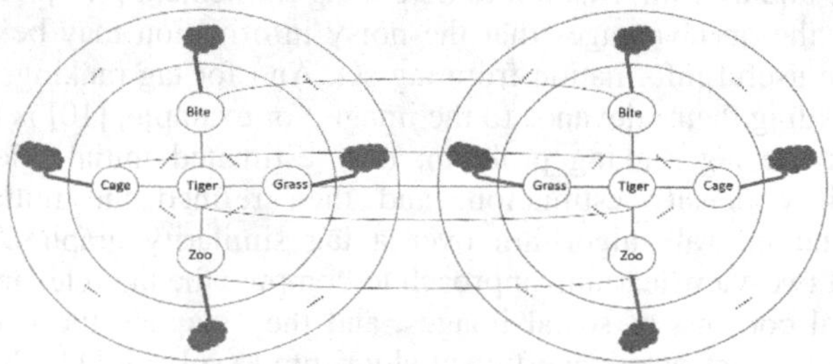

Fig. 2. The multimodal association network

Our multimodal association network consists of two key components, i.e., the co-occurrence association network and the visual association network. As shown in Fig. 2, the left part is our co-occurrence association network, in which to better express what we mean, not all the tags are listed in the figure. Taking the tag "*tiger*" as an example, {"*bite*", "*cage*", "*grass*", "*zoo*" ...} are all the tags co-occurring with "*tiger*" in at least one image, and all these tags and their neighbors constitute the entire association network. This network is formalized with a four-tuple <T, E, W_t, W_e>, where T represents a tag set that contains all the tags occur in the image database, and each tag can be seen as a node on the network, E represents a set of edges, which means if two tags co-occur in at least one image, we assume that there exist an edge between these two tag nodes. W_t represents the weight of the tag node t in T, and its corresponding value is set as the occurrence times of the tag *t*. Since each tag usually occurs only once in one image, this weight can be explained as the number of images which contain the tag t, as described in Formula (1). W_e represents the weight of the edge e in E, and its corresponding value can be set as the occurrence times of the edge e or the tag-tag pair. This weight can also be explained as the number of images that contain both of these two tags, as shown in Formula (2).

$$W_t = |IMG(t)| \quad (1)$$

$$W_e(t_i,t_j) = |IMG(e(t_i,t_j))| \quad (2)$$

The right part of Fig. 2 is our visual association network, which has the same structure with the co-occurrence association network, that is, these two networks have the same tag nodes and edges. The four-tuple <T', E', W'_t, W'_e> is aslo used to represent the visual association network, where T' and E' have the same meaning as in the co-occurrence association network and represent the tag set and the tag-tag pair set respectively; the value of W'_t is set as the visual feature vector of the tag t. which is calculted by using the mean histogram information of the tag; and the value of the W'_t is calculated by Formula (3).

$$W'_t = \frac{\sum_{img \in IMG(t)} HIST(img)}{|IMG(t)|} \quad (3)$$

where HIST(img) is the histogram feature of the image img; and IMG(t) is the image set, in which each image has the tag t. Here we do not use the complex visual feature, because the images from *Flickr* website are flexible and complex and the complex visual features may not be suitable. The value of W'_e is the Euclidean distance between two tags with the edge e, which is calculated by Formiula (4).

$$W'_e(t_i,t_j) = EU\_DIS\left(W'_{t_i}, W'_{t_j}\right) \quad (4)$$

where the function EU_DIS returns the Euclidean distance between the visual feature vectors of two tags of t_i and t_j.

3 Tag Relevance Learning

Our tag relevance measure model consists of two steps, firstly an initial relevance score is obtained through the context analysis for each tag on the basis of our multimodal association network, and then a random-walk algorithm is adopted to make a refinement for the initial score of tag relevance.

3.1 Initial Measure Based on Context Analysis

When we try to understand a certain word in a text, except for the original meaning of this word, the word's context is often utilized to help us and plays an important role for our understanding. Similarly, when we try to measure the tag relevance, the context around the tag can be utilized. For a given tag, the context includes the other tags in the same tag set for the corresponding social image and the image itself. Considering the first image in Fig. 1 as an example, the context of the tag "*tiger*" is shown in Fig. 3, thus we can calculate the initial tag relevance according to the context analysis. Here the "*object tag*" and "*context tags*" are used to represent the object tag and other tags in the same tag set for an image. Firstly, for the relationship between the object tag and the context tags, we assume that each tag of the context tags can provide its own contributions for the relevance of the object tag, and the contribution can be measured from two aspects of the co-occurrence frequency and the visual similarity. If two tags often co-occur in the same image, it means that users tend to annotate these two tags simultaneously for the same image. Generally users won't annotate two close-related tags as noises simultaneously, and in fact if the object tag has the higher co-occurrence frequency with the context tags, its relevance will be higher. For the object tag *otag*, the contribution of a tag *t* in the context tags can be calculated by Formlual (5).

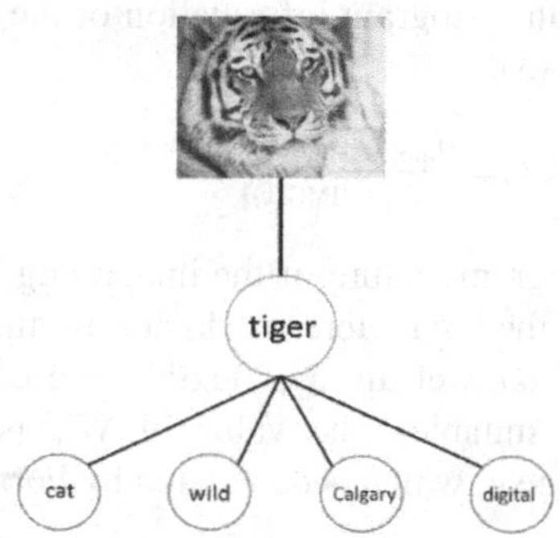

Fig. 3. The context of the tag "tiger" in the image Fig. 1-A

$$\text{Contribute}(t, otag) = \frac{W_e(t, otag)}{W_{otag}} \tag{5}$$

where W_{otag} and W_e are defined in our co-occurrence association network, and can be calculated by Formulae (1) and (2). Since the lengths of different "context tags" are different, we set a normalized weight for each tag in the context tags to avoid the influence of the length, and the value of weight can be calculated by Formula (6).

$$\text{Weight(t, otag)}= \frac{W_e(t, otag)/W_t}{\sum_{T\in ContextTags} W_e(T, otag)/W_T} \quad (6)$$

Thus we can measure the relevance of the object tag from the view of co-occurrence association by Formula (7).

$$\text{TR(otag)}= \sum_{t\in ContextTags} \text{Weight(t,otag)*Contribute(t,otag)} \quad (7)$$

Similarly, we measure the contribution of context tags from the view of visual association in a similar manner. Something different is that we replace the co-occurrence property with the visual similarity, and the exponential function of the Euclidean distance is used to represent the visual similarity, as shown in Formula (8).

$$\text{VR(otag,img)}= \exp(\text{-Dis(otag,img)}) \quad (8)$$

$$\text{Dis(otag,img)}= \sum_{t\in ContextTags} \text{Weight(t,otag)}*W'_e(t,otag)$$

where *img* means the corresponding image to the object tag. Expect the relationship between the object tag and context tags, the relevance of object tag is also affected by the relationship with the image itself, and the visual similarity between them can be calculated by Formula (9).

$$\text{VR'(otag,img)}= \exp(\text{-Dis'(otag,img)}) \quad (9)$$

$$\text{Dis'(otag,img)}= \text{EU\_DIS(tag,img)}$$

where *EU_DIS* is the Euclidean distance between the object tag and the image. Since Formulae (8) and (9) are all about the visual similarity, for simplifying our model we combine Formulae (8) and (9) as Formula (10).

$$VR_f\text{(otag,img)}= \exp(-Dis_f\text{(otag,img)}) \quad (10)$$

$$Dis_f\text{(otag,img)}= 0.5* \sum_{t\in ContextTags} \text{Weight(t, otag)}*W'e\text{(t, otag)} +0.5*\text{EU\_DIS(tag,img)}$$

Finally we combine Formulae (7) and (10) and get the final initial relevance measure for the object tag, as shown in Formula (11).

$$\text{Relvance(otag, img)}= \alpha TR(otag)+(1-\alpha)VR_f(otag,img) \quad (11)$$

where α is a weight parameter ranging from 0 to 1.

3.2 Tag Relevance Refinement through Random Walk

After acquiring the initial relevance score for each tag in the image annotation, we make a further refinement for the tag relevance using an approximate random-walk algorithm. Here, we refer the method implemented in [10], and accomplish some change in our work for the purpose of getting globally-comparable tag relevance. First, we see the tag set in each image as a full-connected graph, and the tag is the node in the graph, then a random-walk process is run on the graph based on the similarity between the tags, and finally more refined tag relevance can be obtained. We use the exponential function of the Google Distance [13] to compute the similarity between tags, as shown in Formula (12).

$$S(t_i, t_j)=\exp(-d(t_i, t_j)) \tag{12}$$

$$d(t_i, t_j)=\frac{\max(\log W_{t_i}, \log W_{t_j})-\log W_e(t_i, t_j)}{\log G-\min(\log W_{t_i}, \log W_{t_j})}$$

where G is the total image numbers in the database. Based on this similarity measure, we can give the transition probabilities used in the process of random walk, as shown in Formula (13).

$$p_{ij}=\frac{S(t_i,t_j)}{\sum_k S(t_i,t_k)} \tag{13}$$

where p_{ij} is the transition probability from the tag t_i to the tag t_j; k is the total number of the neighbor tags of the tag t_i. Hence this formula can be seen a normalization process. We then run the random walk process on each image individually, as shown in Formula (14).

$$r_k(j)=\frac{1}{2m}\sum_i r_{k-1}(i)p_{ij}+\frac{1}{2}v_j \tag{14}$$

where $r_k(j)$ represents the relevance of the tag t_j in the k_{th} iteration; p_{ij} is the transition probability; V_j is the initial relevance of the tag t_j, and m is the total number of context tags for tag t_j. The reasons for using parameter m is that we want to exclude the impact of the tag set length, and it is fair to the images have different tag set length. For the same reason, we don't consider the convergence of Formula (13), and just conducted a limited number of iterations. Another reason for this is that our initial relevance is relatively accurate, thus just a small number of iterations are needed to refine the relevance. On the contrary, too much iteration will reduce the accuracy.

4 Experiment and Analysis

4.1 Dataset and Query Definition

Our dataset is established based on *MIR Flickr Data* constructed by [14] and further development by [15] which have been used in *ImageCLEF*. It consists of 1,000,000 annotated images collected from *Flickr* with unconstrained contents, and these images have all the original user annotations. In our experiment, we use a subset dataset with about 200,000 images for retrieval just as in *ImageCLEF 2012*, which contains about 37863 tags after filtration. We choose 26 queries as the test query in our experiment, as shown in table 1, these queries cover various categories like *Animal, Building,*

Human, Event, Object, and so on. Except 20 single-word queries, we also introduce 6 multi-word queries to see the performance of our model on different kinds of queries. As for ground truth collection, due to the large collection of 200 thousand images, we don't obtain all the ground truth relevance assessments for each query. We first get the retrieval results for each query using all the models we use in our experiment, and then we form a pool for each query by aggregating all these returned images and obtained the relevance assessments by annotating manually. Each image was labeled "relevant" or "irrelevant", which we then used to evaluate the results of each model.

Table 1. The test queries in our experiment

single-word query	*bride, church, fish, ring, piano, pizza, tiger, mother, bus, rainbow, football, couple, bedroom, winter, bike, sheep, lion, monkey, fire, reading*
multi-word query	*old man, apple cellphone phone, beach sunset sunrise, flower bee, girl reading book, horse riding*

4.2 Evaluation Metrics and Model Selection

In our work, we choose two evaluation metrics to assess the performance of social image retrieval via more effective tag relevance measurement.

- *AP@X*: This evaluation measure the average precision when a certain number of images are encountered. In our work, we use AP@5, AP@10, AP@50, AP@100 respectively to measure the experiment results.
- *MAP*: Here we focus on the non-interpolated MAP, that is, each time a relevant image is encountered from top to bottom, we compute the precision, and finally get the mean of these precision values.

For the model selection, there are two parameters we need to set: α in Formula (12) and the iteration numbers for Formula (13), When we set $\alpha = 0.7$ and iter = 5, the best retrieval performance can be acquired, as shown in Fig. 4.

4.3 Experimental Result

To investigate the effect of each part on the whole retrieval performance, we introduce four evaluation patterns.

- TEXT: use only textual information, which means we set the parameter $\alpha = 1$ in Formula (11).
- VISUAL: using only the visual information, which means we set the parameter $\alpha = 0$ in Formula (11).
- TEXT+VISUAL: using both textual and visual information, which means we choose the optimal value of α. As Fig. 4 shows, here we set $\alpha = 0.7$.
- TEXT+VISUAL+RANDOM: Making further refinement by using our random-walk algorithm based on the result of Formula (11).

Fig. 5 shows the results of above four patterns. It can be seen that the performance is 4) > 3) > 1) > 2) and this result can illustrate that each part in our model can contribute for the final performance. We can find that the performance is poor by only using the visual information. However, when combining with the textual information, the result is much better than only using the textual information. It can be also observed that the random-walk process is able to further improve the final result.

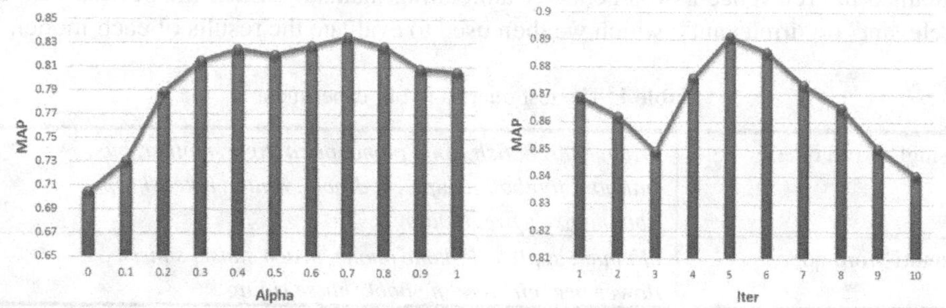

Fig. 4. The performance curves of our approach with respect to the parameters α and iterations

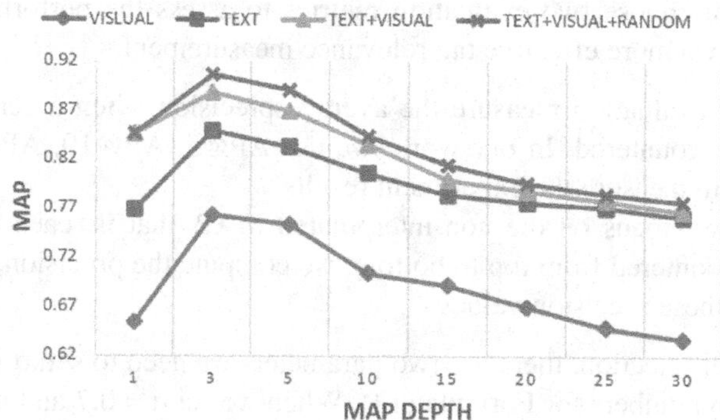

Fig. 5. The experiment results for the four cases in our approach

To give full exhibition to the superiority of our alignment model, we have also performed a comparison between our and the other classical approaches in recent years. Since our work is mainly for social image retrieval, we choose two categories of existing approaches as our comparative experiments: one is traditional text retrieval model for annotation-based image retrieval, the other is tag ranking approaches for social image retrieval. For the first category, we choose two retrieval model, one is a language model implemented in [16], the other is a information-based model implemented in [17]. As for the tag ranking method, we also choose two methods, one is the tag ranking model in [10], for the other method, we combine our method with the method in [10].

- ***Language Model (LM):*** The tags for each image can be viewed as a document, the basic idea is to estimate a language model for each document, and documents are ranked by the likelihood of the query according to the estimated language model.
- ***Information-Based Model (IBM):*** This model is based on a hypothesis that the significance of a tag in the document can benefit from the difference of the behaviors of this tag at the document and collection levels.
- ***Tag Ranking Model (TRM):*** This model first gets local relevance scores using the probability density estimation and random walk algorithm and ranks the tags using these scores, and then use the rank information to get the global relevance for image retrieval by Formula (15).

$$\text{relevance(t)}=\text{-rank}_t+1/\text{N}_t \tag{15}$$

where $rank_t$ denotes the rank value of tag t, and N_t denotes the number of tags in the corresponding tag set.

- ***Joint Model (JM):*** We first get the tag relevance by using our method, however, just use these relevance values to rank the tags and then refer Formula (15) to compute the new relevance. We want to show the advantage of our approach in using more rich information to improve the retrieval performance.

In addition, method 3 and 4 both use the vector space model as the retrieval model, just as our approach. This means for single-word queries, we just rank the images according to the relevance of the word; for multi-word queries, we use the sum of the relevances to rank the images. Since the work in [Liu et al., 2009] used only single-word queries, for fairness, we first use the twenty single-word queries in Table 1 in our experiment, and the final results can be seen in Table 2. We can see that our approach outperforms other approaches obviously, and the comparison result between *JM* and our approach confirms the global comparability of our relevance and the advantage of our model in capturing the appropriate information to compute the relevance. We then implement the experiments on each query in Table 1. For the purpose of clarity, we just list the results of *LM, TRM* and our approach in Fig. 7, here we choose *AP@10* as our evaluation metrics since we usually pay attention to the top images of the return list. It can be seen that for single-word queries, our approach outperforms other approaches obviously, and our approach's performance is the best for almost all the queries. As for multi-word queries, our approach is more robust than tag ranking method *TRM* and has roughly the same results with *LM*. the reason for this is probably because that the presence of all query words in a tagged image largely guarantees the high relevance for the image, and the poor peformance of *TRM* once again verified the coarse of the rank information for image retrieval. At last, we show the top 5 retrieval results of these models in Fig. 6 for the query *"lion"*, *"sheep"*. It can be seen that generally our approach can exactly return the better retrieval results.

Table 2. The comparison between our and the existing methods

	AP@5	AP@10	AP@50	AP@100	MAP(100)
LM	0.63	0.595	0.607	0.596	0.623
IBM	0.63	0.595	0.607	0.596	0.623
TRM	0.63	0.62	0.61	0.6	0.631
CM	0.61	0.63	0.646	0.605	0.654
Our Approach	**0.8**	**0.77**	**0.694**	**0.642**	**0.722**

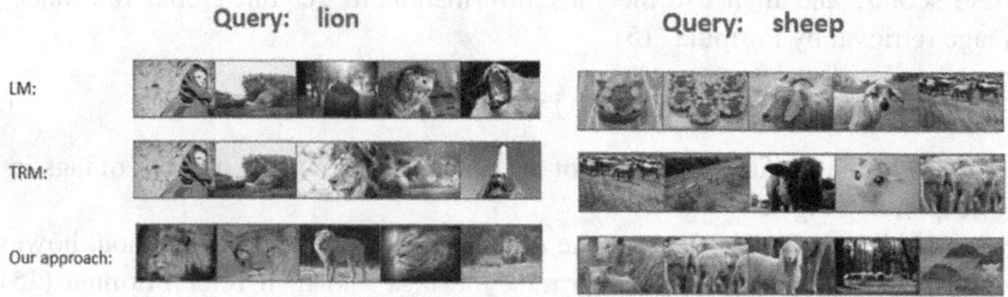

Fig. 6. The top 5 images returned by different approaches for the queries "lion", "sheep"

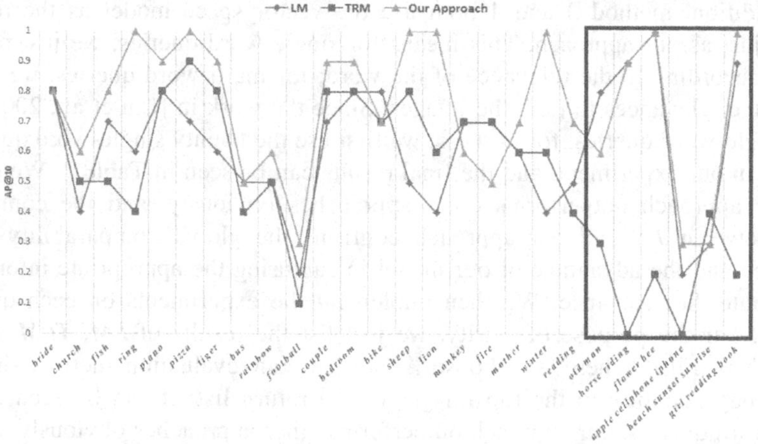

Fig. 7. The experiment results of different approaches on all the queries

5 Conclusions

In this paper, we build a relevance learning model for the tags associated with the social images, and use the tag relevance to improve the performance of image retrieval. Our model considers the user tagging habits and try to compute the tag relevance by analyzing the context of the tag. For computing the relevance, a multi-model association network is constructed as our knowledge source and a random-walk algorithm is adopted to refine the relevance. The experiment results demonstrate that our approach can make use of rich information to compute the relevance and our tag relevance can help improving the retrieval performance significantly. For the future work, we will put more focus on multi-word queries, since different query words are not independent, simply consider the sum of the relevances of the query words are not enough, so our future work will consider the semantic relationships between them to further improve the performance.

Acknowledgments. This work is supported by National Science & Technology Pillar Program of China (No. 2012BAH59F04), National Natural Science Fund of China (No. 61170095; No. 71171126), and Shanghai Municipal R&D Foundation (No. 12dz1500203, 12511505300).

References

1. Datta, R., Joshi, D., Li, J., Wang, J.Z.: Image retrieval: Ideas, influences, and trends of the new age. ACM Computing Surveys (CSUR), 40(2), Article 5 (2008)
2. Carneiro, G., Chan, A.B., Moreno, P.J., Vasconcelos, N.: Supervised learning of semantic classes for image annotation and retrieval. IEEE Transactions on Pattern Analysis and Machine Intelligence 29(3), 394–410 (2007)
3. Sun, A., Bhowmick, S.S., Tran, K., Nguyen, N., Bai, G.: Tag-Based social image retrieval: An empirical evaluation. Journal of the American Society for Information Science and Technology 62(12), 2364–2381 (2011)
4. Goh, D.H., Ang, R.P., Lee, C.S., Chua, A.Y.K.: Fight or unite: Investigating game genres for image tagging. Journal of the American Society for Information Science and Technology 62(7), 1311–1324 (2011)
5. Jain, R., Sinha, P.: Content without context is meaningless. In: Proceedings of MM 2010, pp. 1259–1268 (2010)
6. Qian, X., Hua, X.: Graph-cut based tag enrichment. In: Proceedings of SIGIR 2011, pp. 1111–1112 (2011)
7. Xu, H., Wang, J.D., Hua, X.S., Li, P.: Tag refinement by regularized LDA. In: Proceedings of MM 2009, pp. 573–576 (2009)
8. Xia, Z., Peng, J., Feng, X., Fan, J.: Social Tag Enrichment via Automatic Abstract Tag Refinement. In: Lin, W., Xu, D., Ho, A., Wu, J., He, Y., Cai, J., Kankanhalli, M., Sun, M.-T. (eds.) PCM 2012. LNCS, vol. 7674, pp. 198–209. Springer, Heidelberg (2012)
9. Sang, J.T., Liu, J., Xu, C.S.: Exploiting user information for image tag refinement. In: Proceedings of MM 2011, pp. 1129–1132 (2011)
10. Liu, D., Hua, X.S., Yang, L.J., Wang, M., Zhang, H.J.: Tag ranking. In: Proceedings of WWW 2009, pp. 351–360 (2009)
11. Zhuang, J.F., Hoi, S.C.H.: A two-view learning approach for image tag ranking. In: Proceedings of WSDM 2011, pp. 625–634 (2011)
12. Xiao, J., Zhou, W.G., Tian, Q.: Exploring tag relevance for image tag re-ranking. In: Proceedings of SIGIR 2012, pp. 1069–1070 (2012)
13. Cilibrasi, R.L., Vitanyi, P.M.B.: The Google Similarity Distance. IEEE Transactions on Knowledge and Data Engineering 19(3), 370–383 (2007)
14. Huiskes, M.J., Lew, M.S.: The MIR flickr retrieval evaluation. In: Proceedings of MIR 2008, pp. 39–43 (2008)
15. Huiskes, M.J., Thomee, B., Lew, M.S.: New trends and ideas in visual concept detection: the MIR flickr retrieval evaluation initiative. In: Proceedings of MIR 2010, pp. 527–536 (2010)
16. Zhai, C.X., Lafferty, J.: A study of smoothing methods for language models applied to Ad Hoc Information retrieval. In: Proceedings of SIGIR 2001, pp. 334–342 (2001)
17. Clinchant, S., Gaussier, E.: Information-based models for ad hoc IR. In: Proceedings of SIGIR 2010, pp. 234–241 (2010)

ASR-Based Input Method for Postal Address Recognition in Chinese Mandarin

Ling Feng Wei and Sun Maosong

School of Computer Science and Technology
Tsinghua University, China
andrew.l.wei@gmail.com, sms@tsinghua.edu.cn

Abstract. As the automatic speech recognition technology (ASR) has becoming more and more mature, especially with statistical language modeling built with web scale data, and with the utilization of Hidden Markov Model probabilistic framework, speech recognition has become applicable to many domains and usage scenarios. In particular, speech recognition can be applied to task such as Chinese postal address recognition. This paper presents the first attempt ever, in both academic and commercial settings, to create an ASR-based input method for postal address recognition in Chinese Mandarin. By customizing the statistical language model to such domain, and incorporating the knowledge from the structural information provided by geo-topology, our language model successfully captures the signals from geographical contextual information and self-correct possible mis-recognitions. Experiment results provide evident that our approach based on speech recognition achieves a faster and a more accuracy input method compare to traditional keyboard-based input.

Keywords: Automatic Speech Recognition, Postal Address Recognition, Statistical Language Modeling, Chinese Speech Recognition.

1 Introduction

The market of postal services in China has increased significantly over past few decades. According to National Bureau of Statistics of the People's Republic of China, the total number of workforce behind this market has reached beyond 700,000 people outputting a total delivery of mail and packages of more than 61 billion pieces annually. In order to provide a more reliable postal service in such a large scale, postal tracking for mail and packages has become a standard service provided by many of the shipping and postal companies today. However, to enable such service, the shipping and postal companies often need to first hire a large amount of workers to manually type in the mailing address into their logistic information system before enabling the tracking service.

Currently, there is no special input method developed dedicated to postal address input in Chinese. According to the hand written address provided by the sender, the typist then enters the address by hand using PC based input

M. Sun et al. (Eds.): CCL and NLP-NABD 2014, LNAI 8801, pp. 302–312, 2014.

method such as Sogou Pinyin into the logistic system. Such input process is insufficient because keyboard based Pinyin input method is slow, and Pinyin to Hanzi conversion is not perfect. Furthermore, any error made during this data entry process will introduce additional costs to the service provider.

This paper is motivated to provide an alternative, and a more efficient way of entering Chinese postal address based on using automatic speech recognition technology (ASR). A new ASR-based input method, namely Voice Postal Input (VPI) system, built from this research, will provide a faster and more accuracy input method compare to traditional keyboard typing. Therefore, shipping service providers can lower the costs needed to hire large number of typist. Ultimately, this will translate to a cheaper shipping service for everyone in China. To our knowledge, this will be the first attempt, both in academic and commercial settings, to apply ASR technology to postal address recognition in Chinese Mandarin. Our experiment results have proven the feasibility of our approach, and have shown that high recognition accuracy can be achieved.

2 Background

Data entry process has always been human intensive and time consuming. Especially in Chinese language, typing in Chinese has been a difficult task due to the nature of the language[1]. Because of its facility to learn and use, Pinyin is by far the most popular keyboard input method in China [1]. However, Pinyin input suffers from several challenges. It is slow in terms of input speed compared to voice [2], and the Pinyin to Hanzi character conversion is error prone due to typographical errors during typing and the conversion itself is far from perfect [3]. There are 410 syllables in Chinese and they correspond to over 6000 common Chinese characters. This implies that on average, each syllable corresponds to about 17 characters. As the result, a Chinese typist must then select a choice from a multiple candidate list by typing an extra number key to identify the correct character from the list [4].

Furthermore, previous study has shown that a Chinese character' s Pinyin contains 4.2 Roman characters. Based on a skilled typist, an average keystroke takes 200 ms. Then the Pinyin typing time for a Chinese character would be about 840 ms. An extra time of 450 to 600 ms is also required to identify the correct choice of character from the pinyin candidate lists [4]. Finally, the total time spend to type a Chinese character with Pinyin input method would then fall into the range of 1290 ms to 1440 ms per character.

To improve the data entry process for Chinese postal address, a new input method by voice therefore is proposed. An ASR-based input method will avoid the typographical errors from user as well as the error-prone Pinyin to Hanzi conversion. Knowing that speech is the most effective and fastest form of human communication [6], ASR-based input method will introduce significant improvement to postal address entry process.

3 The Proposed Approach

The Voice Postal Input (VPI) system we created is based on client-server based software architecture where the client captures the audio data from end user, and the computational intensive speech recognition resides on the server. Our server end integrated with two of the most popular ASR products for Chinese Mandarin, namely iFLyTek Voice Cloud and Nuance Recognizer. Although iFlyTek Voice Cloud has been successfully integrated into many products in China, and has proven to have high recognition accuracy for open speech dictation [5], but it is lacking the flexibility for the developer to customize a language model for a domain specific task. In later section, we will show customizing a language model becomes very in postal address recognition. Nuance Recognizer, on the other hand, gives the developer the ability to customize a language model for domain specific task. For flexibility and future studies, our VPI system can easily be expanded to include any additional recognizer from its server end.

Taking advantages of the structural information of Chinese postal addresses, we also introduced a process named Geo-Topology Realignment (GTR) which takes the recognition results as an input, and makes corrections to possible misrecognitions through the knowledge learned from the Chinese geographical topology. GTR correlates the relationship between province, city, district and street information and form a geographical topology offline. When GTR receives the results from the recognizers during run time, it tries to match the recognized string against the knowledge from this topology to identify possible invalid address combinations and makes correction accordingly. Finally, the output of GTR will be sent back to the web client and will be presented as final result.

4 Experiment Setup

4.1 Evaluation Data Set

The evaluation data used to test the VPI system consists of 5170 recordings. Each audio recording contains exactly one postal address randomly picked from 150 thousand valid postal addresses collected. Each postal address is read out by both male and female voice in official Chinese Mandarin without carrying any local accent. The recording session was done in a control environment with minimal background noise, and each participant was asked to speak with their normal speaking rate. Due to the business requirement from postal companies, house numbers were to be ignored. This evaluation data set is used throughout this paper to provide consistent measurements and meaningful comparisons between different processes and features.

4.2 Evaluation Metrics

Two common methods were used to evaluate the performance of recognition accuracy. word accuracy, W_{Acc} which is derived from Levenstein distance, or Edit Distance, is used to measure word level accuracy, and Sentence Accuracy, S_{Acc} , is used to measure how well the recognizer perform in terms of the whole address. To provide further insight to how well the recognition is in terms of different geographical level, the following metrics are also introduced each measuring the accuracy at province, city, district and street level respectively.

- P_{Acc} word accuracy at province level only
- C_{Acc} word accuracy at city level only
- D_{Acc} word accuracy at district level only
- St_{Acc} word accuracy at street level only

5 Experiment Results and Analysis

5.1 Using Open Speech Recognition

In first attempt, we first establish a baseline from using iFLyTek Voice Cloud. Using such an open-speech recognizer, our system suffers from confusing similar or identical sound characters. In extreme cases, out-of-context vocabularies, in this case, being the non-postal address related words, are found in the recognition result. Table below shows some of the errors produced by iFlyTek Voice Cloud.

Table 1. Recognition errors produced by iFlyTek Voice Cloud

ID	Ortho String	Recognized String
I-1	山东省青岛市胶南市旺富路	山东省青岛市胶南市王府路
I-2	天津市东丽区川铁路	天津市东丽区穿铁路
I-3	吉林省白城市洮北区洮河大路	吉林省白城市姚北区辽河大路
I-4	浙江省杭州市桐庐县定大线	浙江省杭州市桐庐县顶大仙
I-5	上海市闵行区墨江路	上海区民航路漠江路
I-6	天津市武清区丰收路	天是无情去丰收路
I-7	四川省成都市郫县禹庙下街	对方声称都市郫县与标赛杰
I-8	四川省成都市郫县汇川街三段	吃饭尚成东是背线绘春街三段

In cases like the ID I-1 , the recognizers were confused with acoustically similar or identical street names such as “旺富路” with “王府路” while both being valid street names. In I-2, “川铁路” with “穿铁路” were phonetically identical words. However, the term “穿铁路” would most likely not to be a name of a street because of the term “穿铁” does not make much sense in Chinese language. Case I-3 and I-4 suffers the similar misrecognition issues. I-7 and I-8 demonstrate more severe errors where terms like “对方声称都市” and “吃饭尚成东是背线绘春”, which makes very little sense in Chinese language, and are out of context of postal address, were found in the recognition result. We observed that iFlyTek Voice Cloud, being an open-speech recognizer, is trying to predict a sequence of words which are most likely to generate the observed acoustic feature without specifically considering the postal address context. More specifically, a character like “川” and “穿”, which are phonetically identical, was misrecognized since “穿” is a more popular character in Chinese language. Since open speech recognizer such as iFlyTek Voice Cloud is designed to handle general dictation task, its language model would most likely be trained with common Chinese vocabularies. As a result, Chinese common terms such as “吃饭”, “对方” and “声称” might appear many times in its training corpus, and therefore most likely have a higher probability compare to terms or characters appears in Chinese postal address.

5.2 Customized SLM for Postal Address Recognition

We further investigate on recognition performance using Nuance Recognizer, and to explore the benefits of ngram customization. In a domain specific task such as postal address recognition, being able to customize the language model become useful because it gives a better approximation on priori probability of how words are connected in the context of Chinese postal address. The intuition behind ngram customization is to train a language model with words only appeared in postal addresses in China. As the result, terms related to postal address like the city “成都市” will have a higher probability compare to a similar sounding term “声称都市” which was previously produced as a misrecognition by iFlyTek Voice Cloud.

We developed two bigram models based on Chinese character or Chinese word as a feature. In the case of Chinese postal address, we take the complete province, city, district or street name such as the province “广东省”, or the district “朝阳区” as a Chinese word. These two language models were generated from 150 thousand valid postal addresses in China. Good-turing smoothing technique was applied to both language models. Table below shows the recognition results from our character bigram model, and word bigram model.

Table 2. Comparison of errors produced by character and word model

ID	Ortho String	Character Bigram Model	Word Bigram Model
N-1	山东省青岛市胶南市旺富路	山 东 省 青 岛 市 胶 南 市 王 府 路	山东省 青岛市 胶南市 旺富路
N-2	天津市东丽区川铁路	天 津 市 东 丽 区 川 街	天津市 东丽区 川铁路
N-3	吉林省白城市洮北区洮河大路	吉 林 省 白 城 市 窑 北 区 蛟 河 大 路	吉林省 白城市 洮北区 辽河大路
N-4	上海市闵行区墨江路	上 海 区 民 航 路 墨 江 路	上海市 闵行路 墨江路
N-5	四川省成都市郫县禹庙下街	四 川 省 成 都 市 郫 县 庙 下 街	四川省 成都市 郫县 禹庙下街
N-6	上海市闸北区公兴路	上 海 市 夏 北 区 共 兴 路	上海市 闸北区 公兴路

Both character and word bigram model eliminates the out-of-context misrecognition. However, when model with character as feature, the recognizer still tends to produce errors with characters sound very similar to each other, and performs poorly compare to word bigram model. For instance, ID N1 of table x.x, the street name “王府路” sounds similar to “旺富路”, a character bigram model have seen both the term “王府”, and “府路” as well as “旺富” and “富路”. Using Baidu’s search result as a measuring baseline, the term “王府” occurred 77 million times in the search result, and the term “府路” appeared 8.3 million times. “旺富” appeared 330 thousand times, and “富路” appeared 85 million times. A character bigram model favors the more popular term of “王府路” over the less popular “旺富路”, which leads to a misrecognition. Similarly, “川街” can be found 16 million times from Baidu’s search result compared to the less popular “川铁” appearing 865 thousand times in the result. Using character as a feature lacks of the contextual information of the previous postal address term. A word bigram model overcome the errors produced by the character bigram. For example, knowing the city name being “胶南市” can help to increase the probability of street name “旺富路” over the street name of “王府路” because “王府路” never appeared in the city “胶南市.” Similar cases can be found for street name “民航路” and “闵行路”, and the district and street combination of “夏北区共兴路” and “闸北区公兴路”

5.3 Geo-Topology Realignment

A word bigram model significantly improve the recognition accuracy. However, due to the lack of geographical knowledge, ngram model still suffers from some of the mis-recognition errors listed below. We have identified the following five major types of mis-recognition errors from our bigram model.

Table 3. Recognition errors produced by word bigram model

ID	Ortho String	Recognized String
C-1	浙江省衡州市江山市丰新线	浙江省杭州市江山市丰新线
C-2	上海市闵行区天星路	上海市闵行区田兴路
C-3	重庆市渝中区罗汉寺街	重庆市渝中区罗汉寺
C-4	四川省成都市锦江区洗瓦堰路	四川省成都市锦江区洗瓦**路
C-5	香港特别行政区屯门区青麟路	香港潮南区青岭路

C1 - Invalid address combination
Valid address related words are correctly recognized, but does not form a single valid address. For example, both the city “衡州市” and “杭州市” belongs to the province “浙江省,” and they are phonetically similar to each other. However, the sub-district of “江山市” only belongs to the city “衡州市.” Therefore, the city and sub-district combination of " 杭州市江山市” does not form a valid address.

C2 - Similar sounding words
Although a word-based bigram significantly eliminates some of the confusion between similar sounding words, but it still produces mis-recognition such as

the similar sounding street names of “天星路” and “田兴路.” Due to the popularity of the street name, a street “田兴路” might appear more often in the training set than “天星路.” Such empirical approach ultimately leads to mis-recognition.

C3 - Missing words
The end user interface built for this system has a push-to-talk button to allow a user to input by voice. Sometimes the user talks before pushing the button or release the button before finishing the voice input. This would cause the recognizer to miss words at the beginning or end of the sentence.

C4 - Encoding issue
The Nuance Recognizer integrated into our VPI system has a software level issue that it sometimes produces Chinese character with encoding issue.

C5 - Other errors
We observe a very small amount of errors were introduced from human interference such as noises created from recorder adjusting the microphone during recording, and low recording volume due to inappropriate microphone position. We choose not to focus to solve this type of error in this paper.

To tackle the misrecognition errors from our ngram model, a geo-topology was generated offline based on 198853 valid addresses in China. 33 province level nodes, 1320 city level nodes, 30972 district level nodes and 103446 street level nodes were created with appropriate links between each level of nodes in the geo-topology. This geo-topology forms a set of rules to validate the recongition result, and to correct possible misrecognition errors based on the relation between each node in the geo-topology. Two correction methods below are designed for the GTR process.

- Skip Match. If two words, w_x,w_y in the recognized string can match to two nodes, n1 and n2 in the geo-topology, and if these two nodes are not immediately connected, meaning one is not the parent of the other, then the GTR process will find the union set of n1’s child nodes and n2’s parent nodes, or vice versa. If such union set has only one unique node, we then replace or insert the name of this node with the string between w_x, and w_y. Figure xx below shows the logic of Skip match. In this example, which is taken from C1 of Table 3., the city “衡州市” was misrecognized as “杭州市”. These two cities have almost identical sounds, and therefore easily be misrecognized. Although both cities belong to “浙江省” province, but the sub district “江山市” only belongs to “衡州市”, but not “杭州市.” GTR takes advantage of the knowledge from geo-topology to automatically correct such misrecognition.
- Pinyin Match. If the union of two nodes in geo-topology, n1 and n2, has more than one node, we cannot directly apply Skip Therefore, a Pinyin Match is proposed. The union nodes of n1 and n2 will be converted into Pinyin, and then the node whose Pinyin has closest phonetic edit distance to the misrecognized string will replace the recognize string. The example below which comes from a real misrecognition string in our experiment is corrected by GTR. The street “旺富路” was misrecognized as the more

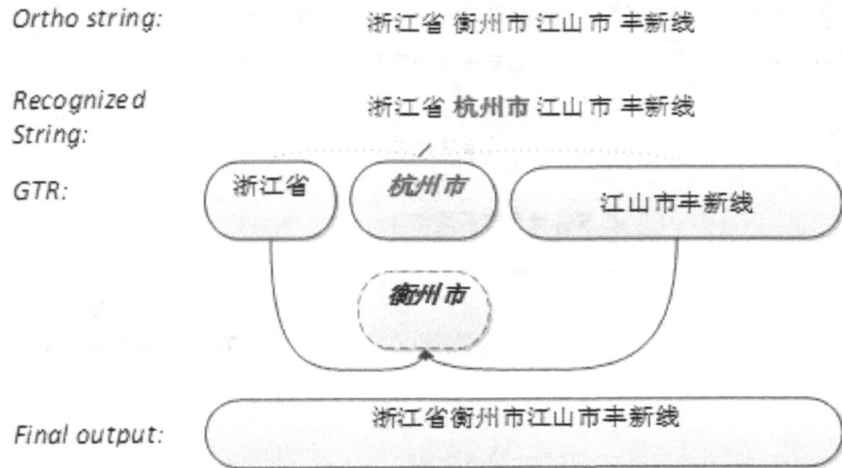

Fig. 1. GTR Skip Match Logic

popular street "王府路" The Pinyin representation of these two words are "Wang4Fu2Lu4" and "Wang2Fu3Lu4" respectively. The city node "胶南市" in the geo-topology contains more than one child whose value represents the street names belonging to this city. GTR performs a fuzzy match based on edit distance on the Pinyin of these street names and finds the street "旺富路" being the closest match. GTR then replace the correct term "旺富路" with the misrecognized "王府路" to "旺富路". The figure blow is the graphical representation of the Pinyin match logic of GTR.

5.4 Overall Recognition Accuracy

We consolidate our experiment results and provide a summary on recognition accuracy using different techniques below.

When using iFlyTek Voice Cloud, experiment iFlyTek, our system performs poorly with a word level accuracy of 87.79%. In experiment iFlyTek+GTR, GTR is applied to the results from iFlyTek Voice Cloud, there is about 2% absolute improvement is observed. When GTR is applied to the results produced by Nuance Recognizer with a customized word bigram (Experiment Word.Bigram+GTR), there is approximately 4% absolute improvement compare to the original bigram results reaching 96.54%.

In iFlyTek+word.bigram+GTR experiment, The best accuracy performance is observed when GTR is applied to the results produced by both iFlyTek and word bigram model achieving 96.93% word accuracy rate, and with the sentence accuracy is at 85.07%. This means for every 100 addresses inputted using VPI system, only about 15 addresses will contain errors. There is less than 1% that the misrecognition error will occur at province or city level, and about 2% chance that the error will occur in district level. Street level accuracy is slightly lowered to 93.57%.

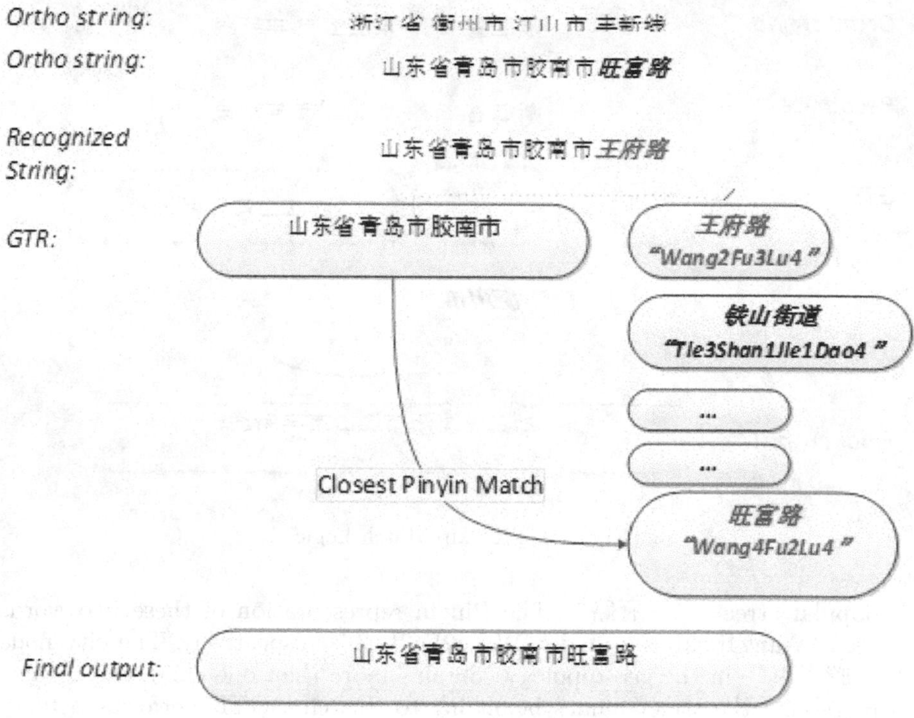

Fig. 2. GTR Fuzzy Pinyin Match Logic

Table 4. Recognition errors produced by iFlyTek Voice Cloud

Experiment Name	S_{Acc}	W_{Acc}	P_{Acc}	C_{Acc}	D_{Acc}	St_{Acc}
iFlyTek	41.86%	87.79%	98.16%	97.80%	89.39%	74.50%
iFlyTek+GTR	66.01%	89.68%	96.01%	98.42%	91.16%	83.94%
Character.Bigram	28.28%	78.44%	94.70%	88.96%	76.31%	72.50%
Word.Bigram	68.45%	92.42%	98.96%	96.82%	92.23%	89.51%
Word.Bigram+GTR	83.27%	96.54%	99.74%	99.23%	96.59%	92.77%
iFlyTek+Word.Bigram + GTR	85.07%	96.93%	99.66%	99.53%	97.12%	93.57%

5.5 Speed Performance

As described earlier in this section, our VPI system consists of a web client to collect audio data from end user, and then the voice data will feed into two recognizers, the result of the recognition will be passed to a post process of GTR. Separate measurements have been taken for each of the individual subtask, including:

t_1 time it takes to read an address
t_2 transmission time for voice data from client to server

t_3 processing time required by iFlyTek Voice Cloud
t_4 processing time required by Nuance Recognizer
t_5 processing time required by GTR
t_6 transmission time of results from server to client

The total time to input an address through VPI system is then,

$$T = t_1 + t_2 + t_3 + t_4 + t_5 + t_6 \tag{1}$$

A complete breakdown of VPI system processing time is shown in table below.

Table 5. Recognition errors produced by iFlyTek Voice Cloud

Process ID	Process Name	Avg. Time (ms)
t_1	Voice Recording	2676
t_2	Transmission from Client to Server	5
t_3	iFlyTek Recognition	1592
t_4	Nuance Recogntion	3543
t_5	GTR	569
t_6	Transmission from Server to Client	5
t_7	Total Process Time	8380

The average input speed using VPI system is about 762 ms per character derives from the average process time of 8390 ms for an 11 character Chinese postal address. VPI system performance can further be enhanced. Current version of runs the speech recognition in serial process, meaning it will run iFlyTek first and wait for the recognition complete before running Nuance Recognizer. This workflow can be further improved by running both iFlyTek and Nuance recognition in parallel with a multithreaded module. It is estimated that 1951 ms of processing time can be saved. In addition, audio streaming allows further time saving. Instead of spending 2682 ms to record an input, audio streaming allows VPI system to start capturing voice data and start the recognition process right away. With a buffer size of 1 second, audio streaming will send the recorded data to server every second. This will also significantly cut down the processing time of VPI system. By entering postal address through voice using VPI system, the data entry person is estimated to be 33.15% - 63% faster than by using traditional keyboard with Pinyin input based on the estimation of 1129 ms per character typing speed for an average user [4].

6 Conclusion

We focuses on implementing an ASR-based input system for Chinese postal addresses. We aim to examine the feasibility and usability of such system for the commercial settings. With a proper language model trained specifically with address specific data, and integrating geo-topology knowledge, the VPI system is able to achieve very high recognition accuracy. On the other hand, using VPI system, the input rate per character is estimated to be 762 ms per character, which is about 33% faster compare to keyboard based Pinyin input method. To our knowledge, our ASR-based input method is the first attempt ever to applied speech recognition accuracy in the domain of postal address recognition. The implication of this work is that using speech as an input for Chinese postal address is indeed feasible. Shipping and postal companies in China can use VPI system to improve their data entry process to reduce operation costs. Ultimately, people in China can also be benefitted with a cheaper shipping service due to such reduction.

Acknowledgements. This work is supported by the National Natural Science Foundation of China (NSFC) under Grant No. 61170196, 61133012 and National Program on Key Basic Research Project (973 Program) under Grant 2014CB340501.

References

1. Chen, Z., Lee, K.-F.: A new statistical approach to Chinese Pinyin input. In: Proceedings of the 38th Annual Meeting on Association for Computational Linguistics, pp. 241–247. Association for Computational Linguistics (2000)
2. Hartley, J., Sotto, E., Pennebaker, J.: Speaking versus typing: a case-study of the effects of using voice-recognition software on academic correspondence. British Journal of Educational Technology 34(1), 5–16 (2003)
3. Chen, Z., Han, J., Lee, K.-F.: Language input architecture for converting one text form to another text form with tolerance to spelling, typographical, and conversion errors. U.S. Patent 6,848,080 (issued January 25, 2005)
4. Wang, J., Zhai, S., Su, H.: Chinese input with keyboard and eye-tracking: an anatomical study. In: Proceedings of the SIGCHI Conference on Human Factors in Computing Systems, pp. 349–356. ACM (2001)
5. iFlyTek Voice Cloud, iFlyTek (May 2, 2014), http://open.voicecloud.cn/ (accessed May 2, 2014)
6. Erden, M., Arslan, L.M.: Automatic Detection of Anger in Human-Human Call Center Dialogs. In: INTERSPEECH, pp. 81–84 (2011)

Author Index